ROUTLEDGE
STUDENT STATUTES

....

Criminal Law Statutes
2012–2013

'Focused content, layout and price – Routledge competes and wins in relation to all of these factors' – Craig Lind, University of Sussex, UK

'The best value and best format books on the market' – Ed Bates, Southampton University, UK

Routledge Student Statutes present all the legislation students need in one easy-to-use volume. Developed in response to feedback from lecturers and students, this book offers a fully up-to-date, comprehensive, and clearly presented collection of legislation – ideal for LLB and GDL course and exam use.

Routledge Student Statutes are:

- **Exam Friendly:** un-annotated and conforming to exam regulations

- **Tailored to fit your course:** 80% of lecturers we surveyed agree that *Routledge Student Statutes* match their course and cover the relevant legislation

- **Trustworthy:** *Routledge Student Statutes* are compiled by subject experts, updated annually and have been developed to meet student needs through extensive market research

- **Easy to use:** a clear text design, comprehensive table of contents, multiple indexes and highlighted amendments to the law make these books the more student-friendly Statutes on the market

- **Competitively Priced:** *Routledge Student Statutes* offer content and usability rated as good or better than our major competitor, but at a more competitive price

- **Supported by a Companion Website:** presenting scenario questions for interpreting Statutes, annotated web links, and multiple-choice questions, these resources are designed to help students to be confident and prepared.

Jonathan Herring is a Fellow at Exeter College, Oxford University.

ROUTLEDGE STUDENT STATUTES

Titles in the series:

Company Law Statutes 2012–2013
  MARC MOORE

Contract, Tort and Restitution Statutes 2012–2013
  JAMES DEVENNEY AND HOWARD JOHNSON

Criminal Law Statutes 2012–2013
  JONATHAN HERRING

European Union Legislation 2012–2013
  JEFFREY KENNER

Evidence Statutes 2012–2013
  CLAIRE McGOURLAY

Family Law Statutes 2012–2013
  PHIL BATES

International Trade Law Statutes and Conventions 2011–2013
  INDIRA CARR AND MIRIAM GOLDBY

Property Law Statutes 2012–2013
  RUSSELL HEWITSON

Public Law and Human Rights 2012–2013
  PHILIP JONES

www.routledge.com/cw/statutes

Praise for Routledge Student Statutes

'The best value and best format books on the market' – Ed Bates, University of Southampton, UK

'Focused content, layout and price – Routledge competes and wins in relation to all of these factors' – Craig Lind, University of Sussex, UK

'comprehensive and reliable' – Andromachi Georgosouli, University of Leicester, UK

'user friendly and sensibly laid out' – John Stanton, Kingston University, UK

'An exciting and valuable selection of the key legislative material' – David Radlett, University of Kent, UK

'I prefer the layout of the Routledge statute book to other statute books that I have seen' – Nicola Haralambous, University of Hertfordshire, UK

'Well-presented and has thorough content [. . .] clearly a good competitor' – Brian Coggon, University of Lincoln, UK

'. . . given the addition of the useful web resource and the easy to read section headings, I would be more inclined to recommend this book than other statute texts' – Emma Warner-Reed, Leeds Metropolitan University, UK

'excellent and relevant' – Sarwan Singh, City University London, UK

'I personally prefer the Routledge series as it is better laid out and more accessible' – Jonathan Doak, University of Nottingham, UK

'*Routledge Student Statutes* are practical and carefully designed for the needs of the students' – Stelios Andreadakis, Oxford Brookes University, UK

'an excellent statute text' – Fang Ma, University of Hertfordshire, UK

'Other statute books are not as attractive in look or feel, not as easy to navigate, more expensive and amendments are less clear' – Jason Lowther, University of Plymouth, UK

'Gives good coverage and certainly includes all elements addressed on our current syllabus. I personally think this statute is more clearly set out than other statute books and is more user friendly for it' – Samantha Pegg, Nottingham Trent University, UK

'This statute book is a student friendly material. Index features as well as the overall content make this book a valuable contribution to student reading lists' – Orkun Akseli, Newcastle University, UK

'A very welcome publication' – Simon Barnett, University of Hertfordshire, UK

'I am sticking with *Routledge Student Statutes*' – Francis Tansinda, Manchester Metropolitan University, UK

ROUTLEDGE
STUDENT STATUTES

Criminal Law Statutes
2012–2013

JONATHAN HERRING
Fellow at Exeter College, Oxford University

LONDON AND NEW YORK

First published 2013
by Routledge
2 Park Square, Milton Park, Abingdon, Oxon OX14 4RN

Simultaneously published in the USA and Canada
by Routledge
711 Third Avenue, New York, NY 10017

Routledge is an imprint of the Taylor & Francis Group, an informa business

British Library Cataloguing in Publication Data
A catalogue record for this book is available from the British Library

Library of Congress Cataloging in Publication Data
A catalog record for this book has been requested

ISBN: 978–0–415–63382–6 (pbk)

Typeset in Sabon
by RefineCatch Limited, Bungay, Suffolk

MIX
Paper from
responsible sources
FSC www.fsc.org   FSC® C004839

Printed and bound in Great Britain by
TJ International Ltd, Padstow, Cornwall

Contents

Preface   x
Guide to the Companion Website   xi
Alphabetical Index   xii–xiii
Chronological Index   xiv–xv

Accessories and Abettors Act 1861   1
Offences Against the Person Act 1861   1–6
Explosive Substances Act 1883   6–8
Trial of Lunatics Act 1883   8
Official Secrets Act 1911   8–9
Perjury Act 1911   9–10
Criminal Justice Act 1925   10
Infant Life (Preservation) Act 1929   10–11
Children and Young Persons Act 1933   11–12
Public Order Act 1936   12
Infanticide Act 1938   12–13
Prevention of Crime Act 1953   13
Sexual Offences Act 1956   13–14
Homicide Act 1957   14–15
Obscene Publications Act 1959   15–17
Street Offences Act 1959   17–18
Suicide Act 1961   18–19
Criminal Procedure (Insanity) Act 1964   19
Murder (Abolition of Death Penalty) Act 1965   19
Abortion Act 1967   20–21
Criminal Justice Act 1967   21
Criminal Law Act 1967   21–24
Sexual Offences Act 1967   24
Criminal Appeals Act 1968   24–26
Firearms Act 1968   27–39
Theft Act 1968   40–51
Tattooing of Minors Act 1969   51
Criminal Damage Act 1971   51–53
Misuse of Drugs Act 1971   54–59
Criminal Law Act 1977   59–62
Interpretation Act 1978   62–63
Protection of Children Act 1978   63–64
Theft Act 1978   64–65
Magistrates' Courts Act 1980   65
Criminal Attempts Act 1981   65–68

Forgery and Counterfeiting Act 1981   68–71
Taking of Hostages Act 1982   71
Child Abduction Act 1984   71–73
Intoxicating Substances (Supply) Act 1985   73–74
Sexual Offences Act 1985   74–75
Public Order Act 1986   75–82
Criminal Justice Act 1987   82–85
Firearms (Amendment) Act 1988   85–86
Malicious Communications Act 1988   86
Road Traffic Act 1988   86–89
Official Secrets Act 1989   89–97
Computer Misuse Act 1990   97–102
Criminal Procedure (Insanity and Unfitness to Plead) Act 1991   102
Dangerous Dogs Act 1991   102–105
Football (Offences) Act 1991   105–106
Sexual Offences Act 1993   106
Criminal Justice and Public Order Act 1994   107
Family Law Act 1996   107–108
Law Reform (Year and a Day Rule) Act 1996   108
Police Act 1996   108–109
Protection from Harassment Act 1997   110–112
Firearms (Amendment) Act 1997   112–113
Knives Act 1997   113–115
Crime and Disorder Act 1998   115–118
Human Rights Act 1998   118–126
Youth Justice and Criminal Evidence Act 1999   126–133
Finance Act 2000   134
Terrorism Act 2000   134–143
Anti-Terrorism, Crime and Security Act 2001   143–145
Mobile Telephones (Re-programming) Act 2002   145–146
Communications Act 2003   146–147
Female Genital Mutilation Act 2003   147–148
Licensing Act 2003   148–150
Sexual Offences Act 2003   151–187
Children Act 2004   187
Domestic Violence, Crime and Victims Act 2004   187–188
Gender Recognition Act 2004   189
Hunting Act 2004   189–194
Gambling Act 2005   194
Mental Capacity Act 2005   194–198
Serious Organised Crime and Police Act 2005   198–202
Violent Crime Reduction Act 2006   203–205
Fraud Act 2006   205–208
Terrorism Act 2006   208–218
Wireless Telegraphy Act 2006   218–219
Corporate Manslaughter and Corporate Homicide Act 2007   219–224
Serious Crime Act 2007   225–229
UK Borders Act 2007   229
Criminal Justice and Immigration Act 2008   229–233
Coroners and Justice Act 2009   233–237
Policing and Crime Act 2009   237–238
Bribery Act 2010   238–245

Crime and Security Act 2010   245–248
Sunbeds (Regulation) Act 2010   248–249
Protection of Freedoms Act 2012   249

Thematic Index   250–251

Preface

The aim of this book is to provide the key criminal law statutes that apply to English criminal law. They are printed incorporating any amendments made by 1st May 2012. At the end of each statute I have referred to the legislation which has amended the original legislation. The statutes are published in chronological order. However, there are also indices of them alphabetically and thematically.

There are over 10,000 offences in English law and, of course, it has not been possible to include them all. I have selected those which most commonly are used in undergraduate criminal law courses or are of general interest. I am grateful to Damian Mitchell and Emma Nugent at Routledge for their help and advice in preparing this book.

Jonathan Herring

Guide to the Companion Website

www.routledge.com/cw/statutes

Visit the Companion Website for *Routledge Student Statutes* in order to:

- Understand how to use a statute book in tutorials and exams;

- Learn how to interpret statutes and other legislation to maximum effect;

- Gain essential practice in statute interpretation prior to your exams, through unique problem-based scenarios;

- Test your understanding of statutes through a set of Multiple Choice Questions for revision or to check your own progress;

- Understand how the law is developing with updates, additional information and links to useful websites.

Alphabetical Index

Abortion Act 1967 — 20–21

Accessories and Abettors Act 1861 — 1

Anti-Terrorism, Crime and Security
Act 2001 — 143–145

Bribery Act 2010 — 238–245

Child Abduction Act 1984 — 71–72

Children Act 2004 — 187

Children and Young Persons
Act 1933 — 11–12

Communications Act 2003 — 146–147

Computer Misuse Act 1990 — 97–102

Coroners and Justice Act 2009 — 233–237

Corporate Manslaughter and
Corporate Homicide
Act 2007 — 219–224

Crime and Disorder Act 1998 — 115–118

Crime and Security Act 2010 — 245–248

Criminal Appeals Act 1968 — 24–26

Criminal Attempts Act 1981 — 65–68

Criminal Damage Act 1971 — 51–53

Criminal Justice Act 1925 — 10

Criminal Justice Act 1967 — 21

Criminal Justice Act 1987 — 82–85

Criminal Justice and Immigration
Act 2008 — 229–233

Criminal Justice and Public
Order Act 1994 — 107

Criminal Law Act 1967 — 21–24

Criminal Law Act 1977 — 59–62

Criminal Procedure (Insanity)
Act 1964 — 19

Criminal Procedure (Insanity and
Unfitness to Plead) Act 1991 — 102

Dangerous Dogs Act 1991 — 102–105

Domestic Violence, Crime and
Victims Act 2004 — 187–188

Explosive Substances Act 1883 — 6–8

Family Law Act 1996 — 107–108

Female Genital Mutilation
Act 2003 — 147–148

Finance Act 2000 — 134

Firearms Act 1968 — 27–39

Firearms (Amendment) Act 1988 — 85–86

Firearms (Amendment) Act 1997 — 112–113

Football (Offences) Act 1991 — 105–106

Forgery and Counterfeiting
Act 1981 — 68–71

Fraud Act 2006 — 205–208

Gambling Act 2005 — 194

Gender Recognition Act 2004 — 189

Homicide Act 1957 — 14–15

Human Rights Act 1998 — 118–126

Hunting Act 2004 — 189–194

Infant Life (Preservation) Act 1929 — 10–11

Infanticide Act 1938 — 12–13

Interpretation Act 1978 — 62–63

Intoxicating Substances (Supply)
Act 1985 — 73–74

Knives Act 1997 — 113–115

Law Reform (Year and a Day Rule)
Act 1996 — 108

Licensing Act 2003 — 148–150

Magistrates' Courts Act 1980 — 65

Malicious Communications Act 1988 — 86

Mental Capacity Act 2005 — 194–198

Misuse of Drugs Act 1971 — 54–59

Mobile Telephones (Re-programming)
Act 2002 — 145–146

Murder (Abolition of Death Penalty)
Act 1965 — 19

Obscene Publications Act 1959 — 15–17

Offences Against the Person Act 1861 — 1–6

Official Secrets Act 1911 — 8–9

Official Secrets Act 1989 — 89–97

Perjury Act 1911 — 9–10

Police Act 1996 — 108–109

Policing and Crime Act 2009 — 237–238

Prevention of Crime Act 1953 — 13

Protection from Harassment Act 1997 — 110–112

Protection of Children Act 1978 — 63–64

Protection of Freedoms Act 2012 — 249

Public Order Act 1936 — 12

Public Order Act 1986 — 75–82

Road Traffic Act 1988   86–89

Serious Crime Act 2007   225–229
Serious Organised Crime and Police
    Act 2005   198–202
Sexual Offences Act 1956   13–14
Sexual Offences Act 1967   24
Sexual Offences Act 1985   74–75
Sexual Offences Act 1993   106
Sexual Offences Act 2003   151–187
Street Offences Act 1959   17–18
Suicide Act 1961   18–19
Sunbeds (Regulation) Act 2010   248–249

Taking of Hostages Act 1982   71

Tattooing of Minors Act 1969   51
Terrorism Act 2000   134–143
Terrorism Act 2006   208–218
Theft Act 1968   40–51
Theft Act 1978   64–65
Trial of Lunatics Act 1883   8

UK Borders Act 2007   229

Violent Crime Reduction Act 2006   203–205

Wireless Telegraphy Act 2006   218–219

Youth Justice and Criminal Evidence
    Act 1999   126–133

Chronological Index

1861	Accessories and Abettors Act	1
	Offences Against the Person Act	1–6
1883	Explosive Substances Act	6–8
	Trial of Lunatics Act	8
1911	Official Secrets Act	8–9
	Perjury Act	9–10
1925	Criminal Justice Act	10
1929	Infant Life (Preservation) Act	10–11
1933	Children and Young Persons Act	11–12
1936	Public Order Act	12
1938	Infanticide Act	12–13
1953	Prevention of Crime Act	13
1956	Sexual Offences Act	13–14
1957	Homicide Act	14–15
1959	Obscene Publications Act	15–17
	Street Offences Act	17–18
1961	Suicide Act	18–19
1964	Criminal Procedure (Insanity) Act	19
1965	Murder (Abolition of Death Penalty) Act	19
1967	Abortion Act	20–21
	Criminal Justice Act	21
	Criminal Law Act	21–24
	Sexual Offences Act	24
1968	Criminal Appeals Act	24–26
	Firearms Act	27–39
	Theft Act	40–51
1969	Tattooing of Minors Act	51
1971	Criminal Damage Act	51–53
	Misuse of Drugs Act	54–59
1977	Criminal Law Act	59–62
1978	Interpretation Act	62–63
	Protection of Children Act	63–64
	Theft Act	64–65
1980	Magistrates' Courts Act	65
1981	Criminal Attempts Act	65–68
	Forgery and Counterfeiting Act	68–71
1982	Taking of Hostages Act	71
1984	Child Abduction Act	71–73
1985	Intoxicating Substances (Supply) Act	73–74
	Sexual Offences Act	74–75
1986	Public Order Act	75–82
1987	Criminal Justice Act	82–85
1988	Firearms (Amendment) Act	85–86
	Malicious Communications Act	86
	Road Traffic Act	86–89
1989	Official Secrets Act	89–97
1990	Computer Misuse Act	97–102
1991	Criminal Procedure (Insanity and Unfitness to Plead) Act	102
	Dangerous Dogs Act	102–105
	Football (Offences) Act	105–106
1993	Sexual Offences Act	106
1994	Criminal Justice and Public Order Act	107
1996	Family Law Act	107–108
	Law Reform (Year and a Day Rule) Act	108
	Police Act	108–109
1997	Protection from Harassment Act	110–112
	Firearms (Amendment) Act	112–113
	Knives Act	113–115
1998	Crime and Disorder Act	115–118
	Human Rights Act	118–126
1999	Youth Justice and Criminal Evidence Act 1999	126–133
2000	Finance Act	134
	Terrorism Act	134–143
2001	Anti-Terrorism, Crime and Security Act	143–145
2002	Mobile Telephones (Re-programming) Act	145–146
2003	Communications Act	146–147
	Female Genital Mutilation Act	147–148
	Licensing Act	148–150
	Sexual Offences Act	151–187
2004	Children Act	187
	Domestic Violence, Crime and Victims Act	187–188
	Gender Recognition Act	189
	Hunting Act	189–194
2005	Gambling Act	194
	Mental Capacity Act	194–198
	Serious Organised Crime and Police Act	198–202
2006	Fraud Act	205–208
	Terrorism Act	208–218
	Violent Crime Reduction Act	203–205
	Wireless Telegraphy Act	218–219

2007   Corporate Manslaughter
       and Corporate
       Homicide Act   219–224
       Serious Crime Act   225–229
       UK Borders Act   229
2008   Criminal Justice and
       Immigration Act   229–233
2009   Coroners and Justice
       Act 2009   233–237

       Policing and Crime
       Act 2009   237–238
2010   Bribery Act   238–245
       Crime and Security
       Act 2010   245–248
       Sunbeds (Regulation)
       Act 2010   248–249
2012   Protection of Freedoms
       Act 2012   249

Statutes

ACCESSORIES AND ABETTORS ACT 1861

8 ABETTORS

Whosoever shall aid, abet, counsel, or procure the commission of any indictable offence, whether the same be an offence at common law or by virtue of any Act passed or to be passed, shall be liable to be tried, indicted, and punished as a principal offender.

As amended Criminal Law Act 1977, s65(7), Schedule 12.

OFFENCES AGAINST THE PERSON ACT 1861

4 CONSPIRING OR SOLICITING TO COMMIT MURDER

Whosoever shall solicit, encourage, persuade, or endeavour to persuade, or shall propose to any person, to murder any other person, whether he be a subject of Her Majesty or not, and whether he be within the Queen's dominions or not, shall be guilty of an offence, and being convicted thereof shall be liable to imprisonment for life.

9 MURDER OR MANSLAUGHTER ABROAD

Where any murder or manslaughter shall be committed on land out of the United Kingdom, whether within the Queen's dominions or without, and whether the person killed were a subject of Her Majesty or not, every offence committed by any subject of Her Majesty in respect of any such case, whether the same shall amount to the offence of murder or of manslaughter, may be dealt with, inquired of, tried, determined, and punished in England or Ireland. Provided, that nothing herein contained shall prevent any person from being tried in any place out of England or Ireland for any murder or manslaughter committed out of England or Ireland, in the same manner as such person might have been tried before the passing of this Act.

16 THREATS TO KILL

A person who without lawful excuse makes to another a threat, intending that that other would fear it would be carried out, to kill that other or a third person shall be guilty of an offence and liable on conviction on indictment to imprisonment for a term not exceeding ten years.

17 IMPEDING A PERSON ENDEAVOURING TO SAVE HIMSELF OR ANOTHER FROM SHIPWRECK

Whosoever shall unlawfully and maliciously prevent or impede any person, being on board of or having quitted any ship or vessel which shall be in distress, or wrecked, stranded, or cast on shore, in his endeavour to save his life, or shall unlawfully and maliciously prevent or impede any person in his endeavour to save the life of any such person as in this section first aforesaid, shall be guilty of an offence, and being convicted thereof shall be liable . . . to [imprisonment] for life . . .

18 SHOOTING OR ATTEMPTING TO SHOOT, OR WOUNDING, WITH INTENT TO DO GRIEVOUS BODILY HARM, OR TO RESIST APPREHENSION

Whosoever shall unlawfully and maliciously by any means whatsoever wound or cause any grievous bodily harm to any person with intent to do some grievous bodily harm to any person, or with intent to resist or prevent the lawful apprehension or detainer of any person, shall be guilty of an offence, and being convicted thereof shall be liable, to be [imprisonment] for life.

20 INFLICTING BODILY INJURY, WITH OR WITHOUT WEAPON

Whosoever shall unlawfully and maliciously wound or inflict any grievous bodily harm upon any other person, either with or without any weapon or instrument, shall be guilty of an offence, and being convicted thereof shall be liable to [imprisonment for a term not exceeding five years]

21 ATTEMPTING TO CHOKE, ETC, IN ORDER TO COMMIT OR ASSIST IN THE COMMITTING OF ANY INDICTABLE OFFENCE

Whosoever shall, by any means whatsoever, attempt to choke, suffocate, or strangle any other person, or shall by any means calculated to choke, suffocate, or strangle, attempt to render any other person insensible, unconscious, or incapable of resistance, with intent in any of such cases thereby to enable himself or any other person to commit, or with intent in any of such cases thereby to assist any other person in committing any indictable offence, shall be guilty of an offence, and being convicted thereof shall be liable to [imprisonment] for life.

22 USING CHLOROFORM, ETC, TO COMMIT OR ASSIST IN THE COMMITTING OF ANY INDICTABLE OFFENCE

Whosoever shall unlawfully apply or administer to or cause to be taken by, or attempt to apply or administer to or attempt to cause to be administered to or taken by, any person, any chloroform, laudanum, or other stupefying or overpowering drug, matter, or thing, with intent in any of such cases thereby to enable himself or any other person to commit, or with intent in any of such cases thereby to assist any other person in committing, any indictable offence, shall be guilty of an offence, and being convicted thereof shall be liable to be [imprisonment] for life.

23 MALICIOUSLY ADMINISTERING POISON, ETC, SO AS TO ENDANGER LIFE OR INFLICT GRIEVOUS BODILY HARM

Whosoever shall unlawfully and maliciously administer to or cause to be administered to or taken by any other person any poison or other destructive or noxious thing, so as thereby to endanger the life of such person, or so as thereby to inflict upon such person any grievous bodily harm, shall be guilty of an offence, and being convicted thereof shall be liable to [imprisonment] for any term not exceeding ten years.

24 MALICIOUSLY ADMINISTERING POISON, ETC, WITH INTENT TO INJURE, AGGRIEVE, OR ANNOY ANY OTHER PERSON

Whosoever shall unlawfully and maliciously administer to or cause to be administered to or taken by any other person any poison or other destructive or noxious thing, with intent to injure, aggrieve, or annoy such person, shall be guilty of an offence, and being convicted thereof shall be liable to [imprisonment for a term not exceeding five years] . . .

26 NOT PROVIDING APPRENTICES OR SERVANTS WITH FOOD, ETC, OR DOING BODILY HARM, WHEREBY LIFE IS ENDANGERED, OR HEALTH PERMANENTLY INJURED

Whosoever, being legally liable, either as a master or mistress, to provide for any apprentice or servant necessary food, clothing, or lodging, shall wilfully and without lawful excuse refuse or neglect to provide the same, or shall unlawfully and maliciously do or cause to be done any bodily harm to any such apprentice or servant, so that the life of such apprentice or servant shall be endangered, or the health of such apprentice or servant shall have been or shall be likely to be permanently injured, shall be guilty of an offence, and being convicted thereof shall be liable. to [imprisonment for a term not exceeding five years].

27 EXPOSING CHILD, WHEREBY LIFE IS ENDANGERED, OR HEALTH PERMANENTLY INJURED

Whosoever shall unlawfully abandon or expose any child, being under the age of two years, whereby the life of such child shall be endangered, or the health of such child shall have been or shall be likely to be permanently injured, shall be guilty of an offence, and being convicted thereof shall be liable to [imprisonment for a term not exceeding five years].

28 CAUSING BODILY INJURY BY GUNPOWDER

Whosoever shall unlawfully and maliciously, by the explosion of gunpowder or other explosive substance, burn, maim, disfigure, disable, or do any grievous bodily harm to any person, shall be guilty of an offence, and being convicted thereof shall be liable, at the discretion of the court, to [imprisonment for life].

29 CAUSING GUNPOWDER TO EXPLODE, OR SENDING TO ANY PERSON AN EXPLOSIVE SUBSTANCE, OR THROWING CORROSIVE FLUID ON A PERSON, WITH INTENT TO DO GRIEVOUS BODILY HARM

Whosoever shall unlawfully and maliciously cause any gunpowder or other explosive substance to explode, or send or deliver to or cause to be taken or received by any person any explosive substance or any other dangerous or noxious thing, or put or lay at any place, or cast or throw at or upon or otherwise apply to any person, any corrosive fluid or any destructive or explosive substance, with intent in any of the cases aforesaid to burn, maim, disfigure, or disable any person, or to do some grievous bodily harm to any person, shall, whether any bodily injury be effected or not, be guilty of an offence, and being convicted thereof shall be liable at the discretion of the court, to [imprisonment for life].

30 PLACING GUNPOWDER NEAR A BUILDING, ETC, WITH INTENT TO DO BODILY INJURY TO ANY PERSON

Whosoever shall unlawfully and maliciously place or throw in, into, upon, against, or near any building, ship, or vessel any gunpowder or other explosive substance, with intent to do any bodily injury to any person, shall, whether or not any explosion take place, and whether or not any bodily injury be effected, be guilty of an offence, and being convicted thereof shall be liable, at the discretion of the court, [imprisonment] for any term not exceeding fourteen years or to be imprisoned.

31 SETTING OR ALLOWING TO REMAIN SPRING GUNS, ETC, WITH INTENT TO INFLICT GRIEVOUS BODILY HARM

Whosoever shall set or place, or cause to be set or placed, any spring gun, man trap, or other engine calculated to destroy human life or inflict grievous bodily harm, with the intent that the same or whereby the same may destroy or inflict grievous bodily harm upon a trespasser or other person coming in contact therewith, shall be guilty of an offence, and being convicted thereof shall be liable to [imprisonment for a term not exceeding five years]; and whosoever shall knowingly and wilfully permit any such spring gun, man trap, or other engine which may have been set or placed in any place then being in or afterwards coming into his possession or occupation by some other person to continue so set or placed, shall be deemed to have set and placed such gun, trap, or engine with such intent as aforesaid: Provided, that nothing in this section contained shall extend to make it illegal to set or place any gin or trap such as may have been or may be usually set or placed with the intent of destroying vermin: Provided also, that nothing in this section shall be deemed to make it unlawful to set or place, or cause to be set or placed, or to be continued set or placed, from sunset to sunrise, any spring gun, man trap, or other engine which shall be set or placed, or caused or continued to be set or placed, in a dwelling-house, for the protection thereof.

32 PLACING WOOD, ETC, ON RAILWAY, TAKING UP RAILS, TURNING POINTS, SHOWING OR HIDING SIGNALS, ETC, WITH INTENT TO ENDANGER PASSENGERS

Whosoever shall unlawfully and maliciously put or throw upon or across any railway any wood, stone, or other matter or thing, or shall unlawfully and maliciously take up, remove, or displace any rail, sleeper, or other matter or thing belonging to any railway, or shall unlawfully and maliciously turn, move, or divert any points or other machinery belonging to any railway, or shall unlawfully and maliciously make or show, hide or remove, any signal or light upon or near to any railway, or shall unlawfully and maliciously do or cause to be done any other matter or thing, with intent, in any of the cases aforesaid, to endanger the safety of any person travelling or being upon such railway, shall be guilty of an offence, and being convicted thereof shall be liable, at the discretion of the court, to [imprisonment for life].

33 CASTING STONE, ETC, UPON A RAILWAY CARRIAGE, WITH INTENT TO ENDANGER THE SAFETY OF ANY PERSON THEREIN, OR IN PART OF THE SAME TRAIN

Whosoever shall unlawfully and maliciously throw, or cause to fall or strike, at, against, into, or upon any engine, tender, carriage, or truck used upon any railway, any wood, stone, or other matter or thing, with intent to injure or endanger the safety of any person being in or upon such engine, tender, carriage, or truck, or in or upon any other engine, tender, carriage, or truck of any train of which such first-mentioned engine, tender, carriage, or truck shall form part, shall be guilty of an offence, and being convicted thereof shall be liable to be [imprisonment for life].

34 DOING OR OMITTING ANYTHING SO AS TO ENDANGER PASSENGERS BY RAILWAY

Whosoever, by any unlawful act, or by any wilful omission or neglect, shall endanger or cause to be endangered the safety of any person conveyed or being in or upon a railway, or shall aid or assist therein, shall be guilty of an offence, and being convicted thereof shall be liable, at the discretion of the court, to be imprisoned for any term not exceeding two years, with or without hard labour.

35 DRIVERS OF CARRIAGES INJURING PERSONS BY FURIOUS DRIVING

Whosoever, having the charge of any carriage or vehicle, shall by wanton or furious driving or racing, or other wilful misconduct, or by wilful neglect, do or cause to be done any bodily harm to any person whatsoever, shall be guilty of an offence, and being convicted thereof shall be liable, at the discretion of the court, to be imprisoned for any term not exceeding two years, with or without hard labour.

36 OBSTRUCTING OR ASSAULTING A CLERGYMAN OR OTHER MINISTER IN THE DISCHARGE OF HIS DUTIES IN PLACE OF WORSHIP OR BURIAL PLACE, OR ON HIS WAY THITHER

Whosoever shall, by threats or force, obstruct or prevent or endeavour to obstruct or prevent, any clergyman or other minister in or from celebrating divine service or otherwise officiating in any church, chapel, meeting house, or other place of divine worship, or in or from the performance of his duty in the lawful burial of the dead in any churchyard or other burial place, or shall strike or offer any violence to, or shall, upon any civil process, or under the pretence of executing any civil process, arrest any clergyman or other minister who is engaged in, or to the knowledge of the offender is about to engage in, any of the rites or duties in this section aforesaid, or who to the knowledge of the offender shall be going to perform the same or returning from the performance thereof, shall be guilty of a an offence and being convicted thereof shall be liable, at the discretion of the court, to be imprisoned for any term not exceeding two years.

37 ASSAULTING A MAGISTRATE, ETC, ON ACCOUNT OF HIS PRESERVING WRECK

Whosoever shall assault and strike or wound any magistrate, officer, or other person whatsoever lawfully authorized, in or on account of the exercise of his duty in or concerning the preservation of any vessel in distress, or of any vessel, goods, or effects wrecked, stranded, or cast on shore, or lying under water, shall be guilty of an offence, and being convicted thereof shall be liable . . . [to a term of imprisonment not exceeding seven years].

38 ASSAULT WITH INTENT TO RESIST ARREST

Whosoever . . . shall assault any person with intent to resist or prevent the lawful apprehension or detainer of himself or of any other person for any offence, shall be guilty of an offence, and being convicted thereof shall be liable, at the discretion of the court, to be imprisoned for any term not exceeding two years.

47 ASSAULT OCCASIONING BODILY HARM—COMMON ASSAULT

Whosoever shall be convicted upon an indictment of any assault occasioning actual bodily harm shall be liable to be [imprisoned for any term not exceeding five years].

57 BIGAMY

Whosoever, being married, shall marry any other person during the life of the former husband or wife, whether the second marriage shall have taken place in England or Ireland or elsewhere, shall be guilty of an offence, and being convicted thereof shall be liable to be [imprisoned] for any term not exceeding seven years: Provided, that nothing in this section contained shall extend to any second marriage contracted elsewhere than in England and Ireland by any other than a subject of Her Majesty, or to any person marrying a second time whose husband or wife shall have been continually absent from such person for the space of seven years then last past, and shall not have been known by such person to be living within that time, or shall extend to any person who, at the time of such second marriage, shall have been divorced from the bond of the first marriage, or to any person whose former marriage shall have been declared void by the sentence of any court of competent jurisdiction.

58 ADMINISTERING DRUGS OR USING INSTRUMENTS TO PROCURE ABORTION

Every woman, being with child, who, with intent to procure her own miscarriage, shall unlawfully administer to herself any poison or other noxious thing, or shall unlawfully use any instrument or other means whatsoever with the like intent, and whosoever, with intent to procure the miscarriage of any woman, whether she be or be not with child, shall unlawfully administer to her or cause to be taken by her any poison or other noxious thing, or shall unlawfully use any instrument or other means whatsoever with the like intent, shall be guilty of an offence, and being convicted thereof shall be liable to be [imprisoned] for life.

59 PROCURING DRUGS, ETC, TO CAUSE ABORTION

Whosoever shall unlawfully supply or procure any poison or other noxious thing, or any instrument or thing whatsoever, knowing that the same is intended to be unlawfully used or employed with intent to procure the miscarriage of any woman, whether she be or be not with child, shall be guilty of an offence, and being convicted thereof shall be liable to [a term of imprisonment not exceeding five years].

60 CONCEALING THE BIRTH OF A CHILD

If any woman shall be delivered of a child, every person who shall, by any secret disposition of the dead body of the said child, whether such child died before, at, or after its birth, endeavour to conceal the birth thereof, shall be guilty of an offence, and being convicted thereof shall be liable, at the discretion of the court, to be imprisoned for any term not exceeding two years.

As amended Statute Law Revision Act 1892, the Statute Law Revision (No 2) Act 1893; Criminal Law Act 1967, s 10(2), and the Criminal Law Act 1967, s 10(2); Criminal Law Act 1977, s 65.

EXPLOSIVE SUBSTANCES ACT 1883

2 CAUSING EXPLOSION LIKELY TO ENDANGER LIFE OR PROPERTY

A person who in the United Kingdom or (being a citizen of the United Kingdom and Colonies) in the Republic of Ireland unlawfully and maliciously causes by any explosive substance an explosion of a nature likely to endanger life or to cause serious injury to property shall, whether any injury to person or property has been actually caused or not, be guilty of an offence and on conviction on indictment shall be liable to imprisonment for life.

3 ATTEMPT TO CAUSE EXPLOSION, OR MAKING OR KEEPING EXPLOSIVE WITH INTENT TO ENDANGER LIFE OR PROPERTY

(1)   A person who in the United Kingdom or a dependency or (being a citizen of the United Kingdom and Colonies) elsewhere unlawfully and maliciously—

(a)   does any act with intent to cause, or conspires to cause, by an explosive substance an explosion of a nature likely to endanger life, or cause serious injury to property, whether in the United Kingdom or the Republic of Ireland, or

(b)   makes or has in his possession or under his control an explosive substance with intent by means thereof to endanger life, or cause serious injury to property, whether in the United Kingdom or the Republic of Ireland, or to enable any other person so to do,

shall, whether any explosion does or does not take place, and whether any injury to person or property is actually caused or not, be guilty of an offence and on conviction on indictment shall be liable to imprisonment for life, and the explosive substance shall be forfeited.

(2)   In this section "dependency" means the Channel Islands, the Isle of Man and any colony, other than a colony for whose external relations a country other than the United Kingdom is responsible.

4 PUNISHMENT FOR MAKING OR POSSESSION OF EXPLOSIVE UNDER SUSPICIOUS CIRCUMSTANCES

(1)   Any person who makes or knowingly has in his possession or under his control any explosive substance, under such circumstances as to give rise to a reasonable suspicion that he is not making it or does not have it in his possession or under his control for a lawful object, shall, unless he can show that he made it or had it in his possession or under his control for a lawful object, be guilty of an offence, and, on conviction, shall be liable to imprisonment for a term not exceeding fourteen years, or to imprisonment for a term not exceeding two years, and the explosive substance shall be forfeited.

(2)   In any proceeding against any person for a crime under this section, such person and his wife, or husband, as the case may be, may, if such person thinks fit, be called, sworn, examined, and cross-examined as an ordinary witness in the case.

5 PUNISHMENT OF ACCESSORIES

Any person who within or (being a subject of Her Majesty) without Her Majesty's dominions by the supply of or solicitation for money, the providing of premises, the supply of materials, or in any manner whatsoever, procures, counsels, aids, abets, or is accessory to, the commission of any crime under this Act, shall be guilty of felony, and shall be liable to be tried and punished for that crime, as if he had been guilty as a principal.

9 DEFINITIONS, AND APPLICATION TO SCOTLAND

(1)   In this Act, unless the context otherwise requires—

The expression "explosive substance" shall be deemed to include any materials for making any explosive substance; also any apparatus, machine, implement, or materials used, or intended to be used, or adapted for causing, or aiding in causing, any explosion in or with any explosive substance; also any part of any such apparatus, machine, or implement. . . .

As amended by Criminal Jurisdiction Act 1975, s7, 13; Criminal Law Act 1977; Police and Criminal Evidence Act 1984, s. 119.

TRIAL OF LUNATICS ACT 1883

2 SPECIAL VERDICT WHERE ACCUSED FOUND GUILTY, BUT INSANE AT DATE OF ACT OR OMISSION CHARGED, AND ORDERS THEREUPON

(1)   Where in any indictment or information any act or omission is charged against any person as an offence, and it is given in evidence on the trial of such person for that offence that he was insane, so as not to be responsible, according to law, for his actions at the time when the act was done or omission made, then, if it appears to the jury before whom such person is tried that he did the act or made the omission charged, but was insane as aforesaid at the time when he did or made the same, the jury shall return a special verdict that the accused is not guilty by reason of insanity.

OFFICIAL SECRETS ACT 1911

1 PENALTIES FOR SPYING

(1)   If any person for any purpose prejudicial to the safety or interests of the State—
  (a) approaches inspects, passes over or is in the neighbourhood of, or enters any prohibited place within the meaning of this Act; or
  (b) makes any sketch, plan, model, or note which is calculated to be or might be or is intended to be directly or indirectly useful to an enemy; or
  (c) obtains, collects, records, or publishes, or communicates to any other person any secret official code word or pass word, or any sketch, plan, model, article, or note, or other document or information which is calculated to be or might be or is intended to be directly or indirectly useful to an enemy;
he shall be guilty of an offence . . .

(2)   On a prosecution under this section, it shall not be necessary to show that the accused person was guilty of any particular act tending to show a purpose prejudicial to the safety or interests of the State, and, notwithstanding that no such act is proved against him, he may be convicted if, from the circumstances of the case, or his conduct, or his known character as proved, it appears that his purpose was a purpose prejudicial to the safety or interests of the State; and if any sketch, plan, model, article, note, document, or information relating to or used in any prohibited place within the meaning of this Act, or anything in such a place or any secret official code word or pass word, is made, obtained, collected, recorded, published, or communicated by any person other than a person acting under lawful authority, it shall be deemed to have been made, obtained, collected, recorded, published or communicated for a purpose prejudicial to the safety or interests of the State unless the contrary is proved.

3 DEFINITION OF PROHIBITED PLACE

For the purposes of this Act, the expression "prohibited place" means—

(a)   any work of defence, arsenal, naval or air force establishment or station, factory, dockyard, mine, minefield, camp, ship, or aircraft belonging to or occupied by or on behalf of His Majesty, or any telegraph, telephone, wireless or signal station, or office so belonging or occupied, and any place belonging to or occupied by or on behalf of His Majesty and used for the purpose of building, repairing, making, or storing any munitions of war, or any sketches, plans, models, or documents relating thereto, or for the purpose of getting any metals, oil, or minerals of use in time of war;

(b)   any place not belonging to His Majesty where any munitions of war, or any sketches, models, plans or documents relating thereto, are being made, repaired, gotten or stored under contract with, or with any person on behalf of, His Majesty, or otherwise on behalf of His Majesty; and

(c)   any place belonging to or used for the purposes of His Majesty which is for the time being declared by order of a Secretary of State to be a prohibited place for the purposes of this section on the ground that information with respect thereto, or damage thereto, would be useful to an enemy; and

(d)   any railway, road, way, or channel, or other means of communication by land or water (including any works or structures being part thereof or connected therewith), or any place used for gas, water, or electricity works or other works for purposes of a public character, or any place where any munitions of war, or any sketches, models, plans or documents relating thereto, are being made, repaired, or stored otherwise than on behalf of His Majesty, which is for the time being declared by order of a Secretary of State to be a prohibited place for the purposes of this section, on the ground that information with respect thereto, or the destruction or obstruction thereof, or interference therewith, would be useful to an enemy.

As amended by Official Secrets Act 1920, s10; Official Secrets Act 1989, s 16.

PERJURY ACT 1911

1 PERJURY

(1)   If any person lawfully sworn as a witness or as an interpreter in a judicial proceeding wilfully makes a statement material in that proceeding, which he knows to be false or does not believe to be true, he shall be guilty of perjury, and shall, on conviction thereof on indictment, be liable to imprisonment for a term not exceeding seven years, or to imprisonment with or without hard labour for a term not exceeding two years, or to a fine or to both such imprisonment and fine.

(2)   The expression "judicial proceeding" includes a proceeding before any court, tribunal, or person having by law power to hear, receive, and examine evidence on oath.

(3)   Where a statement made for the purposes of a judicial proceeding is not made before the tribunal itself, but is made on oath before a person authorised by law to administer an oath to the person who makes the statement, and to record or authenticate the statement, it shall, for the purposes of this section, be treated as having been made in a judicial proceeding.

(4)   A statement made by a person lawfully sworn in England for the purposes of a judicial proceeding—
(a) in another part of His Majesty's dominions; or
(b) in a British tribunal lawfully constituted in any place by sea or land outside His Majesty's dominions; or
(c) in a tribunal of any foreign state,
shall, for the purposes of this section, be treated as a statement made in a judicial proceeding in England.

(5)   Where, for the purposes of a judicial proceeding in England, a person is lawfully sworn under the authority of an Act of Parliament—
(a) in any other part of His Majesty's dominions; or
(b) before a British tribunal or a British officer in a foreign country, or within the jurisdiction of the Admiralty of England;
a statement made by such person so sworn as aforesaid (unless the Act of Parliament under which it was made otherwise specifically provides) shall be treated for the purposes of this section as having been made in the judicial proceeding in England for the purposes whereof it was made.

(6)   The question whether a statement on which perjury is assigned was material is a question of law to be determined by the court of trial.

CRIMINAL JUSTICE ACT 1925

47 ABOLITION OF PRESUMPTION OF COERCION OF MARRIED WOMAN BY HUSBAND

Any presumption of law that an offence committed by a wife in the presence of her husband is committed under the coercion of the husband is hereby abolished, but on a charge against a wife for any offence other than treason or murder it shall be a good defence to prove that the offence was committed in the presence of, and under the coercion of, the husband.

INFANT LIFE (PRESERVATION) ACT 1929

1 PUNISHMENT FOR CHILD DESTRUCTION

(1)   Subject as hereinafter in this subsection provided, any person who, with intent to destroy the life of a child capable of being born alive, by any wilful act causes a child to die before it has an existence independent of its mother, shall be guilty of felony, to wit, of child destruction, and shall be liable on conviction thereof on indictment to imprisonment for life:

Provided that no person shall be found guilty of an offence under this section unless it is proved that the act which caused the death of the child was not done in good faith for the purpose only of preserving the life of the mother.

(2)   For the purposes of this Act, evidence that a woman had at any material time been pregnant for a period of twenty-eight weeks or more shall be prima facie proof that she was at that time pregnant of a child capable of being born alive.

2 PROSECUTION OF OFFENCES

(2) Where upon the trial of any person for the murder or manslaughter of any child, or for infanticide, or for an offence under section 58 of the Offences against the Person Act 1861 (which relates to administering drugs or using instruments to procure abortion), the jury are of opinion that the person charged is not guilty of murder, manslaughter or infanticide, or of an offence under the said section fifty-eight, as the case may be, but that he is shown by the evidence to be guilty of the felony of child destruction, the jury may find him guilty of that felony, and thereupon the person convicted shall be liable to be punished as if he had been convicted upon an indictment for child destruction.

(3) Where upon the trial of any person for the felony of child destruction the jury are of opinion that the person charged is not guilty of that felony, but that he is shown by the evidence to be guilty of an offence under the said section 58 of the Offences against the Person Act 1861 the jury may find him guilty of that offence, and thereupon the person convicted shall be liable to be punished as if he had been convicted upon an indictment under that section.

CHILDREN AND YOUNG PERSONS ACT 1933

1 CRUELTY TO PERSONS UNDER SIXTEEN

(1) If any person who has attained the age of sixteen years and has responsibility for any child or young person under that age, wilfully assaults, ill-treats, neglects, abandons, or exposes him, or causes or procures him to be assaulted, ill-treated, neglected, abandoned, or exposed, in a manner likely to cause him unnecessary suffering or injury to health (including injury to or loss of sight, or hearing, or limb, or organ of the body, and any mental derangement), that person shall be guilty of a crime, and shall be liable—
   (a) on conviction on indictment, to a fine or alternatively, or in addition thereto, to imprisonment for any term not exceeding ten years;
   (b) on summary conviction, to a fine not exceeding £400 pounds, or alternatively, or in addition thereto, to imprisonment for any term not exceeding six months.
(2) For the purposes of this section—
   (a) a parent or other person legally liable to maintain a child or young person or the legal guardian of a child or young person, shall be deemed to have neglected him in a manner likely to cause injury to his health if he has failed to provide adequate food, clothing, medical aid or lodging for him, or if, having been unable otherwise to provide such food, clothing, medical aid or lodging, he has failed to take steps to procure it to be provided under the enactments applicable in that behalf;
   (b) where it is proved that the death of an infant under three years of age was caused by suffocation (not being suffocation caused by disease or the presence of any foreign body in the throat or air passages of the infant) while the infant was in bed with some other person who has attained the age of sixteen years, that other person shall, if he was, when he went to bed, under the influence of drink, be deemed to have neglected the infant in a manner likely to cause injury to its health.
(3) A person may be convicted of an offence under this section—
   (a) notwithstanding that actual suffering or injury to health, or the liklihood of actual suffering or injury to health, was obviated by the action of another person;
   (b) notwithstanding the death of the child or young person in question. . . .

50 AGE OF CRIMINAL RESPONSIBILITY

It shall be conclusively presumed that no child under the age of ten years can be guilty of any offence.

As amended by Children and Young Person Act 1963, s.64, Criminal Law Act 1967, s. 12, Children Act 1975, schedules 3 and 4, Criminal Justice Act 1988, ss 45, 170 Children Act 1989, s. 108, Sch 13; Children and Young Persons (Protection from Tobacco) Act 1991, s1.

PUBLIC ORDER ACT 1936

1 PROHIBITION OF UNIFORMS IN CONNECTION WITH POLITICAL OBJECTS

(1)   Subject as hereinafter provided, any person who in any public place or at any public meeting wears uniform signifying his association with any political organisation or with the promotion of any political object shall be guilty of an offence:

Provided that, if the chief officer of police is satisfied that the wearing of any such uniform as aforesaid on any ceremonial, anniversary, or other special occasion will not be likely to involve risk of public disorder, he may, with the consent of a Secretary of State, by order permit the wearing of such uniform on that occasion either absolutely or subject to such conditions as may be specified in the order.

(2)   Where any person is charged before any court with an offence under this section, no further proceedings in respect thereof shall be taken against him without the consent of the Attorney-General except such as are authorised by section 6 of the Prosecution of Offences Act 1979) so, however, that if that person is remanded in custody he shall, after the expiration of a period of eight days from the date on which he was so remanded, be entitled to be released on bail without sureties unless within that period the Attorney-General has consented to such further proceedings as aforesaid.

As amended Criminal Jurisdiction 1975, s 14; Bail Act 1976, s12.

INFANTICIDE ACT 1938

1 OFFENCE OF INFANTICIDE

(1)   Where a woman by any wilful act or omission causes the death of her child being a child under the age of twelve months, but at the time of the act or omission the balance of her mind was disturbed by reason of her not having fully recovered from the effect of giving birth to the child or by reason of the effect of lactation consequent upon the birth of the child, then, if the circumstances were such that but for this Act the offence would have amounted to murder or manslaughter, she shall be guilty of felony, to wit of infanticide, and may for such offence be dealt with and punished as if she had been guilty of the offence of manslaughter of the child.

(2)   Where upon the trial of a woman for the murder of her child, being a child under the age of twelve months, the jury are of opinion that she by any wilful act or omission caused its death, but that at the time of the act or omission the balance of her mind was disturbed by reason of her not having fully recovered from the effect of giving birth to the child or by reason of the effect of lactation consequent upon the birth of the child, then the jury may, if the circumstances were such that but for the provisions of this Act they might have returned a verdict of murder or manslaughter, return in lieu thereof a verdict of infanticide.

(3)   Nothing in this Act shall affect the power of the jury upon an indictment for the murder of a child to return a verdict of manslaughter, or a verdict of guilty but insane.

As amended by Coroners and Justice Act 2009.

PREVENTION OF CRIME ACT 1953

1 PROHIBITION OF THE CARRYING OF OFFENSIVE WEAPONS WITHOUT LAWFUL AUTHORITY OR REASONABLE EXCUSE

(1)   Any person who without lawful authority or reasonable excuse, the proof whereof shall lie on him, has with him in any public place any offensive weapon shall be guilty of an offence, and shall be liable—
   (a)   on summary conviction, to imprisonment for a term not exceeding six months or a fine not exceeding the prescribed sum or both;
   (b)   on conviction on indictment, to imprisonment for a term not exceeding four years or a fine or both.

(2)   Where any person is convicted of an offence under subsection (1) of this section the court may make an order for the forfeiture or disposal of any weapon in respect of which the offence was committed.

(4)   In this section "public place" includes any highway and any other premises or place to which at the material time the public have or are permitted to have access, whether on payment or otherwise; and "offensive weapon" means any article made or adapted for use for causing injury to the person, or intended by the person having it with him for such use by him or by some other person.

SEXUAL OFFENCES ACT 1956

33 KEEPING A BROTHEL

It is an offence for a person to keep a brothel, or to manage, or act or assist in the management of, a brothel.

33A KEEPING A BROTHEL USED FOR PROSTITUTION

(1)   It is an offence for a person to keep, or to manage, or act or assist in the management of, a brothel to which people resort for practices involving prostitution (whether or not also for other practices).

(2)   In this section "prostitution" has the meaning given by section 51(2) of the Sexual Offences Act 2003.

34 LANDLORD LETTING PREMISES FOR USE AS BROTHEL

It is an offence for the lessor or landlord of any premises or his agent to let the whole or part of the premises with the knowledge that it is to be used, in whole or in part, as a brothel, or, where the whole or part of the premises is used as a brothel, to be wilfully a party to that use continuing.

35 TENANT PERMITTING PREMISES TO BE USED AS A BROTHEL

(1)   It is an offence for the tenant or occupier, or person in charge, of any premises knowingly to permit the whole or part of the premises to be used as a brothel.

(2)   Where the tenant or occupier of any premises is convicted . . . of knowingly permitting the whole or part of the premises to be used as a brothel, the First Schedule to this Act shall apply to enlarge the rights of the lessor or landlord with respect to the assignment or determination of the lease or other contract under which the premises are held by the person convicted.

(3)   Where the tenant or occupier of any premises is so convicted, and either—
    (a) the lessor or landlord, after having the conviction brought to his notice, fails or failed to exercise his statutory rights in relation to the lease or contract under which the premises are or were held by the person convicted; or
    (b) the lessor or landlord, after exercising his statutory rights so as to determine that lease or contract, grants or granted a new lease or enters or entered into a new contract of tenancy of the premises to, with or for the benefit of the same person, without having all reasonable provisions to prevent the recurrence of the offence inserted in the new lease or contract;
    then, if subsequently an offence under this section is committed in respect of the premises during the subsistence of the lease or contract referred to in paragraph (a) of this subsection or (where paragraph (b) applies) during the subsistence of the new lease or contract, the lessor or landlord shall be deemed to be a party to that offence unless he shows that he took all reasonable steps to prevent the recurrence of the offence.
    . . .

36 TENANT PERMITTING PREMISES TO BE USED FOR PROSTITUTION

It is an offence for the tenant or occupier of any premises knowingly to permit the whole or part of the premises to be used for the purposes of habitual prostitution (whether any prostitute involved is male or female).

As amended Sexual Offences Act 2003, s55;. Statute Law (Repeals) Act 2008, s1.

HOMICIDE ACT 1957

1 ABOLITION OF "CONSTRUCTIVE MALICE"

(1)   Where a person kills another in the course or furtherance of some other offence, the killing shall not amount to murder unless done with the same malice aforethought (express or implied) as is required for a killing to amount to murder when not done in the course or furtherance of another offence.

(2)   For the purposes of the foregoing subsection, a killing done in the course or for the purpose of resisting an officer of justice, or of resisting or avoiding or preventing a lawful arrest, or of effecting or assisting an escape or rescue from legal custody, shall be treated as a killing in the course or furtherance of an offence.

2 PERSONS SUFFERING FROM DIMINISHED RESPONSIBILITY

(1)   A person ("D") who kills or is a party to the killing of another is not to be convicted of murder if D was suffering from an abnormality of mental functioning which—
    (a)   arose from a recognised medical condition,
    (b)   substantially impaired D's ability to do one or more of the things mentioned in subsection (1A), and
    (c)   provides an explanation for D's acts and omissions in doing or being a party to the killing.

(1A)   Those things are—
    (a)   to understand the nature of D's conduct;
    (b)   to form a rational judgment;
    (c)   to exercise self-control.

(1B)   For the purposes of subsection (1)(c), an abnormality of mental functioning provides an explanation for D's conduct if it causes, or is a significant contributory factor in causing, D to carry out that conduct.

(2)   On a charge of murder, it shall be for the defence to prove that the person charged is by virtue of this section not liable to be convicted of murder.

(3)   A person who but for this section would be liable, whether as principal or as accessory, to be convicted of murder shall be liable instead to be convicted of manslaughter.

(4)   The fact that one party to a killing is by virtue of this section not liable to be convicted of murder shall not affect the question whether the killing amounted to murder in the case of any party to it.

4 SUICIDE PACTS

(1)   It shall be manslaughter, and shall not be murder, for a person acting in pursuance of a suicide pact between him and another to kill the other or be a party to the other . . . being killed by a third person.

(2)   Where it is shown that a person charged with the murder of another killed the other or was a party to his . . . being killed, it shall be for the defence to prove that the person charged was acting in pursuance of a suicide pact between him and the other.

(3)   For the purposes of this section "suicide pact" means a common agreement between two or more persons having for its object the death of all of them, whether or not each is to take his own life, but nothing done by a person who enters into a suicide pact shall be treated as done by him in pursuance of the pact unless it is done while he has the settled intention of dying in pursuance of the pact.

As amended by Coroners and Justice Act 2009.

OBSCENE PUBLICATIONS ACT 1959

1 TEST OF OBSCENITY

(1)   For the purposes of this Act an article shall be deemed to be obscene if its effect or (where the article comprises two or more distinct items) the effect of any one of its items is, if taken as a whole, such as to tend to deprave and corrupt persons who are likely, having regard to all relevant circumstances, to read, see or hear the matter contained or embodied in it.

(2)   In this Act "article" means any description of article containing or embodying matter to be read or looked at or both, any sound record, and any film or other record of a picture or pictures.

(3)   For the purposes of this Act a person publishes an article who—
   (a) distributes, circulates, sells, lets on hire, gives, or lends it, or who offers it for sale or for letting on hire; or
   (b) in the case of an article containing or embodying matter to be looked at or a record, shows, plays or projects it, or, where the matter is data stored electronically, transmits that data.

(4)   For the purposes of this Act a person also publishes an article to the extent that any matter recorded on it is included by him in a programme included in a programme service.

(5)   Where the inclusion of any matter in a programme so included would, if that matter were recorded matter, constitute the publication of an obscene article for the purposes of this Act by virtue of subsection (4) above, this Act shall have effect in relation to the inclusion of that matter in that programme as if it were recorded matter.

(6)   In this section "programme" and "programme service" have the same meaning as in the Broadcasting Act 1990.

2 PROHIBITION OF PUBLICATION OF OBSCENE MATTER

(1)   Subject as hereinafter provided, any person who, whether for gain or not publishes an obscene article or who has an obscene article for publication for gain (whether gain to himself or gain to another) shall be liable—
   (a) on summary conviction to a fine not exceeding the prescribed sum or to imprisonment for a term not exceeding six months;
   (b) on conviction on indictment to a fine or to imprisonment for a term not exceeding five years or both.

(3)   A prosecution . . . for an offence against this section shall not be commenced more than two years after the commission of the offence.

(3A) Proceedings for an offence under this section shall not be instituted except by or with the consent of the Director of Public Prosecutions in any case where the article in question is a moving picture film of a width of not less than sixteen millimetres and the relevant publication or the only other publication which followed or could reasonably have been expected to follow from the relevant publication took place or (as the case may be) was to take place in the course of an exhibition of a film; and in this subsection "the relevant publication" means—
   (a) in the case of any proceedings under this section for publishing an obscene article, the publication in respect of which the defendant would be charged if the proceedings were brought; and
   (b) in the case of any proceedings under this section for having an obscene article for publication for gain, the publication which, if the proceedings were brought, the defendant would be alleged to have had in contemplation.

. . .

(5)   A person shall not be convicted of an offence against this section if he proves that he had not examined the article in respect of which he is charged and had no reasonable cause to suspect that it was such that his publication of it would make him liable to be convicted of an offence against this section.

(6)   In any proceedings against a person under this section the question whether an article is obscene shall be determined without regard to any publication by another person unless it

could reasonably have been expected that the publication by the other person would follow from publication by the person charged.

4 DEFENCE OF PUBLIC GOOD

(1)   Subject to subsection (1A) of this section a person shall not be convicted of an offence against section two of this Act, and an order for forfeiture shall not be made under the foregoing section, if it is proved that publication of the article in question is justified as being for the public good on the ground that it is in the interests of science, literature, art or learning, or of other objects of general concern.

(1A) Subsection (1) of this section shall not apply where the article in question is a moving picture film or soundtrack, but—
       (a) a person shall not be convicted of an offence against section 2 of this Act in relation to any such film or soundtrack, and

. . .

       if it is proved that publication of the film or soundtrack is justified as being for the public good on the ground that it is in the interests of drama, opera, ballet or any other art, or of literature or learning.

(2)   It is hereby declared that the opinion of experts as to the literary, artistic, scientific or other merits of an article may be admitted in any proceedings under this Act either to establish or to negative the said ground.

As amended Broadcasting Act 1990; Criminal Law Act 1977.

STREET OFFENCES ACT 1959

1 LOITERING OR SOLICITING FOR PURPOSES OF PROSTITUTION

(1)   It shall be an offence for a person (whether male or female) persistently to loiter or solicit in a street or public place for the purpose of prostitution.

(2)   A person guilty of an offence under this section shall be liable on summary conviction to a fine of an amount not exceeding level 2 on the standard scale, or, for an offence committed after a previous conviction, to a fine of an amount not exceeding level 3 on that scale.

(4)   For the purposes of this section
       (a) conduct is persistent if it takes place on two or more occasions in any period of three months;
       (b) any reference to a person loitering or soliciting for the purposes of prostitution is a reference to a person loitering or soliciting for the purposes of offering services as a prostitute;
       (c) "street" includes any bridge, road, lane, footway, subway, square, court, alley or passage, whether a thoroughfare or not, which is for the time being open to the public; and the doorways and entrances of premises abutting on a street (as hereinbefore defined), and any ground adjoining and open to a street, shall be treated as forming part of the street.

As amended Sexual Offences Act 2003, s56; Policing and Crime Act 2009.

SUICIDE ACT 1961

1 SUICIDE TO CEASE TO BE A CRIME

The rule of law whereby it is a crime for a person to commit suicide is hereby abrogated.

2 CRIMINAL LIABILITY FOR COMPLICITY IN ANOTHER'S SUICIDE

(1)   A person ("D") commits an offence if—
   (a) D does an act capable of encouraging or assisting the suicide or attempted suicide of another person, and
   (b) D's act was intended to encourage or assist suicide or an attempt at suicide.

(1A)   The person referred to in subsection (1)(a) need not be a specific person (or class of persons) known to, or identified by, D.

(1B)   D may commit an offence under this section whether or not a suicide, or an attempt at suicide, occurs.

(1C)   An offence under this section is triable on indictment and a person convicted of such an offence is liable to imprisonment for a term not exceeding 14 years.

(2)   If on the trial of an indictment for murder or manslaughter it is proved that the accused aided, abetted, counselled or procured the suicide of the person in question, the jury may find him guilty of that offence.

. . .

(4)   . . . no proceedings shall be instituted for an offence under this section except by or with the consent of the Director of Public Prosecutions.

2A ACTS CAPABLE OF ENCOURAGING OR ASSISTING

(1)   If D arranges for a person ("D2") to do an act that is capable of encouraging or assisting the suicide or attempted suicide of another person and D2 does that act, D is also to be treated for the purposes of this Act as having done it.

(2)   Where the facts are such that an act is not capable of encouraging or assisting suicide or attempted suicide, for the purposes of this Act it is to be treated as so capable if the act would have been so capable had the facts been as D believed them to be at the time of the act or had subsequent events happened in the manner D believed they would happen (or both).

(3)   A reference in this Act to a person ("P") doing an act that is capable of encouraging the suicide or attempted suicide of another person includes a reference to P doing so by threatening another person or otherwise putting pressure on another person to commit or attempt suicide.

2B COURSE OF CONDUCT

A reference in this Act to an act includes a reference to a course of conduct, and a reference to doing an act is to be read accordingly

As amended Criminal Law Act 1967, s10; Coroners and Justice Act 2009, s. 59.

CRIMINAL PROCEDURE (INSANITY) ACT 1964

5 POWERS TO DEAL WITH PERSONS NOT GUILTY BY REASON OF INSANITY OR UNFIT TO PLEAD ETC

(1) This section applies where—
  (a) a special verdict is returned that the accused is not guilty by reason of insanity; or
  (b) findings have been made that the accused is under a disability and that he did the act or made the omission charged against him.

(2) The court shall make in respect of the accused—
  (a) a hospital order (with or without a restriction order);
  (b) a supervision order; or
  (c) an order for his absolute discharge.

(3) Where—
  (a) the offence to which the special verdict or the findings relate is an offence the sentence for which is fixed by law, and
  (b) the court have power to make a hospital order,
    the court shall make a hospital order with a restriction order (whether or not they would have power to make a restriction order apart from this subsection).

(4) In this section—

  "hospital order" has the meaning given in section 37 of the Mental Health Act 1983;

  "restriction order" has the meaning given to it by section 41 of that Act;

  "supervision order" has the meaning given in Part 1 of Schedule 1A to this Act.

As amended by Criminal Procedure (Insanity and Unfitness to Plead) Act 1991, s. 2, 3, 8; Criminal Appeal Act 1968, schedule 7.

MURDER (ABOLITION OF DEATH PENALTY) ACT 1965

1 ABOLITION OF DEATH PENALTY FOR MURDER

(1) No person shall suffer death for murder, and a person convicted of murder shall be sentenced to imprisonment for life.

(2) On sentencing any person convicted of murder to imprisonment for life the Court may at the same time declare the period which it recommends to the Secretary of State as the minimum period which in its view should elapse before the Secretary of State orders the release of that person on licence under section 61 of the Criminal Justice Act 1967

As amended by Powers of Criminal Courts (Sentencing) Act 2000 and Criminal Justice Act 2003.

ABORTION ACT 1967

1 MEDICAL TERMINATION OF PREGNANCY

(1)   Subject to the provisions of this section, a person shall not be guilty of an offence under the law relating to abortion when a pregnancy is terminated by a registered medical practitioner if two registered medical practitioners are of the opinion, formed in good faith—

    (a)   that the pregnancy has not exceeded its twenty-fourth week and that the continuance of the pregnancy would involve risk, greater than if the pregnancy were terminated, of injury to the physical or mental health of the pregnant woman or any existing children of her family; or

    (b)   that the termination is necessary to prevent grave permanent injury to the physical or mental health of the pregnant woman; or

    (c)   that the continuance of the pregnancy would involve risk to the life of the pregnant woman, greater than if the pregnancy were terminated; or

    (d)   that there is a substantial risk that if the child were born it would suffer from such physical or mental abnormalities as to be seriously handicapped.

(2)   In determining whether the continuance of a pregnancy would involve such risk of injury to health as is mentioned in paragraph (a) or (b) of subsection (1) of this section, account may be taken of the pregnant woman's actual or reasonably foreseeable environment.

(3)   Except as provided by subsection (4) of this section, any treatment for the termination of pregnancy must be carried out in a hospital vested in the Secretary of State for the purposes of his functions under the National Health Service Act 1977 or the National Health Service (Scotland) Act 1978 or in a hospital vested in a Primary Care Trust or a National Health Service trust or in a place approved for the purposes of this section by the Secretary of State.

(3A)   The power under subsection (3) of this section to approve a place includes power, in relation to treatment consisting primarily in the use of such medicines as may be specified in the approval and carried out in such manner as may be so specified, to approve a class of places.

(4)   Subsection (3) of this section, and so much of subsection (1) as relates to the opinion of two registered medical practitioners, shall not apply to the termination of a pregnancy by a registered medical practitioner in a case where he is of the opinion, formed in good faith, that the termination is immediately necessary to save the life or to prevent grave permanent injury to the physical or mental health of the pregnant woman.

5 SUPPLEMENTARY PROVISIONS

(1)   No offence under the Infant Life (Preservation) Act 1929 shall be committed by a registered medical practitioner who terminates a pregnancy in accordance with the provisions of this Act.

(2)   For the purposes of the law relating to abortion, anything done with intent to procure a woman's miscarriage (or, in the case of a woman carrying more than one foetus, her miscarriage of any foetus) is unlawfully done unless authorised by section 1 of this Act and, in the case of a woman carrying more than one foetus, anything done with intent to procure her miscarriage of any foetus is authorised by that section if-

    (a)   the ground for termination of the pregnancy specified in subsection (1)(d) of that section applies in relation to any foetus and the thing is done for the purpose of procuring the miscarriage of that foetus, or

    (b)   any of the other grounds for termination of the pregnancy specified in that section applies

6 INTERPRETATION

In this Act, the following expressions have meanings hereby assigned to them:—

"the law relating to abortion" means sections 58 and 59 of the Offences against the Person Act 1861, and any rule of law relating to the procurement of abortion;

As amended Health Services Act 1980, s 1,2; Human Fertilisation and Embryology Act 1990, s37, 39, 43; National Health Service and Community Care Act 1990, s.66, Schedule 9, para 8.

CRIMINAL JUSTICE ACT 1967

8 PROOF OF CRIMINAL INTENT

A court or jury, in determining whether a person has committed an offence,—

(a)   shall not be bound in law to infer that he intended or foresaw a result of his actions by reason only of its being a natural and probable consequence of those actions; but

(b)   shall decide whether he did intend or foresee that result by reference to all the evidence, drawing such inferences from the evidence as appear proper in the circumstances.

91 DRUNKENNESS IN A PUBLIC PLACE

(1)   Any person who in any public place is guilty, while drunk, of disorderly behaviour may be arrested without warrant by any person and shall be liable on summary conviction to a fine not exceeding level 3 on the standard scale.

. . .

(4)   In this section "public place" includes any highway and any other premises or place to which at the material time the public have or are permitted to have access, whether on payment or otherwise.

As amended by Criminal Justice Act 1982, s. 34, 38, 46; Criminal Law Act 1977, sch 13.

CRIMINAL LAW ACT 1967

1 ABOLITION OF DISTINCTION BETWEEN FELONY AND MISDEMEANOUR

(1)   All distinctions between felony and misdemeanour are hereby abolished.

(2)   Subject to the provisions of this Act, on all matters on which a distinction has previously been made between felony and misdemeanour, including mode of trial, the law and practice in relation to all offences cognisable under the law of England and Wales (including piracy) shall be the law and practice applicable at the commencement of this Act in relation to misdemeanour.

3 USE OF FORCE IN MAKING ARREST, ETC

(1)   A person may use such force as is reasonable in the circumstances in the prevention of crime, or in effecting or assisting in the lawful arrest of offenders or suspected offenders or of persons unlawfully at large.

(2)   Subsection (1) above shall replace the rules of the common law on the question when force used for a purpose mentioned in the subsection is justified by that purpose.

4 PENALTIES FOR ASSISTING OFFENDERS

(1)   Where a person has committed an arrestable offence, any other person who, knowing or believing him to be guilty of the offence or of some other arrestable offence, does without lawful authority or reasonable excuse any act with intent to impede his apprehension or prosecution shall be guilty of an offence.

(1A) In this section and section 5 below "arrestable offence" has the meaning assigned to it by section 24 of the Police and Criminal Evidence Act 1984.

(2)   If on the trial of an indictment for an arrestable offence the jury are satisfied that the offence charged (or some other offence of which the accused might on that charge be found guilty) was committed, but find the accused not guilty of it, they may find him guilty of any offence under subsection (1) above of which they are satisfied that he is guilty in relation to the offence charged (or that other offence).

(3)   A person committing an offence under subsection (1) above with intent to impede another person's apprehension or prosecution shall on conviction on indictment be liable to imprisonment according to the gravity of the other person's offence, as follows:—
  (a) if that offence is one for which the sentence is fixed by law, he shall be liable to imprisonment for not more than ten years;
  (b) if it is one for which a person (not previously convicted) may be sentenced to imprisonment for a term of fourteen years, he shall be liable to imprisonment for not more than seven years;
  (c) if it is not one included above but is one for which a person (not previously convicted) may be sentenced to imprisonment for a term of ten years, he shall be liable to imprisonment for not more than five years;
  (d) in any other case, he shall be liable to imprisonment for not more than three years.

(4)   No proceedings shall be instituted for an offence under subsection (1) above except by or with the consent of the Director of Public Prosecutions: . . .

5 PENALTIES FOR CONCEALING OFFENCES OR GIVING FALSE INFORMATION

(1)   Where a person has committed an arrestable offence, any other person who, knowing or believing that the offence or some other arrestable offence has been committed, and that he has information which might be of material assistance in securing the prosecution or conviction of an offender for it, accepts or agrees to accept for not disclosing that information any consideration other than the making good of loss or injury caused by the offence, or the making of reasonable compensation for that loss or injury, shall be liable on conviction on indictment to imprisonment for not more that two years.

(2)   Where a person causes any wasteful employment of the police by knowingly making to any person a false report tending to show that an offence has been committed, or to give rise to apprehension for the safety of any persons or property, or tending to show that he has information material to any police inquiry, he shall be liable on summary conviction

to imprisonment for not more than six months or to a fine of not more than two hundred pounds or to both.

(3) No proceedings shall be instituted for an offence under this section except by or with the consent of the Director of Public Prosecutions.

(5) The compounding of an offence other than treason shall not be an offence otherwise than under this section.

6 TRIAL OF OFFENCES

(1) Where a person is arraigned on an indictment—
   (a) he shall in all cases be entitled to make a plea of not guilty in addition to any demurrer or special plea;
   (b) he may plead not guilty of the offence specifically charged in the indictment but guilty of another offence of which he might be found guilty on that indictment;
   (c) if he stands mute of malice or will not answer directly to the indictment, the court may order a plea of not guilty to be entered on his behalf, and he shall then be treated as having pleaded not guilty.

(2) On an indictment for murder a person found not guilty of murder may be found guilty—
   (a) of manslaughter, or of causing grievous bodily harm with intent to do so; or
   (b) of any offence of which he may be found guilty under an enactment specifically so providing, or under section 4(2) of this Act; or
   (c) of an attempt to commit murder, or of an attempt to commit any other offence of which he might be found guilty;
   but may not be found guilty of any offence not included above.

(3) Where, on a person's trial on indictment for any offence except treason or murder, the jury find him not guilty of the offence specifically charged in the indictment, but the allegations in the indictment amount to or include (expressly or by implication) an allegation of another offence falling within the jurisdiction of the court of trial, the jury may find him guilty of that other offence or of an offence of which he could be found guilty on an indictment specifically charging that other offence.

(4) For purposes of subsection (3) above any allegation of an offence shall be taken as including an allegation of attempting to commit that offence; and where a person is charged on indictment with attempting to commit an offence or with any assault or other act preliminary to an offence, but not with the completed offence, then (subject to the discretion of the court to discharge the jury with a view to the preferment of an indictment for the completed offence) he may be convicted of the offence charged notwithstanding that he is shown to be guilty of the completed offence.

(5) Where a person arraigned on an indictment pleads not guilty of an offence charged in the indictment but guilty of some other offence of which he might be found guilty on that charge, and he is convicted on that plea of guilty without trial for the offence of which he has pleaded not guilty, then (whether or not the two offences are separately charged in distinct counts) his conviction of the one offence shall be an acquittal of the other.

(6) Any power to bring proceedings for an offence by criminal information in the High Court is hereby abolished.

(7) Subsections (1) to (3) above shall apply to an indictment containing more than one count as if each count were a separate indictment.

As amended by Powers of Criminal Courts Act 1973, Sch 6; Criminal Law Act 1977, s.65; Police and Criminal Evidence Act 1984 s. 119, Sch. 6 para. 17; Theft Act 1968, Schdeule 3; Extradition Act 1989, s65; Criminal Jurisdiction Act 1975.

SEXUAL OFFENCES ACT 1967

6 PREMISES RESORTED TO FOR HOMOSEXUAL PRACTICES

Premises shall be treated for purposes of sections 33 to 35 of the [Sexual Offences] Act of 1956 as a brothel if people resort to it for the purpose of lewd homosexual practices in circumstances in which resort thereto for lewd heterosexual practices would have led to its being treated as a brothel for the purposes of those sections.

CRIMINAL APPEALS ACT 1968

1 RIGHT OF APPEAL

(1)   Subject to subsection (3) below a person convicted of an offence on indictment may appeal to the Court of Appeal against his conviction.

(2)   An appeal under this section lies only—
    (a) with the leave of the Court of Appeal; or
    (b) if, within 28 days from the date of the conviction, the judge of the court of trial grants a certificate that the case if fit for appeal.

(3)   Where a person is convicted before the Crown Court of a scheduled offence it shall not be open to him to appeal to the Court of Appeal against the conviction on the ground that the decision of the court which committed him sent him to the Crown Court for trial as to the value involved was mistaken.

(4)   In subsection (3) above "scheduled offence" and "the value involved" have the same meanings as they have in section 22 of the Magistrates' Courts Act 1980 (certain offences against property to be tried summarily if value of property or damage is small).

2 GROUNDS FOR ALLOWING AN APPEAL UNDER S 1

(1)   Subject to the provisions of this Act, the Court of Appeal—
    (a) shall allow an appeal against conviction if they think that the conviction is unsafe; and
    (b) shall dismiss such an appeal in any other case.

(2)   In the case of an appeal against conviction the Court shall, if they allow the appeal, quash the conviction.

(3)   An order of the Court of Appeal quashing a conviction shall, except when under section 7 below the appellant is ordered to be retried, operate as a direction to the court of trial to enter, instead of the record of conviction, a judgment and verdict of acquittal.

3 POWER TO SUBSTITUTE CONVICTION OF ALTERNATIVE OFFENCE

(1)   This section applies on an appeal against conviction, where the appellant has been convicted of an offence to which he did not plead guilty and the jury could on the

indictment have found him guilty of some other offence, and on the finding of the jury it appears to the Court of Appeal that the jury must have been satisfied of facts which proved him guilty of the other offence.

(2)   The Court may, instead of allowing or dismissing the appeal, substitute for the verdict found by the jury a verdict of guilty of the other offence, and pass such sentence in substitution for the sentence passed at the trial as may be authorised by law for the other offence, not being a sentence of greater severity.

3A POWER TO SUBSTITUTE CONVICTION OF ALTERNATIVE OFFENCE AFTER GUILTY PLEA

(1)   This section applies on an appeal against conviction where—
    (a) an appellant has been convicted of an offence to which he pleaded guilty,
    (b) if he had not so pleaded, he could on the indictment have pleaded, or been found, guilty of some other offence, and
    (c) it appears to the Court of Appeal that the plea of guilty indicates an admission by the appellant of facts which prove him guilty of the other offence.

(2)   The Court of Appeal may, instead of allowing or dismissing the appeal, substitute for the appellant's plea of guilty a plea of guilty of the other offence and pass such sentence in substitution for the sentence passed at the trial as may be authorised by law for the other offence, not being a sentence of greater severity.

12 APPEAL AGAINST VERDICT OF NOT GUILTY BY REASON OF INSANITY

A person in whose case there is returned a verdict of not guilty by reason of insanity may appeal to the Court of Appeal against the verdict—
(a)   with the leave of the Court of Appeal; or
(b)   if, within 28 days from the date of the verdict, the judge of the court of trial grants a certificate that the case if fit for appeal.

13 DISPOSAL OF APPEAL UNDER S 12

(1)   Subject to the provisions of this section, the Court of Appeal—
    (a) shall allow an appeal under section 12 of this Act if they think that the verdict is unsafe; and
    (b) shall dismiss such an appeal in any other case.

(3)   Where apart from this subsection—
    (a) an appeal under section 12 of this Act would fall to be allowed; and
    (b) none of the grounds for allowing it relates to the question of the insanity of the accused,
the Court of Appeal may dismiss the appeal if they are of opinion that, but for the insanity of the accused, the proper verdict would have been that he was guilty of an offence other than the offence charged.

(4)   Where an appeal under section 12 of this Act is allowed, the following provisions apply:—
    (a) if the ground, or one of the grounds, for allowing the appeal is that the finding of the jury as to the insanity of the accused ought not to stand and the Court of Appeal are of opinion that the proper verdict would have been that he was guilty of an offence (whether the offence charged or any other offence of which the jury could have found him guilty), the Court—

(i)   shall substitute for the verdict of not guilty by reason of insanity a verdict of guilty of that offence; and

(ii) shall, subject to subsection (5) below, have the like powers of punishing or otherwise dealing with the appellant, and other powers, as the court of trial would have had if the jury had come to the substituted verdict; and

(b) in any other case, the Court of Appeal shall substitute for the verdict of the jury a verdict of acquittal.

(5)   The Court of Appeal shall not by virtue of subsection (4)(a) above sentence any person to death; but where under that paragraph they substitute a verdict of guilty of an offence for which apart from this subsection they would be required to sentence the appellant to death, their sentence shall (whatever the circumstances) be one of imprisonment for life.

(6)   An order of the Court of Appeal allowing an appeal in accordance with this section shall operate as a direction to the court of trial to amend the record to conform with the order.

14   SUBSTITUTION OF FINDINGS OF UNFITNESS TO PLEAD ETC

(1)   This section applies where, on an appeal under section 12 of this Act, the Court of Appeal, on the written or oral evidence of two or more registered medical practitioners at least one of whom is duly approved, are of opinion that—
(a) the case is not one where there should have been a verdict of acquittal; but
(b) there should have been findings that the accused was under a disability and that he did the act or made the omission charged against him.

(2)   The Court of Appeal shall make in respect of the accused—
(a) a hospital order (with or without a restriction order);
(b) a supervision order; or
(c) an order for his absolute discharge.

(3)   Where—
(a) the offence to which the appeal relates is an offence the sentence for which is fixed by law, and
(b) the court have power to make a hospital order,
       the court shall make a hospital order with a restriction order (whether or not they would have power to make a restriction order apart from this subsection).

(4)   Section 5A of the Criminal Procedure (Insanity) Act 1964 ("the 1964 Act") applies in relation to this section as it applies in relation to section 5 of that Act.

(6)   Where the Court of Appeal make a supervision order by virtue of this section, any power of revoking or amending it shall be exercisable as if the order had been made by the court below.

(7)   In this section—

"hospital order" has the meaning given in section 37 of the Mental Health Act 1983;

. . .

"restriction order" has the meaning given to it by section 41 of that Act;

"supervision order" has the meaning given in Part 1 of Schedule 1A to the 1964 Act.

As amended by Criminal Justice Act 1988, s. 43, 157, schedule 8; Criminal Procedure (Insanity and Unfitness to Plead) Act 1991, s4, 8; Magistrates' Courts Act 1980, sch 1; Crimianl Appeal Act 1995, s.1; Criminal Justice and Immigration Act 2008, s47.

FIREARMS ACT 1968

1 REQUIREMENT OF FIREARM CERTIFICATE

(1)   Subject to any exemption under this Act, it is an offence for a person—
    (a) to have in his possession, or to purchase or acquire, a firearm to which this section applies without holding a firearm certificate in force at the time, or otherwise than as authorised by such a certificate;
    (b) to have in his possession, or to purchase or acquire, any ammunition to which this section applies without holding a firearm certificate in force at the time, or otherwise than as authorised by such a certificate, or in quantities in excess of those so authorised.

(2)   It is an offence for a person to fail to comply with a condition subject to which a firearm certificate is held by him.

(3)   This section applies to every firearm except—
    (a) a shot gun within the meaning of this Act, that is to say a smooth-bore gun (not being an air gun) which—
        (i)   has a barrel not less than 24 inches in length and does not have any barrel with a bore exceeding 2 inches in diameter;
        (ii) either has no magazine or has a non-detachable magazine incapable of holding more than two cartridges; and
        (iii) is not a revolver gun; and,
    (b) an air weapon (that is to say, an air rifle, air gun or air pistol which does not fall within section 5(1) and which is not of a type declared by rules made by the Secretary of State under section 53 of this Act to be specially dangerous).

(3A) A gun which has been adapted to have such a magazine as is mentioned in subsection (3)(a) (ii) above shall not be regarded as falling within that provision unless the magazine bears a mark approved by the Secretary of State for denoting that fact and that mark has been made, and the adaptation has been certified in writing as having been carried out in a manner approved by him, either by one of the two companies mentioned in section 58(1) of this Act or by such other person as may be approved by him for that purpose.

(4)   This section applies to any ammunition for a firearm, except the following articles, namely:—
    (a) cartridges containing five or more shot, none of which exceeds .36 inch in diameter;
    (b) ammunition for an air gun, air rifle or air pistol; and
    (c) blank cartridges not more than one inch in diameter measured immediately in front of the rim or cannelure of the base of the cartridge.

2 REQUIREMENT OF CERTIFICATE FOR POSSESSION OF SHOT GUNS

(1)   Subject to any exemption under this Act, it is an offence for a person to have in his possession, or to purchase or acquire, a shot gun without holding a certificate under this Act authorising him to possess shot guns.

(2)   It is an offence for a person to fail to comply with a condition subject to which a shot gun certificate is held by him.

3 BUSINESS AND OTHER TRANSACTIONS WITH FIREARMS AND AMMUNITION

(1)   A person commits an offence if, by way of trade or business, he—
    (a) manufactures, sells, transfers, repairs, tests or proves any firearm or ammunition to which section 1 of this Act applies, or a shot gun;

(b) exposes for sale or transfer, or has in his possession for sale, transfer, repair, test or proof any such firearm or ammunition, or a shot gun, or

(c) sells or transfers an air weapon, exposes such a weapon for sale or transfer or has such a weapon in his possession for sale or transfer,

without being registered under this Act as a firearms dealer.

(2) It is an offence for a person to sell or transfer to any other person in the United Kingdom, other than a registered firearms dealer, any firearm or ammunition to which section 1 of this Act applies, or a shot gun, unless that other produces a firearm certificate authorising him to purchase or acquire it or, as the case may be, his shot gun certificate, or shows that he is by virtue of this Act entitled to purchase or acquire it without holding a certificate.

(3) It is an offence for a person to undertake the repair, test or proof of a firearm or ammunition to which section 1 of this Act applies, or of a shot gun, for any other person in the United Kingdom other than a registered firearms dealer as such, unless that other produces or causes to be produced a firearm certificate authorising him to have possession of the firearm or ammunition or, as the case may be, his shot gun certificate, or shows that he is by virtue of this Act entitled to have possession of it without holding a certificate.

(4) Subsections (1) to (3) above have effect subject to any exemption under subsequent provisions of this Part of this Act.

(5) A person commits an offence if, with a view to purchasing or acquiring, or procuring the repair, test or proof of, any firearm or ammunition to which section 1 of this Act applies, or a shot gun, he produces a false certificate or a certificate in which any false entry has been made, or personates a person to whom a certificate has been granted, or knowingly or recklessly makes a statement false in any material particular.

(6) It is an offence for a pawnbroker to take in pawn any firearm or ammunition to which section 1 of this Act applies, or a shot gun.

4 CONVERSION OF WEAPONS

(1) Subject to this section, it is an offence to shorten the barrel of a shot gun to a length less than 24 inches.

(2) It is not an offence under subsection (1) above for a registered firearms dealer to shorten the barrel of a shot gun for the sole purpose of replacing a defective part of the barrel so as to produce a barrel not less than 24 inches in length.

(3) It is an offence for a person other than a registered firearms dealer to convert into a firearm anything which, though having the appearance of being a firearm, is so constructed as to be incapable of discharging any missile through its barrel.

(4) A person who commits an offence under section 1 of this Act by having in his possession, or purchasing or acquiring, a shot gun which has been shortened contrary to subsection (1) above or a firearm which has been converted as mentioned in subsection (3) above (whether by a registered firearms dealer or not), without holding a firearm certificate authorising him to have it in his possession, or to purchase or acquire it, shall be treated for the purposes of provisions of this Act relating to the punishment of offences as committing that offence in an aggravated form.

5 WEAPONS SUBJECT TO GENERAL PROHIBITION

(1) A person commits an offence if, without the authority of the Secretary of State . . ., he has in his possession, or purchases or acquires, or manufactures, sells or transfers—

(a)   any firearm which is so designed or adapted that two or more missiles can be successively discharged without repeated pressure on the trigger;

(ab)   any self-loading or pump-action rifled gun other than one which is chambered for .22 rim-fire cartridges;

(aba)   any firearm which either has a barrel less than 30 centimetres in length or is less than 60 centimetres in length overall, other than an air weapon, . . ., a muzzle-loading gun or a firearm designed as signalling apparatus;

(ac)   any self-loading or pump-action smooth-bore gun which is not an air weapon or chambered for .22 rim-fire cartridges and either has a barrel less than 24 inches in length or . . . is less than 40 inches in length overall;

(ad)   any smooth-bore revolver gun other than one which is chambered for 9 mm rim-fire cartridges or a muzzle-loading gun;

(ae)   any rocket launcher, or any mortar, for projecting a stabilised missile, other than a launcher or mortar designed for line-throwing or pyrotechnic purposes or as signalling apparatus;

(af)   any air rifle, air gun or air pistol which uses, or is designed or adapted for use with, a self-contained gas cartridge system;

(b)   any weapon of whatever description designed or adapted for the discharge of any noxious liquid, gas or other thing; and

(c)   any cartridge with a bullet designed to explode on or immediately before impact, any ammunition containing or designed or adapted to contain any such noxious thing as is mentioned in paragraph (b) above and, if capable of being used with a firearm of any description, any grenade, bomb (or other like missile), or rocket or shell designed to explode as aforesaid.

(1A)   Subject to section 5A of this Act, a person commits an offence if, without the authority of the Secretary of State . . ., he has in his possession, or purchases or acquires or sells or transfers—

(a)   any firearm which is disguised as another object;

(b)   any rocket or ammunition not falling within paragraph (c) of subsection (1) of this section which consists in or incorporates a missile designed to explode on or immediately before impact and is for military use;

(c)   any launcher or other projecting apparatus not falling within paragraph (ae) of that subsection which is designed to be used with any rocket or ammunition falling within paragraph (b) above or with ammunition which would fall within that paragraph but for its being ammunition falling within paragraph (c) of that subsection;

(d)   any ammunition for military use which consists in or incorporates a missile designed so that a substance contained in the missile will ignite on or immediately before impact;

(e)   any ammunition for military use which consists in or incorporates a missile designed, on account of its having a jacket and hard-core, to penetrate armour plating, armour screening or body armour;

(f)   any ammunition which incorporates a missile designed or adapted to expand on impact;

(g)   anything which is designed to be projected as a missile from any weapon and is designed to be, or has been, incorporated in—
        (i)   any ammunition falling within any of the preceding paragraphs; or
        (ii)   any ammunition which would fall within any of those paragraphs but for its being specified in subsection (1) of this section.

(2)   The weapons and ammunition specified in subsections (1) and (1A) of this section (including, in the case of ammunition, any missiles falling within subsection (1A)(g) of this section) are referred to in this Act as "prohibited weapons" and "prohibited ammunition" respectively.

(3)   An authority given to a person by the Secretary of State . . . under this section shall be in writing and be subject to conditions specified therein.

. . .

(5)   It is an offence for a person to whom an authority is given under this section to fail to comply with any condition of the authority.

(7)   For the purposes of this section and section 5A of this Act—
(a)   any rocket or ammunition which is designed to be capable of being used with a military weapon shall be taken to be for military use;
(b)   references to a missile designed so that a substance contained in the missile will ignite on or immediately before impact include references to any missile containing a substance that ignites on exposure to air; and
(c)   references to a missile's expanding on impact include references to its deforming in any predictable manner on or immediately after impact.

(8)   For the purposes of subsection (1)(aba) and (ac) above, any detachable, folding, retractable or other movable butt-stock shall be disregarded in measuring the length of any firearm.

(9)   Any reference in this section to a muzzle-loading gun is a reference to a gun which is designed to be loaded at the muzzle end of the barrel or chamber with a loose charge and a separate ball (or other missile).

5A   EXEMPTIONS FROM REQUIREMENT OF AUTHORITY UNDER S. 5

(1)   Subject to subsection (2) below, the authority of the Secretary of State . . . shall not be required by virtue of subsection (1A) of section 5 of this Act for any person to have in his possession, or to purchase, acquire, sell or transfer, any prohibited weapon or ammunition if he is authorised by a certificate under this Act to possess, purchase or acquire that weapon or ammunition subject to a condition that he does so only for the purpose of its being kept or exhibited as part of a collection.

(2)   No sale or transfer may be made under subsection (1) above except to a person who—
(a)   produces the authority of the Secretary of State . . . under section 5 of this Act for his purchase or acquisition; or
(b)   shows that he is, under this section or a licence under the Schedule to the Firearms (Amendment) Act 1988 (museums etc), entitled to make the purchase or acquisition without the authority of the Secretary of State . . .

(3)   The authority of the Secretary of State or the Scottish Ministers (by virtue of provision made under section 63 of the Scotland Act 1998) shall not be required by virtue of subsection (1A) of section 5 of this Act for any person to have in his possession, or to purchase or acquire, any prohibited weapon or ammunition if his possession, purchase or acquisition is exclusively in connection with the carrying on of activities in respect of which—
(a)   that person; or
(b)   the person on whose behalf he has possession, or makes the purchase or acquisition, is recognised, for the purposes of the law of another member State relating to firearms, as a collector of firearms or a body concerned in the cultural or historical aspects of weapons.

(4)   The authority of the Secretary of State . . . shall not be required by virtue of subsection (1A) of section 5 of this Act for any person to have in his possession, or to purchase or acquire, or to sell or transfer, any expanding ammunition or the missile for any such ammunition if—
(a)   he is authorised by a firearm certificate or visitor's firearm permit to possess, or purchase or acquire, any expanding ammunition; and
(b)   the certificate or permit is subject to a condition restricting the use of any expanding ammunition to use in connection with any one or more of the following, namely—

      (i) the lawful shooting of deer;

      (ii) the shooting of vermin or, in the course of carrying on activities in connection with the management of any estate, other wildlife;

      (iii) the humane killing of animals;

      (iv) the shooting of animals for the protection of other animals or humans.

(5) The authority of the Secretary of State or the Scottish Ministers (by virtue of provision made under section 63 of the Scotland Act 1998) shall not be required by virtue of subsection (1A) of section 5 of this Act for any person to have in his possession any expanding ammunition or the missile for any such ammunition if—

    (a) he is entitled, under section 10 of this Act, to have a slaughtering instrument and the ammunition for it in his possession; and

    (b) the ammunition or missile in question is designed to be capable of being used with a slaughtering instrument.

(6) The authority of the Secretary of State . . . shall not be required by virtue of subsection (1A) of section 5 of this Act for the sale or transfer of any expanding ammunition or the missile for any such ammunition to any person who produces a certificate by virtue of which he is authorised under subsection (4) above to purchase or acquire it without the authority of the Secretary of State . . .

(7) The authority of the Secretary of State . . . shall not be required by virtue of subsection (1A) of section 5 of this Act for a person carrying on the business of a firearms dealer, or any servant of his, to have in his possession, or to purchase, acquire, sell or transfer, any expanding ammunition or the missile for any such ammunition in the ordinary course of that business.

(8) In this section—

    (a) references to expanding ammunition are references to any ammunition which incorporates a missile which is designed to expand on impact; and

    (b) references to the missile for any such ammunition are references to anything which, in relation to any such ammunition, falls within section 5(1A)(g) of this Act.

7 POLICE PERMIT

(1) A person who has obtained from the chief officer of police for the area in which he resides a permit for the purpose in the prescribed form may, without holding a certificate under this Act, have in his possession a firearm and ammunition in accordance with the terms of the permit.

(2) It is an offence for a person knowingly or recklessly to make a statement false in any material particular for the purpose of procuring, whether for himself or for another person, the grant of a permit under this section.

11 SPORTS, ATHLETICS AND OTHER APPROVED ACTIVITIES

(1) A person carrying a firearm or ammunition belonging to another person holding a certificate under this Act may, without himself holding such a certificate, have in his possession that firearm or ammunition under instructions from, and for the use of, that other person for sporting purposes only.

    . . .

12 THEATRE AND CINEMA

(1)   A person taking part in a theatrical performance or a rehearsal thereof, or in the production of a cinematograph film, may, without holding a certificate, have a firearm in his possession during and for the purpose of the performance, rehearsal or production.

...

16 POSSESSION OF FIREARM WITH INTENT TO INJURE

It is an offence for a person to have in his possession any firearm or ammunition with intent by means thereof to endanger life or to enable another person by means thereof to endanger life whether any injury has been caused or not.

16A POSSESSION OF FIREARM WITH INTENT TO CAUSE FEAR OF VIOLENCE

It is an offence for a person to have in his possession any firearm or imitation firearm with intent—

(a)   by means thereof to cause, or

(b)   to enable another person by means thereof to cause,

any person to believe that unlawful violence will be used against him or another person.

17 USE OF FIREARM TO RESIST ARREST

(1)   It is an offence for a person to make or attempt to make any use whatsoever of a firearm or imitation firearm with intent to resist or prevent the lawful arrest or detention of himself or another person.

(2)   If a person, at the time of his committing or being arrested for an offence specified in Schedule 1 to this Act, has in his possession a firearm or imitation firearm, he shall be guilty of an offence under this subsection unless he shows that he had it in his possession for a lawful object.

(4)   For purposes of this section, the definition of "firearm" in section 57(1) of this Act shall apply without paragraphs (b) and (c) of that subsection, and "imitation firearm" shall be construed accordingly.

18 CARRYING FIREARM WITH CRIMINAL INTENT

(1)   It is an offence for a person to have with him a firearm or imitation firearm with intent to commit an indictable offence, or to resist arrest or prevent the arrest of another, in either case while he has the firearm or imitation firearm with him.

(2)   In proceedings for an offence under this section proof that the accused had a firearm or imitation firearm with him and intended to commit an offence, or to resist or prevent arrest, is evidence that he intended to have it with him while doing so.

(3)   In the application of this section to Scotland, for the reference to an indictable offence there shall be substituted a reference to any offence specified in paragraphs 1 to 18 of Schedule 2 to this Act.

19 CARRYING A FIREARM IN A PUBLIC PLACE

A person commits an offence if, without lawful authority or reasonable excuse (the proof whereof lies on him) he has with him in a public place—

(a)   a loaded shot gun,

(b)   an air weapon (whether loaded or not),

(c)   any other firearm (whether loaded or not) together with ammunition suitable for use in that firearm, or

(d)   an imitation firearm.

20 TRESPASSING WITH FIREARM

(1)   A person commits an offence if, while he has a firearm or imitation firearm with him, he enters or is in any building or part of a building as a trespasser and without reasonable excuse (the proof whereof lies on him).

(2)   A person commits an offence if, while he has a firearm or imitation firearm with him, he enters or is on any land as a trespasser and without reasonable excuse (the proof whereof lies on him).

(3)   In subsection (2) of this section the expression "land" includes land covered with water.

21 POSSESSION OF FIREARMS BY PERSONS PREVIOUSLY CONVICTED OF CRIME

(1)   A person who has been sentenced to custody for life or to preventive detention, or to imprisonment or to corrective training for a term of three years or more or to youth custody or detention in a young offender institution for such a term, or who has been sentenced to be detained for such a term in a young offenders institution in Scotland, shall not at any time have a firearm or ammunition in his possession.

(2)   A person who has been sentenced . . . to imprisonment for a term of three months or more but less than three years or to youth custody or detention in a young offender institution for such a term, or who has been sentenced to be detained for such a term in a detention centre . . . or who has been subject to a secure training order or a detention and training order, shall not at any time before the expiration of the period of five years from the date of his release have a firearm or ammunition in his possession.

(2A) For the purposes of subsection (2) above, "the date of his release" means—
    (a)   in the case of a person sentenced to imprisonment with an order under section 47(1) of the Criminal Law Act 1977 (prison sentence partly served and partly suspended), the date on which he completes service of so much of the sentence as was by that order required to be served in prison;
    (b)   in the case of a person who has been subject to a secure training order—
        (i)   the date on which he is released from detention under the order;
        (ii)   the date on which he is released from detention ordered under section 4 of the Criminal Justice and Public Order Act 1994; or
        (iii) the date halfway through the total period specified by the court in making the order, whichever is the later;
    (c)   in the case of a person who has been subject to a detention and training order—
        (i)   the date on which he is released from detention under the order;

          (ii) the date on which he is released from detention ordered under section 104 of the Powers of Criminal Courts (Sentencing) Act 2000; or

          (iii) the date of the half-way point of the term of the order, whichever is the later;

  (d) in the case of a person who has been subject to a sentence of imprisonment to which an intermittent custody order under section 183(1)(b) of the Criminal Justice Act 2003 relates, the date of his final release.

(2B) A person who is serving a sentence of imprisonment to which an intermittent custody order under section 183 of the Criminal Justice Act 2003 relates shall not during any licence period specified for the purposes of subsection (1)(b)(i) of that section have a firearm or ammunition in his possession.

(3) A person who—

  (a) is the holder of a licence issued under section 53 of the Children and Young Persons Act 1933 . . .; or

  (b) is subject to a recognizance to keep the peace or to be of good behaviour, a condition of which is that he shall not possess, use or carry a firearm, or is subject to a community order containing a requirement that he shall not possess, use or carry a firearm . . .

shall not, at any time during which he holds the licence or is so subject or has been so ordained, have a firearm or ammunition in his possession.

(4) It is an offence for a person to contravene any of the foregoing provisions of this section.

(5) It is an offence for a person to sell or transfer a firearm or ammunition to, or to repair, test or prove a firearm or ammunition for, a person whom he knows or has reasonable ground for believing to be prohibited by this section from having a firearm or ammunition in his possession.

21A FIRING AN AIR WEAPON BEYOND PREMISES

(1) A person commits an offence if—

  (a) he has with him an air weapon on any premises; and

  (b) he uses it for firing a missile beyond those premises.

(2) In proceedings against a person for an offence under this section it shall be a defence for him to show that the only premises into or across which the missile was fired were premises the occupier of which had consented to the firing of the missile (whether specifically or by way of a general consent).

22 ACQUISITION AND POSSESSION OF FIREARMS BY MINORS

(1) It is an offence—

  (a) for a person under the age of eighteen to purchase or hire an air weapon or ammunition for an air weapon;

  (b) for a person under the age of seventeen to purchase or hire a firearm or ammunition of any other description.

(1A) Where a person under the age of eighteen is entitled, as the holder of a certificate under this Act, to have a firearm in his possession, it is an offence for that person to use that firearm for a purpose not authorised by the European weapons directive.

(2) It is an offence for a person under the age of fourteen to have in his possession any firearm or ammunition to which section 1 of this Act or section 15 of the Firearms (Amendment) Act 1988 applies, except in circumstances where under section 11(1), (3) or (4) of this Act he is entitled to have possession of it without holding a firearm certificate.

(3)   It is an offence for a person under the age of fifteen to have with him an assembled shot gun except while under the supervision of a person of or over the age of twenty-one, or while the shot gun is so covered with a securely fastened gun cover that it cannot be fired.

(4)   Subject to section 23 below, it is an offence for a person under the age of eighteen to have with him an air weapon or ammunition for an air weapon.

23 EXCEPTIONS FROM S 22(4)

(1)   It is not an offence under section 22(4) of this Act for a person to have with him an air weapon or ammunition while he is under the supervision of a person of or over the age of twentyone; but where a person has with him an air weapon on any premises in circumstances where he would be prohibited from having it with him but for this subsection, it is an offence for the person under whose supervision he is to allow him to use it for firing any missile beyond those premises.

(1A) In proceedings against a person for an offence under subsection (1) it shall be a defence for him to show that the only premises into or across which the missile was fired were premises the occupier of which had consented to the firing of the missile (whether specifically or by way of a general consent).

(2)   It is not an offence under section 22(4) . . . of this Act for a person to have with him an air weapon or ammunition at a time when—
(a) being a member of a rifle club or miniature rifle club for the time being approved by the Secretary of State for the purposes of this section or section 15 of the Firearms (Amendment) Act 1988, he is engaged as such a member . . . in connection with target shooting; or
(b) he is using the weapon or ammunition at a shooting gallery where the only firearms used are either air weapons or miniature rifles not exceeding .23 inch calibre.

(3)   It is not an offence under section 22(4) of this Act for a person of or over the age of fourteen to have with him an air weapon or ammunition on private premises with the consent of the occupier.

24 SUPPLYING FIREARMS TO MINORS

(1)   It is an offence—
(a) to sell or let on hire an air weapon or ammunition for an air weapon to a person under the age of eighteen;
(b) to sell or let on hire a firearm or ammunition of any other description to a person under the age of seventeen.

(2)   It is an offence—
(a) to make a gift of or lend any firearm or ammunition to which section 1 of this Act applies to a person under the age of fourteen; or
(b) to part with the possession of any such firearm or ammunition to a person under that age, except in circumstances where that person is entitled under section 11(1), (3) or (4) of this Act or section 15 of the Firearms (Amendment) Act 1988 to have possession thereof without holding a firearm certificate.

(3)   It is an offence to make a gift of a shot gun or ammunition for a shot gun to a person under the age of fifteen.

(4)   It is an offence—
(a) to make a gift of an air weapon or ammunition for an air weapon to a person under the age of eighteen; or

(b) to part with the possession of an air weapon or ammunition for an air weapon to a person under the age of eighteen except where by virtue of section 23 of this Act the person is not prohibited from having it with him.

(5) In proceedings for an offence under any provision of this section it is a defence to prove that the person charged with the offence believed the other person to be of or over the age mentioned in that provision and had reasonable ground for the belief.

24A SUPPLYING IMITATION FIREARMS TO MINORS

(1) It is an offence for a person under the age of eighteen to purchase an imitation firearm.

(2) It is an offence to sell an imitation firearm to a person under the age of eighteen.

(3) In proceedings for an offence under subsection (2) it is a defence to show that the person charged with the offence—
(a) believed the other person to be aged eighteen or over; and
(b) had reasonable ground for that belief.

(4) For the purposes of this section a person shall be taken to have shown the matters specified in subsection (3) if—
(a) sufficient evidence of those matters is adduced to raise an issue with respect to them; and
(b) the contrary is not proved beyond a reasonable doubt.

24ZA FAILING TO PREVENT MINORS FROM HAVING AIR WEAPONS

(1) It is an offence for a person in possession of an air weapon to fail to take reasonable precautions to prevent any person under the age of eighteen from having the weapon with him.

(2) Subsection (1) does not apply where by virtue of section 23 of this Act the person under the age of eighteen is not prohibited from having the weapon with him.

(3) In proceedings for an offence under subsection (1) it is a defence to show that the person charged with the offence—
(a) believed the other person to be aged eighteen or over; and
(b) had reasonable ground for that belief.

(4) For the purposes of this section a person shall be taken to have shown the matters specified in subsection (3) if—
(a) sufficient evidence of those matters is adduced to raise an issue with respect to them; and
(b) the contrary is not proved beyond a reasonable doubt.

25 SUPPLYING FIREARM TO PERSON DRUNK OR INSANE

It is an offence for a person to sell or transfer any firearm or ammunition to, or to repair, prove or test any firearm or ammunition for, another person whom he knows or has reasonable cause for believing to be drunk or of unsound mind.

57 INTERPRETATION

(1) In this Act, the expression "firearm" means a lethal barrelled weapon of any description from which any shot, bullet or other missile can be discharged and includes—

(a) any prohibited weapon, whether it is such a lethal weapon as aforesaid or not; and

(b) any component part of such a lethal or prohibited weapon; and

(c) any accessory to any such weapon designed or adapted to diminish the noise or flash caused by firing the weapon;

and so much of section 1 of this Act as excludes any description of firearm from the category of firearms to which that section applies shall be construed as also excluding component parts of, and accessories to, firearms of that description.

(2) In this Act, the expression "ammunition" means ammunition for any firearm and includes grenades, bombs and other like missiles, whether capable of use with a firearm or not, and also includes prohibited ammunition.

(2A) In this Act "self-loading" and "pump-action" in relation to any weapon mean respectively that it is designed or adapted (otherwise than as mentioned in section 5(1)(a)) so that it is automatically re-loaded or that it is so designed or adapted that it is re-loaded by the manual operation of the fore-end or forestock of the weapon.

(2B) In this Act "revolver", in relation to a smooth-bore gun, means a gun containing a series of chambers which revolve when the gun is fired.

(3) For purposes of sections 45, 46, 50, 51(4) and 52 of this Act, the offences under this Act relating specifically to air weapons are those under sections 22(4), 22(5), 23(1) and 24(4).

(4) In this Act—

"acquire" means hire, accept as a gift or borrow and "acquisition" shall be construed accordingly;

"air weapon" has the meaning assigned to it by section 1(3)(b) of this Act;

. . .

"certificate" (except in a context relating to the registration of firearms dealers) and

"certificate under this Act" mean a firearm certificate or a shot gun certificate and—

(a) "firearm certificate" means a certificate granted by a chief officer of police under this Act in respect of any firearm or ammunition to which section 1 of this Act applies and includes a certificate granted in Northern Ireland under section 1 of the Firearms Act 1920 or under an enactment of the Parliament of Northern Ireland amending or substituted for that section; and

(b) "shot gun certificate" means a certificate granted by a chief officer of police under this Act and authorising a person to possess shot guns;

. . .

"firearms dealer" means a person who, by way of trade or business,

(a) manufactures, sells, transfers, repairs, tests or proves firearms or ammunition to which section 1 of this Act applies or shot guns; or

(b) sells or transfers air weapons;

"imitation firearm" means any thing which has the appearance of being a firearm (other than such a weapon as is mentioned in section 5(1)(b) of this Act) whether or not it is capable of discharging any shot, bullet or other missile;

. . .

"premises" includes any land;

"prescribed" means prescribed by rules made by the Secretary of State under section 53 of this Act;

"prohibited weapon" and "prohibited ammunition" have the meanings assigned to them by section 5(2) of this Act;

"public place" includes any highway and any other premises or place to which at the material time the public have or are permitted to have access, whether on payment or otherwise;

"registered", in relation to a firearms dealer, means registered either—
(a) in Great Britain, under section 33 of this Act, or
(b) in Northern Ireland, under section 8 of the Firearms Act 1920 or
any enactment of the Parliament of Northern Ireland amending or substituted for that section, and references to "the register", "registration" and a "certificate of registration" shall be construed accordingly, except in section 40;

"rifle" includes carbine;

"shot gun" has the meaning assigned to it by section 1(3)(a) of this Act and, in sections 3(1) and 45(2) of this Act and in the definition of "firearms dealer", includes any component part of a shot gun and any accessory to a shot gun designed or adapted to diminish the noise or flash caused by firing the gun;

"slaughtering instrument" means a firearm which is specially designed or adapted for the instantaneous slaughter of animals or for the instantaneous stunning of animals with a view to slaughtering them; and

"transfer" includes let on hire, give, lend and part with possession, and "transferee" and

"transferor" shall be construed accordingly.

(4A) For the purposes of any reference in this Act to the use of any firearm or ammunition for a purpose not authorised by the European weapons directive, the directive shall be taken to authorise the use of a firearm or ammunition as or with a slaughtering instrument and the use of a firearm and ammunition—
(a) for sporting purposes;
(b) for the shooting of vermin, or, in the course of carrying on activities in connection with the management of any estate, of other wildlife; and
(c) for competition purposes and target shooting outside competitions.

(5) The definitions in subsections (1) to (3) above apply to the provisions of this Act except where the context otherwise requires.

(6) For purposes of this Act—
(a) the length of the barrel of a firearm shall be measured from the muzzle to the point at which the charge is exploded on firing; and
(b) a shot gun or an air weapon shall be deemed to be loaded if there is ammunition in the chamber or barrel or in any magazine or other device which is in such a position that the ammunition can be fed into the chamber or barrel by the manual or automatic operation of some part of the gun or weapon.

58 PARTICULAR SAVINGS

. . .

(2) Nothing in this Act relating to firearms shall apply to an antique firearm which is sold, transferred, purchased, acquired or possessed as a curiosity or ornament.

SCHEDULE 1: OFFENCES TO WHICH SECTION 17(2) APPLIES

1.   Offences under section 1 of the Criminal Damage Act 1971.

2.   Offences under any of the following provisions of the Offences Against the Person
     Act 1861:—

     sections 20 to 22 (inflicting bodily injury; garrotting; criminal use of stupefying drugs);
     section 30 (laying explosive to building etc);
     section 32 (endangering railway passengers by tampering with track);
     section 38 (assault with intent to commit felony or resist arrest);
     section 47 (criminal assaults);

2A. Offences under Part I of the Child Abduction Act 1984 (abduction of children).

4.   Theft robbery, burglary, blackmail and any offence under section 12(1) (taking of motor
     vehicle or other conveyance without owner's consent) of the Theft Act 1968.

5.   Offences under section 89(1) of the Police Act 1996. . . .

5A. An offence under section 90(1) of the Criminal Justice Act 1991 (assaulting prisoner
     custody officer).

5B. An offence under section 13(1) of the Criminal Justice and Public Order Act 1994
     (assaulting secure training centre custody officer).

5C. An offence under paragraph 4 of Schedule 11 to the Immigration and Asylum Act 1999
     (assaulting a detainee custody officer).

6.   Offences under any of the following provisions of the Sexual Offences Act 2003—
     (a) section 1 (rape);
     (b) section 2 (assault by penetration);
     (c) section 4 (causing a person to engage in sexual activity without consent), where
          the activity caused involved penetration within subsection (4)(a) to (d) of that
          section;
     (d) section 5 (rape of a child under 13);
     (e) section 6 (assault of a child under 13 by penetration);
     (f) section 8 (causing or inciting a child under 13 to engage in sexual activity), where an
          activity involving penetration within subsection (3)(a) to (d) of that section was
          caused;
     (g) section 30 (sexual activity with a person with a mental disorder impeding choice),
          where the touching involved penetration within subsection (3)(a) to (d) of that
          section;
     (h) section 31 (causing or inciting a person, with a mental disorder impeding choice,
          to engage in sexual activity), where an activity involving penetration within
          subsection (3)(a) to (d) of that section was caused.

8.   Aiding or abetting the commission of any offence specified in paragraphs 1 to 6 of this
     Schedule.

*Amended by Firearms (Amendment) Act 1988, s 1, 2; Firearms (Amendment) Act 1997, s 1(2);
Firearms (Amendment) (No 2) Act 1997, ss 1, 2(7), Anti-social Behaviour Act 2003, s 39(1), (2);
Violent Crime Reduction Act 2006, s 34(1), (2); Crime and Security Act 2010, s 46.*

THEFT ACT 1968

1 BASIC DEFINITION OF THEFT

(1) A person is guilty of theft if he dishonestly appropriates property belonging to another with the intention of permanently depriving the other of it; and "thief" and "steal" shall be construed accordingly.

(2) It is immaterial whether the appropriation is made with a view to gain, or is made for the thief's own benefit.

(3) The five following sections of this Act shall have effect as regards the interpretation and operation of this section (and, except as otherwise provided by this Act, shall apply only for purposes of this section).

2 "DISHONESTLY"

(1) A person's appropriation of property belonging to another is not to be regarded as dishonest—
  (a) if he appropriates the property in the belief that he has in law the right to deprive the other of it, on behalf of himself or of a third person; or
  (b) if he appropriates the property in the belief that he would have the other's consent if the other knew of the appropriation and the circumstances of it; or
  (c) (except where the property came to him as trustee or personal representative) if he appropriates the property in the belief that the person to whom the property belongs cannot be discovered by taking reasonable steps.

(2) A person's appropriation of property belonging to another may be dishonest notwithstanding that he is willing to pay for the property.

3 "APPROPRIATES"

(1) Any assumption by a person of the rights of an owner amounts to an appropriation, and this includes, where he has come by the property (innocently or not) without stealing it, any later assumption of a right to it by keeping or dealing with it as owner.

(2) Where property or a right or interest in property is or purports to be transferred for value to a person acting in good faith, no later assumption by him of rights which he believed himself to be acquiring shall, by reason of any defect in the transferor's title, amount to theft of the property.

4 "PROPERTY"

(1) "Property" includes money and all other property, real or personal, including things in action and other intangible property.

(2) A person cannot steal land, or things forming part of land and severed from it by him or by his directions, except in the following cases, that is to say—
  (a) when he is a trustee or personal representative, or is authorised by power of attorney, or as liquidator of a company, or otherwise, to sell or dispose of land belonging to another, and he appropriates the land or anything forming part of it by dealing with it in breach of the confidence reposed in him; or
  (b) when he is not in possession of the land and appropriates anything forming part of the land by severing it or causing it to be severed, or after it has been severed; or

(c) when, being in possession of the land under a tenancy, he appropriates the whole or part of any fixture or structure let to be used with the land.

For purposes of this subsection "land" does not include incorporeal hereditaments; "tenancy" means a tenancy for years or any less period and includes an agreement for such a tenancy, but a person who after the end of a tenancy remains in possession as statutory tenant or otherwise is to be treated as having possession under the tenancy, and "let" shall be construed accordingly.

(3) A person who picks mushrooms growing wild on any land, or who picks flowers, fruit or foliage from a plant wild on any land, does not (although not in possession of the land) steal what he picks, unless he does it for reward or for sale or other commercial purpose.

For purposes of this subsection "mushroom" includes any fungus, and "plant" includes any shrub or tree.

(4) Wild creatures, tamed or untamed, shall be regarded as property; but a person cannot steal a wild creature not tamed nor ordinarily kept in captivity, or the carcase of any such creature, unless either it has been reduced into possession by or on behalf of another person and possession of it has not since been lost or abandoned, or another person is in course of reducing it into possession.

5 "BELONGING TO ANOTHER"

(1) Property shall be regarded as belonging to any person having possession or control of it, or having in it any proprietary right or interest (not being an equitable interest arising only from an agreement to transfer or grant an interest).

(2) Where property is subject to a trust, the persons to whom it belongs shall be regarded as including any person having a right to enforce the trust, and an intention to defeat the trust shall be regarded accordingly as an intention to deprive of the property any person having that right.

(3) Where a person receives property from or on account of another, and is under an obligation to the other to retain and deal with that property or its proceeds in a particular way, the property or proceeds shall be regarded (as against him) as belonging to the other.

(4) Where a person gets property by another's mistake, and is under an obligation to make restoration (in whole or in part) of the property or its proceeds or of the value thereof, then to the extent of that obligation the property or proceeds shall be regarded (as against him) as belonging to the person entitled to restoration, and an intention not to make restoration shall be regarded accordingly as an intention to deprive that person of the property or proceeds.

(5) Property of a corporation sole shall be regarded as belonging to the corporation notwithstanding a vacancy in the corporation.

6 "WITH THE INTENTION OF PERMANENTLY DEPRIVING THE OTHER OF IT"

(1) A person appropriating property belonging to another without meaning the other permanently to lose the thing itself is nevertheless to be regarded as having the intention of permanently depriving the other of it if his intention is to treat the thing as his own to dispose of regardless of the other's rights; and a borrowing or lending of it may amount to so treating it if, but only if, the borrowing or lending is for a period and in circumstances making it equivalent to an outright taking or disposal.

(2)   Without prejudice to the generality of subsection (1) above, where a person, having possession or control (lawfully or not) of property belonging to another, parts with the property under a condition as to its return which he may not be able to perform, this (if done for purposes of his own and without the other's authority) amounts to treating the property as his own to dispose of regardless of the other's rights.

7 THEFT

A person guilty of theft shall on conviction on indictment be liable to imprisonment for a term not exceeding seven years.

8 ROBBERY

(1)   A person is guilty of robbery if he steals, and immediately before or at the time of doing so, and in order to do so, he uses force on any person or puts or seeks to put any person in fear of being then and there subjected to force.

(2)   A person guilty of robbery, or of an assault with intent to rob, shall on conviction on indictment be liable to imprisonment for life.

9 BURGLARY

(1)   A person is guilty of burglary if—
   (a) he enters any building or part of a building as a trespasser and with intent to commit any such offence as is mentioned in subsection (2) below; or
   (b) having entered any building or part of a building as a trespasser he steals or attempts to steal anything in the building or that part of it or inflicts or attempts to inflict on any person therein any grievous bodily harm.

(2)   The offences referred to in subsection (1)(a) above are offences of stealing anything in the building or part of a building in question, of inflicting on any person therein any grievous bodily harm . . . therein, and of doing unlawful damage to the building or anything therein.

(3)   A person guilty of burglary shall on conviction on indictment be liable to imprisonment for a term not exceeding—
   (a) where the offence was committed in respect of a building or part of a building which is a dwelling, fourteen years;
   (b) in any other case, ten years.

(4)   References in subsections (1) and (2) above to a building, and the reference in subsection (3) above to a building which is a dwelling, shall apply also to an inhabited vehicle or vessel, and shall apply to any such vehicle or vessel at times when the person having a habitation in it is not there as well as at times when he is.

10 AGGRAVATED BURGLARY

(1)   A person is guilty of aggravated burglary if he commits any burglary and at the time has with him any firearm or imitation firearm, any weapon of offence, or any explosive; and for this purpose—
   (a) "firearm" includes an airgun or air pistol, and "imitation firearm" means anything which has the appearance of being a firearm, whether capable of being discharged or not; and

(b) "weapon of offence" means any article made or adapted for use for causing injury to or incapacitating a person, or intended by the person having it with him for such use; and

(c) "explosive" means any article manufactured for the purpose of producing a practical effect by explosion, or intended by the person having it with him for that purpose.

(2) A person guilty of aggravated burglary shall on conviction on indictment be liable to imprisonment for life.

11 REMOVAL OF ARTICLES FROM PLACES OPEN TO THE PUBLIC

(1) Subject to subsections (2) and (3) below, where the public have access to a building in order to view the building or part of it, or a collection or part of a collection housed in it, any person who without lawful authority removes from the building or its grounds the whole or part of any article displayed or kept for display to the public in the building or that part of it or in its grounds shall be guilty of an offence.

For this purpose "collection" includes a collection got together for a temporary purpose, but references in this section to a collection do not apply to a collection made or exhibited for the purpose of effecting sales or other commercial dealings.

(2) It is immaterial for purposes of subsection (1) above, that the public's access to a building is limited to a particular period or particular occasion; but where anything removed from a building or its grounds is there otherwise than as forming part of, or being on loan for exhibition with, a collection intended for permanent exhibition to the public, the person removing it does not thereby commit an offence under this section unless he removes it on a day when the public have access to the building as mentioned in subsection (1) above.

(3) A person does not commit an offence under this section if he believes that he has lawful authority for the removal of the thing in question or that he would have it if the person entitled to give it knew of the removal and the circumstances of it.

(4) A person guilty of an offence under this section shall, on conviction on indictment, be liable to imprisonment for a term not exceeding five years.

12 TAKING MOTOR VEHICLE OR OTHER CONVEYANCE WITHOUT AUTHORITY

(1) Subject to subsections (5) and (6) below, a person shall be guilty of an offence if, without having the consent of the owner or other lawful authority, he takes any conveyance for his own or another's use or, knowing that any conveyance has been taken without such authority, drives it or allows himself to be carried in or on it.

(2) A person guilty of an offence under subsection (1) above shall . . . be liable on summary conviction to a fine not exceeding level 5 on the standard scale, to imprisonment for a term not exceeding six months, or to both.

(4) If on the trial of an indictment for theft the jury are not satisfied that the accused committed theft, but it is proved that the accused committed an offence under subsection (1) above, the jury may find him guilty of the offence under subsection (1) and if he is found guilty of it, he shall be liable as he would have been liable under subsection (2) above on summary conviction.

(4A) Proceedings for an offence under subsection (1) above (but not proceedings of a kind falling within subsection (4) above) in relation to a mechanically propelled vehicle—

(a) shall not be commenced after the end of the period of three years beginning with the day on which the offence was committed; but

(b) subject to that, may be commenced at any time within the period of six months beginning with the relevant day.

(4B) In subsection (4A)(b) above "the relevant day" means—

(a) in the case of a prosecution for an offence under subsection (1) above by a public prosecutor, the day on which sufficient evidence to justify the proceedings came to the knowledge of any person responsible for deciding whether to commence any such prosecution;

(b) in the case of a prosecution for an offence under subsection (1) above which is commenced by a person other than a public prosecutor after the discontinuance of a prosecution falling within paragraph (a) above which relates to the same facts, the day on which sufficient evidence to justify the proceedings came to the knowledge of the person who has decided to commence the prosecution or (if later) the discontinuance of the other prosecution;

(c) in the case of any other prosecution for an offence under subsection (1) above, the day on which sufficient evidence to justify the proceedings came to the knowledge of the person who has decided to commence the prosecution.

(4C) For the purposes of subsection (4A)(b) above a certificate of a person responsible for deciding whether to commence a prosecution of a kind mentioned in subsection (4B)(a) above as to the date on which such evidence as is mentioned in the certificate came to the knowledge of any person responsible for deciding whether to commence any such prosecution shall be conclusive evidence of that fact.

(5) Subsection (1) above shall not apply in relation to pedal cycles; but, subject to subsection (6) below, a person who, without having the consent of the owner or other lawful authority, takes a pedal cycle for his own or another's use, or rides a pedal cycle knowing it to have been taken without such authority, shall on summary conviction be liable to a fine not exceeding level 3 on the standard scale.

(6) A person does not commit an offence under this section by anything done in the belief that he has lawful authority to do it or that he would have the owner's consent if the owner knew of his doing it and the circumstances of it.

(7) For purposes of this section—

(a) "conveyance" means any conveyance constructed or adapted for the carriage of a person or persons whether by land, water or air, except that it does not include a conveyance constructed or adapted for use only under the control of a person not carried in or on it, and "drive" shall be construed accordingly; and

(b) "owner", in relation to a conveyance which is the subject of a hiring agreement or hire-purchase agreement, means the person in possession of the conveyance under that agreement.

12A AGGRAVATED VEHICLE-TAKING

(1) Subject to subsection (3) below, a person is guilty of aggravated taking of a vehicle if—

(a) he commits an offence under section 12(1) above (in this section referred to as a "basic offence") in relation to a mechanically propelled vehicle; and

(b) it is proved that, at any time after the vehicle was unlawfully taken (whether by him or another) and before it was recovered, the vehicle was driven, or injury or damage was caused, in one or more of the circumstances set out in paragraphs (a) to (d) of subsection (2) below.

(2)   The circumstances referred to in subsection (1)(b) above are—
    (a)   that the vehicle was driven dangerously on a road or other public place;
    (b)   that, owing to the driving of the vehicle, an accident occurred by which injury was caused to any person;
    (c)   that, owing to the driving of the vehicle, an accident occurred by which damage was caused to any property, other than the vehicle;
    (d)   that damage was caused to the vehicle.

(3)   A person is not guilty of an offence under this section if he proves that, as regards any such proven driving, injury or damage as is referred to in subsection (1)(b) above, either—
    (a)   the driving, accident or damage referred to in subsection (2) above occurred before he committed the basic offence; or
    (b)   he was neither in nor on nor in the immediate vicinity of the vehicle when that driving, accident or damage occurred.

(4)   A person guilty of an offence under this section shall be liable on conviction on indictment to imprisonment for a term not exceeding two years or, if it is proved that, in circumstances falling within subsection (2)(b) above, the accident caused the death of the person concerned, fourteen years.

(5)   If a person who is charged with an offence under this section is found not guilty of that offence but it is proved that he committed a basic offence, he may be convicted of the basic offence.

(6)   If by virtue of subsection (5) above a person is convicted of a basic offence before the Crown Court, that court shall have the same powers and duties as a magistrates' court would have had on convicting him of such an offence.

(7)   For the purposes of this section a vehicle is driven dangerously if—
    (a)   it is driven in a way which falls far below what would be expected of a competent and careful driver; and
    (b)   it would be obvious to a competent and careful driver that driving the vehicle in that way would be dangerous.

(8)   For the purposes of this section a vehicle is recovered when it is restored to its owner or to other lawful possession or custody; and in this subsection "owner" has the same meaning as in section 12 above.

13 ABSTRACTING OF ELECTRICITY

A person who dishonestly uses without due authority, or dishonestly causes to be wasted or diverted, any electricity shall on conviction on indictment be liable to imprisonment for a term not exceeding five years.

. . .

17 FALSE ACCOUNTING

(1)   Where a person dishonestly, with a view to gain for himself or another or with intent to cause loss to another,—
    (a)   destroys, defaces, conceals or falsifies any account or any record or document made or required for any accounting purpose; or
    (b)   in furnishing information for any purpose produces or makes use of any account, or any such record or document as aforesaid, which to his knowledge is or may be misleading, false or deceptive in a material particular;

he shall, on conviction on indictment, be liable to imprisonment for a term not exceeding seven years.

(2)   For purposes of this section a person who makes or concurs in making in an account or other document an entry which is or may be misleading, false or deceptive in a material particular, or who omits or concurs in omitting a material particular from an account or other document, is to be treated as falsifying the account or document.

18   LIABILITY OF COMPANY OFFICERS FOR CERTAIN OFFENCES BY COMPANY

(1)   Where an offence committed by a body corporate under section . . . 17 of this Act is proved to have been committed with the consent or connivance of any director, manager, secretary or other similar officer of the body corporate, or any person who was purporting to act in any such capacity, he as well as the body corporate shall be guilty of that offence, and shall be liable to be proceeded against and punished accordingly.

(2)   Where the affairs of a body corporate are managed by its members, this section shall apply in relation to the acts and defaults of a member in connection with his functions of management as if he were a director of the body corporate.

19   FALSE STATEMENTS BY COMPANY DIRECTORS, ETC

(1)   Where an officer of a body corporate or unincorporated association (or person purporting to act as such), with intent to deceive members or creditors of the body corporate or association about its affairs, publishes or concurs in publishing a written statement or account which to his knowledge is or may be misleading, false or deceptive in a material particular, he shall on conviction on indictment be liable to imprisonment for a term not exceeding seven years.

(2)   For purposes of this section a person who has entered into a security for the benefit of a body corporate or association is to be treated as a creditor of it.

(3)   Where the affairs of a body corporate or association are managed by its members, this section shall apply to any statement which a member publishes or concurs in publishing in connection with his functions of management as if he were an officer of the body corporate or association.

20   SUPPRESSION, ETC OF DOCUMENTS

(1)   A person who dishonestly, with a view to gain for himself or another or with intent to cause loss to another, destroys, defaces or conceals any valuable security, any will or other testamentary document or any original document of or belonging to, or filed or deposited in, any court of justice or any government department shall on conviction on indictment be liable to imprisonment for a term not exceeding seven years.

(3)   For purposes of this section . . . "valuable security" means any document creating, transferring, surrendering or releasing any right to, in or over property, or authorising the payment of money or delivery of any property, or evidencing the creation, transfer, surrender or release of any such right, or the payment of money or delivery of any property, or the satisfaction of any obligation.

21 BLACKMAIL

(1)   A person is guilty of blackmail if, with a view to gain for himself or another or with intent to cause loss to another, he makes any unwarranted demand with menaces; and for this purpose a demand with menaces is unwarranted unless the person making it does so in the belief—
(a)   that he has reasonable grounds for making the demand; and
(b)   that the use of the menaces is a proper means of reinforcing the demand.

(2)   The nature of the act or omission demanded is immaterial, and it is also immaterial whether the menaces relate to action to be taken by the person making the demand.

(3)   A person guilty of blackmail shall on conviction on indictment be liable to imprisonment for a term not exceeding fourteen years.

22 HANDLING STOLEN GOODS

(1)   A person handles stolen goods if (otherwise than in the course of the stealing) knowing or believing them to be stolen goods he dishonestly receives the goods, or dishonestly undertakes or assists in their retention, removal, disposal or realisation by or for the benefit of another person, or if he arranges to do so.

(2)   A person guilty of handling stolen goods shall on conviction on indictment be liable to imprisonment for a term not exceeding fourteen years.

. . .

24 SCOPE OF OFFENCES RELATING TO STOLEN GOODS

(1)   The provisions of this Act relating to goods which have been stolen shall apply whether the stealing occurred in England or Wales or elsewhere, and whether it occurred before or after the commencement of this Act, provided that the stealing (if not an offence under this Act) amounted to an offence where and at the time when the goods were stolen; and references to stolen goods shall be construed accordingly.

(2)   For purposes of those provisions references to stolen goods shall include, in addition to the goods originally stolen and parts of them (whether in their original state or not),—
(a)   any other goods which directly or indirectly represent or have at any time represented the stolen goods in the hands of the thief as being the proceeds of any disposal or realisation of the whole or part of the goods stolen or of goods so representing the stolen goods; and
(b)   any other goods which directly or indirectly represent or have at any time represented the stolen goods in the hands of a handler of the stolen goods or any part of them as being the proceeds of any disposal or realisation of the whole or part of the stolen goods handled by him or of goods so representing them.

(3)   But no goods shall be regarded as having continued to be stolen goods after they have been restored to the person from whom they were stolen or to other lawful possession or custody, or after that person and any other person claiming through him have otherwise ceased as regards those goods to have any right to restitution in respect of the theft.

(4)   For purposes of the provisions of this Act relating to goods which have been stolen (including subsections (1) to (3) above) goods obtained in England or Wales or elsewhere either by blackmail or, subject to subsection (5) below, by fraud (within the meaning of

the Fraud Act 2006) shall be regarded as stolen; and "steal", "theft" and "thief" shall be construed accordingly.

(5) Subsection (1) above applies in relation to goods obtained by fraud as if—
    (a) the reference to the commencement of this Act were a reference to the commencement of the Fruad Act 2006 and
    (b) the reference to an offence under this Act were a reference to an offence under section 1 of that Act.

24A DISHONESTLY RETAINING A WRONGFUL CREDIT

(1) A person is guilty of an offence if—
    (a) a wrongful credit has been made to an account kept by him or in respect of which he has any right or interest;
    (b) he knows or believes that the credit is wrongful; and
    (c) he dishonestly fails to take such steps as are reasonable in the circumstances to secure that the credit is cancelled.

(2) References to a credit are to a credit of an amount of money.

(2A) A credit to an account is wrongful to the extent that it derives from—
    (a) theft;
    (b) blackmail;
    (c) fraud (contrary to section 1 of the Fraud Act 2006); or
    (d) stolen goods.

(5) In determining whether a credit to an account is wrongful, it is immaterial (in particular) whether the account is overdrawn before or after the credit is made.

(6) A person guilty of an offence under this section shall be liable on conviction on indictment to imprisonment for a term not exceeding ten years.

(7) Subsection (8) below applies for purposes of provisions of this Act relating to stolen goods (including subsection (2A) above).

(8) References to stolen goods include money which is dishonestly withdrawn from an account to which a wrongful credit has been made, but only to the extent that the money derives from the credit.

(9) "Account" means an account kept with—
    (a) a bank;
    (b) a person carrying on a business which falls within subsection (10) below; or
    (c) an issuer of electronic money (as defined for the purposes of Part 2 of the Financial Services and Markets Act 2000).

(10) A business falls within this subsection if—
    (a) in the course of the business money received by way of deposit is lent to others; or
    (b) any other activity of the business is financed, wholly or to any material extent, out of the capital of or the interest on money received by way of deposit.

(11) References in subsection (10) above to a deposit must be read with—
    (a) section 22 of the Financial Services and Markets Act 2000;
    (b) any relevant order under that section; and
    (c) Schedule 2 to that Act;
    but any restriction on the meaning of deposit which arises from the identity of the person making it is to be disregarded.

(12) For the purposes of subsection (10) above—
   (a) all the activities which a person carries on by way of business shall be regarded as a single business carried on by him; and
   (b) "money" includes money expressed in a currency other than sterling.

25 GOING EQUIPPED FOR STEALING, ETC

(1) A person shall be guilty of an offence if, when not at his place of abode, he has with him any article for use in the course of or in connection with any burglary or theft.

(2) A person guilty of an offence under this section shall on conviction on indictment be liable to imprisonment for a term not exceeding three years.

(3) Where a person is charged with an offence under this section, proof that he had with him any article made or adapted for use in committing a burglary or theft shall be evidence that he had it with him for such use.

(5) For purposes of this section an offence under section 12(1) of this Act of taking a conveyance shall be treated as theft. . . .

27 EVIDENCE AND PROCEDURE ON CHARGE OF THEFT OR HANDLING STOLEN GOODS

(1) Any number of persons may be charged in one indictment, with reference to the same theft, with having at different times or at the same time handled all or any of the stolen goods, and the persons so charged may be tried together.

(2) On the trial of two or more persons indicted for jointly handling any stolen goods the jury may find any of the accused guilty if the jury are satisfied that he handled all or any of the stolen goods, whether or not he did so jointly with the other accused or any of them.

(3) Where a person is being proceeded against for handling stolen goods (but not for any offence other than handling stolen goods), then at any stage of the proceedings, if evidence has been given of his having or arranging to have in his possession the goods the subject of the charge, or of his undertaking or assisting in, or arranging to undertake or assist in, their retention, removal, disposal or realisation, the following evidence shall be admissible for the purpose of proving that he knew or believed the goods to be stolen goods:—
   (a) evidence that he has had in his possession, or has undertaken or assisted in the retention, removal, disposal or realisation of, stolen goods from any theft taking place not earlier than twelve months before the offence charged; and
   (b) (provided that seven days' notice in writing has been given to him of the intention to prove the conviction) evidence that he has within the five years preceding the date of the offence charged been convicted of theft or of handling stolen goods.

(4) In any proceedings for the theft of anything in the course of transmission (whether by post or otherwise), or for handling stolen goods from such a theft, a statutory declaration made by any person that he despatched or received or failed to receive any goods or postal packet, or that any goods or postal packet when despatched or received by him were in a particular state or condition, shall be admissible as evidence of the facts stated in the declaration, subject to the following conditions:—
   (a) a statutory declaration shall only be admissible where and to the extent to which oral evidence to the like effect would have been admissible in the proceedings; and
   (b) a statutory declaration shall only be admissible if at least seven days before the hearing or trial a copy of it has been given to the person charged, and he has not, at

least three days before the hearing or trial or within such further time as the court may in special circumstances allow, given the prosecutor written notice requiring the attendance at the hearing or trial of the person making the declaration.

. . .

30 SPOUSES AND CIVIL PARTNERS

(1)   This Act shall apply in relation to the parties to a marriage, and to property belonging to the wife or husband whether or not by reason of an interest derived from the marriage, as it would apply if they were not married and any such interest subsisted independently of the marriage.

(2)   Subject to subsection (4) below, a person shall have the same right to bring proceedings against that person's wife or husband for any offence (whether under this Act or otherwise) as if they were not married, and a person bringing any such proceedings shall be competent to give evidence for the prosecution at every stage of the proceedings.

(4)   Proceedings shall not be instituted against a person for any offence of stealing or doing unlawful damage to property which at the time of the offence belongs to that person's wife or husband or civil partner, or for any attempt, incitement or conspiracy to commit such an offence, unless the proceedings are instituted by or with the consent of the Director of Public Prosecutions:

Provided that—

(a)   this subsection shall not apply to proceedings against a person for an offence—
   (i)   if that person is charged with committing the offence jointly with the wife or husband or civil partner; . . .
   (ii)   if by virtue of any judicial decree or order (wherever made) that person and the wife or husband are at the time of the offence under no obligation to cohabit; . . .; or
   (iii) an order (wherever made) is in force providing for the separation of that person and his or her civil partner.

. . .

34 INTERPRETATION

(1)   Sections 4(1) and 5(1) of this Act shall apply generally for purposes of this Act as they apply for purposes of section 1.

(2)   For purposes of this Act—
   (a)   "gain" and "loss" are to be construed as extending only to gain or loss in money or other property, but as extending to any such gain or loss whether temporary or permanent; and—
      (i)   "gain" includes a gain by keeping what one has, as well as a gain by getting what one has not; and
      (ii)   "loss" includes a loss by not getting what one might get, as well as a loss by parting with what one has;
   (b)   "goods", except in so far as the context otherwise requires, includes money and every other description of property except land, and includes things severed from the land by stealing; and
   (c)   "mail bag" and "postal packet" have the meanings given by section 125(1) of the Postal Services Act 2000.

As amended Police and Criminal Evidence Act 1984, s 119; Criminal Justice Act 1988, s 37; Vehicles (Crime) Act 2001, s 37; Aggravated Vehicle-Taking Act 1992, s 1; Criminal Justice Act 2003, s 285; Civil Partnership Act 2003; Fraud Act 2006.

TATTOOING OF MINORS ACT 1969

1 PROHIBITION OF TATTOOING OF MINORS

It shall be an offence to tattoo a person under the age of eighteen except when the tattoo is performed for medical reasons by a duly qualified medical practitioner or by a person working under his direction, but it shall be a defence for a person charged to show that at the time the tattoo was performed he had reasonable cause to believe that the person tattooed was of or over the age of eighteen and did in fact so believe.

2 PENALTIES

Any person committing such an offence shall be liable on summary conviction to a fine not exceeding level three on the standard scale.

3 DEFINITION

For the purposes of this Act "tattoo" shall mean the insertion into the skin of any colouring material designed to leave a permanent mark.

As amended Criminal Justice Act 1982, s 38, 46.

CRIMINAL DAMAGE ACT 1971

1 DESTROYING OR DAMAGING PROPERTY

(1)   A person who without lawful excuse destroys or damages any property belonging to another intending to destroy or damage any such property or being reckless as to whether any such property would be destroyed or damaged shall be guilty of an offence.

(2)   A person who without lawful excuse destroys or damages any property, whether belonging to himself or another—
   (a) intending to destroy or damage any property or being reckless as to whether any property would be destroyed or damaged; and
   (b) intending by the destruction or damage to endanger the life of another or being reckless as to whether the life of another would be thereby endangered;
   shall be guilty of an offence.

(3)   An offence committed under this section by destroying or damaging property by fire shall be charged as arson.

2 THREATS TO DESTROY OR DAMAGE PROPERTY

A person who without lawful excuse makes to another a threat, intending that that other would fear it would be carried out,—

(a)   to destroy or damage any property belonging to that other or a third person; or

(b)   to destroy or damage his own property in a way which he knows is likely to endanger the life of that other or third person;

shall be guilty of an offence.

3 POSSESSING ANYTHING WITH INTENT TO DESTROY OR DAMAGE PROPERTY

A person who has anything in his custody or under his control intending without lawful excuse to use it or cause or permit another to use it—

(a)   to destroy or damage any property belonging to some other person; or

(b)   to destroy or damage his own or the user's property in a way which he knows is likely to endanger the life of some other person;

shall be guilty of an offence.

4 PUNISHMENT OF OFFENCES

(1)   A person guilty of arson under section 1 above or of an offence under section 1(2) above (whether arson or not) shall on conviction on indictment be liable to imprisonment for life.

(2)   A person guilty of any other offence under this Act shall on conviction on indictment be liable to imprisonment for a term not exceeding ten years.

5 "WITHOUT LAWFUL EXCUSE"

(1)   This section applies to any offence under section 1(1) above and any offence under section 2 or 3 above other than one involving a threat by the person charged to destroy or damage property in a way which he knows is likely to endanger the life of another or involving an intent by the person charged to use or cause or permit the use of something in his custody or under his control so to destroy or damage property.

(2)   A person charged with an offence to which this section applies, shall, whether or not he would be treated for the purposes of this Act as having a lawful excuse apart from this subsection, be treated for those purposes as having a lawful excuse—
    (a) if at the time of the act or acts alleged to constitute the offence he believed that the person or persons whom he believed to be entitled to consent to the destruction of or damage to the property in question had so consented, or would have so consented to it if he or they had known of the destruction or damage and its circumstances; or
    (b) if he destroyed or damaged or threatened to destroy or damage the property in question or, in the case of a charge of an offence under section 3 above, intended to use or cause or permit the use of something to destroy or damage it, in order to protect property belonging to himself or another or a right or interest in property which was or which he believed to be vested in himself or another, and at the time of the act or acts alleged to constitute the offence he believed—
        (i)   that the property, right or interest was in immediate need of protection; and
        (ii) that the means of protection adopted or proposed to be adopted were or would be reasonable having regard to all the circumstances.

(3)   For the purposes of this section it is immaterial whether a belief is justified or not if it is honestly held.

(4)   For the purposes of subsection (2) above a right or interest in property includes any right or privilege in or over land, whether created by grant, licence or otherwise.

(5)   This section shall not be construed as casting doubt on any defence recognised by law as a defence to criminal charges.

6 SEARCH FOR THINGS INTENDED FOR USE IN COMMITTING OFFENCES OF CRIMINAL DAMAGE

(1)   If it is made to appear by information on oath before a justice of the peace that there is reasonable cause to believe that any person has in his custody or under his control or on his premises anything which there is reasonable cause to believe has been used or is intended for use without lawful excuse—
(a) to destroy or damage property belonging to another; or
(b) to destroy or damage any property in a way likely to endanger the life of another, the justice may grant a warrant authorising any constable to search for and seize that thing.

(2)   A constable who is authorised under this section to search premises for anything, may enter (if need be by force) and search the premises accordingly and may seize anything which he believes to have been used or to be intended to be used as aforesaid.

(3)   The Police (Property) Act 1897 (disposal of property in the possession of the police) shall apply to property which has come into the possession of the police under this section as it applies to property which has come into the possession of the police in the circumstances mentioned in that Act.

10 INTERPRETATION

(1)   In this Act "property" means property of a tangible nature, whether real or personal, including money and—
(a) including wild creatures which have been tamed or are ordinarily kept in captivity, and any other wild creatures or their carcasses if, but only if, they have been reduced into possession which has not been lost or abandoned or are in the course of being reduced into possession; but
(b) not including mushrooms growing wild on any land or flowers, fruit or foliage of a plant growing wild on any land.
For the purposes of this subsection "mushroom" includes any fungus and "plant" includes any shrub or tree.

(2)   Property shall be treated for the purposes of this Act as belonging to any person—
(a) having the custody or control of it;
(b) having in it any proprietary right or interest (not being an equitable interest arising only from an agreement to transfer or grant an interest); or
(c) having a charge on it.

(3)   Where property is subject to a trust, the persons to whom it belongs shall be so treated as including any person having a right to enforce the trust.

(4)   Property of a corporation sole shall be so treated as belonging to the corporation notwithstanding a vacancy in the corporation.

As amended by Criminal Justice Act 1972, sch 6; Magistrates' Courts Act 1980 (c. 43, SIF 82), Sch. 1.

MISUSE OF DRUGS ACT 1971

2 CONTROLLED DRUGS AND THEIR CLASSIFICATION FOR PURPOSES OF THIS ACT

(1)   In this Act—
   (a)   the expression "controlled drug" means any substance or product for the time being specified in Part I, II, or III of Schedule 2 to this Act; and
   (b)   the expressions "Class A drug", "Class B drug" and "Class C drug" mean any of the substances and products for the time being specified respectively in Part I, Part II and Part III of that Schedule;
   and the provisions of Part IV of that Schedule shall have effect with respect to the meanings of expressions used in that Schedule.

3 RESTRICTION OF IMPORTATION AND EXPORTATION OF CONTROLLED DRUGS

(1)   Subject to subsection (2) below—
   (a)   the importation of a controlled drug; and
   (b)   the exportation of a controlled drug,
   are hereby prohibited.

(2)   Subsection (1) above does not apply—
   (a)   to the importation or exportation of a controlled drug which is for the time being excepted from paragraph (a) or, as the case may be, paragraph (b) of subsection (1) above by regulations under section 7 of this Act; or
   (b)   to the importation or exportation of a controlled drug under and in accordance with the terms of a licence issued by the Secretary of State and in compliance with any conditions attached thereto.

4 RESTRICTION OF PRODUCTION AND SUPPLY OF CONTROLLED DRUGS

(1)   Subject to any regulations under section 7 of this Act for the time being in force, it shall not be lawful for a person—
   (a)   to produce a controlled drug; or
   (b)   to supply or offer to supply a controlled drug to another.

(2)   Subject to section 28 of this Act, it is an offence for a person—
   (a)   to produce a controlled drug in contravention of subsection (1) above; or
   (b)   to be concerned in the production of such a drug in contravention of that subsection by another.

(3)   Subject to section 28 of this Act, it is an offence for a person—
   (a)   to supply or offer to supply a controlled drug to another in contravention of subsection (1) above; or
   (b)   to be concerned in the supplying of such a drug to another in contravention of that subsection; or
   (c)   to be concerned in the making to another in contravention of that subsection of an offer to supply such a drug.

4A AGGRAVATION OF OFFENCE OF SUPPLY OF CONTROLLED DRUG

(1)   This section applies if—

(a) a court is considering the seriousness of an offence under section 4(3) of this Act, and

(b) at the time the offence was committed the offender had attained the age of 18.

(2) If either of the following conditions is met the court—

(a) must treat the fact that the condition is met as an aggravating factor (that is to say, a factor that increases the seriousness of the offence), and

(b) must state in open court that the offence is so aggravated.

(3) The first condition is that the offence was committed on or in the vicinity of school premises at a relevant time.

(4) The second condition is that in connection with the commission of the offence the offender used a courier who, at the time the offence was committed, was under the age of 18.

(5) In subsection (3), a relevant time is—

(a) any time when the school premises are in use by persons under the age of 18;

(b) one hour before the start and one hour after the end of any such time.

(6) For the purposes of subsection (4), a person uses a courier in connection with an offence under section 4(3) of this Act if he causes or permits another person (the courier)—

(a) to deliver a controlled drug to a third person, or

(b) to deliver a drug related consideration to himself or a third person.

(7) For the purposes of subsection (6), a drug related consideration is a consideration of any description which—

(a) is obtained in connection with the supply of a controlled drug, or

(b) is intended to be used in connection with obtaining a controlled drug.

(8) In this section—

"school premises" means land used for the purposes of a school excluding any land occupied solely as a dwelling by a person employed at the school; and

"school" has the same meaning—

(a) in England and Wales, as in section 4 of the Education Act 1996 . . .

5 RESTRICTION OF POSSESSION OF CONTROLLED DRUGS

(1) Subject to any regulations under section 7 of this Act for the time being in force, it shall not be lawful for a person to have a controlled drug in his possession.

(2) Subject to section 28 of this Act and to subsection (4) below, it is an offence for a person to have a controlled drug in his possession in contravention of subsection (1) above.

(3) Subject to section 28 of this Act, it is an offence for a person to have a controlled drug in his possession, whether lawfully or not, with intent to supply it to another in contravention of section 4(1) of this Act.

(4) In any proceedings for an offence under subsection (2) above in which it is proved that the accused had a controlled drug in his possession, it shall be a defence for him to prove—

(a) that, knowing or suspecting it to be a controlled drug, he took possession of it for the purpose of preventing another from committing or continuing to commit an offence in connection with that drug and that as soon as possible after taking possession of it he took all such steps as were reasonably open to him to destroy the drug or to deliver it into the custody of a person lawfully entitled to take custody of it; or

(b) that, knowing or suspecting it to be a controlled drug, he took possession of it for the purpose of delivering it into the custody of a person lawfully entitled to take custody of it and that as soon as possible after taking possession of it he took all such steps as were reasonably open to him to deliver it into the custody of such a person.

(4A) In any proceedings for an offence under subsection (3) above, if it is proved that the accused had an amount of a controlled drug in his possession which is not less than the prescribed amount, the court or jury must assume that he had the drug in his possession with the intent to supply it as mentioned in subsection (3).

(4B) Subsection (4A) above does not apply if evidence is adduced which is sufficient to raise an issue that the accused may not have had the drug in his possession with that intent.

. . .

(6)   Nothing in subsection (4) . . . above shall prejudice any defence which it is open to a person charged with an offence under this section to raise apart from that subsection.

6 RESTRICTIONS OF CULTIVATION OF CANNABIS PLANT

(1)   Subject to any regulations under section 7 of this Act for the time being in force, it shall not be lawful for a person to cultivate any plant of the genus *Cannabis*.

(2)   Subject to section 28 of this Act, it is an offence to cultivate any such plant in contravention of subsection (1) above.

7 AUTHORISATION OF ACTIVITIES OTHERWISE UNLAWFUL UNDER FOREGOING PROVISIONS

(1)   The Secretary of State may by regulations—
    (a) except from section 3(1)(a) or (b), 4(1)(a) or (b) or 5(1) of this Act such controlled drugs as may be specified in the regulations; and
    (b) make such other provision as he thinks fit for the purpose of making it lawful for persons to do things which under any of the following provisions of this Act, that is to say section 4(1), 5(1) and 6(1), it would otherwise be unlawful for them to do.

(2)   Without prejudice to the generality of paragraph (b) of subsection (1) above, regulations under that subsection authorising the doing of any such thing as is mentioned in that paragraph may in particular provide for the doing of that thing to be lawful—
    (a) if it is done under and in accordance with the terms of a licence or other authority issued by the Secretary of State and in compliance with any conditions attached thereto; or
    (b) if it is done in compliance with such conditions as may be prescribed.

(3)   Subject to subsection (4) below, the Secretary of State shall so exercise his power to make regulations under subsection (1) above as to secure—
    (a) that it is not unlawful under section 4 (1) of this Act for a doctor, dentist, veterinary practitioner or veterinary surgeon, acting in his capacity as such, to prescribe, administer, manufacture, compound or supply a controlled drug, or for a pharmacist or a person lawfully conducting a retail pharmacy business, acting in either case in his capacity as such, to manufacture, compound or supply a controlled drug; and
    (b) that it is not unlawful under section 5 (1) of this Act for a doctor, dentist, veterinary practitioner, veterinary surgeon, pharmacist or person lawfully conducting a retail pharmacy business to have a controlled drug in his possession for the purpose of acting in his capacity as such.

(4)   If in the case of any controlled drug the Secretary of State is of the opinion that it is in the public interest—

(a) for production, supply and possession of that drug to be either wholly unlawful or unlawful except for purposes of research or other special purposes; or

(b) for it to be unlawful for practitioners, pharmacists and persons lawfully conducting retail pharmacy businesses to do in relation to that drug any of the things mentioned in subsection (3) above except under a licence or other authority issued by the Secretary of State,

he may by order designate that drug as a drug to which this subsection applies; and while there is in force an order under this subsection designating a controlled drug as one to which this subsection applies, subsection (3) above shall not apply as regards that drug.

. . .

(8) References in this section to a person's "doing" things include references to his having things in his possession.

8 OCCUPIERS ETC OF PREMISES TO BE PUNISHABLE FOR PERMITTING CERTAIN ACTIVITIES TO TAKE PLACE THERE

A person commits an offence if, being the occupier or concerned in the management of any premises, he knowingly permits or suffers any of the following activities to take place on those premises, that is to say—

(a) producing or attempting to produce a controlled drug in contravention of section 4(1) of this Act;

(b) supplying or attempting to supply a controlled drug to another in contravention of section 4(1) of this Act, or offering to supply a controlled drug to another in contravention of section 4(1);

(c) preparing opium for smoking;

(d) administering or using a controlled drug which is unlawfully in any person's possession at or immediately before the time when it is administered or used.

9 PROHIBITION OF CERTAIN ACTIVITIES ETC RELATING TO OPIUM

Subject to section 28 of this Act, it is an offence for a person—

(a) to smoke or otherwise use prepared opium; or

(b) to frequent a place used for the purpose of opium smoking; or

(c) to have in his possession
  (i)   any pipes or other utensils made or adapted for use in connection with the smoking of opium, being pipes or utensils which have been used by him or with his knowledge and permission in that connection or which he intends to use or permit others to use in that connection; or
  (ii) any utensils which have been used by him or with his knowledge and permission in connection with the preparation of opium for smoking.

9A PROHIBITION OF SUPPLY ETC OF ARTICLES FOR ADMINISTERING OR PREPARING CONTROLLED DRUGS

(1) A person who supplies or offers to supply any article which may be used or adapted to be used (whether by itself or in combination with another article or other articles) in the administration by any person of a controlled drug to himself or another, believing that the article (or the article as adapted) is to be so used in circumstances where the administration is unlawful, is guilty of an offence.

(2)   It is not an offence under subsection (1) above to supply or offer to supply a hypodermic syringe, or any part of one.

(3)   A person who supplies or offers to supply any article which may be used to prepare a controlled drug for administration by any person to himself or another believing that the article is to be so used in circumstances where the administration is unlawful is guilty of an offence.

(4)   For the purposes of this section, any administration of a controlled drug is unlawful except—
    (a)   the administration by any person of a controlled drug to another in circumstances where the administration of the drug is not unlawful under section 4(1) of this Act, or
    (b)   the administration by any person of a controlled drug to himself in circumstances where having the controlled drug in his possession is not unlawful under section 5(1) of this Act.

(5)   In this section, references to administration by any person of a controlled drug to himself include a reference to his administering it to himself with the assistance of another.

28 PROOF OF LACK OF KNOWLEDGE ETC TO BE A DEFENCE IN PROCEEDINGS FOR CERTAIN OFFENCES

(1)   This section applies to offences under any of the following provisions of this Act, that is to say section 4(2) and (3), section 5(2) and (3), section 6(2) and section 9.

(2)   Subject to subsection (3) below, in any proceedings for an offence to which this section applies it shall be a defence for the accused to prove that he neither knew of nor suspected nor had reason to suspect the existence of some fact alleged by the prosecution which it is necessary for the prosecution to prove if he is to be convicted of the offence charged.

(3)   Where in any proceedings for an offence to which this section applies it is necessary, if the accused is to be convicted of the offence charged, for the prosecution to prove that some substance or product involved in the alleged offence was the controlled drug which the prosecution alleges it to have been, and it is proved that the substance or product in question was that controlled drug, the accused—
    (a)   shall not be acquitted of the offence charged by reason only of proving that he neither knew nor suspected nor had reason to suspect that the substance or product in question was the particular controlled drug alleged; but
    (b)   shall be acquitted thereof—
        (i)   if he proves that he neither believed nor suspected nor had reason to suspect that the substance or product in question was a controlled drug; or
        (ii)   if he proves that he believed the substance or product in question to be a controlled drug, or a controlled drug of a description, such that, if it had in fact been that controlled drug or a controlled drug of that description, he would not at the material time have been committing any offence to which this section applies.

(4)   Nothing in this section shall prejudice any defence which it is open to a person charged with an offence to which this section applies to raise apart from this section.

37 INTERPRETATION

(1)   In this Act, except in so far as the context otherwise requires, the following expressions have the meanings hereby assigned to them respectively, that is to say:—

    "cannabis" (except in the expression "cannabis resin") means any plant of the genus *Cannabis* or any part of any such plant (by whatever name designated) except that it does

not include cannabis resin or any of the following products after separation from the rest of the plant, namely—
  (a) mature stalk of any such plant,
  (b) fibre produced from mature stalk of any such plant, and
  (c) seed of any such plant;
"cannabis resin" means the separated resin, whether crude or purified, obtained from any plant of the genus *Cannabis*;

"controlled drug" has the meaning assigned by section 2 of this Act;

(2) References in this Act to misusing a drug are references to misusing it by taking it; and the reference in the foregoing provision to the taking of a drug is a reference to the taking of it by a human being by way of any form of self-administration, whether or not involving assistance by another.

(3) For the purposes of this Act the things which a person has in his possession shall be taken to include any thing subject to his control which is in the custody of another.

As amended by Drugs Act 2005, s 1. Criminal Justice and Police Act 2001, s 38. Inserted by the Drug Trafficking Offences Act 1986, s 34(1).

CRIMINAL LAW ACT 1977

1 THE OFFENCE OF CONSPIRACY

(1) Subject to the following provisions of this part of this Act, if a person agrees with any other person or persons that a course of conduct shall be pursued which, if the agreement is carried out in accordance with their intentions, either—
  (a) will necessarily amount to or involve the commission of any offence or offences by one or more of the parties to the agreement, or
  (b) would do so but for the existence of facts which render the commission of the offence or any of the offences impossible,
he is guilty of conspiracy to commit the offence or offences in question.

(2) Where liability for any offence may be incurred without knowledge on the part of the person committing it of any particular fact or circumstance necessary for the commission of the offence, a person shall nevertheless not be guilty of conspiracy to commit that offence by virtue of subsection (1) above unless he and at least one other party to the agreement intend or know that that fact or circumstance shall or will exist at the time when the conduct constituting the offence is to take place.

(4) In this Part of this Act "offence" means an offence triable in England and

1A CONSPIRACY TO COMMIT OFFENCES OUTSIDE THE UNITED KINGDOM

(1) Where each of the following conditions is satisfied in the case of an agreement, this Part of this Act has effect in relation to the agreement as it has effect in relation to an agreement falling within section 1(1) above.

(2) The first condition is that the pursuit of the agreed course of conduct would at some stage involve—
  (a) an act by one or more of the parties, or

(b) the happening of some other event,
intended to take place in a country or territory outside the United Kingdom.

(3)   The second condition is that that act or other event constitutes an offence under the law in force in that country or territory.

(4)   The third condition is that the agreement would fall within section 1(1) above as an agreement relating to the commission of an offence but for the fact that the offence would not be an offence triable in England and Wales if committed in accordance with the parties' intentions.

(5)   The fourth condition is that—
(a) a party to the agreement, or a party's agent, did anything in England and Wales in relation to the agreement before its formation, or
(b) a party to the agreement became a party in England and Wales (by joining it either in person or through an agent), or
(c) a party to the agreement, or a party's agent, did or omitted anything in England and Wales in pursuance of the agreement.

(6)   In the application of this Part of this Act to an agreement in the case of which each of the above conditions is satisfied, a reference to an offence is to be read as a reference to what would be the offence in question but for the fact that it is not an offence triable in England and Wales.

(7)   Conduct punishable under the law in force in any country or territory is an offence under that law for the purposes of this section, however it is described in that law.

(8)   Subject to subsection (9) below, the second condition is to be taken to be satisfied unless, not later than rules of court may provide, the defence serve on the prosecution a notice—
(a) stating that, on the facts as alleged with respect to the agreed course of conduct, the condition is not in their opinion satisfied,
(b) showing their grounds for that opinion, and
(c) requiring the prosecution to show that it is satisfied.

(9)   The court may permit the defence to require the prosecution to show that the second condition is satisfied without the prior service of a notice under subsection (8) above.

(10) In the Crown Court the question whether the second condition is satisfied shall be decided by the judge alone, and shall be treated as a question of law for the purposes of—
(a) section 9(3) of the Criminal Justice Act 1987 (preparatory hearing in fraud cases), and
(b) section 31(3) of the Criminal Procedure and Investigations Act 1996 (preparatory hearing in other cases).

(11) Any act done by means of a message (however communicated) is to be treated for the purposes of the fourth condition as done in England and Wales if the message is sent or received in England and Wales.

(12) In any proceedings in respect of an offence triable by virtue of this section, it is immaterial to guilt whether or not the accused was a British citizen at the time of any act or other event proof of which is required for conviction of the offence.

(13) References in any enactment, instrument or document (except those in this Part of this Act) to an offence of conspiracy to commit an offence include an offence triable in England and Wales as such a conspiracy by virtue of this section (without prejudice to subsection (6) above).

(14) Nothing in this section applies to an agreement entered into before 4 September 1998.

(15) In relation to an agreement entered into during the period beginning with that date and ending with the commencement of section 72(1) of the Coroners and Justice Act 2009, this section applies as if in subsection (2) for "England and Wales" there were substituted "the United Kingdom".

(16) Nothing in this section imposes criminal liability on any person acting on behalf of, or holding office under, the Crown.

2 EXEMPTIONS FROM LIABILITY FOR CONSPIRACY

(1) A person shall not by virtue of section 1 above be guilty of conspiracy to commit any offence if he is an intended victim of that offence.

(2) A person shall not by virtue of section 1 above be guilty of conspiracy to commit any offence or offences if the only other person or persons with whom he agrees are (both initially and at all times during the currency of the agreement) persons of any one or more of the following descriptions, that is to say—
(a) his spouse or civil partner;
(b) a person under the age of criminal responsibility; and
(c) an intended victim of that offence or of each of those offences.

(3) A person is under the age of criminal responsibility for the purposes of subsection (2)(b) above so long as it is conclusively presumed, by virtue of section 50 of the Children and Young Persons Act 1933, that he cannot be guilty of any offence.

3 PENALTIES FOR CONSPIRACY

(1) A person guilty by virtue of section 1 above of conspiracy to commit any offence or offences shall be liable on conviction on indictment—
(a) in a case falling within subsection (2) or (3) below, to imprisonment for a term related in accordance with that subsection to the gravity of the offence or offences in question (referred to below in this section as the relevant offence or offences); and
(b) in any other case, to a fine.
Paragraph (b) above shall not be taken as prejudicing the application of section 163 Criminal Justice Act 2003 (general power of court to fine offender convicted on indictment) in a case falling within subsection (2) or (3) below.

(2) Where the relevant offence or any of the relevant offences is an offence of any of the following descriptions, that is to say—
(a) murder, or any other offence the sentence for which is fixed by law;
(b) an offence for which a sentence extending to imprisonment for life is provided; or
(c) an indictable offence punishable with imprisonment for which no maximum term of imprisonment is provided,
the person convicted shall be liable to imprisonment for life.

(3) Where in a case other than one to which subsection (2) above applies the relevant offence or any of the relevant offences is punishable with imprisonment, the person convicted shall be liable to imprisonment for a term not exceeding the maximum term provided for that offence or (where more than one such offence is in question) for any one of those offences (taking the longer or the longest term as the limit for the purposes of this section where the terms provided differ).

In the case of an offence triable either way the references above in this subsection to the maximum term provided for that offence are references to the maximum term so provided on conviction on indictment.

As amended Criminal Attempts Act 1981, s. 5; Computer Misuse Act 1990, s. 7; Criminal Justice (Terrorism and Conspiracy) Act 1998, s. 9; Civil Partnership Act 2004 Trade Union and Labour Relations (Consolidation) Act 1992 (c. 52), ss. 300(1), 302, Sch. 1; Criminal Attempts Act 1981, s. 47; Coroners and Justice Act 2009, s. 72.

INTERPRETATION ACT 1978

5 DEFINITIONS

In any Act, unless the contrary intention appears, words and expressions listed in Schedule 1 to this Act are to be construed according to that Schedule.

6 GENDER AND NUMBER

In any Act, unless the contrary intention appears,—

(a)   words importing the masculine gender include the feminine;

(b)   words importing the feminine gender include the masculine;

(c)   words in the singular include the plural and words in the plural include the singular.

15 REPEAL OF REPEAL

Where an Act repeals a repealing enactment, the repeal does not revive any enactment previously repealed unless words are inserted reviving it.

16 GENERAL SAVINGS

(1)   Without prejudice to section 15, where an Act repeals an enactment, the repeal does not, unless the contrary intention appears,—
    (a) revive anything not in force or existing at the time at which the repeal takes effect;
    (b) affect the previous operation of the enactment repealed or anything duly done or suffered under that enactment;
    (c) affect any right, privilege, obligation or liability acquired, accrued or incurred under that enactment;
    (d) affect any penalty, forfeiture or punishment incurred in respect of any offence committed against that enactment;
    (e) affect any investigation, legal proceeding or remedy in respect of any such right, privilege, obligation, liability, penalty, forfeiture or punishment;
and any such investigation, legal proceeding or remedy may be instituted, continued or enforced, and any such penalty, forfeiture or punishment may be imposed, as if the repealing Act had not been passed.

(2)   This section applies to the expiry of a temporary enactment as if it were repealed by an Act.

17 REPEAL AND RE-ENACTMENT

(1)   Where an Act repeals a previous enactment and substitutes provisions for the enactment repealed, the repealed enactment remains in force until the substituted provisions come into force.

(2) Where an Act repeals and re-enacts, with or without modification, a previous enactment then, unless the contrary intention appears,—
  (a) any reference in any other enactment to the enactment so repealed shall be construed as a reference to the provision re-enacted;
  (b) in so far as any subordinate legislation made or other thing done under the enactment so repealed, or having effect as if so made or done, could have been made or done under the provision re-enacted, it shall have effect as if made or done under that provision.

18 DUPLICATED OFFENCES

Where an act or omission constitutes an offence under two or more Acts, or both under an Act and at common law, the offender shall, unless the contrary intention appears, be liable to be prosecuted and punished under either or any of those Acts or at common law, but shall not be liable to be punished more than once for the same offence.

SCHEDULE 1 WORDS AND EXPRESSIONS DEFINED

DEFINITIONS

"Act" means an Act of Parliament.

. . .

"Statutory maximum", with reference to a fine or penalty on summary conviction for an offence,—
(a) in relation to England and Wales, means the prescribed sum within the meaning of section 32 of the Magistrates' Courts Act 1980;

  . . .

. . .

Construction of certain expressions relating to offences
In relation to England and Wales—

(a) "indictable offence" means an offence which, if committed by an adult, is triable on indictment, whether it is exclusively so triable or triable either way;

(b) "summary offence" means an offence which, if committed by an adult, is triable only summarily;

(c) "offence triable either way" means an offence, other than an offence triable on indictment only by virtue of Part V of the Criminal Justice Act 1988 which, if committed by an adult, is triable either on indictment or summarily;

and the terms "indictable", "summary" and "triable either way", in their application to offences, are to be construed accordingly.

PROTECTION OF CHILDREN ACT 1978

1 INDECENT PHOTOGRAPHS OF CHILDREN

(1) Subject to sections 1A and 1B, it is an offence for a person—
  (a) to take, or permit to be taken or to make, any indecent photograph or pseudo-photograph of a child . . .; or

(b) to distribute or show such indecent photographs or pseudo-photographs; or

(c) to have in his possession such indecent photographs or pseudo-photographs, with a view to their being distributed or shown by himself or others; or

(d) to publish or cause to be published any advertisement likely to be understood as conveying that the advertiser distributes or shows such indecent photographs or pseudo-photographs, or intends to do so.

(2) For purposes of this Act, a person is to be regarded as distributing an indecent photograph or pseudo-photograph if he parts with possession of it to, or exposes or offers it for acquisition by, another person.

(3) Proceedings for an offence under this Act shall not be instituted except by or with the consent of the Director of Public Prosecutions.

(4) Where a person is charged with an offence under subsection (1)(b) or (c), it shall be a defence for him to prove—

(a) that he had a legitimate reason for distributing or showing the photographs or pseudo-photographs or (as the case may be) having them in his possession; or

(b) that he had not himself seen the photographs or pseudo-photographs and did not know, nor had any cause to suspect, them to be indecent.

. . .

2 EVIDENCE

(1) In proceedings under this Act relating to indecent photographs of children a person is to be taken as having been a child at any material time if it appears from the evidence as a whole that he was then under the age of 18.

As amended Sexual Offences Act 2003; Criminal Justice and Public Order Act 1994, s 84, 168.

THEFT ACT 1978

3 MAKING OFF WITHOUT PAYMENT

(1) Subject to subsection (3) below, a person who, knowing that payment on the spot for any goods supplied or service done is required or expected from him, dishonestly makes off without having paid as required or expected and with intent to avoid payment of the amount due shall be guilty of an offence.

(2) For purposes of this section "payment on the spot" includes payment at the time of collecting goods on which work has been done or in respect of which service has been provided.

(3) Subsection (1) above shall not apply where the supply of the goods or the doing of the service is contrary to law, or where the service done is such that payment is not legally enforceable.

4 PUNISHMENTS

(1) Offences under this Act shall be punishable either on conviction on indictment or on summary conviction.

(2)   A person convicted on indictment shall be liable—
(b) for an offence under section 3 of this Act, to imprisonment for a term not exceeding two years.

(3)   A person convicted summarily of any offence under this Act shall be liable—
(a) to imprisonment for a term not exceeding six months; or
(b) to a fine not exceeding the prescribed sum for the purposes of section 32 of the Magistrates' Courts Act 1980 (punishment on summary conviction of offences triable either way: £1,000 or other sum substituted by order under that Act) or to both.

As amended by the Fraud Act 2006, s 14.

MAGISTRATES' COURTS ACT 1980

44 AIDERS AND ABETTORS

(1)   A person who aids, abets, counsels or procures the commission by another person of a summary offence shall be guilty of the like offence and may be tried (whether or not he is charged as a principal) either by a court having jurisdiction to try that other person or by a court having by virtue of his own offence jurisdiction to try him.

(2)   Any offence consisting in aiding, abetting, counselling or procuring the commission of an offence triable either way (other than an offence listed in Schedule 1 to this Act) shall by virtue of this subsection be triable either way.

CRIMINAL ATTEMPTS ACT 1981

1 ATTEMPTING TO COMMIT AN OFFENCE

(1)   If, with intent to commit an offence to which this section applies, a person does an act which is more than merely preparatory to the commission of the offence, he is guilty of attempting to commit the offence.

(1A)   Subject to section 8 of the Computer Misuse Act 1990 (relevance of external law), if this subsection applies to an act, what the person doing it had in view shall be treated as an offence to which this section applies.

(1B)   Subsection (1A) above applies to an act if—
(a) it is done in England and Wales; and
(b) it would fall within subsection (1) above as more than merely preparatory to the commission of an offence under section 3 of the Computer Misuse Act 1990 but for the fact that the offence, if completed, would not be an offence triable in England and Wales.

(2)   A person may be guilty of attempting to commit an offence to which this section applies even though the facts are such that the commission of the offence is impossible.

(3)   In any case where—
(a) apart from this subsection a person's intention would not be regarded as having amounted to an intent to commit an offence; but
(b) if the facts of the case had been as he believed them to be, his intention would be so regarded,

then, for the purposes of subsection (1) above, he shall be regarded as having had an intent to commit that offence.

(4)   This section applies to any offence which, if it were completed, would be triable in England and Wales as an indictable offence, other than—
(a) conspiracy (at common law or under section 1 of the Criminal Law Act 1977 or any other enactment);
(b) aiding, abetting, counselling, procuring or suborning the commission of an offence;
(ba) an offence under section 2(1) of the Suicide Act 1961 (c. 60) (encouraging or assisting suicide);
(c) offences under section 4(1) (assisting offenders) or 5(1) (accepting or agreeing to accept consideration for not disclosing information about an arrestable offence) of the Criminal Law Act 1967.

1A EXTENDED JURISDICTION IN RELATION TO CERTAIN ATTEMPTS

(1)   If this section applies to an act, what the person doing the act had in view shall be treated as an offence to which section 1(1) above applies.

(2)   This section applies to an act if—
(a) it is done in England and Wales, and
(b) it would fall within section 1(1) above as more than merely preparatory to the commission of a Group A offence but for the fact that that offence, if completed, would not be an offence triable in England and Wales.

(3)   In this section "Group A offence" has the same meaning as in Part I of the Criminal Justice Act 1993.

(4)   Subsection (1) above is subject to the provisions of section 6 of the Act of 1993 (relevance of external law).

(5)   Where a person does any act to which this section applies, the offence which he commits shall for all purposes be treated as the offence of attempting to commit the relevant Group A offence.

3 OFFENCES OF ATTEMPT UNDER OTHER ENACTMENTS

(1)   Subsections (2) to (5) below shall have effect, subject to subsection (6) below and to any inconsistent provision in any other enactment, for the purpose of determining whether a person is guilty of an attempt under a special statutory provision.

(2)   For the purposes of this Act an attempt under a special statutory provision is an offence which—
(a) is created by an enactment other than section 1 above, including an enactment passed after this Act; and
(b) is expressed as an offence of attempting to commit another offence (in this section referred to as "the relevant full offence").

(3)   A person is guilty of an attempt under a special statutory provision if, with intent to commit the relevant full offence, he does an act which is more than merely preparatory to the commission of that offence.

(4)   A person may be guilty of an attempt under a special statutory provision even though the facts are such that the commission of the relevant full offence is impossible.

(5)   In any case where—
(a) apart from this subsection a person's intention would not be regarded as having amounted to an intent to commit the relevant full offence; but

(b) if the facts of the case had been as he believed them to be, his intention would be so regarded, then, for the purposes of subsection (3) above, he shall be regarded as having had an intent to commit that offence.

(6)   Subsections (2) to (5) above shall not have effect in relation to an act done before the commencement of this Act.

4 TRIAL AND PENALTIES

(1)   A person guilty by virtue of section 1 above of attempting to commit an offence shall—
(a) if the offence attempted is murder or any other offence the sentence for which is fixed by law, be liable on conviction on indictment to imprisonment for life; and
(b) if the offence attempted is indictable but does not fall within paragraph (a) above, be liable on conviction on indictment to any penalty to which he would have been liable on conviction on indictment of that offence; and
(c) if the offence attempted is triable either way, be liable on summary conviction to any penalty to which he would have been liable on summary conviction of that offence.

(2)   In any case in which a court may proceed to summary trial of an information charging a person with an offence and an information charging him with an offence under section 1 above of attempting to commit it or an attempt under a special statutory provision, the court may, without his consent, try the informations together.

(3)   Where, in proceedings against a person for an offence under section 1 above, there is evidence sufficient in law to support a finding that he did an act falling within subsection (1) of that section, the question whether or not his act fell within that subsection is a question of fact.

(4)   Where, in proceedings against a person for an attempt under a special statutory provision, there is evidence sufficient in law to support a finding that he did an act falling within subsection (3) of section 3 above, the question whether or not his act fell within that subsection is a question of fact.

(5)   Subsection (1) above shall have effect—
(a) . . .
(b) notwithstanding anything—
(i)   in section 32(1) (no limit to fine on conviction on indictment) of the Criminal Law Act 1977; or
(ii) in section 78(1) and (2) (maximum of six months' imprisonment on summary conviction unless express provision made to the contrary) of the Powers of Criminal Courts (Sentencing) Act 2000
(iii) in section 154(1) and (2) (general limit on magistrates' court's powers to impose imprisonment) of the Criminal Justice Act 2003.

9 INTERFERENCE WITH VEHICLES

(1)   A person is guilty of the offence of vehicle interference if he interferes with a motor vehicle or trailer or with anything carried in or on a motor vehicle or trailer with the intention that an offence specified in subsection (2) below shall be committed by himself or some other person.

(2)   The offences mentioned in subsection (1) above are—
(a) theft of the motor vehicle or trailer or part of it;
(b) theft of anything carried in or on the motor vehicle or trailer; and
(c) an offence under section 12(1) of the Theft Act 1968 (taking and driving away without consent);

and, if it is shown that a person accused of an offence under this section intended that one of those offences should be committed, it is immaterial that it cannot be shown which it was.

(3) A person guilty of an offence under this section shall be liable on summary conviction to imprisonment for a term not exceeding 51 weeks or to a fine not exceeding level 4 on the standard scale or to both.

(5) In this section "motor vehicle" and "trailer" have the meanings assigned to them by section 185(1) of the Road Traffic Act 1988.

As amended Criminal Justice Act 1993, s 6; Computer Misuse Act 1990, s. 1; Criminal Justice Act 2003, s 304; Coroners and Justice Act 2009, sch 21.

FORGERY AND COUNTERFEITING ACT 1981

1 THE OFFENCE OF FORGERY

A person is guilty of forgery if he makes a false instrument, with the intention that he or another shall use it to induce somebody to accept it as genuine, and by reason of so accepting it to do or not to do some act to his own or any other person's prejudice.

2 THE OFFENCE OF COPYING A FALSE INSTRUMENT

It is an offence for a person to make a copy of an instrument which is, and which he knows or believes to be, a false instrument, with the intention that he or another shall use it to induce somebody to accept it as a copy of a genuine instrument, and by reason of so accepting it to do or not to do some act to his own or any other person's prejudice.

3 THE OFFENCE OF USING A FALSE INSTRUMENT

It is an offence for a person to use an instrument which is, and which he knows or believes to be, false, with the intention of inducing somebody to accept it as genuine, and by reason of so accepting it to do or not to do some act to his own or any other person's prejudice.

4 THE OFFENCE OF USING A COPY OF A FALSE INSTRUMENT

It is an offence for a person to use a copy of an instrument which is, and which he knows or believes to be, a false instrument, with the intention of inducing somebody to accept it as a copy of a genuine instrument, and by reason of so accepting it to do or not to do some act to his own or any other person's prejudice.

5 OFFENCES RELATING TO MONEY ORDERS, SHARE CERTIFICATES, PASSPORTS, ETC

(1) It is an offence for a person to have in his custody or under his control an instrument to which this section applies which is, and which he knows or believes to be, false, with the intention that he or another shall use it to induce somebody to accept it as genuine, and by reason of so accepting it to do or not to do some act to his own or any other person's prejudice.

(2)   It is an offence for a person to have in his custody or under his control, without lawful authority or excuse, an instrument to which this section applies which is, and which he knows or believes to be, false.

(3)   It is an offence for a person to make or to have in his custody or under his control a machine or implement, or paper or any other material, which to his knowledge is or has been specially designed or adapted for the making of an instrument to which this section applies, with the intention that he or another shall make an instrument to which this section applies which is false and that he or another shall use the instrument to induce somebody to accept it as genuine, and by reason of so accepting it to do or not to do some act to his own or any other person's prejudice.

(4)   It is an offence for a person to make or to have in his custody or under his control any such machine, implement, paper or material, without lawful authority or excuse.

(5)   The instruments to which this section applies are—
      (a) money orders;
      (b) postal orders;
      (c) United Kingdom postage stamps;
      (d) Inland Revenue stamps;
      (e) share certificates;
      (g) cheques and other bills of exchange;
      (h) travellers' cheques;
           (ha) bankers' drafts;
           (hb) promissory notes;
      (j) cheque cards;
           (ja) debit cards;
      (k) credit cards;
      (l) certified copies relating to an entry in a register of births, adoptions, marriages, civil partnerships or deaths and issued by the Registrar General . . .; and
      (m) certificates relating to entries in such registers.

(6)   In subsection (5)(e) above "share certificate" means an instrument entitling or evidencing the title of a person to a share or interest—
      (a) in any public stock, annuity, fund or debt of any government or state, including a state which forms part of another state; or
      (b) in any stock, fund or debt of a body (whether corporate or unincorporated) established in the United Kingdom or elsewhere.

(7)   An instrument is also an instrument to which this section applies if it is a monetary instrument specified for the purposes of this section by an order made by the Secretary of State.

(8)   The power under subsection (7) above is exercisable by statutory instrument subject to annulment in pursuance of a resolution of either House of Parliament.

8 MEANING OF "INSTRUMENT"

(1)   Subject to subsection (2) below, in this Part of this Act "instrument" means—
      (a) any document, whether of a formal or informal character;
      (b) any stamp issued or sold by a postal operator;
      (c) any Inland Revenue stamp; and
      (d) any disc, tape, sound track or other device on or in which information is recorded or stored by mechanical, electronic or other means.

(2)   A currency note within the meaning of Part II of this Act is not an instrument for the purposes of this Part of this Act.

(3)   A mark denoting payment of postage which a postal operator authorises to be used instead of an adhesive stamp is to be treated for the purposes of this Part of this Act as if it were a stamp issued by the postal operator concerned.

(3A) In this section "postal operator" has the same meaning as in the Postal Services Act 2000.

(4)   In this Part of this Act "Inland Revenue stamp" means a stamp as defined in section 27 of the Stamp Duties Management Act 1891.

9 MEANING OF "FALSE" AND "MAKING"

(1)   An instrument is false for the purposes of this Part of this Act—
      (a) if it purports to have been made in the form in which it is made by a person who did not in fact make it in that form; or
      (b) if it purports to have been made in the form in which it is made on the authority of a person who did not in fact authorise its making in that form; or
      (c) if it purports to have been made in the terms in which it is made by a person who did not in fact make it in those terms; or
      (d) if it purports to have been made in the terms in which it is made on the authority of a person who did not in fact authorise its making in those terms; or
      (e) if it purports to have been altered in any respect by a person who did not in fact alter it in that respect; or
      (f) if it purports to have been altered in any respect on the authority of a person who did not in fact authorise the alteration in that respect; or
      (g) if it purports to have been made or altered on a date on which, or at a place at which, or otherwise in circumstances in which, it was not in fact made or altered; or
      (h) if it purports to have been made or altered by an existing person but he did not in fact exist.

(2)   A person is to be treated for the purposes of this Part of this Act as making a false instrument if he alters an instrument so as to make it false in any respect (whether or not it is false in some other respect apart from that alteration).

10 MEANING OF "PREJUDICE" AND "INDUCE"

(1)   Subject to subsections (2) and (4) below, for the purposes of this Part of this Act an act or omission intended to be induced is to a person's prejudice if, and only if, it is one which, if it occurs—
      (a) will result—
          (i)   in his temporary or permanent loss of property; or
          (ii) in his being deprived of an opportunity to earn remuneration or greater remuneration; or
          (iii) in his being deprived of an opportunity to gain a financial advantage otherwise than by way of remuneration; or
      (b) will result in somebody being given an opportunity—
          (i)   to earn remuneration or greater remuneration from him; or
          (ii) to gain a financial advantage from him otherwise than by way of remuneration; or
      (c) will be the result of his having accepted a false instrument as genuine, or a copy of a false instrument as a copy of a genuine one, in connection with his performance of any duty.

(2)   An act which a person has an enforceable duty to do and an omission to do an act which a person is not entitled to do shall be disregarded for the purposes of this Part of this Act.

(3)   In this Part of this Act references to inducing somebody to accept a false instrument as genuine, or a copy of a false instrument as a copy of a genuine one, include references to inducing a machine to respond to the instrument or copy as if it were a genuine instrument or, as the case may be, a copy of a genuine one.

(4)   Where subsection (3) above applies, the act or omission intended to be induced by the machine responding to the instrument or copy shall be treated as an act or omission to a person's prejudice.

(5)   In this section "loss" includes not getting what one might get as well as parting with what one has.

As amended Isle of Man Act 1979, s 9; Identity Cards Act 2006, s 44; Asylum and Immigration (Treatment of Claimants etc) Act 2004, s 3; Crime (International Co-operation) Act 2003, s 88; Civil Partnership Act 2004, s 261.

TAKING OF HOSTAGES ACT 1982

1 HOSTAGE-TAKING

(1)   A person, whatever his nationality, who, in the United Kingdom or elsewhere,—
    (a)   detains any other person ("the hostage"), and
    (b)   in order to compel a State, international governmental organisation or person to do or abstain from doing any act, threatens to kill, injure or continue to detain the hostage, commits an offence.

(2)   A person guilty of an offence under this Act shall be liable, on conviction on indictment, to imprisonment for life.

CHILD ABDUCTION ACT 1984

1 OFFENCE OF ABDUCTION OF CHILD BY PARENT, ETC

(1)   Subject to subsections (5) and (8) below, a person connnected with a child under the age of sixteen commits an offence if he takes or sends the child out of the United Kingdom without the appropriate consent.

(2)   A person is connected with a child for the purposes of this section if—
    (a)   he is a parent of the child; or
    (b)   in the case of a child whose parents were not married to each other at the time of his birth, there are reasonable grounds for believing that he is the father of the child; or
    (c)   he is a guardian of the child; or
    (d)   he is a person in whose favour a residence order is in force with respect to the child; or
    (e)   he has custody of the child.

(3)   In this section "the appropriate consent", in relation to a child, means—
    (a)   the consent of each of the following—

(i)   the child's mother;

(ii) the child's father, if he has parental responsibility for him;

(iii) any guardian of the child;

(iv) any person in whose favour a residence order is in force with respect to the child;

(v)   any person who has custody of the child; or

(b)   the leave of the court granted under or by virtue of any provision of Part II of the Children Act 1989; or

(c)   if any person has custody of the child, the leave of the court which awarded custody to him.

(4)   A person does not commit an offence under this section by taking or sending a child out of the United Kingdom without obtaining the appropriate consent if—

(a)   he is a person in whose favour there is a residence order in force with respect to the child, and

(b)   he takes or sends him out of the United Kingdom for a period of less than one month.

(4A) Subsection (4) above does not apply if the person taking or sending the child out of the United Kingdom does so in breach of an order under Part II of the Children Act 1989.

(5)   A person does not commit an offence under this section by doing anything without the consent of another person whose consent is required under the foregoing provisions if—

(a)   he does it in the belief that the other person—

(i)   has consented; or

(ii) would consent if he was aware of all the relevant circumstances; or

(b)   he has taken all reasonable steps to communicate with the other person but has been unable to communicate with him; or

(c)   the other person has unreasonably refused to consent,

(5A) Subsection (5)(c) above does not apply if—

(a)   the person who refused to consent is a person—

(i)   in whose favour there is a residence order in force with respect to the child; or

(ii) who has custody of the child; or

(b)   the person taking or sending the child out of the United Kingdom is, by so acting, in breach of an order made by a court in the United Kingdom.

(6)   Where, in proceedings for an offence under this section, there is sufficient evidence to raise an issue as to the application of subsection (5) above, it shall be for the prosecution to prove that that subsection does not apply.

(7)   For the purposes of this section—

(a)   "guardian of a child", "residence order" and "parental responsibility" have the same meaning as in the Children Act 1989; and

(b)   a person shall be treated as having custody of a child if there is in force an order of a court in the United Kingdom awarding him (whether solely or jointly with another person) custody, legal custody or care and control of the child.

(8)   This section shall have effect subject to the provisions of the Schedule to this Act in relation to a child who is in the care of a local authority detained in a place of safety, remanded to a local authority accommodation or the subject of proceedings or an order relating to adoption.

2 OFFENCE OF ABDUCTION OF CHILD BY OTHER PERSONS

(1)   Subject to subsection (3) below, a person, other than one mentioned in subsection (2) below. commits an offence if, without lawful authority or reasonable excuse, he takes or detains a child under the age of sixteen—

(a) so as to remove him from the lawful control of any person having lawful control of the child; or

(b) so as to keep him out of the lawful control of any person entitled to lawful control of the child.

(2) The persons are—

(a) where the father and mother of the child in question were married to each other at the time of his birth, the child's father and mother;

(b) where the father and mother of the child in question were not married to each other at the time of his birth, the child's mother; and

(c) any other person mentioned in section 1(2)(c) to (e) above.

(3) In proceedings against any person for an offence under this section, it shall be a defence for that person to prove—

(a) where the father and mother of the child in question were not married to each other at the time of his birth—

(i) that he is the child's father; or

(ii) that, at the time of the alleged offence, he believed, on reasonable grounds, that he was the child's father; or

(b) that, at the time of the alleged offence, he believed that the child had attained the age of sixteen.

3 CONSTRUCTION OF REFERENCES TO TAKING, SENDING AND DETAINING

For the purposes of this Part of this Act—

(a) a person shall be regarded as taking a child if he causes or induces the child to accompany him or any other person or causes the child to be taken;

(b) a person shall be regarded as sending a child if he causes the child to be sent;

(c) a person shall be regarded as detaining a child if he causes the child to be detained or induces the child to remain with him or any other person; and

(d) references to a child's parents and to a child whose parents were (or were not) married to each other at the time of his birth shall be construed in accordance with section 1 of the Family Law Reform Act 1987 (which extends their meaning).

As amended by Children Act 1989, s. 51(7)(d).

INTOXICATING SUBSTANCES (SUPPLY) ACT 1985

1 OFFENCE OF SUPPLYING INTOXICATING SUBSTANCE

(1) It is an offence for a person to supply or offer to supply a substance other than a controlled drug—

(a) to a person under the age of eighteen whom he knows, or has reasonable cause to believe, to be under that age; or

(b) to a person—

(i) who is acting on behalf of a person under that age; and

(ii) whom he knows, or has reasonable cause to believe, to be acting, if he knows or has reasonable cause to believe that the substance is, or its fumes are, likely to be inhaled by the person under the age of eighteen for the purpose of causing intoxication.

(2) In proceedings against any person for an offence under subsection (1) above it is a defence for him to show that at the time he made the supply or offer he was under the age of eighteen and was acting otherwise than in the course or furtherance of a business.

(3) A person guilty of an offence under this section shall be liable on summary conviction to imprisonment for a term not exceeding six months or to a fine not exceeding level 5 on the standard scale . . ., or to both.

As amended by the Statute Law (Repeals) Act 1993.

SEXUAL OFFENCES ACT 1985

1 KERB-CRAWLING

(1) A person commits an offence if he solicits another person (or different persons) for the purpose of prostitution—
(a) from a motor vehicle while it is in a street or public place; or
(b) in a street or public place while in the immediate vicinity of a motor vehicle that he has just got out of or off,
persistently or, in such manner or in such circumstances as to be likely to cause annoyance to the person (or any of the persons) solicited, or nuisance to other persons in the neighbourhood.

(2) A person guilty of an offence under this section shall be liable on summary conviction to a fine not exceeding level 3 on the standard scale . . .

(3) In this section "motor vehicle" has the same meaning as in the Road Traffic Act 1988.

2 PERSISTENT SOLICITING

(1) A person commits an offence if in a street or public place he persistently solicits another person (or different persons) for the purpose of prostitution.

(2) A person guilty of an offence under this section shall be liable on summary conviction to a fine not exceeding level 3 on the standard scale.

4 INTERPRETATION

(1) References in this Act to a person soliciting another person for the purpose of prostitution are references to his soliciting that person for the purpose of obtaining that person's services as a prostitute.

(4) For the purposes of this Act "street" includes any bridge, road, lane, footway, subway, square, court, alley or passage, whether a thoroughfare or not, which is for the time being open to the public; and the doorways and entrances of premises abutting on a street (as hereinbefore defined), and any ground adjoining and open to a street, shall be treated as forming part of the street.

As amended Sexual Offences Act 2003, s 56; Statute Law (Repeals).

PUBLIC ORDER ACT 1986

1 RIOT

(1) Where 12 or more persons who are present together use or threaten unlawful violence for a common purpose and the conduct of them (taken together) is such as would cause a person of reasonable firmness present at the scene to fear for his personal safety, each of the persons using unlawful violence for the common purpose is guilty of riot.

(2) It is immaterial whether or not the 12 or more use or threaten unlawful violence simultaneously.

(3) The common purpose may be inferred from conduct.

(4) No person of reasonable firmness need actually be, or be likely to be, present at the scene.

(5) Riot may be committed in private as well as in public places.

(6) A person guilty of riot is liable on conviction on indictment to imprisonment for a term not exceeding ten years or a fine or both.

2 VIOLENT DISORDER

(1) Where 3 or more persons who are present together use or threaten unlawful violence and the conduct of them (taken together) is such as would cause a person of reasonable firmness present at the scene to fear for personal safety, each of the persons using or threatening unlawful violence is guilty of violent disorder.

(2) It is immaterial whether or not the 3 or more use or threaten unlawful violence simultaneously.

(3) No person of reasonable firmness need actually be, or be likely to be, present at the scene.

(4) Violent disorder may be committed in private as well as in public places.

(5) A person guilty of violent disorder is liable on conviction on indictment to imprisonment for a term not exceeding 5 years or a fine or both, or on summary conviction to imprisonment for a term not exceeding 6 months or a fine not exceeding the statutory maximum or both.

3 AFFRAY

(1) A person is guilty of affray if he uses or threatens unlawful violence towards another and his conduct is such as would cause a person of reasonable firmness present at the scene to fear for his personal safety.

(2) Where 2 or more persons use or threaten the unlawful violence, it is the conduct of them taken together that must be considered for the purposes of subsection (1).

(3) For the purposes of this section a threat cannot be made by the use of words alone.

(4) No person of reasonable firmness need actually be, or be likely to be, present at the scene.

(5) Affray may be committed in private as well as in public places.

(7)   A person guilty of affray is liable on conviction on indictment to imprisonment for a term not exceeding 3 years or a fine or both, or on summary conviction to imprisonment for a term not exceeding 6 months or a fine not exceeding the statutory maximum or both.

4 FEAR OR PROVOCATION OF VIOLENCE

(1)   A person is guilty of an offence if he—
   (a) uses towards another person threatening, abusive or insulting words or behaviour, or
   (b) distributes or displays to another person any writing, sign or other visible representation which is threatening, abusive or insulting,
   with intent to cause that person to believe that immediate unlawful violence will be used against him or another by any person, or to provoke the immediate use of unlawful violence by that person or another, or whereby that person is likely to believe that such violence will be used or it is likely that such violence will be provoked.

(2)   An offence under this section may be committed in a public or a private place, except that no offence is committed where the words or behaviour are used, or the writing, sign or other visible representation is distributed or displayed, by a person inside a dwelling and the other person is also inside that or another dwelling.

(4)   A person guilty of an offence under this section is liable on summary conviction to imprisonment for a term not exceeding 6 months or a fine not exceeding level 5 on the standard scale or both.

4A INTENTIONAL HARASSMENT, ALARM OR DISTRESS

(1)   A person is guilty of an offence if, with intent to cause a person harassment, alarm or distress, he—
   (a) uses threatening, abusive or insulting words or behaviour, or disorderly behaviour, or
   (b) displays any writing, sign or other visible representation which is threatening, abusive or insulting,
   thereby causing that or another person harassment, alarm or distress.

(2)   An offence under this section may be committed in a public or a private place, except that no offence is committed where the words or behaviour are used, or the writing, sign or other visible representation is displayed, by a person inside a dwelling and the person who is harassed, alarmed or distressed is also inside that or another dwelling.

(3)   It is a defence for the accused to prove—
   (a) that he was inside a dwelling and had no reason to believe that the words or behaviour used, or the writing, sign or other visible representation displayed, would be heard or seen by a person outside that or any other dwelling, or
   (b) that his conduct was reasonable.

(5)   A person guilty of an offence under this section is liable on summary conviction to imprisonment for a term not exceeding 6 months or a fine not exceeding level 5 on the standard scale or both.

5 HARASSMENT, ALARM OR DISTRESS

(1)   A person is guilty of an offence if he—
   (a) uses threatening, abusive or insulting words or behaviour, or disorderly behaviour, or
   (b) displays any writing, sign or other visible representation which is threatening, abusive or insulting,

within the hearing or sight of a person likely to be caused harassment, alarm or distress thereby.

(2)   An offence under this section may be committed in a public or a private place, except that no offence is committed where the words or behaviour are used, or the writing, sign or other visible representation is displayed, by a person inside a dwelling and the other person is also inside that or another dwelling.

(3)   It is a defence for the accused to prove—
   (a)   that he had no reason to believe that there was any person within hearing or sight who was likely to be caused harassment, alarm or distress, or
   (b)   that he was inside a dwelling and had no reason to believe that the words or behaviour used, or the writing, sign or other visible representation displayed, would be heard or seen by a person outside that or any other dwelling, or
   (c)   that his conduct was reasonable.

(6)   A person guilty of an offence under this section is liable on summary conviction to a fine not exceeding level 3 on the standard scale.

6 MENTAL ELEMENT: MISCELLANEOUS

(1)   A person is guilty of riot only if he intends to use violence or is aware that his conduct may be violent.

(2)   A person is guilty of violent disorder or affray only if he intends to use or threaten violence or is aware that his conduct may be violent or threaten violence.

(3)   A person is guilty of an offence under section 4 only if he intends his words or behaviour, or the writing, sign or other visible representation, to be threatening, abusive or insulting, or is aware that it may be threatening, abusive or insulting.

(4)   A person is guilty of an offence under section 5 only if he intends his words or behaviour, or the writing, sign or other visible representation, to be threatening, abusive or insulting, or is aware that it may be threatening, abusive or insulting or (as the case may be) he intends his behaviour to be or is aware that it may be disorderly.

(5)   For the purposes of this section a person whose awareness is impaired by intoxication shall be taken to be aware of that of which he would be aware if not intoxicated, unless he shows either that his intoxication was not self-induced or that it was caused solely by the taking or administration of a substance in the course of medical treatment.

(6)   In subsection (5) "intoxication" means any intoxication, whether caused by drink, drugs or other means, or by a combination of means.

(7)   Subsections (1) and (2) do not affect the determination for the purposes of riot or violent disorder of the number of persons who use or threaten violence.

8 INTERPRETATION

(1)   In this Part—

"dwelling" means any structure or part of a structure occupied as a person's home or as other living accommodation (whether the occupation is separate or shared with others) but does not include any part not so occupied, and for his purpose "structure" includes a tent, caravan, vehicle, vessel or other temporary or movable structure;

"violence" means any violent conduct, so that—

(a) except in the context of affray, it includes violent conduct towards property as well as violent conduct towards persons, and

(b) it is not restricted to conduct causing or intended to cause injury or damage but includes any other violent conduct (for example, throwing at or towards a person a missile of a kind capable of causing injury which does not hit or falls short).

17 MEANING OF "RACIAL HATRED"

In this Part "racial hatred" means hatred against a group of persons . . . defined by reference to colour, race, nationality (including citizenship) or ethnic or national origins.

18 USE OF WORDS OR BEHAVIOUR OR DISPLAY OF WRITTEN MATERIAL

(1) A person who uses threatening, abusive or insulting words or behaviour, or displays any written material which is threatening, abusive or insulting, is guilty of an offence if—
(a) he intends thereby to stir up racial hatred, or
(b) having regard to all the circumstances racial hatred is likely to be stirred up thereby.

(2) An offence under this section may be committed in a public or a private place, except that no offence is committed where the words or behaviour are used, or the written material is displayed, by a person inside a dwelling and are not heard or seen except by other persons in that or another dwelling.

(4) In proceedings for an offence under this section it is a defence for the accused to prove that he was inside a dwelling and had no reason to believe that the words or behaviour used, or the written material displayed, would be heard or seen by a person outside that or any other dwelling.

(5) A person who is not shown to have intended to stir up racial hatred is not guilty of an offence under this section if he did not intend his words or behaviour, or the written material, to be, and was not aware that it might be, threatening, abusive or insulting.

(6) This section does not apply to words or behaviour used, or written material displayed, solely for the purpose of being included in a programme service.

19 PUBLISHING OR DISTRIBUTING WRITTEN MATERIAL

(1) A person who publishes or distributes written material which is threatening, abusive or insulting is guilty of an offence if—
(a) he intends thereby to stir up racial hatred, or
(b) having regard to all the circumstances racial hatred is likely to be stirred up thereby.

(2) In proceedings for an offence under this section it is a defence for an accused who is not shown to have intended to stir up racial hatred to prove that he was not aware of the content of the material and did not suspect, and had no reason to suspect, that it was threatening, abusive or insulting.

(3) References in this Part to the publication or distribution of written material are to its publication or distribution to the public or a section of the public.

29 INTERPRETATION

In this Part—

"distribute", and related expressions, shall be construed in accordance with section 19(3) (written material) and section 21(2) (recordings);

"dwelling" means any structure or part of a structure occupied as a person's home or other living accommodation (whether the occupation is separate or shared with others) but does not include any part not so occupied, and for this purpose "structure" includes a tent, caravan, vehicle, vessel or other temporary or movable structure;

"programme" means any item which is included in a programme service;

"programme service" has the same meaning as in the Broadcasting Act 1990;

"publish", and related expressions, in relation to written material, shall be construed in accordance with section 19(3);

"racial hatred" has the meaning given by section 17;

. . .

"written material" includes any sign or other visible representation.

29A MEANING OF "RELIGIOUS HATRED"

In this Part "religious hatred" means hatred against a group of persons defined by reference to religious belief or lack of religious belief.

29AB MEANING OF "HATRED ON THE GROUNDS OF SEXUAL ORIENTATION"

In this Part "hatred on the grounds of sexual orientation" means hatred against a group of persons defined by reference to sexual orientation (whether towards persons of the same sex, the opposite sex or both).

29B USE OF WORDS OR BEHAVIOUR OR DISPLAY OF WRITTEN MATERIAL

(1) A person who uses threatening words or behaviour, or displays any written material which is threatening, is guilty of an offence if he intends thereby to stir up religious hatred or hatred on the grounds of sexual orientation.

(2) An offence under this section may be committed in a public or a private place, except that no offence is committed where the words or behaviour are used, or the written material is displayed, by a person inside a dwelling and are not heard or seen except by other persons in that or another dwelling.

(4) In proceedings for an offence under this section it is a defence for the accused to prove that he was inside a dwelling and had no reason to believe that the words or behaviour used, or the written material displayed, would be heard or seen by a person outside that or any other dwelling.

(5) This section does not apply to words or behaviour used, or written material displayed, solely for the purpose of being included in a programme service.

29C PUBLISHING OR DISTRIBUTING WRITTEN MATERIAL

(1) A person who publishes or distributes written material which is threatening is guilty of an offence if he intends thereby to stir up religious hatred or hatred on the grounds of sexual orientation.

(2)   References in this Part to the publication or distribution of written material are to its publication or distribution to the public or a section of the public.

29D PUBLIC PERFORMANCE OF PLAY

(1)   If a public performance of a play is given which involves the use of threatening words or behaviour, any person who presents or directs the performance is guilty of an offence if he intends thereby to stir up religious hatred or hatred on the grounds of sexual orientation.

(2)   This section does not apply to a performance given solely or primarily for one or more of the following purposes—
(a) rehearsal,
(b) making a recording of the performance, or
(c) enabling the performance to be included in a programme service;
but if it is proved that the performance was attended by persons other than those directly connected with the giving of the performance or the doing in relation to it of the things mentioned in paragraph (b) or (c), the performance shall, unless the contrary is shown, be taken not to have been given solely or primarily for the purpose mentioned above.

(3)   For the purposes of this section—
(a) a person shall not be treated as presenting a performance of a play by reason only of his taking part in it as a performer,
(b) a person taking part as a performer in a performance directed by another shall be treated as a person who directed the performance if without reasonable excuse he performs otherwise than in accordance with that person's direction, and
(c) a person shall be taken to have directed a performance of a play given under his direction notwithstanding that he was not present during the performance;
and a person shall not be treated as aiding or abetting the commission of an offence under this section by reason only of his taking part in a performance as a performer.

(4)   In this section "play" and "public performance" have the same meaning as in the Theatres Act 1968.

. . .

29E DISTRIBUTING, SHOWING OR PLAYING A RECORDING

(1)   A person who distributes, or shows or plays, a recording of visual images or sounds which are threatening is guilty of an offence if he intends thereby to stir up religious hatred or hatred on the grounds of sexual orientation.

(2)   In this Part "recording" means any record from which visual images or sounds may, by any means, be reproduced; and references to the distribution, showing or playing of a recording are to its distribution, showing or playing to the public or a section of the public.

(3)   This section does not apply to the showing or playing of a recording solely for the purpose of enabling the recording to be included in a programme service.

29F BROADCASTING OR INCLUDING PROGRAMME IN PROGRAMME SERVICE

(1)   If a programme involving threatening visual images or sounds is included in a programme service, each of the persons mentioned in subsection (2) is guilty of an offence if he intends thereby to stir up religious hatred or hatred on the grounds of sexual orientation.

(2)   The persons are—
    (a) the person providing the programme service,
    (b) any person by whom the programme is produced or directed, and
    (c) any person by whom offending words or behaviour are used.

29G POSSESSION OF INFLAMMATORY MATERIAL

(1)   A person who has in his possession written material which is threatening, or a recording of visual images or sounds which are threatening, with a view to—
    (a) in the case of written material, its being displayed, published, distributed, or included in a programme service whether by himself or another, or
    (b) in the case of a recording, its being distributed, shown, played, or included in a programme service, whether by himself or another, is guilty of an offence if he intends religious hatred to be stirred up thereby to stir up religious hatred or hatred on the grounds of sexual orientation.

(2)   For this purpose regard shall be had to such display, publication, distribution, showing, playing, or inclusion in a programme service as he has, or it may be reasonably be inferred that he has, in view.

. . .

29J PROTECTION OF FREEDOM OF EXPRESSION

Nothing in this Part shall be read or given effect in a way which prohibits or restricts discussion, criticism or expressions of antipathy, dislike, ridicule, insult or abuse of particular religions or the beliefs or practices of their adherents, or of any other belief system or the beliefs or practices of its adherents, or proselytising or urging adherents of a different religion or belief system to cease practising their religion or belief system.

29JA PROTECTION OF FREEDOM OF EXPRESSION (SEXUAL ORIENTATION)

In this Part, for the avoidance of doubt, the discussion or criticism of sexual conduct or practices or the urging of persons to refrain from or modify such conduct or practices shall not be taken of itself to be threatening or intended to stir up hatred.

. . .

29L PROCEDURE AND PUNISHMENT

(1)   No proceedings for an offence under this Part may be instituted . . . except by or with the consent of the Attorney General.

(2)   For the purposes of the rules . . . against charging more than one offence in the same count or information, each of sections 29B to 29G creates one offence.

(3)   A person guilty of an offence under this Part is liable—
    (a) on conviction on indictment to imprisonment for a term not exceeding seven years or a fine or both;
    (b) on summary conviction to imprisonment for a term not exceeding 12 months or a fine not exceeding the statutory maximum or both.

As amended Public Order Act 1994, s 154; Serious Organised Crime and Police Act 2005, ss 111, 172; Criminal Justice and Immigration Act 2008, s 74; Racial and Religious Hatred Act 2006, s 1.

CRIMINAL JUSTICE ACT 1987

39 COMMON ASSAULT AND BATTERY TO BE SUMMARY OFFENCES

Common assault and battery shall be summary offences and a person guilty of either of them shall be liable to a fine not exceeding level 5 on the standard scale, to imprisonment for a term not exceeding six months, or to both.

134 TORTURE

(1)   A public official or person acting in an official capacity, whatever his nationality, commits the offence of torture if in the United Kingdom or elsewhere he intentionally inflicts severe pain or suffering on another in the performance or purported performance of his official duties.

(2)   A person not falling within subsection (1) above commits the offence of torture, whatever his nationality, if—
(a)   in the United Kingdom or elsewhere he intentionally inflicts severe pain or suffering on another at the instigation or with the consent or acquiescence—
(i)   of a public official; or
(ii)   of a person acting in an official capacity; and
(b)   the official or other person is performing or purporting to perform his official duties when he instigates the commission of the offence or consents to or acquiesces in it.

(3)   It is immaterial whether the pain or suffering is physical or mental and whether it is caused by an act or an omission.

(4)   It shall be a defence for a person charged with an offence under this section in respect of any conduct of his to prove that he had lawful authority, justification or excuse for that conduct.

(5)   For the purposes of this section "lawful authority, justification or excuse" means—
(a)   in relation to pain or suffering inflicted in the United Kingdom, lawful authority, justification or excuse under the law of the part of the United Kingdom where it was inflicted;
(b)   in relation to pain or suffering inflicted outside the United Kingdom—
(i)   if it was inflicted by a United Kingdom official acting under the law of the United Kingdom or by a person acting in an official capacity under that law, lawful authority, justification or excuse under that law;
(ii)   if it was inflicted by a United Kingdom official acting under the law of any part of the United Kingdom or by a person acting in an official capacity under such law, lawful authority, justification or excuse under the law of the part of the United Kingdom under whose law he was acting; and
(iii)   in any other case, lawful authority, justification or excuse under the law of the place where it was inflicted.

(6)   A person who commits the offence of torture shall be liable on conviction on indictment to imprisonment for life.

139 OFFENCE OF HAVING ARTICLE WITH BLADE OR POINT IN PUBLIC PLACE

(1)   Subject to subsections (4) and (5) below, any person who has an article to which this section applies with him in a public place shall be guilty of an offence.

(2)   Subject to subsection (3) below, this section applies to any article which has a blade or is sharply pointed except a folding pocketknife.

(3)   This section applies to a folding pocketknife if the cutting edge of its blade exceeds 3 inches.

(4)   It shall be a defence for a person charged with an offence under this section to prove that he had good reason or lawful authority for having the article with him in a public place.

(5)   Without prejudice to the generality of subsection (4) above, it shall be a defence for a person charged with an offence under this section to prove that he had the article with him—
(a)   for use at work;
(b)   for religious reasons; or
(c)   as part of any national costume.

(6)   A person guilty of an offence under subsection (1) shall be liable—
(a)   on summary conviction, to imprisonment for a term not exceeding 12 months or to a fine not exceeding the statutory maximum, or to both;
(b)   on conviction on indictment, to imprisonment for a term not exceeding 4 years, or to a fine, or to both.

(7)   In this section "public place" includes any place to which at the material time the public have or are permitted access, whether on payment or otherwise.

(8)   This section shall not have effect in relation to anything done before it comes into force.

139A OFFENCE OF HAVING ARTICLE WITH BLADE OR POINT (OR OFFENSIVE WEAPON) ON SCHOOL PREMISES

(1)   Any person who has an article to which section 139 of this Act applies with him on school premises shall be guilty of an offence.

(2)   Any person who has an offensive weapon within the meaning of section 1 of the Prevention of Crime Act 1953 with him on school premises shall be guilty of an offence.

(3)   It shall be a defence for a person charged with an offence under subsection (1) or (2) above to prove that he had good reason or lawful authority for having the article or weapon with him on the premises in question.

(4)   Without prejudice to the generality of subsection (3) above, it shall be a defence for a person charged with an offence under subsection (1) or (2) above to prove that he had the article or weapon in question with him—
(a)   for use at work,
(b)   for educational purposes,
(c)   for religious reasons, or
(d)   as part of any national costume.

(5)   A person guilty of an offence—
(a)   under subsection (1) above shall be liable—
(i)   on summary conviction to imprisonment for a term not exceeding six months, or a fine not exceeding the statutory maximum, or both;
(ii)   on conviction on indictment, to imprisonment for a term not exceeding four years, or a fine, or both;

(b) under subsection (2) above shall be liable—
  (i) on summary conviction, to imprisonment for a term not exceeding six months, or a fine not exceeding the statutory maximum, or both;
  (ii) on conviction on indictment, to imprisonment for a term not exceeding four years, or a fine, or both.

(6) A person guilty of an offence under subsection (1) shall be liable—
  (a) on summary conviction, to imprisonment for a term not exceeding 12 months or to a fine not exceeding the statutory maximum, or to both;
  (b) on conviction on indictment, to imprisonment for a term not exceeding 4 years, or to a fine, or to both.

160 POSSESSION OF INDECENT PHOTOGRAPH OF CHILD

(1) Subject to section 160A, it is an offence for a person to have any indecent photograph or pseudo-photograph of a child in his possession.

(2) Where a person is charged with an offence under subsection (1) above, it shall be a defence for him to prove—
  (a) that he had a legitimate reason for having the photograph or pseudo-photograph in his possession; or
  (b) that he had not himself seen the photograph or pseudo-photograph and did not know, nor had any cause to suspect, it to be indecent; or
  (c) that the photograph or pseudo-photograph was sent to him without any prior request made by him or on his behalf and that he did not keep it for an unreasonable time.

(2A) A person shall be liable on conviction on indictment of an offence under this section to imprisonment for a term not exceeding five years or a fine, or both.

(3) A person shall be liable on summary conviction of an offence under this section to imprisonment for a term not exceeding six months or a fine not exceeding level 5 on the standard scale, or both.

160A MARRIAGE AND OTHER RELATIONSHIPS

(1) This section applies where, in proceedings for an offence under section 160 relating to an indecent photograph of a child, the defendant proves that the photograph was of the child aged 16 or over, and that at the time of the offence charged the child and he—
  (a) were married or civil partners of each other, or
  (b) lived together as partners in an enduring family relationship.

(2) This section also applies where, in proceedings for an offence under section 160 relating to an indecent photograph of a child, the defendant proves that the photograph was of the child aged 16 or over, and that at the time when he obtained it the child and he—
  (a) were married or civil partners of each other, or
  (b) lived together as partners in an enduring family relationship.

(3) This section applies whether the photograph showed the child alone or with the defendant, but not if it showed any other person.

(4) If sufficient evidence is adduced to raise an issue as to whether the child consented to the photograph being in the defendant's possession, or as to whether the defendant reasonably believed that the child so consented, the defendant is not guilty of the offence unless it is proved that the child did not so consent and that the defendant did not reasonably believe that the child so consented.

As amended Offensive Weapons Act 1996, s 4, Violent Crime Reduction act 2006, s 42; Criminal Justice and Court Services Act 2000, s 41; Criminal Justice and Public Order Act 1994, s. 84; Civil Partnership Act 2004, s. 261.

FIREARMS (AMENDMENT) ACT 1988

5 RESTRICTION ON SALE OF AMMUNITION FOR SMOOTH-BORE GUNS

(1) This section applies to ammunition to which section 1 of the principal Act does not apply and which is capable of being used in a shot gun or in a smooth-bore gun to which that section applies.

(2) It is an offence for a person to sell any such ammunition to another person in the United Kingdom who is neither a registered firearms dealer nor a person who sells such ammunition by way of trade or business unless that other person—
   (a) produces a certificate authorising him to possess a gun of a kind mentioned in subsection (1) above; or
   (b) shows that he is by virtue of that Act or this Act entitled to have possession of such a gun without holding a certificate; or
   (c) produces a certificate authorising another person to possess such a gun, together with that person's written authority to purchase the ammunition on his behalf.

(3) An offence under this section shall be punishable on summary conviction with imprisonment for a term not exceeding six months or a fine not exceeding level 5 on the standard scale or both.

6 SHORTENING OF BARRELS

(1) Subject to subsection (2) below, it is an offence to shorten to a length less than 24 inches the barrel of any smooth-bore gun to which section 1 of the principal Act applies other than one which has a barrel with a bore exceeding 2 inches in diameter; and that offence shall be punishable—
   (a) on summary conviction, with imprisonment for a term not exceeding six months or a fine not exceeding the statutory maximum or both;
   (b) on indictment, with imprisonment for a term not exceeding five years or a fine or both.

(2) It is not an offence under this section for a registered firearms dealer to shorten the barrel of a gun for the sole purpose of replacing a defective part of the barrel so as to produce a barrel not less than 24 inches in length.

8 DE-ACTIVATED WEAPONS

For the purposes of the principal Act and this Act it shall be presumed, unless the contrary is shown, that a firearm has been rendered incapable of discharging any shot, bullet or other missile, and has consequently ceased to be a firearm within the meaning of those Acts, if—

(a) it bears a mark which has been approved by the Secretary of State for denoting that fact and which has been made either by one of the two companies mentioned in section 58(1) of the principal Act or by such other person as may be approved by the Secretary of State for the purposes of this section; and

(b) that company or person has certified in writing that work has been carried out on the firearm in a manner approved by the Secretary of State for rendering it incapable of discharging any shot, bullet or other missile.

MALICIOUS COMMUNICATIONS ACT 1988

1 OFFENCE OF SENDING LETTERS ETC WITH INTENT TO CAUSE DISTRESS OR ANXIETY

(1) Any person who sends to another person—
  (a) a letter, electronic communication or article of any description which conveys—
    (i) a message which is indecent or grossly offensive;
    (ii) a threat; or
    (iii) information which is false and known or believed to be false by the sender; or
  (b) any article or electronic communication which is, in whole or part, of an indecent or grossly offensive nature,
  is guilty of an offence if his purpose, or one of his purposes, in sending it is that it should, so far as falling within paragraph (a) or (b) above, cause distress or anxiety to the recipient or to any other person to whom he intends that it or its contents or nature should be communicated.

(2) A person is not guilty of an offence by virtue of subsection (1)(a)(ii) above if he shows—
  (a) that the threat was used to reinforce a demand made by him on reasonable grounds; and
  (b) that he believed, and had reasonable grounds for believing, that the use of the threat was a proper means of reinforcing the demand.

(2A) In this section "electronic communication" includes—
  (a) any oral or other communication by means of an electronic communications network; and
  (b) any communication (however sent) that is in electronic form.

(3) In this section references to sending include references to delivering or transmitting and to causing to be sent, delivered or transmitted and "sender" shall be construed accordingly.

(4) A person guilty of an offence under this section shall be liable on summary conviction to imprisonment for a term not exceeding six months or to a fine not exceeding level 5 on the standard scale, or to both.

As amended Criminal Justice and Police Act 2001, s 43; Communications Act 2003, s 406.

ROAD TRAFFIC ACT 1988

1 CAUSING DEATH BY DANGEROUS DRIVING

A person who causes the death of another person by driving a mechanically propelled vehicle dangerously on a road or other public place is guilty of an offence.

2 DANGEROUS DRIVING

A person who drives a mechanically propelled vehicle dangerously on a road or other public place is guilty of an offence.

2A MEANING OF DANGEROUS DRIVING

(1)   For the purposes of sections 1 and 2 above a person is to be regarded as driving
        dangerously if (and, subject to subsection (2) below, only if)—
        (a) the way he drives falls far below what would be expected of a competent and careful
              driver, and
        (b) it would be obvious to a competent and careful driver that driving in that way would
              be dangerous.

(2)   A person is also to be regarded as driving dangerously for the purposes of sections 1 and 2
        above if it would be obvious to a competent and careful driver that driving the vehicle in
        its current state would be dangerous.

(3)   In subsections (1) and (2) above "dangerous" refers to danger either of injury to any
        person or of serious damage to property; and in determining for the purposes of those
        subsections what would be expected of, or obvious to, a competent and careful driver in a
        particular case, regard shall be had not only to the circumstances of which he could be
        expected to be aware but also to any circumstances shown to have been within the
        knowledge of the accused.

(4)   In determining for the purposes of subsection (2) above the state of a vehicle, regard may
        be had to anything attached to or carried on or in it and to the manner in which it is
        attached or carried.

2B CAUSING DEATH BY CARELESS, OR INCONSIDERATE, DRIVING

A person who causes the death of another person by driving a mechanically propelled vehicle on
a road or other public place without due care and attention, or without reasonable
consideration for other persons using the road or place, is guilty of an offence.

3 CARELESS, AND INCONSIDERATE, DRIVING

If a person drives a mechanically propelled vehicle on a road or other public place without due
care and attention, or without reasonable consideration for other persons using the road or
place, he is guilty of an offence.

3ZA MEANING OF CARELESS, OR INCONSIDERATE, DRIVING

(1)   This section has effect for the purposes of sections 2B and 3 above and section 3A below.

(2)   A person is to be regarded as driving without due care and attention if (and only if) the
        way he drives falls below what would be expected of a competent and careful driver.

(3)   In determining for the purposes of subsection (2) above what would be expected of a
        careful and competent driver in a particular case, regard shall be had not only to the
        circumstances of which he could be expected to be aware but also to any circumstances
        shown to have been within the knowledge of the accused.

(4)   A person is to be regarded as driving without reasonable consideration for other persons
        only if those persons are inconvenienced by his driving.

3ZB CAUSING DEATH BY DRIVING: UNLICENSED, DISQUALIFIED OR UNINSURED DRIVERS

A person is guilty of an offence under this section if he causes the death of another person by
driving a motor vehicle on a road and, at the time when he is driving, the circumstances are
such that he is committing an offence under—

(a)   section 87(1) of this Act (driving otherwise than in accordance with a licence),

(b)   section 103(1)(b) of this Act (driving while disqualified), or

(c)   section 143 of this Act (using motor vehicle while uninsured or unsecured against third party risks).

3A CAUSING DEATH BY CARELESS DRIVING WHEN UNDER INFLUENCE OF DRINK OR DRUGS

(1)   If a person causes the death of another person by driving a mechanically propelled vehicle on a road or other public place without due care and attention, or without reasonable consideration for other persons using the road or place, and—
  (a) he is, at the time when he is driving, unfit to drive through drink or drugs, or
  (b) he has consumed so much alcohol that the proportion of it in his breath, blood or urine at that time exceeds the prescribed limit, or
  (c) he is, within 18 hours after that time, required to provide a specimen in pursuance of section 7 of this Act, but without reasonable excuse fails to provide it, or
  (d) he is required by a constable to give his permission for a laboratory test of a specimen of blood taken from him under section 7A of this Act, but without reasonable excuse fails to do so,
  he is guilty of an offence.

(2)   For the purposes of this section a person shall be taken to be unfit to drive at any time when his ability to drive properly is impaired.

(3)   Subsection (1)(b), (c) and (d) above shall not apply in relation to a person driving a mechanically propelled vehicle other than a motor vehicle.

4 DRIVING, OR BEING IN CHARGE, WHEN UNDER INFLUENCE OF DRINK OR DRUGS

(1)   A person who, when driving or attempting to drive a mechanically propelled vehicle on a road or other public place, is unfit to drive through drink or drugs is guilty of an offence.

(2)   Without prejudice to subsection (1) above, a person who, when in charge of a mechanically propelled vehicle which is on a road or other public place, is unfit to drive through drink or drugs is guilty of an offence.

(3)   For the purposes of subsection (2) above, a person shall be deemed not to have been in charge of a mechanically propelled vehicle if he proves that at the material time the circumstances were such that there was no likelihood of his driving it so long as he remained unfit to drive through drink or drugs.

(4)   The court may, in determining whether there was such a likelihood as is mentioned in subsection (3) above, disregard any injury to him and any damage to the vehicle.

(5)   For the purposes of this section, a person shall be taken to be unfit to drive if his ability to drive properly is for the time being impaired.

5 DRIVING OR BEING IN CHARGE OF A MOTOR VEHICLE WITH ALCOHOL CONCENTRATION ABOVE PRESCRIBED LIMIT

(1)   If a person—
  (a) drives or attempts to drive a motor vehicle on a road or other public place, or

(b) is in charge of a motor vehicle on a road or other public place, after consuming so much alcohol that the proportion of it in his breath, blood or urine exceeds the prescribed limit he is guilty of an offence.

(2) It is a defence for a person charged with an offence under subsection (1)(b) above to prove that at the time he is alleged to have committed the offence the circumstances were such that there was no likelihood of his driving the vehicle whilst the proportion of alcohol in his breath, blood or urine remained likely to exceed the prescribed limit.

(3) The court may, in determining whether there was such a likelihood as is mentioned in subsection (2) above, disregard any injury to him and any damage to the vehicle.

OFFICIAL SECRETS ACT 1989

1 SECURITY AND INTELLIGENCE

(1) A person who is or has been—
(a) a member of the security and intelligence services; or
(b) a person notified that he is subject to the provisions of this subsection,
is guilty of an offence if without lawful authority he discloses any information, document or other article relating to security or intelligence which is or has been in his possession by virtue of his position as a member of any of those services or in the course of his work while the notification is or was in force.

(2) The reference in subsection (1) above to disclosing information relating to security or intelligence includes a reference to making any statement which purports to be a disclosure of such information or is intended to be taken by those to whom it is addressed as being such a disclosure.

(3) A person who is or has been a Crown servant or government contractor is guilty of an offence if without lawful authority he makes a damaging disclosure of any information, document or other article relating to security or intelligence which is or has been in his possession by virtue of his position as such but otherwise than as mentioned in subsection (1) above.

(4) For the purposes of subsection (3) above a disclosure is damaging if—
(a) it causes damage to the work of, or of any part of, the security and intelligence services; or
(b) it is of information or a document or other article which is such that its unauthorised disclosure would be likely to cause such damage or which falls within a class or description of information, documents or articles the unauthorised disclosure of which would be likely to have that effect.

(5) It is a defence for a person charged with an offence under this section to prove that at the time of the alleged offence he did not know, and had no reasonable cause to believe, that the information, document or article in question related to security or intelligence or, in the case of an offence under subsection (3), that the disclosure would be damaging within the meaning of that subsection.

(6) Notification that a person is subject to subsection (1) above shall be effected by a notice in writing served on him by a Minister of the Crown; and such a notice may be served if, in the Minister's opinion, the work undertaken by the person in question is or includes work connected with the security and intelligence services and its nature is such that the interests of national security require that he should be subject to the provisions of that subsection.

(7)   Subject to subsection (8) below, a notification for the purposes of subsection (1) above shall be in force for the period of five years beginning with the day on which it is served but may be renewed by further notices under subsection (6) above for periods of five years at a time.

(8)   A notification for the purposes of subsection (1) above may at any time be revoked by a further notice in writing served by the Minister on the person concerned; and the Minister shall serve such a further notice as soon as, in his opinion, the work undertaken by that person ceases to be such as is mentioned in subsection (6) above.

(9)   In this section "security or intelligence" means the work of, or in support of, the security and intelligence services or any part of them, and references to information relating to security or intelligence include references to information held or transmitted by those services or by persons in support of, or of any part of, them.

2 DEFENCE

(1)   A person who is or has been a Crown servant or government contractor is guilty of an offence if without lawful authority he makes a damaging disclosure of any information, document or other article relating to defence which is or has been in his possession by virtue of his position as such.

(2)   For the purposes of subsection (1) above a disclosure is damaging if—
   (a) it damages the capability of, or of any part of, the armed forces of the Crown to carry out their tasks or leads to loss of life or injury to members of those forces or serious damage to the equipment or installations of those forces; or
   (b) otherwise than as mentioned in paragraph (a) above, it endangers the interests of the United Kingdom abroad, seriously obstructs the promotion or protection by the United Kingdom of those interests or endangers the safety of British citizens abroad; or
   (c) it is of information or of a document or article which is such that its unauthorised disclosure would be likely to have any of those effects.

(3)   It is a defence for a person charged with an offence under this section to prove that at the time of the alleged offence he did not know, and had no reasonable cause to believe, that the information, document or article in question related to defence or that its disclosure would be damaging within the meaning of subsection (1) above.

(4)   In this section "defence" means—
   (a) the size, shape, organisation, logistics, order of battle, deployment, operations, state of readiness and training of the armed forces of the Crown;
   (b) the weapons, stores or other equipment of those forces and the invention, development, production and operation of such equipment and research relating to it;
   (c) defence policy and strategy and military planning and intelligence;
   (d) plans and measures for the maintenance of essential supplies and services that are or would be needed in time of war.

3 INTERNATIONAL RELATIONS

(1)   A person who is or has been a Crown servant or government contractor is guilty of an offence if without lawful authority he makes a damaging disclosure of—
   (a) any information, document or other article relating to international relations; or
   (b) any confidential information, document or other article which was obtained from a State other than the United Kingdom or an international organisation,

being information or a document or article which is or has been in his possession by virtue of his position as a Crown servant or government contractor.

(2) For the purposes of subsection (1) above a disclosure is damaging if—
   (a) it endangers the interests of the United Kingdom abroad, seriously obstructs the promotion or protection by the United Kingdom of those interests or endangers the safety of British citizens abroad; or
   (b) it is of information or of a document or article which is such that its unauthorised disclosure would be likely to have any of those effects.

(3) In the case of information or a document or article within subsection (1)(b) above—
   (a) the fact that it is confidential, or
   (b) its nature or contents,
   may be sufficient to establish for the purposes of subsection (2)(b) above that the information, document or article is such that its unauthorised disclosure would be likely to have any of the effects there mentioned.

(4) It is a defence for a person charged with an offence under this section to prove that at the time of the alleged offence he did not know, and had no reasonable cause to believe, that the information, document or article in question was such as is mentioned in subsection (1) above or that its disclosure would be damaging within the meaning of that subsection.

(5) In this section "international relations" means the relations between States, between international organisations or between one or more States and one or more such organisations and includes any matter relating to a State other than the United Kingdom or to an international organisation which is capable of affecting the relations of the United Kingdom with another State or with an international organisation.

(6) For the purposes of this section any information, document or article obtained from a State or organisation is confidential at any time while the terms on which it was obtained require it to be held in confidence or while the circumstances in which it was obtained make it reasonable for the State or organisation to expect that it would be so held.

4 CRIME AND SPECIAL INVESTIGATION POWERS

(1) A person who is or has been a Crown servant or government contractor is guilty of an offence if without lawful authority he discloses any information, document or other article to which this section applies and which is or has been in his possession by virtue of his position as such.

(2) This section applies to any information, document or other article—
   (a) the disclosure of which—
      (i)   results in the commission of an offence; or
      (ii) facilitates an escape from legal custody or the doing of any other act prejudicial to the safekeeping of persons in legal custody; or
      (iii) impedes the prevention or detection of offences or the apprehension or prosecution of suspected offenders; or
   (b) which is such that its unauthorised disclosure would be likely to have any of those effects.

(3) This section also applies to—
   (a) any information obtained by reason of the interception of any communication in obedience to a warrant issued under section 2 of the Interception of Communications Act 1985 or under the authority of an interception warrant under section 5 of the Regulation of Investigatory Powers Act 2000, any information relating to the

obtaining of information by reason of any such interception and any document or other article which is or has been used or held for use in, or has been obtained by reason of, any such interception; and

(b) any information obtained by reason of action authorised by a warrant issued under section 3 of the Security Service Act 1989 or under section 5 of the Intelligence Services Act 1994 or by an authorisation given under section 7 of that Act, any information relating to the obtaining of information by reason of any such action and any document or other article which is or has been used or held for use in, or has been obtained by reason of, any such action.

(4) It is a defence for a person charged with an offence under this section in respect of a disclosure falling within subsection (2)(a) above to prove that at the time of the alleged offence he did not know, and had no reasonable cause to believe, that the disclosure would have any of the effects there mentioned.

(5) It is a defence for a person charged with an offence under this section in respect of any other disclosure to prove that at the time of the alleged offence he did not know, and had no reasonable cause to believe, that the information, document or article in question was information or a document or article to which this section applies.

(6) In this section "legal custody" includes detention in pursuance of any enactment or any instrument made under an enactment.

5 INFORMATION RESULTING FROM UNAUTHORISED DISCLOSURES OR ENTRUSTED IN CONFIDENCE

(1) Subsection (2) below applies where—
(a) any information, document or other article protected against disclosure by the foregoing provisions of this Act has come into a person's possession as a result of having been—
  (i) disclosed (whether to him or another) by a Crown servant or government contractor without lawful authority; or
  (ii) entrusted to him by a Crown servant or government contractor on terms requiring it to be held in confidence or in circumstances in which the Crown servant or government contractor could reasonably expect that it would be so held; or
  (iii) disclosed (whether to him or another) without lawful authority by a person to whom it was entrusted as mentioned in sub-paragraph (ii) above; and
(b) the disclosure without lawful authority of the information, document or article by the person into whose possession it has come is not an offence under any of those provisions.

(2) Subject to subsections (3) and (4) below, the person into whose possession the information, document or article has come is guilty of an offence if he discloses it without lawful authority knowing, or having reasonable cause to believe, that it is protected against disclosure by the foregoing provisions of this Act and that it has come into his possession as mentioned in subsection (1) above.

(3) In the case of information or a document or article protected against disclosure by sections 1 to 3 above, a person does not commit an offence under subsection (2) above unless—
(a) the disclosure by him is damaging; and
(b) he makes it knowing, or having reasonable cause to believe, that it would be damaging;
and the question whether a disclosure is damaging shall be determined for the purposes of this subsection as it would be in relation to a disclosure of that information, document or article by a Crown servant in contravention of section 1(3), 2(1) or 3(1) above.

(4) A person does not commit an offence under subsection (2) above in respect of information or a document or other article which has come into his possession as a result of having been disclosed—
(a) as mentioned in subsection (1)(a)(i) above by a government contractor; or
(b) as mentioned in subsection (1)(a)(iii) above,
unless that disclosure was by a British citizen or took place in the United Kingdom, in any of the Channel Islands or in the Isle of Man or a colony.

(5) For the purposes of this section information or a document or article is protected against disclosure by the foregoing provisions of this Act if—
(a) it relates to security or intelligence, defence or international relations within the meaning of section 1, 2 or 3 above or is such as is mentioned in section 3(1)(b) above; or
(b) it is information or a document or article to which section 4 above applies;
and information or a document or article is protected against disclosure by sections 1 to 3 above if it falls within paragraph (a) above.

(6) A person is guilty of an offence if without lawful authority he discloses any information, document or other article which he knows, or has reasonable cause to believe, to have come into his possession as a result of a contravention of section 1 of the Official Secrets Act 1911.

6 INFORMATION ENTRUSTED IN CONFIDENCE TO OTHER STATES OR INTERNATIONAL ORGANISATIONS

(1) This section applies where—
(a) any information, document or other article which—
(i) relates to security or intelligence, defence or international relations; and
(ii) has been communicated in confidence by or on behalf of the United Kingdom to another State or to an international organisation, has come into a person's possession as a result of having been disclosed (whether to him or another) without the authority of that State or organisation or, in the case of an organisation, of a member of it; and
(b) the disclosure without lawful authority of the information, document or article by the person into whose possession it has come is not an offence under any of the foregoing provisions of this Act.

(2) Subject to subsection (3) below, the person into whose possession the information, document or article has come is guilty of an offence if he makes a damaging disclosure of it knowing, or having reasonable cause to believe, that it is such as is mentioned in subsection (1) above, that it has come into his possession as there mentioned and that its disclosure would be damaging.

(3) A person does not commit an offence under subsection (2) above if the information, document or article is disclosed by him with lawful authority or has previously been made available to the public with the authority of the State or organisation concerned or, in the case of an organisation, of a member of it.

(4) For the purposes of this section "security or intelligence", "defence" and "international relations" have the same meaning as in section 1, 2 and 3 above and the question whether a disclosure is damaging shall be determined as it would be in relation to a disclosure of the information, document or article in question by a Crown servant in contravention of section 1(3), 2(1) and 3(1) above.

(5)   For the purposes of this section information or a document or article is communicated in confidence if it is communicated on terms requiring it to be held in confidence or in circumstances in which the person communicating it could reasonably expect that it would be so held.

7 AUTHORISED DISCLOSURES

(1)   For the purposes of this Act a disclosure by—
   (a) a Crown servant; or
   (b) a person, not being a Crown servant or government contractor, in whose case a notification for the purposes of section 1(1) above is in force,
   is made with lawful authority if, and only if, it is made in accordance with his official duty.

(2)   For the purposes of this Act a disclosure by a government contractor is made with lawful authority if, and only if, it is made—
   (a) in accordance with an official authorisation; or
   (b) for the purposes of the functions by virtue of which he is a government contractor and without contravening an official restriction.

(3)   For the purposes of this Act a disclosure made by any other person is made with lawful authority if, and only if, it is made—
   (a) to a Crown servant for the purposes of his functions as such; or
   (b) in accordance with an official authorisation.

(4)   It is a defence for a person charged with an offence under any of the foregoing provisions of this Act to prove that at the time of the alleged offence he believed that he had lawful authority to make the disclosure in question and had no reasonable cause to believe otherwise.

(5)   In this section "official authorisation" and "official restriction" mean, subject to subsection (6) below, an authorisation or restriction duly given or imposed by a Crown servant or government contractor or by or on behalf of a prescribed body or a body of a prescribed class.

(6)   In relation to section 6 above "official authorisation" includes an authorisation duly given by or on behalf of the State or organisation concerned or, in the case of an organisation, a member of it.

8 SAFEGUARDING OF INFORMATION

(1)   Where a Crown servant or government contractor, by virtue of his position as such, has in his possession or under his control any document or other article which it would be an offence under any of the foregoing provisions of this Act for him to disclose without lawful authority he is guilty of an offence if—
   (a) being a Crown servant, he retains the document or article contrary to his official duty; or
   (b) being a government contractor, he fails to comply with an official direction for the return or disposal of the document or article,
   or if he fails to take such care to prevent the unauthorised disclosure of the document or article as a person in his position may reasonably be expected to take.

(2)   It is a defence for a Crown servant charged with an offence under subsection (1)(a) above to prove that at the time of the alleged offence he believed that he was acting in accordance with his official duty and had no reasonable cause to believe otherwise.

(3)   In subsections (1) and (2) above references to a Crown servant include any person, not being a Crown servant or government contractor, in whose case a notification for the purposes of section 1(1) above is in force.

(4)   Where a person has in his possession or under his control any document or other article which it would be an offence under section 5 above for him to disclose without lawful authority, he is guilty of an offence if—
   (a) he fails to comply with an official direction for its return or disposal; or
   (b) where he obtained it from a Crown servant or government contractor on terms requiring it to be held in confidence or in circumstances in which that servant or contractor could reasonably expect that it would be so held, he fails to take such care to prevent its unauthorised disclosure as a person in his position may reasonably be expected to take.

(5)   Where a person has in his possession or under his control any document or other article which it would be an offence under section 6 above for him to disclose without lawful authority, he is guilty of an offence if he fails to comply with an official direction for its return or disposal.

(6)   A person is guilty of an offence if he discloses any official information, document or other article which can be used for the purpose of obtaining access to any information, document or other article protected against disclosure by the foregoing provisions of this Act and the circumstances in which it is disclosed are such that it would be reasonable to expect that it might be used for that purposes without authority.

(7)   For the purposes of subsection (6) above a person discloses information or a document or article which is official if—
   (a) he has or has had it in his possession by virtue of his position as a Crown servant or government contractor; or
   (b) he knows or has reasonable cause to believe that a Crown servant or government contractor has or has had it in his possession by virtue of his position as such.

(8)   Subsection (5) of section 5 above applies for the purposes of subsection (6) above as it applies for the purposes of that section.

(9)   In this section "official direction" means a direction duly given by a Crown servant or government contractor or by or on behalf of a prescribed body or a body of a prescribed class.

10 PENALTIES

(1)   A person guilty of an offence under any provision of this Act other than section 8(1), (4) or (5) shall be liable—
   (a) on conviction on indictment, to imprisonment for a term not exceeding two years or a fine or both;
   (b) on summary conviction, to imprisonment for a term not exceeding six months or a fine not exceeding the statutory maximum or both.

(2)   A person guilty of an offence under section 8(1), (4) or (5) above shall be liable on summary conviction to imprisonment for a term not exceeding three months or a fine not exceeding level 5 on the standard scale or both.

12 "CROWN SERVANT" AND "GOVERNMENT CONTRACTOR"

(1)   In this Act "Crown servant" means—
   (a) a Minister of the Crown;

(aa) a member of the Scottish Executive or a junior Scottish Minister;

(ab) the First Minister for Wales, a Welsh Minister appointed under section 48 of the Government of Wales Act 2006, the Counsel General to the Welsh Assembly Government or a Deputy Welsh Minister;

(b) a person appointed under section 8 of the Northern Ireland Constitution Act 1973 (the Northern Ireland Executive etc.);

(c) any person employed in the civil service of the Crown, including Her Majesty's Diplomatic Service, Her Majesty's Overseas Civil Service, the civil service of Northern Ireland and the Northern Ireland Court Service;

(d) any member of the naval, military or air forces of the Crown, including any person employed by an association established for the purposes of Part XI of the Reserve Forces Act 1996;

(e) any constable and any other person employed or appointed in or for the purposes of any police force (including a police force within the meaning of the Police Act (Northern Ireland) 1970) or of the Serious Organised Crime Agency;

(f) any person who is a member or employee of a prescribed body or a body of a prescribed class and either is prescribed for the purposes of this paragraph or belongs to a prescribed class of members or employees of any such body;

(g) any person who is the holder of a prescribed office or who is an employee of such a holder and either is prescribed for the purposes of this paragraph or belongs to a prescribed class of such employees.

(2) In this Act "government contractor" means, subject to subsection (3) below, any person who is not a Crown servant but who provides, or is employed in the provision of, goods or services—

(a) for the purposes of any Minister or person mentioned in paragraph (a), (ab) or (b) of subsection (1) above, of any office-holder in the Scottish Administration, of any of the services, forces or bodies mentioned in that subsection or of the holder of any office prescribed under that subsection;

. . .

(b) under an agreement or arrangement certified by the Secretary of State as being one to which the government of a State other than the United Kingdom or an international organisation is a party or which is subordinate to, or made for the purposes of implementing,any such agreement or arrangement.

(3) Where an employee or class of employees of any body, or of any holder of an office, is prescribed by an order made for the purposes of subsection (1) above—

(a) any employee of that body, or of the holder of that office, who is not prescribed or is not within the prescribed class; and

(b) any person who does not provide, or is not employed in the provision of, goods or services for the purposes of the performance of those functions of the body or the holder of the office in connection with which the employee or prescribed class of employees is engaged,

shall not be a government contractor for the purposes of this Act.

. . .

13 OTHER INTERPRETATION PROVISIONS

(1) In this Act—

"disclose" and "disclosure", in relation to a document or other article, include parting with possession of it;

"international organisation" means, subject to subsections (2) and (3) below, an organisation of which only States are members and includes a reference to any organ of such an organisation;

"prescribed" means prescribed by an order made by the Secretary of State;

"State" includes the government of a State and any organ of its government and references to a State other than the United Kingdom include references to any territory outside the United Kingdom.

(2)   In section 12(2)(b) above the reference to an international organisation includes a reference to any such organisation whether or not one of which only States are members and includes a commercial organisation.

(3)   In determining for the purposes of subsection (1) above whether only States are members of an organisation, any member which is itself an organisation of which only States are members, or which is an organ of such an organisation, shall be treated as a State.

As amended Regulation of Investigatory Powers Act 2000 Schedule 4; Intelligence Services Act 1994 Schedule 4; Scotland Act 1998 Schedule 8; Government of Wales Act 2006 Schedule 10; Reserve Forces Act 1996 Schedule 10; Serious Organised Crime and Police Act 2005 Schedule 4.

COMPUTER MISUSE ACT 1990

1 UNAUTHORISED ACCESS TO COMPUTER MATERIAL

(1)   A person is guilty of an offence if—
   (a) he causes a computer to perform any function with intent to secure access to any program or data held in any computer, or to enable any such access to be secured;
   (b) the access he intends to secure, or to enable to be secured, is unauthorised; and
   (c) he knows at the time when he causes the computer to perform the function that that is the case.

(2)   The intent a person has to have to commit an offence under this section need not be directed at—
   (a) any particular program or data;
   (b) a program or data of any particular kind; or
   (c) a program or data held in any particular computer.

(3)   A person guilty of an offence under this section shall be liable—
   (a) on summary conviction in England and Wales, to imprisonment for a term not exceeding 12 months or to a fine not exceeding the statutory maximum or to both;
   (b) on summary conviction in Scotland, to imprisonment for a term not exceeding six months or to a fine not exceeding the statutory maximum or to both;
   (c) on conviction on indictment, to imprisonment for a term not exceeding two years or to a fine or to both.

2 UNAUTHORISED ACCESS WITH INTENT TO COMMIT OR FACILITATE COMMISSION OF FURTHER OFFENCES

(1)   A person is guilty of an offence under this section if he commits an offence under section 1 above ("the unauthorised access offence") with intent—

(a) to commit an offence to which this section applies; or

(b) to facilitate the commission of such an offence (whether by himself or by any other person);

and the offence he intends to commit or facilitate is referred to below in this section as the further offence.

(2) This section applies to offences—

(a) for which the sentence is fixed by law; or

(b) for which a person of twenty-one years of age or over (not previously convicted) who has attained the age of twenty-one years (eighteen in relation to England and Wales) and has no previous convictions may be sentenced to imprisonment for a term of five years (or, in England and Wales, might be so sentenced but for the restrictions imposed by section 33 of the Magistrates' Courts Act 1980).

(3) It is immaterial for the purposes of this section whether the further offence is to be committed on the same occasion as the unauthorised access offence or on any future occasion.

(4) A person may be guilty of an offence under this section even though the facts are such that the commission of the further offence is impossible.

(5) A person guilty of an offence under this section shall be liable—

(a) on summary conviction in England and Wales, to imprisonment for a term not exceeding 12 months or to a fine not exceeding the statutory maximum or to both;

(b) on summary conviction in Scotland, to imprisonment for a term not exceeding six months or to a fine not exceeding the statutory maximum or to both;

(c) on conviction on indictment, to imprisonment for a term not exceeding five years or to a fine or to both.

3 UNAUTHORISED ACTS WITH INTENT TO IMPAIR, OR WITH RECKLESSNESS AS TO IMPAIRING, OPERATION OF COMPUTER, ETC

(1) A person is guilty of an offence if—

(a) he does any unauthorised act in relation to a computer;

(b) at the time when he does the act he knows that it is unauthorised; and

(c) either subsection (2) or subsection (3) below applies.

(2) This subsection applies if the person intends by doing the act—

(a) to impair the operation of any computer;

(b) to prevent or hinder access to any program or data held in any computer; or

(c) to impair the operation of any such program or the reliability of any such data.

(3) This subsection applies if the person is reckless as to whether the act will do any of the things mentioned in paragraphs (a) to (c) of subsection (2) above.

(4) The intention referred to in subsection (2) above, or the recklessness referred to in subsection (3) above, need not relate to—

(a) any particular computer;

(b) any particular program or data; or

(c) a program or data of any particular kind.

(5) In this section—

(a) a reference to doing an act includes a reference to causing an act to be done;

(b) "act" includes a series of acts;

(c) a reference to impairing, preventing or hindering something includes a reference to doing so temporarily.

(6)   A person guilty of an offence under this section shall be liable—
    (a) on summary conviction in England and Wales, to imprisonment for a term not exceeding 12 months or to a fine not exceeding the statutory maximum or to both;
    (b) on summary conviction in Scotland, to imprisonment for a term not exceeding six months or to a fine not exceeding the statutory maximum or to both;
    (c) on conviction on indictment, to imprisonment for a term not exceeding ten years or to a fine or to both.

3A MAKING, SUPPLYING OR OBTAINING ARTICLES FOR USE IN OFFENCE UNDER SECTION 1 OR 3

(1)   A person is guilty of an offence if he makes, adapts, supplies or offers to supply any article intending it to be used to commit, or to assist in the commission of, an offence under section 1 or 3.

(2)   A person is guilty of an offence if he supplies or offers to supply any article believing that it is likely to be used to commit, or to assist in the commission of, an offence under section 1 or 3.

(3)   A person is guilty of an offence if he obtains any article with a view to its being supplied for use to commit, or to assist in the commission of, an offence under section 1 or 3.

(4)   In this section "article" includes any program or data held in electronic form.

(5)   A person guilty of an offence under this section shall be liable—
    (a) on summary conviction in England and Wales, to imprisonment for a term not exceeding 12 months or to a fine not exceeding the statutory maximum or to both;
    (b) on summary conviction in Scotland, to imprisonment for a term not exceeding six months or to a fine not exceeding the statutory maximum or to both;
    (c) on conviction on indictment, to imprisonment for a term not exceeding two years or to a fine or to both.

4 TERRITORIAL SCOPE OF OFFENCES UNDER SECTIONS 1 TO 3

(1)   Except as provided below in this section, it is immaterial for the purposes of any offence under section 1 or 3 above—
    (a) whether any act or other event proof of which is required for conviction of the offence occurred in the home country concerned; or
    (b) whether the accused was in the home country concerned at the time of any such act or event.

(2)   Subject to subsection (3) below, in the case of such an offence at least one significant link with domestic jurisdiction must exist in the circumstances of the case for the offence to be committed.

(3)   There is no need for any such link to exist for the commission of an offence under section 1 above to be established in proof of an allegation to that effect in proceedings for an offence under section 2 above.

(4)   Subject to section 8 below, where—
    (a) any such link does in fact exist in the case of an offence under section 1 above; and
    (b) commission of that offence is alleged in proceedings for an offence under section 2 above;
section 2 above shall apply as if anything the accused intended to do or facilitate in any place outside the home country concerned which would be an offence to which section 2 applies if it took place in the home country concerned were the offence in question.

. . .

(6)   References in this Act to the home country concerned are references—
    (a) in the application of this Act to England and Wales, to England and Wales;
    (b) in the application of this Act to Scotland, to Scotland; and
    (c) in the application of this Act to Northern Ireland, to Northern Ireland.

5 SIGNIFICANT LINKS WITH DOMESTIC JURISDICTION

(1)   The following provisions of this section apply for the interpretation of section 4 above.

(2)   In relation to an offence under section 1, either of the following is a significant link with domestic jurisdiction—
    (a) that the accused was in the home country concerned at the time when he did the act which caused the computer to perform the function; or
    (b) that any computer containing any program or data to which the accused by doing that act secured or intended to secure unauthorised access, or enabled or intended to enable unauthorised access to be secured, was in the home country concerned at that time.

(3)   In relation to an offence under section 3, either of the following is a significant link with domestic jurisdiction—
    (a) that the accused was in the home country concerned at the time when he did the unauthorised act (or caused it to be done); or
    (b) that the unauthorised act was done in relation to a computer in the home country concerned.

6 TERRITORIAL SCOPE OF INCHOATE OFFENCES RELATED TO OFFENCES UNDER SECTIONS 1 TO 3

(1)   On a charge of conspiracy to commit an offence under section 1, 2 or 3 above the following questions are immaterial to the accused's guilt—
    (a) the question where any person became a party to the conspiracy; and
    (b) the question whether any act, omission or other event occurred in the home country concerned.

(2)   On a charge of attempting to commit an offence under section 3 above the following questions are immaterial to the accused's guilt—
    (a) the question where the attempt was made; and
    (b) the question whether it had an effect in the home country concerned.
. . .

8 RELEVANCE OF EXTERNAL LAW

(1)   A person is guilty of an offence triable by virtue of section 4(4) above only if what he intended to do or facilitate would involve the commission of an offence under the law in force where the whole or any part of it was intended to take place.

(3)   A person is guilty of an offence triable by virtue of section 1(1A) of the Criminal Attempts Act 1981 only if what he had in view would involve the commission of an offence under the law in force where the whole or any part of it was intended to take place.

(4)   Conduct punishable under the law in force in any place is an offence under that law for the purposes of this section, however it is described in that law.

(5)   Subject to subsection (7) below, a condition specified in subsection (1) or (3) above shall be taken to be satisfied unless not later than rules of court may provide the defence serve on the prosecution a notice—

(a) stating that, on the facts as alleged with respect to the relevant conduct, the condition is not in their opinion satisfied;

(b) showing their grounds for that opinion; and

(c) requiring the prosecution to show that it is satisfied.

(6) In subsection (5) above "the relevant conduct" means—

(a) where the condition in subsection (1) above is in question, what the accused intended to do or facilitate;

(c) where the condition in subsection (3) above is in question, what the accused had in view.

(7) The court, if it thinks fit, may permit the defence to require the prosecution to show that the condition is satisfied without the prior service of a notice under subsection (5) above.

. . .

17 INTERPRETATION

(1) The following provisions of this section apply for the interpretation of this Act.

(2) A person secures access to any program or data held in a computer if by causing a computer to perform any function he—

(a) alters or erases the program or data;

(b) copies or moves it to any storage medium other than that in which it is held or to a different location in the storage medium in which it is held;

(c) uses it; or

(d) has it output from the computer in which it is held (whether by having it displayed or in any other manner);

and references to access to a program or data (and to an intent to secure such access or to enable such access to be secured) shall be read accordingly.

(3) For the purposes of subsection (2)(c) above a person uses a program if the function he causes the computer to perform—

(a) causes the program to be executed; or

(b) is itself a function of the program.

(4) For the purposes of subsection (2)(d) above—

(a) a program is output if the instructions of which it consists are output; and

(b) the form in which any such instructions or any other data is output (and in particular whether or not it represents a form in which, in the case of instructions, they are capable of being executed or, in the case of data, it is capable of being processed by a computer) is immaterial.

(5) Access of any kind by any person to any program or data held in a computer is unauthorised if—

(a) he is not himself entitled to control access of the kind in question to the program or data; and

(b) he does not have consent to access by him of the kind in question to the program or data from any person who is so entitled but this subsection is subject to section 10.

(6) References to any program or data held in a computer include references to any program or data held in any removable storage medium which is for the time being in the computer; and a computer is to be regarded as containing any program or data held in any such medium.

(8)   An act done in relation to a computer is unauthorised if the person doing the act (or causing it to be done)—
    (a) is not himself a person who has responsibility for the computer and is entitled to determine whether the act may be done; and
    (b) does not have consent to the act from any such person.
    In this subsection "act" includes a series of acts.

(9)   References to the home country concerned shall be read in accordance with section 4(6) above.

(10) References to a program include references to part of a program.

> As amended by *Criminal Justice and Court Services Act 2000, s 74, Police and Justice Act 2006, s 35, Serious Crimes Act 2006.*

CRIMINAL PROCEDURE (INSANITY AND UNFITNESS TO PLEAD) ACT 1991

1 ACQUITTALS ON GROUNDS OF INSANITY

(1)   A jury shall not return a special verdict under section 2 of the Trial of Lunatics Act 1883 (acquittal on ground of insanity) except on the written or oral evidence of two or more registered medical practitioners at least one of whom is duly approved.

(2)   Subsections (2) and (3) of section 54 of the Mental Health Act 1983 ("the 1983 Act") shall have effect with respect to proof of the accused's mental condition for the purposes of the said section 2 as they have effect with respect to proof of an offender's mental condition for the purposes of section 37(2)(a) of that Act.

6 INTERPRETATION ETC

(1)   In this Act—

"duly approved", in relation to a registered medical practitioner, means approved for the purposes of section 12 of the 1983 Act by the Secretary of State as having special experience in the diagnosis or treatment of mental disorder.

DANGEROUS DOGS ACT 1991

1 DOGS BRED FOR FIGHTING

(1)   This section applies to—
    (a) any dog of the type known as the pit bull terrier;
    (b) any dog of the type known as the Japanese tosa; and
    (c) any dog of any type designated for the purposes of this section by an order of the Secretary of State, being a type appearing to him to be bred for fighting or to have the characteristics of a type bred for that purpose.

(2)   No person shall—
    (a) breed, or breed from, a dog to which this section applies;

(b) sell or exchange such a dog or offer, advertise or expose such a dog for sale or exchange;

(c) make or offer to make a gift of such a dog or advertise or expose such a dog as a gift;

(d) allow such a dog of which he is the owner or of which he is for the time being in charge to be in a public place without being muzzled and kept on a lead; or

(e) abandon such a dog of which he is the owner or, being the owner or for the time being in charge of such a dog, allow it to stray.

(7) Any person who contravenes this section is guilty of an offence and liable on summary conviction to imprisonment for a term not exceeding six months or a fine not exceeding level 5 on the standard scale or both except that a person who publishes an advertisement in contravention of subsection (2)(b) or (c)—

(a) shall not on being convicted be liable to imprisonment if he shows that he published the advertisement to the order of someone else and did not himself devise it; and

(b) shall not be convicted if, in addition, he shows that he did not know and had no reasonable cause to suspect that it related to a dog to which this section applies.

2 OTHER SPECIALLY DANGEROUS DOGS

(1) If it appears to the Secretary of State that dogs of any type to which section 1 above does not apply present a serious danger to the public he may by order impose in relation to dogs of that type restrictions corresponding, with such modifications, if any, as he thinks appropriate, to all or any of those in subsection (2)(d) and (e) of that section.

. . .

3 KEEPING DOGS UNDER PROPER CONTROL

(1) If a dog is dangerously out of control in a public place—

(a) the owner; and

(b) if different, the person for the time being in charge of the dog,

is guilty of an offence, or, if the dog while so out of control injures any person, an aggravated offence, under this subsection.

(2) In proceedings for an offence under subsection (1) above against a person who is the owner of a dog but was not at the material time in charge of it, it shall be a defence for the accused to prove that the dog was at the material time in the charge of a person whom he reasonably believed to be a fit and proper person to be in charge of it.

(3) If the owner or, if different, the person for the time being in charge of a dog allows it to enter a place which is not a public place but where it is not permitted to be and while it is there—

(a) it injures any person; or

(b) there are grounds for reasonable apprehension that it will do so,

he is guilty of an offence, or, if the dog injures any person, an aggravated offence, under this subsection.

(4) A person guilty of an offence under subsection (1) or (3) above other than an aggravated offence is liable on summary conviction to imprisonment for a term not exceeding six months or a fine not exceeding level 5 on the standard scale or both; and a person guilty of an aggravated offence under either of those subsections is liable—

(a) on summary conviction, to imprisonment for a term not exceeding six months or a fine not exceeding the statutory maximum or both;

(b) on conviction on indictment, to imprisonment for a term not exceeding two years or a fine or both.

(5)   It is hereby declared for the avoidance of doubt that an order under section 2 of the Dogs Act 1871 (order on complaint that dog is dangerous and not kept under proper control)—

      (a)   may be made whether or not the dog is shown to have injured any person; and

      (b)   may specify the measures to be taken for keeping the dog under proper control, whether by muzzling, keeping on a lead, excluding it from specified places or otherwise.

(6)   If it appears to a court on a complaint under section 2 of the said Act of 1871 that the dog to which the complaint relates is a male and would be less dangerous if neutered the court may under that section make an order requiring it to be neutered.

(7)   The reference in section 1(3) of the Dangerous Dogs Act 1989 (penalties) to failing to comply with an order under section 2 of the said Act of 1871 to keep a dog under proper control shall include a reference to failing to comply with any other order made under that section; but no order shall be made under that section by virtue of subsection (6) above where the matters complained of arose before the coming into force of that subsection.

4 DESTRUCTION AND DISQUALIFICATION ORDERS

(1)   Where a person is convicted of an offence under section 1 or 3(1) or (3) above or of an offence under an order made under section 2 above the court—

      (a)   may order the destruction of any dog in respect of which the offence was committed and shall do so in the case of an offence under section 1 or an aggravated offence under section 3(1) or (3) above; and

      (b)   may order the offender to be disqualified, for such period as the court thinks fit, for having custody of a dog.

(2)   Where a court makes an order under subsection (1)(a) above for the destruction of a dog owned by a person other than the offender, then, unless the order is one that the court is required to make, the owner may appeal to the Crown Court against the order.

(3)   A dog shall not be destroyed pursuant to an order under subsection (1)(a) above—

      (a)   until the end of the period for giving notice of appeal against the conviction or, where the order was not one which the court was required to make, against the order; and

      (b)   if notice of appeal is given within that period, until the appeal is determined or withdrawn,

    unless the offender and, in a case to which subsection (2) above applies, the owner of the dog give notice to the court that made the order that there is to be no appeal.

(4)   Where a court makes an order under subsection (1)(a) above it may—

      (a)   appoint a person to undertake the destruction of the dog and require any person having custody of it to deliver it up for that purpose; and

      (b)   order the offender to pay such sum as the court may determine to be the reasonable expenses of destroying the dog and of keeping it pending its destruction.

(5)   Any sum ordered to be paid under subsection (4)(b) above shall be treated for the purposes of enforcement as if it were a fine imposed on conviction.

(6)   Any person who is disqualified for having custody of a dog by virtue of an order under subsection (1)(b) above may, at any time after the end of the period of one year beginning with the date of the order, apply to the court that made it (or a magistrates' court acting for the same petty sessions area as that court) for a direction terminating the disqualification.

(7)   On an application under subsection (6) above the court may—
   (a) having regard to the applicant's character, his conduct since the disqualification was imposed and any other circumstances of the case, grant or refuse the application; and
   (b) order the applicant to pay all or any part of the costs of the application;
      and where an application in respect of an order is refused no further application in respect of that order shall be entertained if made before the end of the period of one year beginning with the date of the refusal.

(8)   Any person who—
   (a) has custody of a dog in contravention of an order under subsection (1)(b) above; or
   (b) fails to comply with a requirement imposed on him under subsection (4)(a) above,
   is guilty of an offence and liable on summary conviction to a fine not exceeding level 5 on the standard scale.

7 MUZZLING AND LEADS

(1)   In this Act—
   (a) references to a dog being muzzled are to its being securely fitted with a muzzle sufficient to prevent it biting any person; and
   (b) references to its being kept on a lead are to its being securely held on a lead by a person who is not less than sixteen years old.

10 SHORT TITLE, INTERPRETATION, COMMENCEMENT AND EXTENT

. . .

(2)   In this Act—

"advertisement" includes any means of bringing a matter to the attention of the public and "advertise" shall be construed accordingly;

"public place" means any street, road or other place (whether or not enclosed) to which the public have or are permitted to have access whether for payment or otherwise and includes the common parts of a building containing two or more separate dwellings.

(3)   For the purposes of this Act a dog shall be regarded as dangerously out of control on any occasion on which there are grounds for reasonable apprehension that it will injure any person, whether or not it actually does so, but references to a dog injuring a person or there being grounds for reasonable apprehension that it will do so do not include references to any case in which the dog is being used for a lawful purpose by a constable or a person in the service of the Crown.

FOOTBALL (OFFENCES) ACT 1991

1 DESIGNATED FOOTBALL MATCHES

(1)   In this Act a "designated football match" means an association football match designated, or of a description designated, for the purposes of this Act by order of the Secretary of State.

Any such order shall be made by statutory instrument which shall be subject to annulment in pursuance of a resolution of either House of Parliament.

(2)   References in this Act to things done at a designated football match include anything done at the ground—

(a)   within the period beginning two hours before the start of the match or (if earlier) two hours before the time at which it is advertised to start and ending one hour after the end of the match; or

(b)   where the match is advertised to start at a particular time on a particular day but does not take place on that day, within the period beginning two hours before and ending one hour after the advertised starting time.

2 THROWING OF MISSILES

It is an offence for a person at a designated football match to throw anything at or towards—

(a)   the playing area, or any area adjacent to the playing area to which spectators are not generally admitted, or

(b)   any area in which spectators or other persons are or may be present,

without lawful authority or lawful excuse (which shall be for him to prove).

3 INDECENT OR RACIALIST CHANTING

(1)   It is an offence to engage or take part in chanting of an indecent or racialist nature at a designated football match.

(2)   For this purpose—

(a)   "chanting" means the repeated uttering of any words or sounds (whether alone or in concert with one or more others); and

(b)   "of a racialist nature" means consisting of or including matter which is threatening, abusive or insulting to a person by reason of his colour, race, nationality (including citizenship) or ethnic or national origins.

4 GOING ONTO THE PLAYING AREA

It is an offence for a person at a designated football match to go onto the playing area, or any area adjacent to the playing area to which spectators are not generally admitted, without lawful authority or lawful excuse (which shall be for him to prove).

As amended by Football (Offences and Disorder) Act 1999, s 9(1), (2).

SEXUAL OFFENCES ACT 1993

1 ABOLITION OF PRESUMPTION OF SEXUAL INCAPACITY

The presumption of criminal law that a boy under the age of fourteen is incapable of sexual intercourse is hereby abolished.

CRIMINAL JUSTICE AND PUBLIC ORDER ACT 1994

68 OFFENCE OF AGGRAVATED TRESPASS

(1) A person commits the offence of aggravated trespass if he trespasses on land and, in relation to any lawful activity which persons are engaging in or are about to engage in on that or adjoining land . . ., does there anything which is intended by him to have the effect—
  (a) of intimidating those persons or any of them so as to deter them or any of them from engaging in that activity,
  (b) of obstructing that activity, or
  (c) of disrupting that activity.

. . .

(2) Activity on any occasion on the part of a person or persons on land is "lawful" for the purposes of this section if he or they may engage in the activity on the land on that occasion without committing an offence or trespassing on the land.

(3) A person guilty of an offence under this section is liable on summary conviction to imprisonment for a term not exceeding 51 weeks or a fine not exceeding level 4 on the standard scale, or both.

(5) In this section "land" does not include—
  (a) the highways and roads excluded from the application of section 61 by paragraph (b) of the definition of "land" in subsection (9) of that section . . .

As amended Anti-Social Behaviour Act 2003, s. 59, 62, Criminal Justice Act 2003, s. 280.

FAMILY LAW ACT 1996

42A OFFENCE OF BREACHING NON-MOLESTATION ORDER

(1) A person who without reasonable excuse does anything that he is prohibited from doing by a non-molestation order is guilty of an offence.

(2) In the case of a non-molestation order made by virtue of section 45(1), a person can be guilty of an offence under this section only in respect of conduct engaged in at a time when he was aware of the existence of the order.

(3) Where a person is convicted of an offence under this section in respect of any conduct, that conduct is not punishable as a contempt of court.

(4) A person cannot be convicted of an offence under this section in respect of any conduct which has been punished as a contempt of court.

(5) A person guilty of an offence under this section is liable—
  (a) on conviction on indictment, to imprisonment for a term not exceeding five years, or a fine, or both;
  (b) on summary conviction, to imprisonment for a term not exceeding 12 months, or a fine not exceeding the statutory maximum, or both.

(6) A reference in any enactment to proceedings under this Part, or to an order under this Part, does not include a reference to proceedings for an offence under this section or to an order made in such proceedings.

As amended Domestic Violence, Crime Victims Act 2004, s 1.

LAW REFORM (YEAR AND A DAY RULE) ACT 1996

1 ABOLITION OF "YEAR AND A DAY RULE"

The rule known as the "year and a day rule" (that is, the rule that, for the purposes of offences involving death and of suicide, an act or omission is conclusively presumed not to have caused a person's death if more than a year and a day elapsed before he died) is abolished for all purposes.

2 RESTRICTION ON INSTITUTION OF PROCEEDINGS FOR A FATAL OFFENCE

(1)   Proceedings to which this section applies may only be instituted by or with the consent of the Attorney General.

(2)   This section applies to proceedings against a person for a fatal offence if—
    (a)   the injury alleged to have caused the death was sustained more than three years before the death occurred, or
    (b)   the person has previously been convicted of an offence committed in circumstances alleged to be connected with the death.

(3)   In subsection (2) "fatal offence" means—
    (a)   murder, manslaughter, infanticide or any other offence of which one of the elements is causing a person's death, . . .
    (b)   the offence of aiding, abetting, counselling or procuring a person's suicide, or
    (c)   an offence under section 5 of the Domestic Violence, Crime and Victims Act 2004 (causing or allowing the death of a child or vulnerable adult).

(4)   No provision that proceedings may be instituted only by or with the consent of the Director of Public Prosecutions shall apply to proceedings to which this section applies.

As amended by the Domestic Violence, Crime and Victims Act 2004, s 58.

POLICE ACT 1996

89 ASSAULTS ON CONSTABLES

(1)   Any person who assaults a constable in the execution of his duty, or a person assisting a constable in the execution of his duty, shall be guilty of an offence and liable on summary conviction to imprisonment for a term not exceeding six months or to a fine not exceeding level 5 on the standard scale, or to both.

(2)   Any person who resists or wilfully obstructs a constable in the execution of his duty, or a person assisting a constable in the execution of his duty, shall be guilty of an offence and liable on summary conviction to imprisonment for a term not exceeding *one month* 51 weeks or to a fine not exceeding level 3 on the standard scale, or to both.

. . .

(4)   In this section references to a person assisting a constable in the execution of his duty include references to any person who is neither a constable nor in the company of a constable but who—
    (a) is a member of an international joint investigation team that is led by a member of a police force; and
    (b) is carrying out his functions as a member of that team.

(5)   In this section "international joint investigation team" means any investigation team formed in accordance with—
    (a) any framework decision on joint investigation teams adopted under Article 34 of the Treaty on European Union;
    (b) the Convention on Mutual Assistance in Criminal Matters between the Member States of the European Union, and the Protocol to that Convention, established in accordance with that Article of that Treaty; or
    (c) any international agreement to which the United Kingdom is a party and which is specified for the purposes of this section in an order made by the Secretary of State.

(6)   A statutory instrument containing an order under subsection (5) shall be subject to annulment in pursuance of a resolution of either House of Parliament.

90 IMPERSONATION, ETC

(1)   Any person who with intent to deceive impersonates a member of a police force or special constable, or makes any statement or does any act calculated falsely to suggest that he is such a member or constable, shall be guilty of an offence and liable on summary conviction to imprisonment for a term not exceeding six months or to a fine not exceeding level 5 on the standard scale, or to both.

(2)   Any person who, not being a constable, wears any article of police uniform in circumstances where it gives him an appearance so nearly resembling that of a member of a police force as to be calculated to deceive shall be guilty of an offence and liable on summary conviction to a fine not exceeding level 3 on the standard scale.

(3)   Any person who, not being a member of a police force or special constable, has in his possession any article of police uniform shall, unless he proves that he obtained possession of that article lawfully and has possession of it for a lawful purpose, be guilty of an offence and liable on summary conviction to a fine not exceeding level 1 on the standard scale.

(4)   In this section—
    (a) "article of police uniform" means any article of uniform or any distinctive badge or mark or document of identification usually issued to members of police forces or special constables, or anything having the appearance of such an article, badge, mark or document,
    (ab) "member of a police force" includes a member of the staff of the National Policing Improvement Agency who is a constable, and
    (b) "special constable" means a special constable appointed for a police area.

As amended Anti-Terrorism, Crime and Security Act 2001, s 101, Police and Justice Act 2006, s 1(3), Criminal Justice Act 2003, s 336(3); Police Reform Act 2002, s 104(1); Serious Organised Crime and Police Act 2005, ss 59.

PROTECTION FROM HARASSMENT ACT 1997

1 PROHIBITION OF HARASSMENT

(1)   A person must not pursue a course of conduct—
    (a) which amounts to harassment of another, and
    (b) which he knows or ought to know amounts to harassment of the other.

(1A) A person must not pursue a course of conduct—
    (a) which involves harassment of two or more persons, and
    (b) which he knows or ought to know involves harassment of those persons, and
    (c) by which he intends to persuade any person (whether or not one of those mentioned above)—
        (i) not to do something that he is entitled or required to do, or
        (ii) to do something that he is not under any obligation to do.

(2)   For the purposes of this section, the person whose course of conduct is in question ought to know that it amounts to or involves harassment of another if a reasonable person in possession of the same information would think the course of conduct amounted to or involved harassment of the other.

(3)   Subsection (1) or (1A) does not apply to a course of conduct if the person who pursued it shows—
    (a) that it was pursued for the purpose of preventing or detecting crime,
    (b) that it was pursued under any enactment or rule of law or to comply with any condition or requirement imposed by any person under any enactment, or
    (c) that in the particular circumstances the pursuit of the course of conduct was reasonable.

2 OFFENCE OF HARASSMENT

(1)   A person who pursues a course of conduct in breach of section 1(1) or (1A) is guilty of an offence.

(2)   A person guilty of an offence under this section is liable on summary conviction to imprisonment for a term not exceeding six months, or a fine not exceeding level 5 on the standard scale, or both.

4 PUTTING PEOPLE IN FEAR OF VIOLENCE

(1)   A person whose course of conduct causes another to fear, on at least two occasions, that violence will be used against him is guilty of an offence if he knows or ought to know that his course of conduct will cause the other so to fear on each of those occasions.

(2)   For the purposes of this section, the person whose course of conduct is in question ought to know that it will cause another to fear that violence will be used against him on any occasion if a reasonable person in possession of the same information would think the course of conduct would cause the other so to fear on that occasion.

(3)   It is a defence for a person charged with an offence under this section to show that—
    (a) his course of conduct was pursued for the purpose of preventing or detecting crime,
    (b) his course of conduct was pursued under any enactment or rule of law or to comply with any condition or requirement imposed by any person under any enactment, or
    (c) the pursuit of his course of conduct was reasonable for the protection of himself or another or for the protection of his or another's property.

(4)   A person guilty of an offence under this section is liable—
    (a) on conviction on indictment, to imprisonment for a term not exceeding five years, or a fine, or both, or
    (b) on summary conviction, to imprisonment for a term not exceeding six months, or a fine not exceeding the statutory maximum, or both.

(5)   If on the trial on indictment of a person charged with an offence under this section the jury find him not guilty of the offence charged, they may find him guilty of an offence under section 2.

4A STALKING INVOLVING FEAR OF VIOLENCE OR SERIOUS ALARM OR DISTRESS

(1)   A person ("A") whose course of conduct—
    (a) amounts to stalking, and
    (b) either—
        (i)   causes another ("B") to fear, on at least two occasions, that violence will be used against B, or
        (ii) causes B serious alarm or distress which has a substantial adverse effect on B's usual day-to-day activities,
is guilty of an offence if A knows or ought to know that A's course of conduct will cause B so to fear on each of those occasions or (as the case may be) will cause such alarm or distress.

(2)   For the purposes of this section A ought to know that A's course of conduct will cause B to fear that violence will be used against B on any occasion if a reasonable person in possession of the same information would think the course of conduct would cause B so to fear on that occasion.

(3)   For the purposes of this section A ought to know that A's course of conduct will cause B serious alarm or distress which has a substantial adverse effect on B's usual day-to-day activities if a reasonable person in possession of the same information would think the course of conduct would cause B such alarm or distress.

(4)   It is a defence for A to show that—
    (a) A's course of conduct was pursued for the purpose of preventing or detecting crime,
    (b) A's course of conduct was pursued under any enactment or rule of law or to comply with any condition or requirement imposed by any person under any enactment, or
    (c) the pursuit of A's course of conduct was reasonable for the protection of A or another or for the protection of A's or another's property.

(5)   A person guilty of an offence under this section is liable—
    (a) on conviction on indictment, to imprisonment for a term not exceeding five years, or a fine, or both, or
    (b) on summary conviction, to imprisonment for a term not exceeding twelve months, or a fine not exceeding the statutory maximum, or both.

. . .

7 INTERPRETATION OF THIS GROUP OF SECTIONS

(1)   This section applies for the interpretation of sections 1 to 5A.

(2)   References to harassing a person include alarming the person or causing the person distress.

(3)   A "course of conduct" must involve—

    (a) in the case of conduct in relation to a single person (see section 1(1)), conduct on at least two occasions in relation to that person, or

    (b) in the case of conduct in relation to two or more persons (see section 1(1A)), conduct on at least one occasion in relation to each of those persons.

(3A) A person's conduct on any occasion shall be taken, if aided, abetted, counselled or procured by another—

    (a) to be conduct on that occasion of the other (as well as conduct of the person whose conduct it is); and

    (b) to be conduct in relation to which the other's knowledge and purpose, and what he ought to have known, are the same as they were in relation to what was contemplated or reasonably foreseeable at the time of the aiding, abetting, counselling or procuring.

(4)   "Conduct" includes speech.

(5)   References to a person, in the context of the harassment of a person, are references to a person who is an individual.

As amended Serious Organised Crime and Police Act 2005, s 125; Protection of Freedoms Act 2012, s 111.

FIREARMS (AMENDMENT) ACT 1997

2 SLAUGHTERING INSTRUMENTS

The authority of the Secretary of State . . . is not required by virtue of subsection (1)(aba) of section 5 of the Firearms 1968 Act—

(a)   for a person to have in his possession, or to purchase or acquire, or to sell or transfer, a slaughtering instrument if he is authorised by a firearm certificate to have the instrument in his possession, or to purchase or acquire it;

(b)   for a person to have a slaughtering instrument in his possession if he is entitled, under section 10 of the 1968 Act, to have it in his possession without a firearm certificate.

3 FIREARMS USED FOR HUMANE KILLING OF ANIMALS

The authority of the Secretary of State . . . is not required by virtue of subsection (1)(aba) of section 5 of the 1968 Act for a person to have in his possession, or to purchase or acquire, or to sell or transfer, a firearm if he is authorised by a firearm certificate to have the firearm in his possession, or to purchase or acquire it, subject to a condition that it is only for use in connection with the humane killing of animals.

. . .

6 TROPHIES OF WAR

The authority of the Secretary of State . . . is not required by virtue of subsection (1)(aba) of section 5 of the 1968 Act for a person to have in his possession a firearm which was acquired as a trophy of war before 1st January 1946 if he is authorised by a firearm certificate to have it in his possession.

7 FIREARMS OF HISTORIC INTEREST

(1)   The authority of the Secretary of State . . . is not required by virtue of subsection (1)(aba) of section 5 of the 1968 Act for a person to have in his possession, or to purchase or acquire, or to sell or transfer, a firearm which—
(a) was manufactured before 1st January 1919; and
(b) is of a description specified under subsection (2) below,
if he is authorised by a firearm certificate to have the firearm in his possession, or to purchase or acquire it, subject to a condition that he does so only for the purpose of its being kept or exhibited as part of a collection.

(2)   The Secretary of State may by order made by statutory instrument specify a description of firearm for the purposes of subsection (1) above if it appears to him that—
(a) firearms of that description were manufactured before 1st January 1919; and
(b) ammunition for firearms of that type is not readily available.

(3)   The authority of the Secretary of State . . . is not required by virtue of subsection (1)(aba) of section 5 of the 1968 Act for a person to have in his possession, or to purchase or acquire, or to sell or transfer, a firearm which—
(a) is of particular rarity, aesthetic quality or technical interest, or
(b) is of historical importance,
if he is authorised by a firearm certificate to have the firearm in his possession subject to a condition requiring it to be kept and used only at a place designated for the purposes of this subsection by the Secretary of State. . . .

(4)   This section has effect without prejudice to section 58(2) of the 1968 Act (antique firearms).

8 WEAPONS AND AMMUNITION USED FOR TREATING ANIMALS

The authority of the Secretary of State or the Scottish Ministers (by virtue of provision made under section 63 of the Scotland Act 1998) is not required by virtue of subsection (1)(aba), (b) or (c) of section 5 of the 1968 Act for a person to have in his possession, or to purchase or acquire, or to sell or transfer, any firearm, weapon or ammunition designed or adapted for the purpose of tranquillising or otherwise treating any animal, if he is authorised by a firearm certificate to possess, or to purchase or acquire, the firearm, weapon or ammunition subject to a condition restricting its use to use in connection with the treatment of animals.

KNIVES ACT 1997

1 UNLAWFUL MARKETING OF KNIVES

(1)   A person is guilty of an offence if he markets a knife in a way which—
(a) indicates, or suggests, that it is suitable for combat; or
(b) is otherwise likely to stimulate or encourage violent behaviour involving the use of the knife as a weapon.

(2)   "Suitable for combat" and "violent behaviour" are defined in section 10.

(3)   For the purposes of this Act, an indication or suggestion that a knife is suitable for combat may, in particular, be given or made by a name or description—
(a) applied to the knife;
(b) on the knife or on any packaging in which it is contained; or
(c) included in any advertisement which, expressly or by implication, relates to the knife.

(4)   For the purposes of this Act, a person markets a knife if—
    (a) he sells or hires it;
    (b) he offers, or exposes, it for sale or hire; or
    (c) he has it in his possession for the purpose of sale or hire.

(5)   A person guilty of an offence under this section shall be liable—
    (a) on summary conviction, to imprisonment for a term not exceeding 12 months or to a fine not exceeding the statutory maximum, or to both;
    (b) on conviction on indictment, to imprisonment for a term not exceeding 4 years, or to a fine, or to both.

2 PUBLICATIONS

(1)   A person is guilty of an offence if he publishes any written, pictorial or other material in connection with the marketing of any knife and that material—
    (a) indicates, or suggests, that the knife is suitable for combat; or
    (b) is otherwise likely to stimulate or encourage violent behaviour involving the use of the knife as a weapon.

(2)   A person guilty of an offence under this section shall be liable—
    (a) on summary conviction, to imprisonment for a term not exceeding 12 months or to a fine not exceeding the statutory maximum, or to both;
    (b) on conviction on indictment, to imprisonment for a term not exceeding 4 years, or to a fine, or to both.

3 EXEMPT TRADES

(1)   It is a defence for a person charged with an offence under section 1 to prove that—
    (a) the knife was marketed—
        (i)   for use by the armed forces of any country;
        (ii) as an antique or curio; or
        (iii) as falling within such other category (if any) as may be prescribed;
    (b) it was reasonable for the knife to be marketed in that way; and
    (c) there were no reasonable grounds for suspecting that a person into whose possession the knife might come in consequence of the way in which it was marketed would use it for an unlawful purpose.

(2)   It is a defence for a person charged with an offence under section 2 to prove that—
    (a) the material was published in connection with marketing a knife—
        (i)   for use by the armed forces of any country;
        (ii) as an antique or curio; or
        (iii) as falling within such other category (if any) as may be prescribed;
    (b) it was reasonable for the knife to be marketed in that way; and
    (c) there were no reasonable grounds for suspecting that a person into whose possession the knife might come in consequence of the publishing of the material would use it for an unlawful purpose.

(3)   In this section "prescribed" means prescribed by regulations made by the Secretary of State.

4 OTHER DEFENCES

(1)   It is a defence for a person charged with an offence under section 1 to prove that he did not know or suspect, and had no reasonable grounds for suspecting, that the way in which the knife was marketed—

(a) amounted to an indication or suggestion that the knife was suitable for combat; or

(b) was likely to stimulate or encourage violent behaviour involving the use of the knife as a weapon.

(2) It is a defence for a person charged with an offence under section 2 to prove that he did not know or suspect, and had no reasonable grounds for suspecting, that the material—

(a) amounted to an indication or suggestion that the knife was suitable for combat; or

(b) was likely to stimulate or encourage violent behaviour involving the use of the knife as a weapon.

(3) It is a defence for a person charged with an offence under section 1 or 2 to prove that he took all reasonable precautions and exercised all due diligence to avoid committing the offence.

10 INTERPRETATION

In this Act—
"the court" means—

(a) in relation to England and Wales or Northern Ireland, the Crown Court or a magistrate's court . . .

"knife" means an instrument which has a blade or is sharply pointed;

"marketing" and related expressions are to be read with section 1(4);

"publication" includes a publication in electronic form and, in the case of a publication which is, or may be, produced from electronic data, any medium on which the data are stored;

"suitable for combat" means suitable for use as a weapon for inflicting injury on a person or causing a person to fear injury;

"violent behaviour" means an unlawful act inflicting injury on a person or causing a person to fear injury.

CRIME AND DISORDER ACT 1998

1 ANTI-SOCIAL BEHAVIOUR ORDERS

(1) An application for an order under this section may be made by a relevant authority if it appears to the authority that the following conditions are fulfilled with respect to any person aged 10 or over, namely—

(a) that the person has acted, since the commencement date, in an anti-social manner, that is to say, in a manner that caused or was likely to cause harassment, alarm or distress to one or more persons not of the same household as himself; and

(b) that such an order is necessary to protect relevant persons from further anti-social acts by him.

. . .

(4) If, on such an application, it is proved that the conditions mentioned in subsection (1) above are fulfilled, the magistrates' court may make an order under this section (an "anti-social behaviour order") which prohibits the defendant from doing anything described in the order.

(5) For the purpose of determining whether the condition mentioned in subsection (1)(a) above is fulfilled, the court shall disregard any act of the defendant which he shows was reasonable in the circumstances.

. . .

(6)   The prohibitions that may be imposed by an anti-social behaviour order are those necessary for the purpose of protecting persons (whether relevant persons or persons elsewhere in England and Wales) from further anti-social acts by the defendant.

(7)   An anti-social behaviour order shall have effect for a period (not less than two years) specified in the order or until further order.

(8)   Subject to subsection (9) below, the applicant or the defendant may apply by complaint to the court which made an anti-social behaviour order for it to be varied or discharged by a further order.

(9)   Except with the consent of both parties, no anti-social behaviour order shall be discharged before the end of the period of two years beginning with the date of service of the order.

(10)   If without reasonable excuse a person does anything which he is prohibited from doing by an anti-social behaviour order, he is guilty of an offence and liable—
    (a) on summary conviction, to imprisonment for a term not exceeding six months or to a fine not exceeding the statutory maximum, or to both; or
    (b) on conviction on indictment, to imprisonment for a term not exceeding five years or to a fine, or to both.

28 MEANING OF "RACIALLY OR RELIGIOUSLY AGGRAVATED"

(1)   An offence is racially or religiously aggravated for the purposes of sections 29 to 32 below if—
    (a) at the time of committing the offence, or immediately before or after doing so, the offender demonstrates towards the victim of the offence hostility based on the victim's membership (or presumed membership) of a racial or religious group; or
    (b) the offence is motivated (wholly or partly) by hostility towards members of a racial or religious group based on their membership of that group.

(2)   In subsection (1)(a) above—

    "membership", in relation to a racial or religious group, includes association with members of that group;

    "presumed" means presumed by the offender.

(3)   It is immaterial for the purposes of paragraph (a) or (b) of subsection (1) above whether or not the offender's hostility is also based, to any extent, on any other factor not mentioned in that paragraph.

(4)   In this section "racial group" means a group of persons defined by reference to race, colour, nationality (including citizenship) or ethnic or national origins.

(5)   In this section "religious group" means a group of persons defined by reference to religious belief or lack of religious belief.

29 RACIALLY OR RELIGIOUSLY AGGRAVATED ASSAULTS

(1)   A person is guilty of an offence under this section if he commits—
    (a) an offence under section 20 of the Offences Against the Person Act 1861 (malicious wounding or grievous bodily harm);
    (b) an offence under section 47 of that Act (actual bodily harm); or
    (c) common assault,
    which is racially or religiously aggravated for the purposes of this section.

(2)   A person guilty of an offence falling within subsection (1)(a) or (b) above shall be liable—
  (a)   on summary conviction, to imprisonment for a term not exceeding six months or to a fine not exceeding the statutory maximum, or to both;
  (b)   on conviction on indictment, to imprisonment for a term not exceeding seven years or to a fine, or to both.

(3)   A person guilty of an offence falling within subsection (1)(c) above shall be liable—
  (a)   on summary conviction, to imprisonment for a term not exceeding six months or to a fine not exceeding the statutory maximum, or to both;
  (b)   on conviction on indictment, to imprisonment for a term not exceeding two years or to a fine, or to both.

30 RACIALLY OR RELIGIOUSLY AGGRAVATED CRIMINAL DAMAGE

(1)   A person is guilty of an offence under this section if he commits an offence under section 1(1) of the Criminal Damage Act 1971 (destroying or damaging property belonging to another) which is racially or religiously aggravated for the purposes of this section.

(2)   A person guilty of an offence under this section shall be liable—
  (a)   on summary conviction, to imprisonment for a term not exceeding six months or to a fine not exceeding the statutory maximum, or to both;
  (b)   on conviction on indictment, to imprisonment for a term not exceeding fourteen years or to a fine, or to both.

(3)   For the purposes of this section, section 28(1)(a) above shall have effect as if the person to whom the property belongs or is treated as belonging for the purposes of that Act were the victim of the offence.

31 RACIALLY OR RELIGIOUSLY AGGRAVATED PUBLIC ORDER OFFENCES

(1)   A person is guilty of an offence under this section if he commits—
  (a)   an offence under section 4 of the Public Order Act 1986 (fear or provocation of violence);
  (b)   an offence under section 4A of that Act (intentional harassment, alarm or distress); or
  (c)   an offence under section 5 of that Act (harassment, alarm or distress), which is racially or religiously aggravated for the purposes of this section.

(4)   A person guilty of an offence falling within subsection (1)(a) or (b) above shall be liable—
  (a)   on summary conviction, to imprisonment for a term not exceeding six months or to a fine not exceeding the statutory maximum, or to both;
  (b)   on conviction on indictment, to imprisonment for a term not exceeding two years or to a fine, or to both.

(5)   A person guilty of an offence falling within subsection (1)(c) above shall be liable on summary conviction to a fine not exceeding level 4 on the standard scale.

(6)   If, on the trial on indictment of a person charged with an offence falling within subsection (1)(a) or (b) above, the jury find him not guilty of the offence charged, they may find him guilty of the basic offence mentioned in that provision.

(7)   For the purposes of subsection (1)(c) above, section 28(1)(a) above shall have effect as if the person likely to be caused harassment, alarm or distress were the victim of the offence.

32 RACIALLY OR RELIGIOUSLY AGGRAVATED HARASSMENT ETC

(1)   A person is guilty of an offence under this section if he commits—
    (a)   an offence under section 2 of the Protection from Harassment Act 1997 (offence of harassment); or
    (b)   an offence under section 4 of that Act (putting people in fear of violence),
    which is racially or religiously aggravated for the purposes of this section.

(3)   A person guilty of an offence falling within subsection (1)(a) above shall be liable—
    (a)   on summary conviction, to imprisonment for a term not exceeding six months or to a fine not exceeding the statutory maximum, or to both;
    (b)   on conviction on indictment, to imprisonment for a term not exceeding two years or to a fine, or to both.

(4)   A person guilty of an offence falling within subsection (1)(b) above shall be liable—
    (a)   on summary conviction, to imprisonment for a term not exceeding six months or to a fine not exceeding the statutory maximum, or to both;
    (b)   on conviction on indictment, to imprisonment for a term not exceeding seven years or to a fine, or to both.

(5)   If, on the trial on indictment of a person charged with an offence falling within subsection (1)(a) above, the jury find him not guilty of the offence charged, they may find him guilty of the basic offence mentioned in that provision.

(6)   If, on the trial on indictment of a person charged with an offence falling within subsection (1)(b) above, the jury find him not guilty of the offence charged, they may find him guilty of an offence falling within subsection (1)(a) above.

(7)   Section 5 of the Protection from Harassment Act 1997 (restraining orders) shall have effect in relation to a person convicted of an offence under this section as if the reference in subsection (1) of that section to an offence under section 2 or 4 included a reference to an offence under this section.

34 ABOLITION OF REBUTTABLE PRESUMPTION THAT A CHILD IS DOLI INCAPAX

The rebuttable presumption of criminal law that a child aged 10 or over is incapable of committing an offence is hereby abolished.

As amended by the anti-social behaviour Act 2003, s. 85; Police Reform Act 2002, s. 107; Anti-Terrorism, Crime and Security Act 2001, s. 42, s. 127.

HUMAN RIGHTS ACT 1998

1 THE CONVENTION RIGHTS

(1)   In this Act "the Convention rights" means the rights and fundamental freedoms set out in—
    (a)   Articles 2 to 12 and 14 of the Convention,
    (b)   Articles 1 to 3 of the First Protocol, and
    (c)   Article 1 of the Thirteenth Protocol,
    as read with Articles 16 to 18 of the Convention.

(2)   Those Articles are to have effect for the purposes of this Act subject to any designated derogation or reservation (as to which see sections 14 and 15).

(3)   The Articles are set out in Schedule 1.

2 INTERPRETATION OF CONVENTION RIGHTS

(1)   A court or tribunal determining a question which has arisen in connection with a Convention right must take into account any—
   (a) judgment, decision, declaration or advisory opinion of the European Court of Human Rights,
   (b) opinion of the Commission given in a report adopted under Article 31 of the Convention,
   (c) decision of the Commission in connection with Article 26 or 27(2) of the Convention, or
   (d) decision of the Committee of Ministers taken under Article 46 of the Convention,
   whenever made or given, so far as, in the opinion of the court or tribunal, it is relevant to the proceedings in which that question has arisen.

(2)   Evidence of any judgment, decision, declaration or opinion of which account may have to be taken under this section is to be given in proceedings before any court or tribunal in such manner as may be provided by rules.

(3)   In this section "rules" means rules of court or, in the case of proceedings before a tribunal, rules made for the purposes of this section—
   (a) by . . . the Lord Chancellor or the Secretary of State, in relation to any proceedings outside Scotland . . .

3 INTERPRETATION OF LEGISLATION

(1)   So far as it is possible to do so, primary legislation and subordinate legislation must be read and given effect in a way which is compatible with the Convention rights.

(2)   This section—
   (a) applies to primary legislation and subordinate legislation whenever enacted;
   (b) does not affect the validity, continuing operation or enforcement of any incompatible primary legislation; and
   (c) does not affect the validity, continuing operation or enforcement of any incompatible subordinate legislation if (disregarding any possibility of revocation) primary legislation prevents removal of the incompatibility.

4 DECLARATION OF INCOMPATIBILITY

(1)   Subsection (2) applies in any proceedings in which a court determines whether a provision of primary legislation is compatible with a Convention right.

(2)   If the court is satisfied that the provision is incompatible with a Convention right, it may make a declaration of that incompatibility.

(3)   Subsection (4) applies in any proceedings in which a court determines whether a provision of subordinate legislation, made in the exercise of a power conferred by primary legislation, is compatible with a Convention right.

(4)   If the court is satisfied—
   (a) that the provision is incompatible with a Convention right, and

(b) that (disregarding any possibility of revocation) the primary legislation concerned prevents removal of the incompatibility,

it may make a declaration of that incompatibility.

(5)   In this section "court" means—
   (a) the House of Lords;
   (b) the Judicial Committee of the Privy Council;
   (c) the Courts Martial Appeal Court;
   (d) in Scotland, the High Court of Justiciary sitting otherwise than as a trial court or the Court of Session;
   (e) in England and Wales or Northern Ireland, the High Court or the Court of Appeal;
   (f) the Court of Protection, in any matter being dealt with by the President of the Family Division, the Vice-Chancellor or a puisne judge of the High Court.

(6)   A declaration under this section ("a declaration of incompatibility")—
   (a) does not affect the validity, continuing operation or enforcement of the provision in respect of which it is given; and
   (b) is not binding on the parties to the proceedings in which it is made.

. . .

6 ACTS OF PUBLIC AUTHORITIES

(1)   It is unlawful for a public authority to act in a way which is incompatible with a Convention right.

(2)   Subsection (1) does not apply to an act if—
   (a) as the result of one or more provisions of primary legislation, the authority could not have acted differently; or
   (b) in the case of one or more provisions of, or made under, primary legislation which cannot be read or given effect in a way which is compatible with the Convention rights, the authority was acting so as to give effect to or enforce those provisions.

(3)   In this section "public authority" includes—
   (a) a court or tribunal, and
   (b) any person certain of whose functions are functions of a public nature,
   but does not include either House of Parliament or a person exercising functions in connection with proceedings in Parliament.

(4)   In subsection (3) "Parliament" does not include the House of Lords in its judicial capacity.

(5)   In relation to a particular act, a person is not a public authority by virtue only of subsection (3)(b) if the nature of the act is private.

(6)   "An act" includes a failure to act but does not include a failure to—
   (a) introduce in, or lay before, Parliament a proposal for legislation; or
   (b) make any primary legislation or remedial order.

7 PROCEEDINGS

(1)   A person who claims that a public authority has acted (or proposes to act) in a way which is made unlawful by section 6(1) may—
   (a) bring proceedings against the authority under this Act in the appropriate court or tribunal, or
   (b) rely on the Convention right or rights concerned in any legal proceedings,
   but only if he is (or would be) a victim of the unlawful act.

(2) In subsection (1)(a) "appropriate court or tribunal" means such court or tribunal as may be determined in accordance with rules; and proceedings against an authority include a counterclaim or similar proceeding.

(3) If the proceedings are brought on an application for judicial review, the applicant is to be taken to have a sufficient interest in relation to the unlawful act only if he is, or would be, a victim of that act.

(4) If the proceedings are made by way of a petition for judicial review in Scotland, the applicant shall be taken to have title and interest to sue in relation to the unlawful act only if he is, or would be, a victim of that act.

(5) Proceedings under subsection (1)(a) must be brought before the end of—
 (a) the period of one year beginning with the date on which the act complained of took place; or
 (b) such longer period as the court or tribunal considers equitable having regard to all the circumstances,
 but that is subject to any rule imposing a stricter time limit in relation to the procedure in question.

(6) In subsection (1)(b) "legal proceedings" includes—
 (a) proceedings brought by or at the instigation of a public authority; and
 (b) an appeal against the decision of a court or tribunal.

(7) For the purposes of this section, a person is a victim of an unlawful act only if he would be a victim for the purposes of Article 34 of the Convention if proceedings were brought in the European Court of Human Rights in respect of that act.

(8) Nothing in this Act creates a criminal offence.

. . .

8 JUDICIAL REMEDIES

(1) In relation to any act (or proposed act) of a public authority which the court finds is (or would be) unlawful, it may grant such relief or remedy, or make such order, within its powers as it considers just and appropriate.

(2) But damages may be awarded only by a court which has power to award damages, or to order the payment of compensation, in civil proceedings.

(3) No award of damages is to be made unless, taking account of all the circumstances of the case, including—
 (a) any other relief or remedy granted, or order made, in relation to the act in question (by that or any other court), and
 (b) the consequences of any decision (of that or any other court) in respect of that act,
 the court is satisfied that the award is necessary to afford just satisfaction to the person in whose favour it is made.

(4) In determining—
 (a) whether to award damages, or
 (b) the amount of an award,
 the court must take into account the principles applied by the European Court of Human Rights in relation to the award of compensation under Article 41 of the Convention.

(5) A public authority against which damages are awarded is to be treated—

. . .

(b) for the purposes of the Civil Liability (Contribution) Act 1978 as liable in respect of damage suffered by the person to whom the award is made.

(6)   In this section—

"court" includes a tribunal;

"damages" means damages for an unlawful act of a public authority; and

"unlawful" means unlawful under section 6(1).

12 FREEDOM OF EXPRESSION

(1)   This section applies if a court is considering whether to grant any relief which, if granted, might affect the exercise of the Convention right to freedom of expression.

(2)   If the person against whom the application for relief is made ("the respondent") is neither present nor represented, no such relief is to be granted unless the court is satisfied—
(a) that the applicant has taken all practicable steps to notify the respondent; or
(b) that there are compelling reasons why the respondent should not be notified.

(3)   No such relief is to be granted so as to restrain publication before trial unless the court is satisfied that the applicant is likely to establish that publication should not be allowed.

(4)   The court must have particular regard to the importance of the Convention right to freedom of expression and, where the proceedings relate to material which the respondent claims, or which appears to the court, to be journalistic, literary or artistic material (or to conduct connected with such material), to—
(a) the extent to which—
    (i)   the material has, or is about to, become available to the public; or
    (ii) it is, or would be, in the public interest for the material to be published;
(b) any relevant privacy code.

(5)   In this section—

"court" includes a tribunal; and

"relief" includes any remedy or order (other than in criminal proceedings).

13 FREEDOM OF THOUGHT, CONSCIENCE AND RELIGION

(1)   If a court's determination of any question arising under this Act might affect the exercise by a religious organisation (itself or its members collectively) of the Convention right to freedom of thought, conscience and religion, it must have particular regard to the importance of that right.

(2)   In this section "court" includes a tribunal.

SCHEDULE 1

Part I THE CONVENTION

Article 2 Right to life
1   Everyone's right to life shall be protected by law. No one shall be deprived of his life intentionally save in the execution of a sentence of a court following his conviction of a crime for which this penalty is provided by law.

2   Deprivation of life shall not be regarded as inflicted in contravention of this Article when
     it results from the use of force which is no more than absolutely necessary:
     (a) in defence of any person from unlawful violence;
     (b) in order to effect a lawful arrest or to prevent the escape of a person lawfully
          detained;
     (c) in action lawfully taken for the purpose of quelling a riot or insurrection.

Article 3 Prohibition of torture
No one shall be subjected to torture or to inhuman or degrading treatment or punishment.

Article 4 Prohibition of slavery and forced labour
1   No one shall be held in slavery or servitude.

2   No one shall be required to perform forced or compulsory labour.

3   For the purpose of this Article the term "forced or compulsory labour" shall not include:
     (a) any work required to be done in the ordinary course of detention imposed according
          to the provisions of Article 5 of this Convention or during conditional release from
          such detention;
     (b) any service of a military character or, in case of conscientious objectors in countries
          where they are recognised, service exacted instead of compulsory military service;
     (c) any service exacted in case of an emergency or calamity threatening the life or well-
          being of the community;
     (d) any work or service which forms part of normal civic obligations.

Article 5 Right to liberty and security
1   Everyone has the right to liberty and security of person. No one shall be deprived of his
     liberty save in the following cases and in accordance with a procedure prescribed by law:
     (a) the lawful detention of a person after conviction by a competent court;
     (b) the lawful arrest or detention of a person for non-compliance with the lawful order of
          a court or in order to secure the fulfilment of any obligation prescribed by law;
     (c) the lawful arrest or detention of a person effected for the purpose of bringing him
          before the competent legal authority on reasonable suspicion of having committed an
          offence or when it is reasonably considered necessary to prevent his committing an
          offence or fleeing after having done so;
     (d) the detention of a minor by lawful order for the purpose of educational supervision or
          his lawful detention for the purpose of bringing him before the competent legal
          authority;
     (e) the lawful detention of persons for the prevention of the spreading of infectious
          diseases, of persons of unsound mind, alcoholics or drug addicts or vagrants;
     (f) the lawful arrest or detention of a person to prevent his effecting an unauthorised
          entry into the country or of a person against whom action is being taken with a view
          to deportation or extradition.

2   Everyone who is arrested shall be informed promptly, in a language which he understands,
     of the reasons for his arrest and of any charge against him.

3   Everyone arrested or detained in accordance with the provisions of paragraph 1(c) of this
     Article shall be brought promptly before a judge or other officer authorised by law to
     exercise judicial power and shall be entitled to trial within a reasonable time or to release
     pending trial. Release may be conditioned by guarantees to appear for trial.

4   Everyone who is deprived of his liberty by arrest or detention shall be entitled to take
     proceedings by which the lawfulness of his detention shall be decided speedily by a court
     and his release ordered if the detention is not lawful.

5   Everyone who has been the victim of arrest or detention in contravention of the provisions of this Article shall have an enforceable right to compensation.

Article 6 Right to a fair trial

1   In the determination of his civil rights and obligations or of any criminal charge against him, everyone is entitled to a fair and public hearing within a reasonable time by an independent and impartial tribunal established by law. Judgment shall be pronounced publicly but the press and public may be excluded from all or part of the trial in the interest of morals, public order or national security in a democratic society, where the interests of juveniles or the protection of the private life of the parties so require, or to the extent strictly necessary in the opinion of the court in special circumstances where publicity would prejudice the interests of justice.

2   Everyone charged with a criminal offence shall be presumed innocent until proved guilty according to law.

3   Everyone charged with a criminal offence has the following minimum rights:
   (a) to be informed promptly, in a language which he understands and in detail, of the nature and cause of the accusation against him;
   (b) to have adequate time and facilities for the preparation of his defence;
   (c) to defend himself in person or through legal assistance of his own choosing or, if he has not sufficient means to pay for legal assistance, to be given it free when the interests of justice so require;
   (d) to examine or have examined witnesses against him and to obtain the attendance and examination of witnesses on his behalf under the same conditions as witnesses against him;
   (e) to have the free assistance of an interpreter if he cannot understand or speak the language used in court.

Article 7 No punishment without law

1   No one shall be held guilty of any criminal offence on account of any act or omission which did not constitute a criminal offence under national or international law at the time when it was committed. Nor shall a heavier penalty be imposed than the one that was applicable at the time the criminal offence was committed.

2   This Article shall not prejudice the trial and punishment of any person for any act or omission which, at the time when it was committed, was criminal according to the general principles of law recognised by civilised nations.

Article 8 Right to respect for private and family life

1   Everyone has the right to respect for his private and family life, his home and his correspondence

2   There shall be no interference by a public authority with the exercise of this right except such as is in accordance with the law and is necessary in a democratic society in the interests of national security, public safety or the economic well-being of the country, for the prevention of disorder or crime, for the protection of health or morals, or for the protection of the rights and freedoms of others.

Article 9 Freedom of thought, conscience and religion

1   Everyone has the right to freedom of thought, conscience and religion; this right includes freedom to change his religion or belief and freedom, either alone or in community with others and in public or private, to manifest his religion or belief, in worship, teaching, practice and observance.

2	Freedom to manifest one's religion or beliefs shall be subject only to such limitations as are prescribed by law and are necessary in a democratic society in the interests of public safety, for the protection of public order, health or morals, or for the protection of the rights and freedoms of others.

Article 10 Freedom of expression

1	Everyone has the right to freedom of expression. This right shall include freedom to hold opinions and to receive and impart information and ideas without interference by public authority and regardless of frontiers. This Article shall not prevent States from requiring the licensing of broadcasting, television or cinema enterprises.

2	The exercise of these freedoms, since it carries with it duties and responsibilities, may be subject to such formalities, conditions, restrictions or penalties as are prescribed by law and are necessary in a democratic society, in the interests of national security, territorial integrity or public safety, for the prevention of disorder or crime, for the protection of health or morals, for the protection of the reputation or rights of others, for preventing the disclosure of information received in confidence, or for maintaining the authority and impartiality of the judiciary.

Article 11 Freedom of assembly and association

1	Everyone has the right to freedom of peaceful assembly and to freedom of association with others, including the right to form and to join trade unions for the protection of his interests.

2	No restrictions shall be placed on the exercise of these rights other than such as are prescribed by law and are necessary in a democratic society in the interests of national security or public safety, for the prevention of disorder or crime, for the protection of health or morals or for the protection of the rights and freedoms of others. This Article shall not prevent the imposition of lawful restrictions on the exercise of these rights by members of the armed forces, of the police or of the administration of the State.

Article 12 Right to marry

Men and women of marriageable age have the right to marry and to found a family, according to the national laws governing the exercise of this right.

Article 14 Prohibition of discrimination

The enjoyment of the rights and freedoms set forth in this Convention shall be secured without discrimination on any ground such as sex, race, colour, language, religion, political or other opinion, national or social origin, association with a national minority, property, birth or other status.

Article 16 Restrictions on political activity of aliens

Nothing in Articles 10, 11 and 14 shall be regarded as preventing the High Contracting Parties from imposing restrictions on the political activity of aliens.

Article 17 Prohibition of abuse of rights

Nothing in this Convention may be interpreted as implying for any State, group or person any right to engage in any activity or perform any act aimed at the destruction of any of the rights and freedoms set forth herein or at their limitation to a greater extent than is provided for in the Convention.

Article 18 Limitation on use of restrictions on rights

The restrictions permitted under this Convention to the said rights and freedoms shall not be applied for any purpose other than those for which they have been prescribed.

Part II **THE FIRST PROTOCOL**

Article 1 Protection of property
Every natural or legal person is entitled to the peaceful enjoyment of his possessions. No one shall be deprived of his possessions except in the public interest and subject to the conditions provided for by law and by the general principles of international law.
The preceding provisions shall not, however, in any way impair the right of a State to enforce such laws as it deems necessary to control the use of property in accordance with the general interest or to secure the payment of taxes or other contributions or penalties.

Article 2 Right to education
No person shall be denied the right to education. In the exercise of any functions which it assumes in relation to education and to teaching, the State shall respect the right of parents to ensure such education and teaching in conformity with their own religious and philosophical convictions.

Article 3 Right to free elections
The High Contracting Parties undertake to hold free elections at reasonable intervals by secret ballot, under conditions which will ensure the free expression of the opinion of the people in the choice of the legislature.

Article 1 of the Thirteenth Protocol *Abolition of the Death Penalty*
The death penalty shall be abolished. No one shall be condemned to such penalty or executed.

YOUTH JUSTICE AND CRIMINAL EVIDENCE ACT 1999

Part II **GIVING OF EVIDENCE OR INFORMATION FOR PURPOSES OF CRIMINAL PROCEEDINGS CHAPTER I**

SPECIAL MEASURES DIRECTIONS IN CASE OF VULNERABLE AND INTIMIDATED WITNESSES

Preliminary

16 WITNESSES ELIGIBLE FOR ASSISTANCE ON GROUNDS OF AGE OR INCAPACITY

(1)   For the purposes of this Chapter a witness in criminal proceedings (other than the accused) is eligible for assistance by virtue of this section—
(a) if under the age of 18 at the time of the hearing; or
(b) if the court considers that the quality of evidence given by the witness is likely to be diminished by reason of any circumstances falling within subsection (2).

(2)   The circumstances falling within this subsection are—
(a) that the witness—
(i)   suffers from mental disorder within the meaning of the Mental Health Act 1983, or
(ii) otherwise has a significant impairment of intelligence and social functioning;
(b) that the witness has a physical disability or is suffering from a physical disorder.

(3)   In subsection (1)(a) "the time of the hearing", in relation to a witness, means the time when it falls to the court to make a determination for the purposes of section 19(2) in relation to the witness.

(4)   In determining whether a witness falls within subsection (1)(b) the court must consider any views expressed by the witness.

(5)   In this Chapter references to the quality of a witness's evidence are to its quality in terms of completeness, coherence and accuracy; and for this purpose "coherence" refers to a witness's ability in giving evidence to give answers which address the questions put to the witness and can be understood both individually and collectively.

17 WITNESSES ELIGIBLE FOR ASSISTANCE ON GROUNDS OF FEAR OR DISTRESS ABOUT TESTIFYING

(1)   For the purposes of this Chapter a witness in criminal proceedings (other than the accused) is eligible for assistance by virtue of this subsection if the court is satisfied that the quality of evidence given by the witness is likely to be diminished by reason of fear or distress on the part of the witness in connection with testifying in the proceedings.

(2)   In determining whether a witness falls within subsection (1) the court must take into account, in particular—
   (a)   the nature and alleged circumstances of the offence to which the proceedings relate;
   (b)   the age of the witness;
   (c)   such of the following matters as appear to the court to be relevant, namely—
      (i)   the social and cultural background and ethnic origins of the witness,
      (ii)   the domestic and employment circumstances of the witness, and
      (iii) any religious beliefs or political opinions of the witness;
   (d)   any behaviour towards the witness on the part of—
      (i)   the accused,
      (ii)   members of the family or associates of the accused, or
      (iii) any other person who is likely to be an accused or a witness in the proceedings.

(3)   In determining that question the court must in addition consider any views expressed by the witness.

(4)   Where the complainant in respect of a sexual offence is a witness in proceedings relating to that offence (or to that offence and any other offences), the witness is eligible for assistance in relation to those proceedings by virtue of this subsection unless the witness has informed the court of the witness' wish not to be so eligible by virtue of this subsection.

(5)   A witness in proceedings relating to a relevant offence (or to a relevant offence and any other offences) is eligible for assistance in relation to those proceedings by virtue of this subsection unless the witness has informed the court of the witness's wish not to be so eligible by virtue of this subsection.

(6)   For the purposes of subsection (5) an offence is a relevant offence if it is an offence described in Schedule 1A.

(7)   The Secretary of State may by order amend Schedule 1A.

18 SPECIAL MEASURES AVAILABLE TO ELIGIBLE WITNESSES

(1)   For the purposes of this Chapter—
   (a)   the provision which may be made by a special measures direction by virtue of each of sections 23 to 30 is a special measure available in relation to a witness eligible for assistance by virtue of section 16; and
   (b)   the provision which may be made by such a direction by virtue of each of sections 23 to 28 is a special measure available in relation to a witness eligible for assistance by virtue of section 17;
but this subsection has effect subject to subsection (2).

(2)   Where (apart from this subsection) a special measure would, in accordance with subsection (1)(a) or (b), be available in relation to a witness in any proceedings, it shall not be taken by a court to be available in relation to the witness unless—

    (a) the court has been notified by the Secretary of State that relevant arrangements may be made available in the area in which it appears to the court that the proceedings will take place, and

    (b) the notice has not been withdrawn.

(3)   In subsection (2) "relevant arrangements" means arrangements for implementing the measure in question which cover the witness and the proceedings in question.

(4)   The withdrawal of a notice under that subsection relating to a special measure shall not affect the availability of that measure in relation to a witness if a special measures direction providing for that measure to apply to the witness's evidence has been made by the court before the notice is withdrawn.

(5)   The Secretary of State may by order make such amendments of this Chapter as he considers appropriate for altering the special measures which, in accordance with subsection (1)(a) or (b), are available in relation to a witness eligible for assistance by virtue of section 16 or (as the case may be) section 17, whether—

    (a) by modifying the provisions relating to any measure for the time being available in relation to such a witness,

    (b) by the addition—

       (i) (with or without modifications) of any measure which is for the time being available in relation to a witness eligible for assistance by virtue of the other of those sections, or

       (ii) of any new measure, or

    (c) by the removal of any measure.

Special measures directions

19 SPECIAL MEASURES DIRECTION RELATING TO ELIGIBLE WITNESS

(1)   This section applies where in any criminal proceedings—

    (a) a party to the proceedings makes an application for the court to give a direction under this section in relation to a witness in the proceedings other than the accused, or

    (b) the court of its own motion raises the issue whether such a direction should be given.

(2)   Where the court determines that the witness is eligible for assistance by virtue of section 16 or 17, the court must then—

    (a) determine whether any of the special measures available in relation to the witness (or any combination of them) would, in its opinion, be likely to improve the quality of evidence given by the witness; and

    (b) if so—

       (i) determine which of those measures (or combination of them) would, in its opinion, be likely to maximise so far as practicable the quality of such evidence; and

       (ii) give a direction under this section providing for the measure or measures so determined to apply to evidence given by the witness.

(3)   In determining for the purposes of this Chapter whether any special measure or measures would or would not be likely to improve, or to maximise so far as practicable, the quality of evidence given by the witness, the court must consider all the circumstances of the case, including in particular—

(a) any views expressed by the witness; and

(b) whether the measure or measures might tend to inhibit such evidence being effectively tested by a party to the proceedings.

(4) A special measures direction must specify particulars of the provision made by the direction in respect of each special measure which is to apply to the witness's evidence.

(5) In this Chapter "special measures direction" means a direction under this section.

(6) Nothing in this Chapter is to be regarded as affecting any power of a court to make an order or give leave of any description (in the exercise of its inherent jurisdiction or otherwise)—

(a) in relation to a witness who is not an eligible witness, or

(b) in relation to an eligible witness where (as, for example, in a case where a foreign language interpreter is to be provided) the order is made or the leave is given otherwise than by reason of the fact that the witness is an eligible witness.

20 FURTHER PROVISIONS ABOUT DIRECTIONS: GENERAL

(1) Subject to subsection (2) and section 21(8), a special measures direction has binding effect from the time it is made until the proceedings for the purposes of which it is made are either—

(a) determined (by acquittal, conviction or otherwise), or

(b) abandoned, in relation to the accused or (if there is more than one) in relation to each of the accused.

(2) The court may discharge or vary (or further vary) a special measures direction if it appears to the court to be in the interests of justice to do so, and may do so either—

(a) on an application made by a party to the proceedings, if there has been a material change of circumstances since the relevant time, or

(b) of its own motion.

(3) In subsection (2) "the relevant time" means —

(a) the time when the direction was given, or

(b) if a previous application has been made under that subsection, the time when the application (or last application) was made.

(4) Nothing in section 24(2) and (3), 27(4) to (7) or 28(4) to (6) is to be regarded as affecting the power of the court to vary or discharge a special measures direction under subsection (2).

(5) The court must state in open court its reasons for—

(a) giving or varying,

(b) refusing an application for, or for the variation or discharge of, or

(c) discharging,

a special measures direction and, if it is a magistrates' court, must cause them to be entered in the register of its proceedings.

. . .

21 SPECIAL PROVISIONS RELATING TO CHILD WITNESSES

(1) For the purposes of this section—

(a) a witness in criminal proceedings is a "child witness" if he is an eligible witness by reason of section 16(1)(a) (whether or not he is an eligible witness by reason of any other provision of section 16 or 17); and

(c) a "relevant recording", in relation to a child witness, is a video recording of an interview of the witness made with a view to its admission as evidence in chief of the witness.

(2)   Where the court, in making a determination for the purposes of section 19(2), determines that a witness in criminal proceedings is a child witness, the court must—
(a) first have regard to subsections (3) to (4C) below; and
(b) then have regard to section 19(2);
and for the purposes of section 19(2), as it then applies to the witness, any special measures required to be applied in relation to him by virtue of this section shall be treated as if they were measures determined by the court, pursuant to section 19(2)(a) and (b)(i), to be ones that (whether on their own or with any other special measures) would be likely to maximise, so far as practicable, the quality of his evidence.

(3)   The primary rule in the case of a child witness is that the court must give a special measures direction in relation to the witness which complies with the following requirements—
(a) it must provide for any relevant recording to be admitted under section 27 (video recorded evidence in chief); and
(b) it must provide for any evidence given by the witness in the proceedings which is not given by means of a video recording (whether in chief or otherwise) to be given by means of a live link in accordance with section 24.

(4)   The primary rule is subject to the following limitations—
(a) the requirement contained in subsection (3)(a) or (b) has effect subject to the availability (within the meaning of section 18(2)) of the special measure in question in relation to the witness;
(b) the requirement contained in subsection (3)(a) also has effect subject to section 27(2)
(ba) if the witness informs the court of the witness's wish that the rule should not apply or should apply only in part, the rule does not apply to the extent that the court is satisfied that not complying with the rule would not diminish the quality of the witness's evidence; and
(c) the rule does not apply to the extent that the court is satisfied that compliance with it would not be likely to maximise the quality of the witness's evidence so far as practicable (whether because the application to that evidence of one or more other special measures available in relation to the witness would have that result or for any other reason).

(4A) Where as a consequence of all or part of the primary rule being disapplied under subsection (4)(ba) a witness's evidence or any part of it would fall to be given as testimony in court, the court must give a special measures direction making such provision as is described in section 23 for the evidence or that part of it.

(4B) The requirement in subsection (4A) is subject to the following limitations—
(a) if the witness informs the court of the witness's wish that the requirement in subsection (4A) should not apply, the requirement does not apply to the extent that the court is satisfied that not complying with it would not diminish the quality of the witness's evidence; and
(b) the requirement does not apply to the extent that the court is satisfied that making such a provision would not be likely to maximise the quality of the witness's evidence so far as practicable (whether because the application to that evidence of one or more other special measures available in relation to the witness would have that result or for any other reason).

(4C) In making a decision under subsection (4)(ba) or (4B)(a), the court must take into account the following factors (and any others it considers relevant)—
(a) the age and maturity of the witness;
(b) the ability of the witness to understand the consequences of giving evidence otherwise than in accordance with the requirements in subsection (3) or (as the case may be) inaccordance with the requirement in subsection (4A);

(c) the relationship (if any) between the witness and the accused;

(d) the witness's social and cultural background and ethnic origins;

(e) the nature and alleged circumstances of the offence to which the proceedings relate.

(8) Where a special measures direction is given in relation to a child witness who is an eligible witness by reason only of section 16(1)(a), then—

(a) subject to subsection (9) below, and

(b) except where the witness has already begun to give evidence in the proceedings,

the direction shall cease to have effect at the time when the witness attains the age of 18.

(9) Where a special measures direction is given in relation to a child witness who is an eligible witness by reason only of section 16(1)(a) and—

(a) the direction provides—

(i)   for any relevant recording to be admitted under section 27 as evidence in chief of the witness, or

(ii) for the special measure available under section 28 to apply in relation to the witness, and

(b) if it provides for that special measure to so apply, the witness is still under the age of 18 when the video recording is made for the purposes of section 28, then, so far as it provides as mentioned in paragraph (a)(i) or (ii) above, the direction shall continue

to have effect in accordance with section 20(1) even though the witness subsequently attains that age.

22 EXTENSION OF PROVISIONS OF SECTION 21 TO CERTAIN WITNESSES OVER 18

(1) For the purposes of this section—

(a) a witness in criminal proceedings (other than the accused) is a "qualifying witness" if he—

(i)   is not an eligible witness at the time of the hearing (as defined by section 16(3)), but

(ii) was under the age of 18 when a relevant recording was made; and

(c) a "relevant recording", in relation to a witness, is a video recording of an interview of the witness made with a view to its admission as evidence in chief of the witness.

(2) Subsections (2) to (4) and (4C) of section 21, so far as relating to the giving of a direction complying with the requirement contained in section 21(3)(a), apply to a qualifying witness in respect of the relevant recording as they apply to a child witness (within the meaning of that section).

22A SPECIAL PROVISIONS RELATING TO SEXUAL OFFENCES

(1) This section applies where in criminal proceedings relating to a sexual offence (or to a sexual offence and other offences) the complainant in respect of that offence is a witness in the proceedings.

(2) This section does not apply if the place of trial is a magistrates' court.

(3) This section does not apply if the complainant is an eligible witness by reason of section 16(1)(a) (whether or not the complainant is an eligible witness by reason of any other provision of section 16 or 17).

(4) If a party to the proceedings makes an application under section 19(1)(a) for a special measures direction in relation to the complainant, the party may request that the direction provide for any relevant recording to be admitted under section 27 (video recorded evidence in chief).

(5)   Subsection (6) applies if—
(a) a party to the proceedings makes a request under subsection (4) with respect to the complainant, and
(b) the court determines for the purposes of section 19(2) that the complainant is eligible for assistance by virtue of section 16(1)(b) or 17.

(6)   The court must—
(a) first have regard to subsections (7) to (9); and
(b) then have regard to section 19(2);
and for the purposes of section 19(2), as it then applies to the complainant, any special measure required to be applied in relation to the complainant by virtue of this section is to be treated as if it were a measure determined by the court, pursuant to section 19(2)(a) and (b)(i), to be one that (whether on its own or with any other special measures) would be likely to maximise, so far as practicable, the quality of the complainant's evidence.

(7)   The court must give a special measures direction in relation to the complainant that provides for any relevant recording to be admitted under section 27.

(8)   The requirement in subsection (7) has effect subject to section 27(2).

(9)   The requirement in subsection (7) does not apply to the extent that the court is satisfied that compliance with it would not be likely to maximise the quality of the complainant's evidence so far as practicable (whether because the application to that evidence of one or more other special measures available in relation to the complainant would have that result or for any other reason).

(10) In this section "relevant recording", in relation to a complainant, is a video recording of an interview of the complainant made with a view to its admission as the evidence in chief of the complainant.

Special measures

23 SCREENING WITNESS FROM ACCUSED

(1)   A special measures direction may provide for the witness, while giving testimony or being sworn in court, to be prevented by means of a screen or other arrangement from seeing the accused.

(2)   But the screen or other arrangement must not prevent the witness from being able to see, and to be seen by—
(a) the judge or justices (or both) and the jury (if there is one);
(b) legal representatives acting in the proceedings; and
(c) any interpreter or other person appointed (in pursuance of the direction or otherwise) to assist the witness.

(3)   Where two or more legal representatives are acting for a party to the proceedings, subsection (2)(b) is to be regarded as satisfied in relation to those representatives if the witness is able at all material times to see and be seen by at least one of them.

24 EVIDENCE BY LIVE LINK

(1)   A special measures direction may provide for the witness to give evidence by means of a live link.

(1A) Such a direction may also provide for a specified person to accompany the witness while the witness is giving evidence by live link.

(1B) In determining who may accompany the witness, the court must have regard to the wishes of the witness.

(2) Where a direction provides for the witness to give evidence by means of a live link, the witness may not give evidence in any other way without the permission of the court.

(3) The court may give permission for the purposes of subsection (2) if it appears to the court to be in the interests of justice to do so, and may do so either—
(a) on an application by a party to the proceedings, if there has been a material change of circumstances since the relevant time, or
(b) of its own motion.

(4) In subsection (3) "the relevant time" means —
(a) the time when the direction was given, or
(b) if a previous application has been made under that subsection, the time when the application (or last application) was made.

(8) In this Chapter "live link" means a live television link or other arrangement whereby a witness, while absent from the courtroom or other place where the proceedings are being held, is able to see and hear a person there and to be seen and heard by the persons specified in section 23(2)(a) to (c).

25 EVIDENCE GIVEN IN PRIVATE

(1) A special measures direction may provide for the exclusion from the court, during the giving of the witness's evidence, of persons of any description specified in the direction.

(2) The persons who may be so excluded do not include—
(a) the accused,
(b) legal representatives acting in the proceedings, or
(c) any interpreter or other person appointed (in pursuance of the direction or otherwise) to assist the witness.

(3) A special measures direction providing for representatives of news gathering or reporting organisations to be so excluded shall be expressed not to apply to one named person who—
(a) is a representative of such an organisation, and
(b) has been nominated for the purpose by one or more such organisations, unless it appears to the court that no such nomination has been made.

(4) A special measures direction may only provide for the exclusion of persons under this section where—
(a) the proceedings relate to a sexual offence; or
(b) it appears to the court that there are reasonable grounds for believing that any person other than the accused has sought, or will seek, to intimidate the witness in connection with testifying in the proceedings.

(5) Any proceedings from which persons are excluded under this section (whether or not those persons include representatives of news gathering or reporting organisations) shall nevertheless be taken to be held in public for the purposes of any privilege or exemption from liability available in respect of fair, accurate and contemporaneous reports of legal proceedings held in public.

26 REMOVAL OF WIGS AND GOWNS

A special measures direction may provide for the wearing of wigs or gowns to be dispensed with during the giving of the witness's evidence.

FINANCE ACT 2000

144 OFFENCE OF FRAUDULENT EVASION OF INCOME TAX

(1) A person commits an offence if he is knowingly concerned in the fraudulent evasion of income tax by him or any other person.

(2) A person guilty of an offence under this section is liable—
   (a) on summary conviction, to imprisonment for a term not exceeding six months or a fine not exceeding the statutory maximum, or both;
   (b) on conviction on indictment, to imprisonment for a term not exceeding seven years or a fine, or both.

(3) This section applies to things done or omitted on or after 1st January 2001.

TERRORISM ACT 2000

1 TERRORISM: INTERPRETATION

(1) In this Act "terrorism" means the use or threat of action where—
   (a) the action falls within subsection (2),
   (b) the use or threat is designed to influence the government or an international governmental organisation or to intimidate the public or a section of the public, and
   (c) the use or threat is made for the purpose of advancing a political, religious, racial or ideological cause.

(2) Action falls within this subsection if it—
   (a) involves serious violence against a person,
   (b) involves serious damage to property,
   (c) endangers a person's life, other than that of the person committing the action,
   (d) creates a serious risk to the health or safety of the public or a section of the public, or
   (e) is designed seriously to interfere with or seriously to disrupt an electronic system.

(3) The use or threat of action falling within subsection (2) which involves the use of firearms or explosives is terrorism whether or not subsection (1)(b) is satisfied.

(4) In this section—
   (a) "action" includes action outside the United Kingdom,
   (b) a reference to any person or to property is a reference to any person, or to property, wherever situated,
   (c) a reference to the public includes a reference to the public of a country other than the United Kingdom, and
   (d) "the government" means the government of the United Kingdom, of a Part of the United Kingdom or of a country other than the United Kingdom.

(5) In this Act a reference to action taken for the purposes of terrorism includes a reference to action taken for the benefit of a proscribed organisation.

3 PROSCRIPTION

(1) For the purposes of this Act an organisation is proscribed if—
   (a) it is listed in Schedule 2, or
   (b) it operates under the same name as an organisation listed in that Schedule.

(2)   Subsection (1)(b) shall not apply in relation to an organisation listed in Schedule 2 if its entry is the subject of a note in that Schedule.

(3)   The Secretary of State may by order—
(a)   add an organisation to Schedule 2;
(b)   remove an organisation from that Schedule;
(c)   amend that Schedule in some other way.

(4)   The Secretary of State may exercise his power under subsection (3)(a) in respect of an organisation only if he believes that it is concerned in terrorism.

(5)   For the purposes of subsection (4) an organisation is concerned in terrorism if it—
(a)   commits or participates in acts of terrorism,
(b)   prepares for terrorism,
(c)   promotes or encourages terrorism, or
(d)   is otherwise concerned in terrorism.

(5A)   The cases in which an organisation promotes or encourages terrorism for the purposes of subsection (5)(c) include any case in which activities of the organisation—
(a)   include the unlawful glorification of the commission or preparation (whether in the past, in the future or generally) of acts of terrorism; or
(b)   are carried out in a manner that ensures that the organisation is associated with statements containing any such glorification.

(5B)   The glorification of any conduct is unlawful for the purposes of subsection (5A) if there are persons who may become aware of it who could reasonably be expected to infer that what is being glorified, is being glorified as—
(a)   conduct that should be emulated in existing circumstances, or
(b)   conduct that is illustrative of a type of conduct that should be so emulated.

(5C)   In this section—
'glorification' includes any form of praise or celebration, and cognate expressions are to be construed accordingly;

'statement' includes a communication without words consisting of sounds or images or both.

. . .

11 MEMBERSHIP

(1)   A person commits an offence if he belongs or professes to belong to a proscribed organisation.

(2)   It is a defence for a person charged with an offence under subsection (1) to prove—
(a)   that the organisation was not proscribed on the last (or only) occasion on which he became a member or began to profess to be a member, and
(b)   that he has not taken part in the activities of the organisation at any time while it was proscribed.

(3)   A person guilty of an offence under this section shall be liable—
(a)   on conviction on indictment, to imprisonment for a term not exceeding ten years, to a fine or to both, or
(b)   on summary conviction, to imprisonment for a term not exceeding six months, to a fine not exceeding the statutory maximum or to both.

(4)   In subsection (2) "proscribed" means proscribed for the purposes of any of the following—

(a) this Act;
(b) the Northern Ireland (Emergency Provisions) Act 1996;
(c) the Northern Ireland (Emergency Provisions) Act 1991;
(d) the Prevention of Terrorism (Temporary Provisions) Act 1989;
(e) the Prevention of Terrorism (Temporary Provisions) Act 1984;
(f) the Northern Ireland (Emergency Provisions) Act 1978;
(g) the Prevention of Terrorism (Temporary Provisions) Act 1976;
(h) the Prevention of Terrorism (Temporary Provisions) Act 1974;
(i) the Northern Ireland (Emergency Provisions) Act 1973.

12 SUPPORT

(1) A person commits an offence if—
   (a) he invites support for a proscribed organisation, and
   (b) the support is not, or is not restricted to, the provision of money or other property (within the meaning of section 15).

(2) A person commits an offence if he arranges, manages or assists in arranging or managing a meeting which he knows is—
   (a) to support a proscribed organisation,
   (b) to further the activities of a proscribed organisation, or
   (c) to be addressed by a person who belongs or professes to belong to a proscribed organisation.

(3) A person commits an offence if he addresses a meeting and the purpose of his address is to encourage support for a proscribed organisation or to further its activities.

(4) Where a person is charged with an offence under subsection (2)(c) in respect of a private meeting it is a defence for him to prove that he had no reasonable cause to believe that the address mentioned in subsection (2)(c) would support a proscribed organisation or further its activities.

(5) In subsections (2) to (4)—
   (a) "meeting" means a meeting of three or more persons, whether or not the public are admitted, and
   (b) a meeting is private if the public are not admitted.

(6) A person guilty of an offence under this section shall be liable—
   (a) on conviction on indictment, to imprisonment for a term not exceeding ten years, to a fine or to both, or
   (b) on summary conviction, to imprisonment for a term not exceeding six months, to a fine not exceeding the statutory maximum or to both.

13 UNIFORM

(1) A person in a public place commits an offence if he—
   (a) wears an item of clothing, or
   (b) wears, carries or displays an article,
   in such a way or in such circumstances as to arouse reasonable suspicion that he is a member or supporter of a proscribed organisation.

. . .

(3) A person guilty of an offence under this section shall be liable on summary conviction to—
   (a) imprisonment for a term not exceeding six months,
   (b) a fine not exceeding level 5 on the standard scale, or
   (c) both.

14 TERRORIST PROPERTY

(1)   In this Act "terrorist property" means—
    (a) money or other property which is likely to be used for the purposes of terrorism (including any resources of a proscribed organisation),
    (b) proceeds of the commission of acts of terrorism, and
    (c) proceeds of acts carried out for the purposes of terrorism.

(2)   In subsection (1)—
    (a) a reference to proceeds of an act includes a reference to any property which wholly or partly, and directly or indirectly, represents the proceeds of the act (including payments or other rewards in connection with its commission), and
    (b) the reference to an organisation's resources includes a reference to any money or other property which is applied or made available, or is to be applied or made available, for use by the organisation.

15 FUND-RAISING

(1)   A person commits an offence if he—
    (a) invites another to provide money or other property, and
    (b) intends that it should be used, or has reasonable cause to suspect that it may be used, for the purposes of terrorism.

(2)   A person commits an offence if he—
    (a) receives money or other property, and
    (b) intends that it should be used, or has reasonable cause to suspect that it may be used, for the purposes of terrorism.

(3)   A person commits an offence if he—
    (a) provides money or other property, and
    (b) knows or has reasonable cause to suspect that it will or may be used for the purposes of terrorism.

(4)   In this section a reference to the provision of money or other property is a reference to its being given, lent or otherwise made available, whether or not for consideration.

16 USE AND POSSESSION

(1)   A person commits an offence if he uses money or other property for the purposes of terrorism.

(2)   A person commits an offence if he—
    (a) possesses money or other property, and
    (b) intends that it should be used, or has reasonable cause to suspect that it may be used, for the purposes of terrorism.

17 FUNDING ARRANGEMENTS

A person commits an offence if—
(a)   he enters into or becomes concerned in an arrangement as a result of which money or other property is made available or is to be made available to another, and

(b)   he knows or has reasonable cause to suspect that it will or may be used for the purposes of terrorism.

18 MONEY LAUNDERING

(1) A person commits an offence if he enters into or becomes concerned in an arrangement which facilitates the retention or control by or on behalf of another person of terrorist property—
   (a) by concealment,
   (b) by removal from the jurisdiction,
   (c) by transfer to nominees, or
   (d) in any other way.

(2) It is a defence for a person charged with an offence under subsection (1) to prove that he did not know and had no reasonable cause to suspect that the arrangement related to terrorist property.

19 DISCLOSURE OF INFORMATION: DUTY

(1) This section applies where a person—
   (a) believes or suspects that another person has committed an offence under any of sections 15 to 18, and
   (b) bases his belief or suspicion on information which comes to his attention—
      (i)   in the course of a trade, profession or business, or
      (ii) in the course of his employment (whether or not in the course of a trade, profession or business).

(1A) But this section does not apply if the information came to the person in the course of a business in the regulated sector.

(2) The person commits an offence if he does not disclose to a constable as soon as is reasonably practicable—
   (a) his belief or suspicion, and
   (b) the information on which it is based.

(3) It is a defence for a person charged with an offence under subsection (2) to prove that he had a reasonable excuse for not making the disclosure.

(4) Where—
   (a) a person is in employment,
   (b) his employer has established a procedure for the making of disclosures of the matters specified in subsection (2), and
   (c) he is charged with an offence under that subsection,
      it is a defence for him to prove that he disclosed the matters specified in that subsection in accordance with the procedure.

(5) Subsection (2) does not require disclosure by a professional legal adviser of—
   (a) information which he obtains in privileged circumstances, or
   (b) a belief or suspicion based on information which he obtains in privileged circumstances.

(6) For the purpose of subsection (5) information is obtained by an adviser in privileged circumstances if it comes to him, otherwise than with a view to furthering a criminal purpose—
   (a) from a client or a client's representative, in connection with the provision of legal advice by the adviser to the client,
   (b) from a person seeking legal advice from the adviser, or from the person's representative, or
   (c) from any person, for the purpose of actual or contemplated legal proceedings.

(7)   For the purposes of subsection (1)(a) a person shall be treated as having committed an offence under one of sections 15 to 18 if—
(a) he has taken an action or been in possession of a thing, and
(b) he would have committed an offence under one of those sections if he had been in the United Kingdom at the time when he took the action or was in possession of the thing.

. . .

(8)   A person guilty of an offence under this section shall be liable—
(a) on conviction on indictment, to imprisonment for a term not exceeding five years, to a fine or to both, or
(b) on summary conviction, to imprisonment for a term not exceeding six months, or to a fine not exceeding the statutory maximum or to both.

. . .

54 WEAPONS TRAINING

(1)   A person commits an offence if he provides instruction or training in the making or use of—
(a) firearms,
(aa) radioactive material or weapons designed or adapted for the discharge of any radioactive material,
(b) explosives, or
(c) chemical, biological or nuclear weapons.

(2)   A person commits an offence if he receives instruction or training in the making or use of—
(a) firearms,
(aa) radioactive material or weapons designed or adapted for the discharge of any radioactive material,
(b) explosives, or
(c) chemical, biological or nuclear weapons.

(3)   A person commits an offence if he invites another to receive instruction or training and the receipt—
(a) would constitute an offence under subsection (2), or
(b) would constitute an offence under subsection (2) but for the fact that it is to take place outside the United Kingdom.

(4)   For the purpose of subsections (1) and (3)—
(a) a reference to the provision of instruction includes a reference to making it available either generally or to one or more specific persons, and
(b) an invitation to receive instruction or training may be either general or addressed to one or more specific persons.

(5)   It is a defence for a person charged with an offence under this section in relation to instruction or training to prove that his action or involvement was wholly for a purpose other than assisting, preparing for or participating in terrorism.

(6)   A person guilty of an offence under this section shall be liable—
(a) on conviction on indictment, to imprisonment for a term not exceeding ten years, to a fine or to both, or
(b) on summary conviction, to imprisonment for a term not exceeding six months, to a fine not exceeding the statutory maximum or to both.

. . .

55 WEAPONS TRAINING: INTERPRETATION

In section 54—

"biological weapon" means a biological agent or toxin (within the meaning of the Biological Weapons Act 1974) in a form capable of use for hostile purposes or anything to which section 1(1)(b) of that Act applies,

"chemical weapon" has the meaning given by section 1 of the Chemical Weapons Act 1996, and

"radioactive material" means radioactive material capable of endangering life or causing harm to human health.

56 DIRECTING TERRORIST ORGANISATION

(1) A person commits an offence if he directs, at any level, the activities of an organisation which is concerned in the commission of acts of terrorism.

(2) A person guilty of an offence under this section is liable on conviction on indictment to imprisonment for life.

57 POSSESSION FOR TERRORIST PURPOSES

(1) A person commits an offence if he possesses an article in circumstances which give rise to a reasonable suspicion that his possession is for a purpose connected with the commission, preparation or instigation of an act of terrorism.

(2) It is a defence for a person charged with an offence under this section to prove that his possession of the article was not for a purpose connected with the commission, preparation or instigation of an act of terrorism.

(3) In proceedings for an offence under this section, if it is proved that an article—
(a) was on any premises at the same time as the accused, or
(b) was on premises of which the accused was the occupier or which he habitually used otherwise than as a member of the public,
the court may assume that the accused possessed the article, unless he proves that he did not know of its presence on the premises or that he had no control over it.

(4) A person guilty of an offence under this section shall be liable—
(a) on conviction on indictment, to imprisonment for a term not exceeding 15 years, to a fine or to both, or
(b) on summary conviction, to imprisonment for a term not exceeding six months, to a fine not exceeding the statutory maximum or to both.

58 COLLECTION OF INFORMATION

(1) A person commits an offence if—
(a) he collects or makes a record of information of a kind likely to be useful to a person committing or preparing an act of terrorism, or
(b) he possesses a document or record containing information of that kind.

(2) In this section "record" includes a photographic or electronic record.

(3) It is a defence for a person charged with an offence under this section to prove that he had a reasonable excuse for his action or possession.

(4)   A person guilty of an offence under this section shall be liable—
    (a)   on conviction on indictment, to imprisonment for a term not exceeding 10 years, to a fine or to both, or
    (b)   on summary conviction, to imprisonment for a term not exceeding six months, to a fine not exceeding the statutory maximum or to both.

. . .

58A ELICITING, PUBLISHING OR COMMUNICATING INFORMATION ABOUT MEMBERS OF ARMED FORCES ETC ﹨

(1)   A person commits an offence who—
    (a)   elicits or attempts to elicit information about an individual who is or has been—
        (i)   a member of Her Majesty's forces,
        (ii)   a member of any of the intelligence services, or
        (iii)   a constable,
            which is of a kind likely to be useful to a person committing or preparing an act of terrorism, or
    (b)   publishes or communicates any such information.

(2)   It is a defence for a person charged with an offence under this section to prove that they had a reasonable excuse for their action.

(3)   A person guilty of an offence under this section is liable—
    (a)   on conviction on indictment, to imprisonment for a term not exceeding 10 years or to a fine, or to both;
    (b)   on summary conviction—
        (i)   in England and Wales or Scotland, to imprisonment for a term not exceeding 12 months or to a fine not exceeding the statutory maximum, or to both; . . .

(4)   In this section "the intelligence services" means the Security Service, the Secret Intelligence Service and GCHQ (within the meaning of section 3 of the Intelligence Services Act 1994 (c 13)).

59 ENGLAND AND WALES

(1)   A person commits an offence if—
    (a)   he incites another person to commit an act of terrorism wholly or partly outside the United Kingdom, and
    (b)   the act would, if committed in England and Wales, constitute one of the offences listed in subsection (2).

(2)   Those offences are—
    (a)   murder,
    (b)   an offence under section 18 of the Offences against the Person Act 1861 (wounding with intent),
    (c)   an offence under section 23 or 24 of that Act (poison),
    (d)   an offence under section 28 or 29 of that Act (explosions), and
    (e)   an offence under section 1(2) of the Criminal Damage Act 1971 (endangering life by damaging property).

(3)   A person guilty of an offence under this section shall be liable to any penalty to which he would be liable on conviction of the offence listed in subsection (2) which corresponds to the act which he incites.

(4)   For the purposes of subsection (1) it is immaterial whether or not the person incited is in the United Kingdom at the time of the incitement.

(5)   Nothing in this section imposes criminal liability on any person acting on behalf of, or holding office under, the Crown.

118 DEFENCES

(1)   Subsection (2) applies where in accordance with a provision mentioned in subsection (5) it is a defence for a person charged with an offence to prove a particular matter.

(2)   If the person adduces evidence which is sufficient to raise an issue with respect to the matter the court or jury shall assume that the defence is satisfied unless the prosecution proves beyond reasonable doubt that it is not.

(3)   Subsection (4) applies where in accordance with a provision mentioned in subsection (5) a court—
    (a) may make an assumption in relation to a person charged with an offence unless a particular matter is proved, or
    (b) may accept a fact as sufficient evidence unless a particular matter is proved.

(4)   If evidence is adduced which is sufficient to raise an issue with respect to the matter mentioned in subsection (3)(a) or (b) the court shall treat it as proved unless the prosecution disproves it beyond reasonable doubt.

(5)   The provisions in respect of which subsections (2) and (4) apply are—
    (a) sections 12(4), 39(5)(a), 54, 57, 58, 58A, 77 and 103 of this Act, and

. . .

121 INTERPRETATION

In this Act—
    "act" and "action" include omission,

    "article" includes substance and any other thing,

    "British Transport Police Force" means the constables appointed under section 53 of the British Transport Commission Act 1949 (cxxix),

    "customs officer" means an officer of Revenue and Customs,

    "dwelling" means a building or part of a building used as a dwelling, and a vehicle which is habitually stationary and which is used as a dwelling,

    "explosive" means—

        (a) an article or substance manufactured for the purpose of producing a practical effect by explosion,
        (b) materials for making an article or substance within paragraph (a),
        (c) anything used or intended to be used for causing or assisting in causing an explosion, and
        (d) a part of anything within paragraph (a) or (c),
    "firearm" includes an air gun or air pistol,

    "immigration officer" means a person appointed as an immigration officer under paragraph 1 of Schedule 2 to the Immigration Act 1971, "the Islands" means the Channel Islands and the Isle of Man,

"organisation" includes any association or combination of persons,

"premises", except in section 63D, includes any place and in particular includes—
   (a) a vehicle,
   (b) an offshore installation within the meaning given in section 44 of the Petroleum Act 1998, and
   (c) a tent or moveable structure,

"property" includes property wherever situated and whether real or personal, heritable or moveable, and things in action and other intangible or incorporeal property,

"public place" means a place to which members of the public have or are permitted to have access, whether or not for payment,

"road" has the same meaning as in the Road Traffic Act 1988 (in relation to England and Wales), . . . and

"vehicle", except in sections 48 to 52 and Schedule 7, includes an aircraft, hovercraft, train or vessel.

As amended Terrorism Act 2006, s 34; Counter-Terrorism Act 2008, s 77.

ANTI-TERRORISM, CRIME AND SECURITY ACT 2001

113 USE OF NOXIOUS SUBSTANCES OR THINGS TO CAUSE HARM AND INTIMIDATE

(1) A person who takes any action which—
   (a) involves the use of a noxious substance or other noxious thing;
   (b) has or is likely to have an effect falling within subsection (2); and
   (c) is designed to influence the government or an international governmental organisation or to intimidate the public or a section of the public,
   is guilty of an offence.

(2) Action has an effect falling within this subsection if it—
   (a) causes serious violence against a person anywhere in the world;
   (b) causes serious damage to real or personal property anywhere in the world;
   (c) endangers human life or creates a serious risk to the health or safety of the public or a section of the public; or
   (d) induces in members of the public the fear that the action is likely to endanger their lives or create a serious risk to their health or safety;
   but any effect on the person taking the action is to be disregarded.

(3) A person who—
   (a) makes a threat that he or another will take any action which constitutes an offence under subsection (1); and
   (b) intends thereby to induce in a person anywhere in the world the fear that the threat is likely to be carried out,
   is guilty of an offence.

(4)   A person guilty of an offence under this section is liable—
    (a) on summary conviction, to imprisonment for a term not exceeding six months or a fine not exceeding the statutory maximum (or both); and
    (b) on conviction on indictment, to imprisonment for a term not exceeding fourteen years or a fine (or both).

(5)   In this section—

"the government" means the government of the United Kingdom, of a part of the United Kingdom or of a country other than the United Kingdom; and

"the public" includes the public of a country other than the United Kingdom.

113A APPLICATION OF SECTION 113

(1)   Section 113 applies to conduct done—
    (a) in the United Kingdom; or
    (b) outside the United Kingdom which satisfies the following two conditions.

(2)   The first condition is that the conduct is done for the purpose of advancing a political, religious, racial or ideological cause.

(3)   The second condition is that the conduct is—
    (a) by a United Kingdom national or a United Kingdom resident;
    (b) by any person done to, or in relation to, a United Kingdom national, a United Kingdom resident or a protected person; or
    (c) by any person done in circumstances which fall within section 63D(1)(b) and (c) or (3)(b) and (c) of the Terrorism Act 2000.

(4)   The following expressions have the same meaning as they have for the purposes of sections 63C and 63D of that Act—
    (a) "United Kingdom national";
    (b) "United Kingdom resident";
    (c) "protected person".

(5)   For the purposes of this section it is immaterial whether a person knows that another is a United Kingdom national, a United Kingdom resident or a protected person.

113B CONSENT TO PROSECUTION FOR OFFENCE UNDER SECTION 113

(1)   Proceedings for an offence committed under section 113 outside the United Kingdom are not to be started—
    (a) in England and Wales, except by or with the consent of the Attorney General;
    (b) in Northern Ireland, except by or with the consent of the Advocate General for Northern Ireland.

(2)   Proceedings for an offence committed under section 113 outside the United Kingdom may be taken, and the offence may for incidental purposes be treated as having been committed, in any part of the United Kingdom.

(3)   In relation to any time before the coming into force of section 27(1) of the Justice (Northern Ireland) Act 2002, the reference in subsection (1)(b) to the Advocate General for Northern Ireland is to be read as a reference to the Attorney General for Northern Ireland.

114 HOAXES INVOLVING NOXIOUS SUBSTANCES OR THINGS

(1)   A person is guilty of an offence if he—
    (a)   places any substance or other thing in any place; or
    (b)   sends any substance or other thing from one place to another (by post, rail or any other means whatever);
with the intention of inducing in a person anywhere in the world a belief that it is likely to be (or contain) a noxious substance or other noxious thing and thereby endanger human life or create a serious risk to human health.

(2)   A person is guilty of an offence if he communicates any information which he knows or believes to be false with the intention of inducing in a person anywhere in the world a belief that a noxious substance or other noxious thing is likely to be present (whether at the time the information is communicated or later) in any place and thereby endanger human life or create a serious risk to human health.

(3)   A person guilty of an offence under this section is liable—
    (a)   on summary conviction, to imprisonment for a term not exceeding six months or a fine not exceeding the statutory maximum (or both); and
    (b)   on conviction on indictment, to imprisonment for a term not exceeding seven years or a fine (or both).

115 SECTIONS 113 AND 114: SUPPLEMENTARY

(1)   For the purposes of sections 113 and 114 "substance" includes any biological agent and any other natural or artificial substance (whatever its form, origin or method of production).

(2)   For a person to be guilty of an offence under section 113(3) or 114 it is not necessary for him to have any particular person in mind as the person in whom he intends to induce the belief in question.

As amended by Crime (International Co-Operation) Act 2003, s 53; Terrorism Act 2006.

MOBILE TELEPHONES (RE-PROGRAMMING) ACT 2002

1 RE-PROGRAMMING MOBILE TELEPHONE ETC

(1)   A person commits an offence if—
    (a)   he changes a unique device identifier, . . .
    (b)   he interferes with the operation of a unique device identifier,
    (c)   he offers or agrees to change, or interfere with the operation of, a unique device identifier, or
    (d)   he offers or agrees to arrange for another person to change, or interfere with the operation of, a unique device identifier.

(2)   A unique device identifier is an electronic equipment identifier which is unique to a mobile wireless communications device.

(3)   But a person does not commit an offence under this section if—
    (a)   he is the manufacturer of the device, or

(b) he does the act mentioned in subsection (1) with the written consent of the manufacturer of the device.

(4) A person guilty of an offence under this section is liable—
   (a) on summary conviction, to imprisonment for a term not exceeding 6 months or to a fine not exceeding the statutory maximum or to both, or
   (b) on conviction on indictment, to imprisonment for a term not exceeding 5 years or to a fine or to both.

2 POSSESSION OR SUPPLY OF ANYTHING FOR RE-PROGRAMMING PURPOSES

(1) A person commits an offence if—
   (a) he has in his custody or under his control anything which may be used for the purpose of changing or interfering with the operation of a unique device identifier, and
   (b) he intends to use the thing unlawfully for that purpose or to allow it to be used unlawfully for that purpose.

(2) A person commits an offence if—
   (a) he supplies anything which may be used for the purpose of changing or interfering with the operation of a unique device identifier, and
   (b) he knows or believes that the person to whom the thing is supplied intends to use it unlawfully for that purpose or to allow it to be used unlawfully for that purpose.

(3) A person commits an offence if—
   (a) he offers to supply anything which may be used for the purpose of changing or interfering with the operation of a unique device identifier, and
   (b) he knows or believes that the person to whom the thing is offered intends if it is supplied to him to use it unlawfully for that purpose or to allow it to be used unlawfully for that purpose.

(4) A unique device identifier is an electronic equipment identifier which is unique to a mobile wireless communications device.

(5) A thing is used by a person unlawfully for a purpose if in using it for that purpose he commits an offence under section 1.

(6) A person guilty of an offence under this section is liable—
   (a) on summary conviction, to imprisonment for a term not exceeding 6 months or to a fine not exceeding the statutory maximum or to both, or
   (b) on conviction on indictment, to imprisonment for a term not exceeding 5 years or to a fine or to both.

As amended Violent Crime Reduction Act 2006, ss 62, 65.

COMMUNICATIONS ACT 2003

127 IMPROPER USE OF PUBLIC ELECTRONIC COMMUNICATIONS NETWORK

(1) A person is guilty of an offence if he—
   (a) sends by means of a public electronic communications network a message or other matter that is grossly offensive or of an indecent, obscene or menacing character; or
   (b) causes any such message or matter to be so sent.

(2)   A person is guilty of an offence if, for the purpose of causing annoyance, inconvenience or needless anxiety to another, he—
(a) sends by means of a public electronic communications network, a message that he knows to be false,
(b) causes such a message to be sent; or
(c) persistently makes use of a public electronic communications network.

(3)   A person guilty of an offence under this section shall be liable, on summary conviction, to imprisonment for a term not exceeding six months or to a fine not exceeding level 5 on the standard scale, or to both.

(4)   Subsections (1) and (2) do not apply to anything done in the course of providing a programme service (within the meaning of the Broadcasting Act 1990 (c. 42)).

FEMALE GENITAL MUTILATION ACT 2003

1 OFFENCE OF FEMALE GENITAL MUTILATION

(1)   A person is guilty of an offence if he excises, infibulates or otherwise mutilates the whole or any part of a girl's labia majora, labia minora or clitoris.

(2)   But no offence is committed by an approved person who performs—
(a) a surgical operation on a girl which is necessary for her physical or mental health, or
(b) a surgical operation on a girl who is in any stage of labour, or has just given birth, for purposes connected with the labour or birth.

(3)   The following are approved persons—
(a) in relation to an operation falling within subsection (2)(a), a registered medical practitioner,
(b) in relation to an operation falling within subsection (2)(b), a registered medical practitioner, a registered midwife or a person undergoing a course of training with a view to becoming such a practitioner or midwife.

(4)   There is also no offence committed by a person who—
(a) performs a surgical operation falling within subsection (2)(a) or (b) outside the United Kingdom, and
(b) in relation to such an operation exercises functions corresponding to those of an approved person.

(5)   For the purpose of determining whether an operation is necessary for the mental health of a girl it is immaterial whether she or any other person believes that the operation is required as a matter of custom or ritual.

2 OFFENCE OF ASSISTING A GIRL TO MUTILATE HER OWN GENITALIA

A person is guilty of an offence if he aids, abets, counsels or procures a girl to excise, infibulate or otherwise mutilate the whole or any part of her own labia majora, labia minora or clitoris.

3 OFFENCE OF ASSISTING A NON-UK PERSON TO MUTILATE OVERSEAS A GIRL'S GENITALIA

(1)   A person is guilty of an offence if he aids, abets, counsels or procures a person who is not a United Kingdom national or permanent United Kingdom resident to do a relevant act of female genital mutilation outside the United Kingdom.

(2)   An act is a relevant act of female genital mutilation if—

    (a) it is done in relation to a United Kingdom national or permanent United Kingdom resident, and

    (b) it would, if done by such a person, constitute an offence under section 1.

(3)   But no offence is committed if the relevant act of female genital mutilation—

    (a) is a surgical operation falling within section 1(2)(a) or (b), and

    (b) is performed by a person who, in relation to such an operation, is an approved person or exercises functions corresponding to those of an approved person.

4 EXTENSION OF SECTIONS 1 TO 3 TO EXTRA-TERRITORIAL ACTS

(1)   Sections 1 to 3 extend to any act done outside the United Kingdom by a United Kingdom national or permanent United Kingdom resident.

(2)   If an offence under this Act is committed outside the United Kingdom—

    (a) proceedings may be taken, and

    (b) the offence may for incidental purposes be treated as having been committed,

in any place in England and Wales or Northern Ireland.

5 PENALTIES FOR OFFENCES

A person guilty of an offence under this Act is liable—

(a)   on conviction on indictment, to imprisonment for a term not exceeding 14 years or a fine (or both),

(b)   on summary conviction, to imprisonment for a term not exceeding six months or a fine not exceeding the statutory maximum (or both).

6 DEFINITIONS

(1)   Girl includes woman.

(2)   A United Kingdom national is an individual who is—

    (a) a British citizen, a British overseas territories citizen, a British National (Overseas) or a British Overseas citizen,

    (b) a person who under the British Nationality Act 1981 (c 61) is a British subject, or

    (c) a British protected person within the meaning of that Act.

(3)   A permanent United Kingdom resident is an individual who is settled in the United Kingdom (within the meaning of the Immigration Act 1971 (c 77)).

(4)   This section has effect for the purposes of this Act.

LICENSING ACT 2003

141 SALE OF ALCOHOL TO A PERSON WHO IS DRUNK

(1)   A person to whom subsection (2) applies commits an offence if, on relevant premises, he knowingly—

    (a) sells or attempts to sell alcohol to a person who is drunk, or

    (b) allows alcohol to be sold to such a person.

(2)   This subsection applies—

(a) to any person who works at the premises in a capacity, whether paid or unpaid, which gives him authority to sell the alcohol concerned,

(b) in the case of licensed premises, to—
   (i)   the holder of a premises licence in respect of the premises, and
   (ii) the designated premises supervisor (if any) under such a licence,

(c) in the case of premises in respect of which a club premises certificate has effect, to any member or officer of the club which holds the certificate who at the time the sale (or attempted sale) takes place is present on the premises in a capacity which enables him to prevent it, and

(d) in the case of premises which may be used for a permitted temporary activity by virtue of Part 5, to the premises user in relation to the temporary event notice in question.

(3) This section applies in relation to the supply of alcohol by or on behalf of a club to or to the order of a member of the club as it applies in relation to the sale of alcohol.

(4) A person guilty of an offence under this section is liable on summary conviction to a fine not exceeding level 3 on the standard scale.

142 OBTAINING ALCOHOL FOR A PERSON WHO IS DRUNK

(1) A person commits an offence if, on relevant premises, he knowingly obtains or attempts to obtain alcohol for consumption on those premises by a person who is drunk.

(2) A person guilty of an offence under this section is liable on summary conviction to a fine not exceeding level 3 on the standard scale.

146 SALE OF ALCOHOL TO CHILDREN

(1) A person commits an offence if he sells alcohol to an individual aged under 18.

(2) A club commits an offence if alcohol is supplied by it or on its behalf—
   (a) to, or to the order of, a member of the club who is aged under 18, or
   (b) to the order of a member of the club, to an individual who is aged under 18.

(3) A person commits an offence if he supplies alcohol on behalf of a club—
   (a) to, or to the order of, a member of the club who is aged under 18, or
   (b) to the order of a member of the club, to an individual who is aged under 18.

(4) Where a person is charged with an offence under this section by reason of his own conduct it is a defence that—
   (a) he believed that the individual was aged 18 or over, and
   (b) either—
      (i)   he had taken all reasonable steps to establish the individual's age, or
      (ii) nobody could reasonably have suspected from the individual's appearance that he was aged under 18.

(5) For the purposes of subsection (4), a person is treated as having taken all reasonable steps to establish an individual's age if—
   (a) he asked the individual for evidence of his age, and
   (b) the evidence would have convinced a reasonable person.

(6) Where a person ("the accused") is charged with an offence under this section by reason of the act or default of some other person, it is a defence that the accused exercised all due diligence to avoid committing it.

(7)   A person guilty of an offence under this section is liable on summary conviction to a fine not exceeding level 5 on the standard scale.

149 PURCHASE OF ALCOHOL BY OR ON BEHALF OF CHILDREN

(1)   An individual aged under 18 commits an offence if—
(a)   he buys or attempts to buy alcohol, or
(b)   where he is a member of a club—
    (i)   alcohol is supplied to him or to his order by or on behalf of the club, as a result of some act or default of his, or
    (ii)   he attempts to have alcohol supplied to him or to his order by or on behalf of the club.

(2)   But subsection (1) does not apply where the individual buys or attempts to buy the alcohol at the request of—
(a)   a constable, or
(b)   a weights and measures inspector, who is acting in the course of his duty.

(3)   A person commits an offence if—
(a)   he buys or attempts to buy alcohol on behalf of an individual aged under 18, or
(b)   where he is a member of a club, on behalf of an individual aged under 18 he—
    (i)   makes arrangements whereby alcohol is supplied to him or to his order by or on behalf of the club, or
    (ii)   attempts to make such arrangements.

(4)   A person ("the relevant person") commits an offence if—
(a)   he buys or attempts to buy alcohol for consumption on relevant premises by an individual aged under 18, or
(b)   where he is a member of a club—
    (i)   by some act or default of his, alcohol is supplied to him, or to his order, by or on behalf of the club for consumption on relevant premises by an individual aged under 18, or
    (ii)   he attempts to have alcohol so supplied for such consumption.

(5)   But subsection (4) does not apply where—
(a)   the relevant person is aged 18 or over,
(b)   the individual is aged 16 or 17,
(c)   the alcohol is beer, wine or cider,
(d)   its purchase or supply is for consumption at a table meal on relevant premises, and
(e)   the individual is accompanied at the meal by an individual aged 18 or over.

(6)   Where a person is charged with an offence under subsection (3) or (4) it is a defence that he had no reason to suspect that the individual was aged under 18.

(7)   A person guilty of an offence under this section is liable on summary conviction—
(a)   in the case of an offence under subsection (1), to a fine not exceeding level 3 on the standard scale, and
(b)   in the case of an offence under subsection (3) or (4), to a fine not exceeding level 5 on the standard scale.

SEXUAL OFFENCES ACT 2003

1 RAPE

(1)   A person (A) commits an offence if—
    (a) he intentionally penetrates the vagina, anus or mouth of another person (B) with his penis,
    (b) B does not consent to the penetration, and
    (c) A does not reasonably believe that B consents.

(2)   Whether a belief is reasonable is to be determined having regard to all the circumstances, including any steps A has taken to ascertain whether B consents.

(3)   Sections 75 and 76 apply to an offence under this section.

(4)   A person guilty of an offence under this section is liable, on conviction on indictment, to imprisonment for life.

2 ASSAULT BY PENETRATION

(1)   A person (A) commits an offence if—
    (a) he intentionally penetrates the vagina or anus of another person (B) with a part of his body or anything else,
    (b) the penetration is sexual,
    (c) B does not consent to the penetration, and
    (d) A does not reasonably believe that B consents.

(2)   Whether a belief is reasonable is to be determined having regard to all the circumstances, including any steps A has taken to ascertain whether B consents.

(3)   Sections 75 and 76 apply to an offence under this section.

(4)   A person guilty of an offence under this section is liable, on conviction on indictment, to imprisonment for life.

3 SEXUAL ASSAULT

(1)   A person (A) commits an offence if—
    (a) he intentionally touches another person (B),
    (b) the touching is sexual,
    (c) B does not consent to the touching, and
    (d) A does not reasonably believe that B consents.

(2)   Whether a belief is reasonable is to be determined having regard to all the circumstances, including any steps A has taken to ascertain whether B consents.

(3)   Sections 75 and 76 apply to an offence under this section.

(4)   A person guilty of an offence under this section is liable—
    (a) on summary conviction, to imprisonment for a term not exceeding 6 months or a fine not exceeding the statutory maximum or both;
    (b) on conviction on indictment, to imprisonment for a term not exceeding 10 years.

4 CAUSING A PERSON TO ENGAGE IN SEXUAL ACTIVITY WITHOUT CONSENT

(1)   A person (A) commits an offence if—
    (a) he intentionally causes another person (B) to engage in an activity,
    (b) the activity is sexual,
    (c) B does not consent to engaging in the activity, and
    (d) A does not reasonably believe that B consents.

(2)   Whether a belief is reasonable is to be determined having regard to all the circumstances, including any steps A has taken to ascertain whether B consents.

(3)   Sections 75 and 76 apply to an offence under this section.

(4)   A person guilty of an offence under this section, if the activity caused involved—
    (a) penetration of B's anus or vagina,
    (b) penetration of B's mouth with a person's penis,
    (c) penetration of a person's anus or vagina with a part of B's body or by B with anything else, or
    (d) penetration of a person's mouth with B's penis,
    is liable, on conviction on indictment, to imprisonment for life.

(5)   Unless subsection (4) applies, a person guilty of an offence under this section is liable—
    (a) on summary conviction, to imprisonment for a term not exceeding 6 months or to a fine not exceeding the statutory maximum or both;
    (b) on conviction on indictment, to imprisonment for a term not exceeding 10 years.

5 RAPE OF A CHILD UNDER 13

(1)   A person commits an offence if—
    (a) he intentionally penetrates the vagina, anus or mouth of another person with his penis, and
    (b) the other person is under 13.

(2)   A person guilty of an offence under this section is liable, on conviction on indictment, to imprisonment for life.

6 ASSAULT OF A CHILD UNDER 13 BY PENETRATION

(1)   A person commits an offence if—
    (a) he intentionally penetrates the vagina or anus of another person with a part of his body or anything else,
    (b) the penetration is sexual, and
    (c) the other person is under 13.

(2)   A person guilty of an offence under this section is liable, on conviction on indictment, to imprisonment for life.

7 SEXUAL ASSAULT OF A CHILD UNDER 13

(1)   A person commits an offence if—
    (a) he intentionally touches another person,
    (b) the touching is sexual, and
    (c) the other person is under 13.

(2)   A person guilty of an offence under this section is liable—
    (a) on summary conviction, to imprisonment for a term not exceeding 6 months or a fine not exceeding the statutory maximum or both;
    (b) on conviction on indictment, to imprisonment for a term not exceeding 14 years.

8 CAUSING OR INCITING A CHILD UNDER 13 TO ENGAGE IN SEXUAL ACTIVITY

(1)   A person commits an offence if—
    (a) he intentionally causes or incites another person (B) to engage in an activity,
    (b) the activity is sexual, and
    (c) B is under 13.

(2)   A person guilty of an offence under this section, if the activity caused or incited involved—
    (a) penetration of B's anus or vagina,
    (b) penetration of B's mouth with a person's penis,
    (c) penetration of a person's anus or vagina with a part of B's body or by B with anything else, or
    (d) penetration of a person's mouth with B's penis,
    is liable, on conviction on indictment, to imprisonment for life.

(3)   Unless subsection (2) applies, a person guilty of an offence under this section is liable—
    (a) on summary conviction, to imprisonment for a term not exceeding 6 months or to a fine not exceeding the statutory maximum or both;
    (b) on conviction on indictment, to imprisonment for a term not exceeding 14 years.

9 SEXUAL ACTIVITY WITH A CHILD

(1)   A person aged 18 or over (A) commits an offence if—
    (a) he intentionally touches another person (B),
    (b) the touching is sexual, and
    (c) either—
        (i)   B is under 16 and A does not reasonably believe that B is 16 or over, or
        (ii) B is under 13.

(2)   A person guilty of an offence under this section, if the touching involved—
    (a) penetration of B's anus or vagina with a part of A's body or anything else,
    (b) penetration of B's mouth with A's penis,
    (c) penetration of A's anus or vagina with a part of B's body, or
    (d) penetration of A's mouth with B's penis,
    is liable, on conviction on indictment, to imprisonment for a term not exceeding 14 years.

(3)   Unless subsection (2) applies, a person guilty of an offence under this section is liable—
    (a) on summary conviction, to imprisonment for a term not exceeding 6 months or to a fine not exceeding the statutory maximum or both;
    (b) on conviction on indictment, to imprisonment for a term not exceeding 14 years.

10 CAUSING OR INCITING A CHILD TO ENGAGE IN SEXUAL ACTIVITY

(1)   A person aged 18 or over (A) commits an offence if—
    (a) he intentionally causes or incites another person (B) to engage in an activity,
    (b) the activity is sexual, and

(c) either—
    (i) B is under 16 and A does not reasonably believe that B is 16 or over, or
    (ii) B is under 13.

(2) A person guilty of an offence under this section, if the activity caused or incited involved—
    (a) penetration of B's anus or vagina,
    (b) penetration of B's mouth with a person's penis,
    (c) penetration of a person's anus or vagina with a part of B's body or by B with anything else, or
    (d) penetration of a person's mouth with B's penis,
is liable, on conviction on indictment, to imprisonment for a term not exceeding 14 years.

(3) Unless subsection (2) applies, a person guilty of an offence under this section is liable—
    (a) on summary conviction, to imprisonment for a term not exceeding 6 months or to a fine not exceeding the statutory maximum or both;
    (b) on conviction on indictment, to imprisonment for a term not exceeding 14 years.

11 ENGAGING IN SEXUAL ACTIVITY IN THE PRESENCE OF A CHILD

(1) A person aged 18 or over (A) commits an offence if—
    (a) he intentionally engages in an activity,
    (b) the activity is sexual,
    (c) for the purpose of obtaining sexual gratification, he engages in it—
        (i) when another person (B) is present or is in a place from which A can be observed, and
        (ii) knowing or believing that B is aware, or intending that B should be aware, that he is engaging in it, and
    (d) either—
        (i) B is under 16 and A does not reasonably believe that B is 16 or over, or
        (ii) B is under 13.

(2) A person guilty of an offence under this section is liable—
    (a) on summary conviction, to imprisonment for a term not exceeding 6 months or a fine not exceeding the statutory maximum or both;
    (b) on conviction on indictment, to imprisonment for a term not exceeding 10 years.

12 CAUSING A CHILD TO WATCH A SEXUAL ACT

(1) A person aged 18 or over (A) commits an offence if—
    (a) for the purpose of obtaining sexual gratification, he intentionally causes another person (B) to watch a third person engaging in an activity, or to look at an image of any person engaging in an activity,
    (b) the activity is sexual, and
    (c) either—
        (i) B is under 16 and A does not reasonably believe that B is 16 or over, or
        (ii) B is under 13.

(2) A person guilty of an offence under this section is liable—
    (a) on summary conviction, to imprisonment for a term not exceeding 6 months or a fine not exceeding the statutory maximum or both;
    (b) on conviction on indictment, to imprisonment for a term not exceeding 10 years.

13 CHILD SEX OFFENCES COMMITTED BY CHILDREN OR YOUNG PERSONS

(1) A person under 18 commits an offence if he does anything which would be an offence under any of sections 9 to 12 if he were aged 18.

(2) A person guilty of an offence under this section is liable—
   (a) on summary conviction, to imprisonment for a term not exceeding 6 months or a fine not exceeding the statutory maximum or both;
   (b) on conviction on indictment, to imprisonment for a term not exceeding 5 years.

14 ARRANGING OR FACILITATING COMMISSION OF A CHILD SEX OFFENCE

(1) A person commits an offence if—
   (a) he intentionally arranges or facilitates something that he intends to do, intends another person to do, or believes that another person will do, in any part of the world, and
   (b) doing it will involve the commission of an offence under any of sections 9 to 13.

(2) A person does not commit an offence under this section if—
   (a) he arranges or facilitates something that he believes another person will do, but that he does not intend to do or intend another person to do, and
   (b) any offence within subsection (1)(b) would be an offence against a child for whose protection he acts.

(3) For the purposes of subsection (2), a person acts for the protection of a child if he acts for the purpose of—
   (a) protecting the child from sexually transmitted infection,
   (b) protecting the physical safety of the child,
   (c) preventing the child from becoming pregnant, or
   (d) promoting the child's emotional well-being by the giving of advice,
   and not for the purpose of obtaining sexual gratification or for the purpose of causing or encouraging the activity constituting the offence within subsection (1)(b) or the child's participation in it.

(4) A person guilty of an offence under this section is liable—
   (a) on summary conviction, to imprisonment for a term not exceeding 6 months or a fine not exceeding the statutory maximum or both;
   (b) on conviction on indictment, to imprisonment for a term not exceeding 14 years.

15 MEETING A CHILD FOLLOWING SEXUAL GROOMING ETC

(1) A person aged 18 or over (A) commits an offence if—
   (a) A has met or communicated with another person (B) on at least two occasions and subsequently—
      (i)   A intentionally meets B,
      (ii) A travels with the intention of meeting B in any part of the world or arranges to meet B in any part of the world, or
      (iii) B travels with the intention of meeting A in any part of the world,
   (b) A intends to do anything to or in respect of B, during or after the meeting mentioned in paragraph (a)(i) to (iii) and in any part of the world, which if done will involve the commission by A of a relevant offence,
   (c) B is under 16, and
   (d) A does not reasonably believe that B is 16 or over.

(2)   In subsection (1)—
    (a)   the reference to A having met or communicated with B is a reference to A having met B in any part of the world or having communicated with B by any means from, to or in any part of the world;
    (b)   "relevant offence" means—
        (i)   an offence under this Part,
        (iii)   anything done outside England and Wales . . . which is not an offence within subparagraph (i) but would be an offence within subparagraph (i) if done in England and Wales.

(4)   A person guilty of an offence under this section is liable—
    (a)   on summary conviction, to imprisonment for a term not exceeding 6 months or a fine not exceeding the statutory maximum or both;
    (b)   on conviction on indictment, to imprisonment for a term not exceeding 10 years.

16 ABUSE OF POSITION OF TRUST: SEXUAL ACTIVITY WITH A CHILD

(1)   A person aged 18 or over (A) commits an offence if—
    (a)   he intentionally touches another person (B),
    (b)   the touching is sexual,
    (c)   A is in a position of trust in relation to B,
    (d)   where subsection (2) applies, A knows or could reasonably be expected to know of the circumstances by virtue of which he is in a position of trust in relation to B, and
    (e)   either—
        (i)   B is under 18 and A does not reasonably believe that B is 18 or over, or
        (ii)   B is under 13.

(2)   This subsection applies where A—
    (a)   is in a position of trust in relation to B by virtue of circumstances within section 21(2), (3), (4) or (5), and
    (b)   is not in such a position of trust by virtue of other circumstances.

(3)   Where in proceedings for an offence under this section it is proved that the other person was under 18, the defendant is to be taken not to have reasonably believed that that person was 18 or over unless sufficient evidence is adduced to raise an issue as to whether he reasonably believed it.

(4)   Where in proceedings for an offence under this section—
    (a)   it is proved that the defendant was in a position of trust in relation to the other person by virtue of circumstances within section 21(2), (3), (4) or (5), and
    (b)   it is not proved that he was in such a position of trust by virtue of other circumstances, it is to be taken that the defendant knew or could reasonably have been expected to know of the circumstances by virtue of which he was in such a position of trust unless sufficient evidence is adduced to raise an issue as to whether he knew or could reasonably have been expected to know of those circumstances.

(5)   A person guilty of an offence under this section is liable—
    (a)   on summary conviction, to imprisonment for a term not exceeding 6 months or a fine not exceeding the statutory maximum or both;
    (b)   on conviction on indictment, to imprisonment for a term not exceeding 5 years.

17 ABUSE OF POSITION OF TRUST: CAUSING OR INCITING A CHILD TO ENGAGE IN SEXUAL ACTIVITY

(1)   A person aged 18 or over (A) commits an offence if—
   (a) he intentionally causes or incites another person (B) to engage in an activity,
   (b) the activity is sexual,
   (c) A is in a position of trust in relation to B,
   (d) where subsection (2) applies, A knows or could reasonably be expected to know of the circumstances by virtue of which he is in a position of trust in relation to B, and
   (e) either—
     (i)   B is under 18 and A does not reasonably believe that B is 18 or over, or
     (ii) B is under 13.

(2)   This subsection applies where A—
   (a) is in a position of trust in relation to B by virtue of circumstances within section 21(2), (3), (4) or (5), and
   (b) is not in such a position of trust by virtue of other circumstances.

(3)   Where in proceedings for an offence under this section it is proved that the other person was under 18, the defendant is to be taken not to have reasonably believed that that person was 18 or over unless sufficient evidence is adduced to raise an issue as to whether he reasonably believed it.

(4)   Where in proceedings for an offence under this section—
   (a) it is proved that the defendant was in a position of trust in relation to the other person by virtue of circumstances within section 21(2), (3), (4) or (5), and
   (b) it is not proved that he was in such a position of trust by virtue of other circumstances,
it is to be taken that the defendant knew or could reasonably have been expected to know of the circumstances by virtue of which he was in such a position of trust unless sufficient evidence is adduced to raise an issue as to whether he knew or could reasonably have been expected to know of those circumstances.

(5)   A person guilty of an offence under this section is liable—
   (a) on summary conviction, to imprisonment for a term not exceeding 6 months or a fine not exceeding the statutory maximum or both;
   (b) on conviction on indictment, to imprisonment for a term not exceeding 5 years.

18 ABUSE OF POSITION OF TRUST: SEXUAL ACTIVITY IN THE PRESENCE OF A CHILD

(1)   A person aged 18 or over (A) commits an offence if—
   (a) he intentionally engages in an activity,
   (b) the activity is sexual,
   (c) for the purpose of obtaining sexual gratification, he engages in it—
     (i)   when another person (B) is present or is in a place from which A can be observed, and
     (ii) knowing or believing that B is aware, or intending that B should be aware, that he is engaging in it,
   (d) A is in a position of trust in relation to B,
   (e) where subsection (2) applies, A knows or could reasonably be expected to know of the circumstances by virtue of which he is in a position of trust in relation to B, and
   (f) either—
     (i)   B is under 18 and A does not reasonably believe that B is 18 or over, or
     (ii) B is under 13.

(2)   This subsection applies where A—
    (a)   is in a position of trust in relation to B by virtue of circumstances within section 21(2), (3), (4) or (5), and
    (b)   is not in such a position of trust by virtue of other circumstances.

(3)   Where in proceedings for an offence under this section it is proved that the other person was under 18, the defendant is to be taken not to have reasonably believed that that person was 18 or over unless sufficient evidence is adduced to raise an issue as to whether he reasonably believed it.

(4)   Where in proceedings for an offence under this section—
    (a)   it is proved that the defendant was in a position of trust in relation to the other person by virtue of circumstances within section 21(2), (3), (4) or (5), and
    (b)   it is not proved that he was in such a position of trust by virtue of other circumstances,
    it is to be taken that the defendant knew or could reasonably have been expected to know of the circumstances by virtue of which he was in such a position of trust unless sufficient evidence is adduced to raise an issue as to whether he knew or could reasonably have been expected to know of those circumstances.

(5)   A person guilty of an offence under this section is liable—
    (a)   on summary conviction, to imprisonment for a term not exceeding 6 months or a fine not exceeding the statutory maximum or both;
    (b)   on conviction on indictment, to imprisonment for a term not exceeding 5 years.

19   ABUSE OF POSITION OF TRUST: CAUSING A CHILD TO WATCH A SEXUAL ACT

(1)   A person aged 18 or over (A) commits an offence if—
    (a)   for the purpose of obtaining sexual gratification, he intentionally causes another person (B) to watch a third person engaging in an activity, or to look at an image of any person engaging in an activity,
    (b)   the activity is sexual,
    (c)   A is in a position of trust in relation to B,
    (d)   where subsection (2) applies, A knows or could reasonably be expected to know of the circumstances by virtue of which he is in a position of trust in relation to B, and
    (e)   either—
        (i)   B is under 18 and A does not reasonably believe that B is 18 or over, or
        (ii)   B is under 13.

(2)   This subsection applies where A—
    (a)   is in a position of trust in relation to B by virtue of circumstances within section 21(2), (3), (4) or (5), and
    (b)   is not in such a position of trust by virtue of other circumstances.

(3)   Where in proceedings for an offence under this section it is proved that the other person was under 18, the defendant is to be taken not to have reasonably believed that that person was 18 or over unless sufficient evidence is adduced to raise an issue as to whether he reasonably believed it.

(4)   Where in proceedings for an offence under this section—
    (a)   it is proved that the defendant was in a position of trust in relation to the other person by virtue of circumstances within section 21(2), (3), (4) or (5), and
    (b)   it is not proved that he was in such a position of trust by virtue of other circumstances,

it is to be taken that the defendant knew or could reasonably have been expected to know of the circumstances by virtue of which he was in such a position of trust unless sufficient evidence is adduced to raise an issue as to whether he knew or could reasonably have been expected to know of those circumstances.

(5)   A person guilty of an offence under this section is liable—
   (a)   on summary conviction, to imprisonment for a term not exceeding 6 months or a fine not exceeding the statutory maximum or both;
   (b)   on conviction on indictment, to imprisonment for a term not exceeding 5 years.

. . .

21 POSITIONS OF TRUST

(1)   For the purposes of sections 16 to 19, a person (A) is in a position of trust in relation to another person (B) if—
   (a)   any of the following subsections applies, or
   (b)   any condition specified in an order made by the Secretary of State is met.

(2)   This subsection applies if A looks after persons under 18 who are detained in an institution by virtue of a court order or under an enactment, and B is so detained in that institution.

(3)   This subsection applies if A looks after persons under 18 who are resident in a home or other place in which—
   (a)   accommodation and maintenance are provided by an authority under section 23(2) in accordance with section 22C(6) of the Children Act 1989 (c 41), or
   (b)   accommodation is provided by a voluntary organisation under section 59(1) of that Act.,
   and B is resident, and is so provided with accommodation and maintenance or accommodation, in that place.

(4)   This subsection applies if A looks after persons under 18 who are accommodated and cared for in one of the following institutions—
   (a)   a hospital,
   (b)   an independent clinic,
   (c)   a care home, . . .,
   (d)   a community home, voluntary home or children's home, or
   (e)   a home provided under section 82(5) of the Children Act 1989,
   and B is accommodated and cared for in that institution.

(5)   This subsection applies if A looks after persons under 18 who are receiving education at an educational institution and B is receiving, and A is not receiving, education at that institution.

(7)   This subsection applies if A is engaged in the provision of services under, or pursuant to anything done under—
   (a)   sections 8 to 10 of the Employment and Training Act 1973 (c 50), or
   (b)   section 68, 70(1)(b) or 74 of the Education and Skills Act 2008,
   and, in that capacity, looks after B on an individual basis.

(8)   This subsection applies if A regularly has unsupervised contact with B (whether face to face or by any other means)—
   (a)   in the exercise of functions of a local authority under section 20 or 21 of the Children Act 1989 (c 41).

(9)   This subsection applies if A, as a person who is to report to the court under section 7 of the Children Act 1989 . . . on matters relating to the welfare of B, regularly has unsupervised contact with B (whether face to face or by any other means).

(10)   This subsection applies if A is a personal adviser appointed for B under—
        (a) section 23B(2) of, or paragraph 19C of Schedule 2 to, the Children Act 1989, and, in that capacity, looks after B on an individual basis.

(11)   This subsection applies if—
        (a) B is subject to a care order, a supervision order or an education supervision order, and
        (b) in the exercise of functions conferred by virtue of the order on an authorised person or the authority designated by the order, A looks after B on an individual basis.

(12)   This subsection applies if A—
        (a) is an officer of the Service or Welsh family proceedings officer (within the meaning given by section 35 of the Children Act 2004) appointed for B under section 41(1) of the Children Act 1989,
        (b) is appointed a children's guardian of B under rule 6 or rule 18 of the Adoption Rules 1984 (SI 1984/265), or
        (c) is appointed to be the guardian ad litem of B under rule 9.5 of the Family Proceedings Rules 1991 (S. I. 1991/1247),
        and, in that capacity, regularly has unsupervised contact with B (whether face to face or by any other means).

(13)   This subsection applies if—
        (a) B is subject to requirements imposed by or under an enactment on his release from detention for a criminal offence, or is subject to requirements imposed by a court order made in criminal proceedings, and (b) A looks after B on an individual basis in pursuance of the requirements.

22 POSITIONS OF TRUST: INTERPRETATION

(1)   The following provisions apply for the purposes of section 21.

(2)   Subject to subsection (3), a person looks after persons under 18 if he is regularly involved in caring for, training, supervising or being in sole charge of such persons.

(3)   A person (A) looks after another person (B) on an individual basis if—
        (a) A is regularly involved in caring for, training or supervising B, and
        (b) in the course of his involvement, A regularly has unsupervised contact with B (whether face to face or by any other means).

(4)   A person receives education at an educational institution if—
        (a) he is registered or otherwise enrolled as a pupil or student at the institution, or
        (b) he receives education at the institution under arrangements with another educational institution at which he is so registered or otherwise enrolled.

(5)   In section 21—
        "authority"—
        (a) in relation to England and Wales, means a local authority;
        "care home" means an establishment which is a care home for the purposes of the Care Standards Act 2000 (c 14);

"care order" has—

(a) in relation to England and Wales, the same meaning as in the Children Act 1989 (c 41);

"children's home" has—

(a) in relation to England and Wales, the meaning given by section 1 of the Care Standards Act 2000;

"community home" has the meaning given by section 53 of the Children Act 1989;

"education supervision order" has—

(a) in relation to England and Wales, the meaning given by section 36 of the Children Act 1989;

"hospital"—

(a) in relation to England and Wales, means a hospital within the meaning given by section 275(1) of the National Health Service Act 2006 or section 206(1) of the National Health Service Act 2006, or any other establishment which is a hospital within the meaning given by section 2(3) of the Care Standards Act 2000 (c 14);

"independent clinic" has—

(a) in relation to England and Wales, the meaning given by section 2 of the Care Standards Act 2000;

"supervision order" has—

(a) in relation to England and Wales, the meaning given by section 31(11) of the Children Act 1989 (c 41);

"voluntary home" has—

(a) in relation to England and Wales, the meaning given by section 60(3) of the Children Act 1989.

23 SECTIONS 16 TO 19: EXCEPTION FOR SPOUSES AND CIVIL PARTNERS

(1) Conduct by a person (A) which would otherwise be an offence under any of sections 16 to 19 against another person (B) is not an offence under that section if at the time—
(a) B is 16 or over, and
(b) A and B are lawfully married or civil partners of each other.

(2) In proceedings for such an offence it is for the defendant to prove that A and B were at the time lawfully married or civil partners of each other.

24 SECTIONS 16 TO 19: SEXUAL RELATIONSHIPS WHICH PRE-DATE POSITION OF TRUST

(1) Conduct by a person (A) which would otherwise be an offence under any of sections 16 to 19 against another person (B) is not an offence under that section if, immediately before the position of trust arose, a sexual relationship existed between A and B.

(2) Subsection (1) does not apply if at that time sexual intercourse between A and B would have been unlawful.

(3)   In proceedings for an offence under any of sections 16 to 19 it is for the defendant to prove that such a relationship existed at that time.

25 SEXUAL ACTIVITY WITH A CHILD FAMILY MEMBER

(1)   A person (A) commits an offence if—
   (a) he intentionally touches another person (B),
   (b) the touching is sexual,
   (c) the relation of A to B is within section 27,
   (d) A knows or could reasonably be expected to know that his relation to B is of a description falling within that section, and
   (e) either—
      (i)   B is under 18 and A does not reasonably believe that B is 18 or over, or
      (ii) B is under 13.

(2)   Where in proceedings for an offence under this section it is proved that the other person was under 18, the defendant is to be taken not to have reasonably believed that that person was 18 or over unless sufficient evidence is adduced to raise an issue as to whether he reasonably believed it.

(3)   Where in proceedings for an offence under this section it is proved that the relation of the defendant to the other person was of a description falling within section 27, it is to be taken that the defendant knew or could reasonably have been expected to know that his relation to the other person was of that description unless sufficient evidence is adduced to raise an issue as to whether he knew or could reasonably have been expected to know that it was.

(4)   A person guilty of an offence under this section, if aged 18 or over at the time of the offence, is liable—
   (a) where subsection (6) applies, on conviction on indictment to imprisonment for a term not exceeding 14 years;
   (b) in any other case—
      (i)   on summary conviction, to imprisonment for a term not exceeding 6 months or a fine not exceeding the statutory maximum or both;
      (ii) on conviction on indictment, to imprisonment for a term not exceeding 14 years.

(5)   Unless subsection (4) applies, a person guilty of an offence under this section is liable—
   (a) on summary conviction, to imprisonment for a term not exceeding 6 months or a fine not exceeding the statutory maximum or both;
   (b) on conviction on indictment, to imprisonment for a term not exceeding 5 years.

(6)   This subsection applies where the touching involved—
   (a) penetration of B's anus or vagina with a part of A's body or anything else,
   (b) penetration of B's mouth with A's penis,
   (c) penetration of A's anus or vagina with a part of B's body, or
   (d) penetration of A's mouth with B's penis.

26 INCITING A CHILD FAMILY MEMBER TO ENGAGE IN SEXUAL ACTIVITY

(1)   A person (A) commits an offence if—
   (a) he intentionally incites another person (B) to touch, or allow himself to be touched by, A,
   (b) the touching is sexual,

(c) the relation of A to B is within section 27,

(d) A knows or could reasonably be expected to know that his relation to B is of a description falling within that section, and

(e) either—

(i) B is under 18 and A does not reasonably believe that B is 18 or over, or

(ii) B is under 13.

(2) Where in proceedings for an offence under this section it is proved that the other person was under 18, the defendant is to be taken not to have reasonably believed that that person was 18 or over unless sufficient evidence is adduced to raise an issue as to whether he reasonably believed it.

(3) Where in proceedings for an offence under this section it is proved that the relation of the defendant to the other person was of a description falling within section 27, it is to be taken that the defendant knew or could reasonably have been expected to know that his relation to the other person was of that description unless sufficient evidence is adduced to raise an issue as to whether he knew or could reasonably have been expected to know that it was.

(4) A person guilty of an offence under this section, if he was aged 18 or over at the time of the offence, is liable—

(a) where subsection (6) applies, on conviction on indictment to imprisonment for a term not exceeding 14 years;

(b) in any other case—

(i) on summary conviction, to imprisonment for a term not exceeding 6 months or a fine not exceeding the statutory maximum or both;

(ii) on conviction on indictment, to imprisonment for a term not exceeding 14 years.

(5) Unless subsection (4) applies, a person guilty of an offence under this section is liable—

(a) on summary conviction, to imprisonment for a term not exceeding 6 months or a fine not exceeding the statutory maximum or both;

(b) on conviction on indictment, to imprisonment for a term not exceeding 5 years.

(6) This subsection applies where the touching to which the incitement related involved—

(a) penetration of B's anus or vagina with a part of A's body or anything else,

(b) penetration of B's mouth with A's penis,

(c) penetration of A's anus or vagina with a part of B's body, or

(d) penetration of A's mouth with B's penis.

27 FAMILY RELATIONSHIPS

(1) The relation of one person (A) to another (B) is within this section if—

(a) it is within any of subsections (2) to (4), or

(b) it would be within one of those subsections but for section 39 of the Adoption Act 1976 or section 67 of the Adoption and Children Act 2002 (c 38) (status conferred by adoption).

(2) The relation of A to B is within this subsection if—

(a) one of them is the other's parent, grandparent, brother, sister, half-brother, half-sister, aunt or uncle, or

(b) A is or has been B's foster parent.

(3) The relation of A to B is within this subsection if A and B live or have lived in the same household, or A is or has been regularly involved in caring for, training, supervising or being in sole charge of B, and—

(a) one of them is or has been the other's step-parent,

(b) A and B are cousins,

(c) one of them is or has been the other's stepbrother or stepsister, or

(d) the parent or present or former foster parent of one of them is or has been the other's foster parent.

(4) The relation of A to B is within this subsection if—

(a) A and B live in the same household, and

(b) A is regularly involved in caring for, training, supervising or being in sole charge of B.

(5) For the purposes of this section—

(a) "aunt" means the sister or half-sister of a person's parent, and "uncle" has a corresponding meaning;

(b) "cousin" means the child of an aunt or uncle;

(c) a person is a child's foster parent if—

(i) he is a person with whom the child has been placed under section 22C of the Children Act 1989 in a placement falling within subsection (6)(a) or (b) of that section (placement with local authority foster parent),

(ia) he is a person with whom the child has been placed under section 59(1)(a) of that Act (placement by voluntary organisation), or

(ii) he fosters the child privately, within the meaning given by section 66(1)(b) of that Act;

(d) a person is another's partner (whether they are of different sexes or the same sex) if they live together as partners in an enduring family relationship;

(e) "step-parent" includes a parent's partner and "stepbrother" and "stepsister" include the child of a parent's partner.

28 SECTIONS 25 AND 26: EXCEPTION FOR SPOUSES AND CIVIL PARTNERS

(1) Conduct by a person (A) which would otherwise be an offence under section 25 or 26 against another person (B) is not an offence under that section if at the time—

(a) B is 16 or over, and

(b) A and B are lawfully married or civil partners of each other.

(2) In proceedings for such an offence it is for the defendant to prove that A and B were at the time lawfully married or civil partners of each other.

29 SECTIONS 25 AND 26: SEXUAL RELATIONSHIPS WHICH PRE-DATE FAMILY RELATIONSHIPS

(1) Conduct by a person (A) which would otherwise be an offence under section 25 or 26 against another person (B) is not an offence under that section if—

(a) the relation of A to B is not within subsection (2) of section 27,

(b) it would not be within that subsection if section 39 of the Adoption Act 1976 or section 67 of the Adoption and Children Act 2002 (c 38) did not apply, and

(c) immediately before the relation of A to B first became such as to fall within section 27, a sexual relationship existed between A and B.

(2) Subsection (1) does not apply if at the time referred to in subsection (1)(c) sexual intercourse between A and B would have been unlawful.

(3) In proceedings for an offence under section 25 or 26 it is for the defendant to prove the matters mentioned in subsection (1)(a) to (c).

30 SEXUAL ACTIVITY WITH A PERSON WITH A MENTAL DISORDER IMPEDING CHOICE

(1)   A person (A) commits an offence if—
    (a) he intentionally touches another person (B),
    (b) the touching is sexual,
    (c) B is unable to refuse because of or for a reason related to a mental disorder, and
    (d) A knows or could reasonably be expected to know that B has a mental disorder and that because of it or for a reason related to it B is likely to be unable to refuse.

(2)   B is unable to refuse if—
    (a) he lacks the capacity to choose whether to agree to the touching (whether because he lacks sufficient understanding of the nature or reasonably foreseeable consequences of what is being done, or for any other reason), or
    (b) he is unable to communicate such a choice to A.

(3)   A person guilty of an offence under this section, if the touching involved—
    (a) penetration of B's anus or vagina with a part of A's body or anything else,
    (b) penetration of B's mouth with A's penis,
    (c) penetration of A's anus or vagina with a part of B's body, or
    (d) penetration of A's mouth with B's penis,
    is liable, on conviction on indictment, to imprisonment for life.

(4)   Unless subsection (3) applies, a person guilty of an offence under this section is liable—
    (a) on summary conviction, to imprisonment for a term not exceeding 6 months or to a fine not exceeding the statutory maximum or both;
    (b) on conviction on indictment, to imprisonment for a term not exceeding 14 years.

31 CAUSING OR INCITING A PERSON, WITH A MENTAL DISORDER IMPEDING CHOICE, TO ENGAGE IN SEXUAL ACTIVITY

(1)   A person (A) commits an offence if—
    (a) he intentionally causes or incites another person (B) to engage in an activity,
    (b) the activity is sexual,
    (c) B is unable to refuse because of or for a reason related to a mental disorder, and
    (d) A knows or could reasonably be expected to know that B has a mental disorder and that because of it or for a reason related to it B is likely to be unable to refuse.

(2)   B is unable to refuse if—
    (a) he lacks the capacity to choose whether to agree to engaging in the activity caused or incited (whether because he lacks sufficient understanding of the nature or reasonably foreseeable consequences of the activity, or for any other reason), or
    (b) he is unable to communicate such a choice to A.

(3)   A person guilty of an offence under this section, if the activity caused or incited involved—
    (a) penetration of B's anus or vagina,
    (b) penetration of B's mouth with a person's penis,
    (c) penetration of a person's anus or vagina with a part of B's body or by B with anything else, or
    (d) penetration of a person's mouth with B's penis,
    is liable, on conviction on indictment, to imprisonment for life.

(4)   Unless subsection (3) applies, a person guilty of an offence under this section is liable—
    (a) on summary conviction, to imprisonment for a term not exceeding 6 months or to a fine not exceeding the statutory maximum or both;
    (b) on conviction on indictment, to imprisonment for a term not exceeding 14 years.

32 ENGAGING IN SEXUAL ACTIVITY IN THE PRESENCE OF A PERSON WITH A MENTAL DISORDER IMPEDING CHOICE

(1)   A person (A) commits an offence if—
  (a) he intentionally engages in an activity,
  (b) the activity is sexual,
  (c) for the purpose of obtaining sexual gratification, he engages in it—
      (i)   when another person (B) is present or is in a place from which A can be observed, and
      (ii) knowing or believing that B is aware, or intending that B should be aware, that he is engaging in it,
  (d) B is unable to refuse because of or for a reason related to a mental disorder, and
  (e) A knows or could reasonably be expected to know that B has a mental disorder and that because of it or for a reason related to it B is likely to be unable to refuse.

(2)   B is unable to refuse if—
  (a) he lacks the capacity to choose whether to agree to being present (whether because he lacks sufficient understanding of the nature of the activity, or for any other reason), or
  (b) he is unable to communicate such a choice to A.

(3)   A person guilty of an offence under this section is liable—
  (a) on summary conviction, to imprisonment for a term not exceeding 6 months or a fine not exceeding the statutory maximum or both;
  (b) on conviction on indictment, to imprisonment for a term not exceeding 10 years.

33 CAUSING A PERSON, WITH A MENTAL DISORDER IMPEDING CHOICE, TO WATCH A SEXUAL ACT

(1)   A person (A) commits an offence if—
  (a) for the purpose of obtaining sexual gratification, he intentionally causes another person (B) to watch a third person engaging in an activity, or to look at an image of any person engaging in an activity,
  (b) the activity is sexual,
  (c) B is unable to refuse because of or for a reason related to a mental disorder, and
  (d) A knows or could reasonably be expected to know that B has a mental disorder and that because of it or for a reason related to it B is likely to be unable to refuse.

(2)   B is unable to refuse if—
  (a) he lacks the capacity to choose whether to agree to watching or looking (whether because he lacks sufficient understanding of the nature of the activity, or for any other reason), or
  (b) he is unable to communicate such a choice to A.

(3)   A person guilty of an offence under this section is liable—
  (a) on summary conviction, to imprisonment for a term not exceeding 6 months or a fine not exceeding the statutory maximum or both;
  (b) on conviction on indictment, to imprisonment for a term not exceeding 10 years.

34 INDUCEMENT, THREAT OR DECEPTION TO PROCURE SEXUAL ACTIVITY WITH A PERSON WITH A MENTAL DISORDER

(1)   A person (A) commits an offence if—
  (a) with the agreement of another person (B) he intentionally touches that person,
  (b) the touching is sexual,

(c) A obtains B's agreement by means of an inducement offered or given, a threat made or a deception practised by A for that purpose,

(d) B has a mental disorder, and

(e) A knows or could reasonably be expected to know that B has a mental disorder.

(2) A person guilty of an offence under this section, if the touching involved—

(a) penetration of B's anus or vagina with a part of A's body or anything else,

(b) penetration of B's mouth with A's penis,

(c) penetration of A's anus or vagina with a part of B's body, or

(d) penetration of A's mouth with B's penis,

is liable, on conviction on indictment, to imprisonment for life.

(3) Unless subsection (2) applies, a person guilty of an offence under this section is liable—

(a) on summary conviction, to imprisonment for a term not exceeding 6 months or a fine not exceeding the statutory maximum or both;

(b) on conviction on indictment, to imprisonment for a term not exceeding 14 years.

35 CAUSING A PERSON WITH A MENTAL DISORDER TO ENGAGE IN OR AGREE TO ENGAGE IN SEXUAL ACTIVITY BY INDUCEMENT, THREAT OR DECEPTION

(1) A person (A) commits an offence if—

(a) by means of an inducement offered or given, a threat made or a deception practised by him for this purpose, he intentionally causes another person (B) to engage in, or to agree to engage in, an activity,

(b) the activity is sexual,

(c) B has a mental disorder, and

(d) A knows or could reasonably be expected to know that B has a mental disorder.

(2) A person guilty of an offence under this section, if the activity caused or agreed to involved—

(a) penetration of B's anus or vagina,

(b) penetration of B's mouth with a person's penis,

(c) penetration of a person's anus or vagina with a part of B's body or by B with anything else, or

(d) penetration of a person's mouth with B's penis,

is liable, on conviction on indictment, to imprisonment for life.

(3) Unless subsection (2) applies, a person guilty of an offence under this section is liable—

(a) on summary conviction, to imprisonment for a term not exceeding 6 months or a fine not exceeding the statutory maximum or both;

(b) on conviction on indictment, to imprisonment for a term not exceeding 14 years.

36 ENGAGING IN SEXUAL ACTIVITY IN THE PRESENCE, PROCURED BY INDUCEMENT, THREAT OR DECEPTION, OF A PERSON WITH A MENTAL DISORDER

(1) A person (Λ) commits an offence if—

(a) he intentionally engages in an activity,

(b) the activity is sexual,

(c) for the purpose of obtaining sexual gratification, he engages in it—

(i) when another person (B) is present or is in a place from which A can be observed, and

(ii) knowing or believing that B is aware, or intending that B should be aware, that he is engaging in it,

(d) B agrees to be present or in the place referred to in paragraph (c)(i) because of an inducement offered or given, a threat made or a deception practised by A for the purpose of obtaining that agreement,

(e) B has a mental disorder, and

(f) A knows or could reasonably be expected to know that B has a mental disorder.

(2) A person guilty of an offence under this section is liable—

(a) on summary conviction, to imprisonment for a term not exceeding 6 months or a fine not exceeding the statutory maximum or both;

(b) on conviction on indictment, to imprisonment for a term not exceeding 10 years.

37 CAUSING A PERSON WITH A MENTAL DISORDER TO WATCH A SEXUAL ACT BY INDUCEMENT, THREAT OR DECEPTION

(1) A person (A) commits an offence if—

(a) for the purpose of obtaining sexual gratification, he intentionally causes another person (B) to watch a third person engaging in an activity, or to look at an image of any person engaging in an activity,

(b) the activity is sexual,

(c) B agrees to watch or look because of an inducement offered or given, a threat made or a deception practised by A for the purpose of obtaining that agreement,

(d) B has a mental disorder, and

(e) A knows or could reasonably be expected to know that B has a mental disorder.

(2) A person guilty of an offence under this section is liable—

(a) on summary conviction, to imprisonment for a term not exceeding 6 months or a fine not exceeding the statutory maximum or both;

(b) on conviction on indictment, to imprisonment for a term not exceeding 10 years.

. . .

47 PAYING FOR SEXUAL SERVICES OF A CHILD

(1) A person (A) commits an offence if—

(a) he intentionally obtains for himself the sexual services of another person (B),

(b) before obtaining those services, he has made or promised payment for those services to B or a third person, or knows that another person has made or promised such a payment, and

(c) either—

(i) B is under 18, and A does not reasonably believe that B is 18 or over, or

(ii) B is under 13.

(2) In this section, "payment" means any financial advantage, including the discharge of an obligation to pay or the provision of goods or services (including sexual services) gratuitously or at a discount.

(3) A person guilty of an offence under this section against a person under 13, where subsection (6) applies, is liable on conviction on indictment to imprisonment for life.

(4) Unless subsection (3) applies, a person guilty of an offence under this section against a person under 16 is liable—

(a) where subsection (6) applies, on conviction on indictment, to imprisonment for a term not exceeding 14 years;

(b) in any other case—

(i) on summary conviction, to imprisonment for a term not exceeding 6 months or a fine not exceeding the statutory maximum or both;

(ii) on conviction on indictment, to imprisonment for a term not exceeding 14 years.

(5) Unless subsection (3) or (4) applies, a person guilty of an offence under this section is liable—

(a) on summary conviction, to imprisonment for a term not exceeding 6 months or a fine not exceeding the statutory maximum or both;

(b) on conviction on indictment, to imprisonment for a term not exceeding 7 years.

(6) This subsection applies where the offence involved—

(a) penetration of B's anus or vagina with a part of A's body or anything else,

(b) penetration of B's mouth with A's penis,

(c) penetration of A's anus or vagina with a part of B's body or by B with anything else, or

(d) penetration of A's mouth with B's penis.

48 CAUSING OR INCITING CHILD PROSTITUTION OR PORNOGRAPHY

(1) A person (A) commits an offence if—

(a) he intentionally causes or incites another person (B) to become a prostitute, or to be involved in pornography, in any part of the world, and

(b) either—

(i) B is under 18, and A does not reasonably believe that B is 18 or over, or

(ii) B is under 13.

(2) A person guilty of an offence under this section is liable—

(a) on summary conviction, to imprisonment for a term not exceeding 6 months or a fine not exceeding the statutory maximum or both;

(b) on conviction on indictment, to imprisonment for a term not exceeding 14 years.

49 CONTROLLING A CHILD PROSTITUTE OR A CHILD INVOLVED IN PORNOGRAPHY

(1) A person (A) commits an offence if—

(a) he intentionally controls any of the activities of another person (B) relating to B's prostitution or involvement in pornography in any part of the world, and

(b) either—

(i) B is under 18, and A does not reasonably believe that B is 18 or over, or

(ii) B is under 13.

(2) A person guilty of an offence under this section is liable—

(a) on summary conviction, to imprisonment for a term not exceeding 6 months or a fine not exceeding the statutory maximum or both;

(b) on conviction on indictment, to imprisonment for a term not exceeding 14 years.

50 ARRANGING OR FACILITATING CHILD PROSTITUTION OR PORNOGRAPHY

(1) A person (A) commits an offence if—

(a) he intentionally arranges or facilitates the prostitution or involvement in pornography in any part of the world of another person (B), and

(b) either—
    (i) B is under 18, and A does not reasonably believe that B is 18 or over, or
    (ii) B is under 13.

(2)   A person guilty of an offence under this section is liable—
    (a) on summary conviction, to imprisonment for a term not exceeding 6 months or a fine not exceeding the statutory maximum or both;
    (b) on conviction on indictment, to imprisonment for a term not exceeding 14 years.

51 SECTIONS 48 TO 50: INTERPRETATION

(1)   For the purposes of sections 48 to 50, a person is involved in pornography if an indecent image of that person is recorded; and similar expressions, and "pornography", are to be interpreted accordingly.

(2)   In those sections "prostitute" means a person (A) who, on at least one occasion and whether or not compelled to do so, offers or provides sexual services to another person in return for payment or a promise of payment to A or a third person; and "prostitution" is to be interpreted accordingly.

(3)   In subsection (2), "payment" means any financial advantage, including the discharge of an obligation to pay or the provision of goods or services (including sexual services) gratuitously or at a discount.

51A SOLICITING

(1)   It is an offence for a person in a street or public place to solicit another (B) for the purpose of obtaining B's sexual services as a prostitute.

(2)   The reference to a person in a street or public place includes a person in a vehicle in a street or public place.

(3)   A person guilty of an offence under this section is liable on summary conviction to a fine not exceeding level 3 on the standard scale.

(4)   In this section "street" has the meaning given by section 1(4) of the Street Offences Act 1959.

52 CAUSING OR INCITING PROSTITUTION FOR GAIN

(1)   A person commits an offence if—
    (a) he intentionally causes or incites another person to become a prostitute in any part of the world, and
    (b) he does so for or in the expectation of gain for himself or a third person.

(2)   A person guilty of an offence under this section is liable—
    (a) on summary conviction, to imprisonment for a term not exceeding 6 months or a fine not exceeding the statutory maximum or both;
    (b) on conviction on indictment, to imprisonment for a term not exceeding 7 years.

53 CONTROLLING PROSTITUTION FOR GAIN

(1)   A person commits an offence if—
    (a) he intentionally controls any of the activities of another person relating to that person's prostitution in any part of the world, and
    (b) he does so for or in the expectation of gain for himself or a third person.

(2)   A person guilty of an offence under this section is liable—
    (a) on summary conviction, to imprisonment for a term not exceeding 6 months or a fine not exceeding the statutory maximum or both;
    (b) on conviction on indictment, to imprisonment for a term not exceeding 7 years.

53A PAYING FOR SEXUAL SERVICES OF A PROSTITUTE SUBJECTED TO FORCE ETC.

(1)   A person (A) commits an offence if—
    (a) A makes or promises payment for the sexual services of a prostitute (B),
    (b) a third person (C) has engaged in exploitative conduct of a kind likely to induce or encourage B to provide the sexual services for which A has made or promised payment, and
    (c) C engaged in that conduct for or in the expectation of gain for C or another person (apart from A or B).

(2)   The following are irrelevant—
    (a) where in the world the sexual services are to be provided and whether those services are provided,
    (b) whether A is, or ought to be, aware that C has engaged in exploitative conduct.

(3)   C engages in exploitative conduct if—
    (a) C uses force, threats (whether or not relating to violence) or any other form of coercion, or
    (b) C practises any form of deception.

(4)   A person guilty of an offence under this section is liable on summary conviction to a fine not exceeding level 3 on the standard scale.

54 SECTIONS 51A TO 53A: INTERPRETATION

(1)   In sections 52, 53 and 53A, "gain" means—
    (a) any financial advantage, including the discharge of an obligation to pay or the provision of goods or services (including sexual services) gratuitously or at a discount; or
    (b) the goodwill of any person which is or appears likely, in time, to bring financial advantage.

(2)   In sections 51A, 52, 53 and 53A "prostitute" and "prostitution" have the meaning given by section 51(2).

(3)   In section 53A "payment" has the meaning given by section 51(3).

. . .

61 ADMINISTERING A SUBSTANCE WITH INTENT

(1)   A person commits an offence if he intentionally administers a substance to, or causes a substance to be taken by, another person (B)—
    (a) knowing that B does not consent, and
    (b) with the intention of stupefying or overpowering B, so as to enable any person to engage in a sexual activity that involves B.

(2)   A person guilty of an offence under this section is liable—

(a) on summary conviction, to imprisonment for a term not exceeding 6 months or a fine not exceeding the statutory maximum or both;

(b) on conviction on indictment, to imprisonment for a term not exceeding 10 years.

62 COMMITTING AN OFFENCE WITH INTENT TO COMMIT A SEXUAL OFFENCE

(1) A person commits an offence under this section if he commits any offence with the intention of committing a relevant sexual offence.

(2) In this section, "relevant sexual offence" means any offence under this Part (including an offence of aiding, abetting, counselling or procuring such an offence).

(3) A person guilty of an offence under this section is liable on conviction on indictment, where the offence is committed by kidnapping or false imprisonment, to imprisonment for life.

(4) Unless subsection (3) applies, a person guilty of an offence under this section is liable—
   (a) on summary conviction, to imprisonment for a term not exceeding 6 months or a fine not exceeding the statutory maximum or both;
   (b) on conviction on indictment, to imprisonment for a term not exceeding 10 years.

63 TRESPASS WITH INTENT TO COMMIT A SEXUAL OFFENCE

(1) A person commits an offence if—
   (a) he is a trespasser on any premises,
   (b) he intends to commit a relevant sexual offence on the premises, and
   (c) he knows that, or is reckless as to whether, he is a trespasser.

(2) In this section—

   "premises" includes a structure or part of a structure;

   "relevant sexual offence" has the same meaning as in section 62;

   "structure" includes a tent, vehicle or vessel or other temporary or movable structure.

(3) A person guilty of an offence under this section is liable—
   (a) on summary conviction, to imprisonment for a term not exceeding 6 months or a fine not exceeding the statutory maximum or both;
   (b) on conviction on indictment, to imprisonment for a term not exceeding 10 years.

64 SEX WITH AN ADULT RELATIVE: PENETRATION

(1) A person aged 16 or over (A) (subject to subsection (3A)) commits an offence if—
   (a) he intentionally penetrates another person's vagina or anus with a part of his body or anything else, or penetrates another person's mouth with his penis,
   (b) the penetration is sexual,
   (c) the other person (B) is aged 18 or over,
   (d) A is related to B in a way mentioned in subsection (2), and
   (e) A knows or could reasonably be expected to know that he is related to B in that way.

(2) The ways that A may be related to B are as parent, grandparent, child, grandchild, brother, sister, half-brother, half-sister, uncle, aunt, nephew or niece.

(3) In subsection (2)—
   (za) "parent" includes an adoptive parent;
   (zb) "child" includes an adopted person within the meaning of Chapter 4 of Part 1 of the Adoption and Children Act 2002;

(a) "uncle" means the brother of a person's parent, and "aunt" has a corresponding meaning;

(b) "nephew" means the child of a person's brother or sister, and "niece" has a corresponding meaning.

(3A) Where subsection (1) applies in a case where A is related to B as B's child by virtue of subsection (3)(zb), A does not commit an offence under this section unless A is 18 or over.

(4) Where in proceedings for an offence under this section it is proved that the defendant was related to the other person in any of those ways, it is to be taken that the defendant knew or could reasonably have been expected to know that he was related in that way unless sufficient evidence is adduced to raise an issue as to whether he knew or could reasonably have been expected to know that he was.

(5) A person guilty of an offence under this section is liable—
   (a) on summary conviction, to imprisonment for a term not exceeding 6 months or a fine not exceeding the statutory maximum or both;
   (b) on conviction on indictment, to imprisonment for a term not exceeding 2 years.

. . .

65 SEX WITH AN ADULT RELATIVE: CONSENTING TO PENETRATION

(1) A person aged 16 or over (A) (subject to subsection (3A)) commits an offence if—
   (a) another person (B) penetrates A's vagina or anus with a part of B's body or anything else, or penetrates A's mouth with B's penis,
   (b) A consents to the penetration,
   (c) the penetration is sexual,
   (d) B is aged 18 or over,
   (e) A is related to B in a way mentioned in subsection (2), and
   (f) A knows or could reasonably be expected to know that he is related to B in that way.

(2) The ways that A may be related to B are as parent, grandparent, child, grandchild, brother, sister, half-brother, half-sister, uncle, aunt, nephew or niece.

(3) In subsection (2)—
   (za) "parent" includes an adoptive parent;
   (zb) "child" includes an adopted person within the meaning of Chapter 4 of Part 1 of the Adoption and Children Act 2002;
   (a) "uncle" means the brother of a person's parent, and "aunt" has a corresponding meaning;
   (b) "nephew" means the child of a person's brother or sister, and "niece" has a corresponding meaning.

(3A) Where subsection (1) applies in a case where A is related to B as B's child by virtue of subsection (3)(zb), A does not commit an offence under this section unless A is 18 or over.

(4) Where in proceedings for an offence under this section it is proved that the defendant was related to the other person in any of those ways, it is to be taken that the defendant knew or could reasonably have been expected to know that he was related in that way unless sufficient evidence is adduced to raise an issue as to whether he knew or could reasonably have been expected to know that he was.

(5) A person guilty of an offence under this section is liable—

(a) on summary conviction, to imprisonment for a term not exceeding 6 months or a fine not exceeding the statutory maximum or both;

(b) on conviction on indictment, to imprisonment for a term not exceeding 2 years.

. . .

66 EXPOSURE

(1)   A person commits an offence if—
(a) he intentionally exposes his genitals, and
(b) he intends that someone will see them and be caused alarm or distress.

(2)   A person guilty of an offence under this section is liable—
(a) on summary conviction, to imprisonment for a term not exceeding 6 months or a fine not exceeding the statutory maximum or both;
(b) on conviction on indictment, to imprisonment for a term not exceeding 2 years.

67 VOYEURISM

(1)   A person commits an offence if—
(a) for the purpose of obtaining sexual gratification, he observes another person doing a private act, and
(b) he knows that the other person does not consent to being observed for his sexual gratification.

(2)   A person commits an offence if—
(a) he operates equipment with the intention of enabling another person to observe, for the purpose of obtaining sexual gratification, a third person (B) doing a private act, and
(b) he knows that B does not consent to his operating equipment with that intention.

(3)   A person commits an offence if—
(a) he records another person (B) doing a private act,
(b) he does so with the intention that he or a third person will, for the purpose of obtaining sexual gratification, look at an image of B doing the act, and
(c) he knows that B does not consent to his recording the act with that intention.

(4)   A person commits an offence if he installs equipment, or constructs or adapts a structure or part of a structure, with the intention of enabling himself or another person to commit an offence under subsection (1).

(5)   A person guilty of an offence under this section is liable—
(a) on summary conviction, to imprisonment for a term not exceeding 6 months or a fine not exceeding the statutory maximum or both;
(b) on conviction on indictment, to imprisonment for a term not exceeding 2 years.

68 VOYEURISM: INTERPRETATION

(1)   For the purposes of section 67, a person is doing a private act if the person is in a place which, in the circumstances, would reasonably be expected to provide privacy, and—
(a) the person's genitals, buttocks or breasts are exposed or covered only with underwear,
(b) the person is using a lavatory, or
(c) the person is doing a sexual act that is not of a kind ordinarily done in public.

(2)   In section 67, "structure" includes a tent, vehicle or vessel or other temporary or movable structure.

69 INTERCOURSE WITH AN ANIMAL

(1)   A person commits an offence if—
    (a)   he intentionally performs an act of penetration with his penis,
    (b)   what is penetrated is the vagina or anus of a living animal, and
    (c)   he knows that, or is reckless as to whether, that is what is penetrated.

(2)   A person (A) commits an offence if—
    (a)   A intentionally causes, or allows, A's vagina or anus to be penetrated,
    (b)   the penetration is by the penis of a living animal, and
    (c)   A knows that, or is reckless as to whether, that is what A is being penetrated by.

(3)   A person guilty of an offence under this section is liable—
    (a)   on summary conviction, to imprisonment for a term not exceeding 6 months or a fine not exceeding the statutory maximum or both;
    (b)   on conviction on indictment, to imprisonment for a term not exceeding 2 years.

70 SEXUAL PENETRATION OF A CORPSE

(1)   A person commits an offence if—
    (a)   he intentionally performs an act of penetration with a part of his body or anything else,
    (b)   what is penetrated is a part of the body of a dead person,
    (c)   he knows that, or is reckless as to whether, that is what is penetrated, and
    (d)   the penetration is sexual.

(2)   A person guilty of an offence under this section is liable—
    (a)   on summary conviction, to imprisonment for a term not exceeding 6 months or a fine not exceeding the statutory maximum or both;
    (b)   on conviction on indictment, to imprisonment for a term not exceeding 2 years.

71 SEXUAL ACTIVITY IN A PUBLIC LAVATORY

(1)   A person commits an offence if—
    (a)   he is in a lavatory to which the public or a section of the public has or is permitted to have access, whether on payment or otherwise,
    (b)   he intentionally engages in an activity, and,
    (c)   the activity is sexual.

(2)   For the purposes of this section, an activity is sexual if a reasonable person would, in all the circumstances but regardless of any person's purpose, consider it to be sexual.

(3)   A person guilty of an offence under this section is liable on summary conviction, to imprisonment for a term not exceeding 6 months or a fine not exceeding level 5 on the standard scale or both.

. . .

73 EXCEPTIONS TO AIDING, ABETTING AND COUNSELLING

(1)   A person is not guilty of aiding, abetting or counselling the commission against a child of an offence to which this section applies if he acts for the purpose of—
    (a)   protecting the child from sexually transmitted infection,
    (b)   protecting the physical safety of the child,

(c) preventing the child from becoming pregnant, or

(d) promoting the child's emotional well-being by the giving of advice,

and not for the purpose of obtaining sexual gratification or for the purpose of causing or encouraging the activity constituting the offence or the child's participation in it.

(2) This section applies to—

(a) an offence under any of sections 5 to 7 (offences against children under 13);

(b) an offence under section 9 (sexual activity with a child);

(c) an offence under section 13 which would be an offence under section 9 if the offender were aged 18;

(d) an offence under any of sections 16, 25, 30, 34 and 38 (sexual activity) against a person under 16.

(3) This section does not affect any other enactment or any rule of law restricting the circumstances in which a person is guilty of aiding, abetting or counselling an offence under this Part.

74 "CONSENT"

For the purposes of this Part, a person consents if he agrees by choice, and has the freedom and capacity to make that choice.

75 EVIDENTIAL PRESUMPTIONS ABOUT CONSENT

(1) If in proceedings for an offence to which this section applies it is proved—

(a) that the defendant did the relevant act,

(b) that any of the circumstances specified in subsection (2) existed, and

(c) that the defendant knew that those circumstances existed,

the complainant is to be taken not to have consented to the relevant act unless sufficient evidence is adduced to raise an issue as to whether he consented, and the defendant is to be taken not to have reasonably believed that the complainant consented unless sufficient evidence is adduced to raise an issue as to whether he reasonably believed it.

(2) The circumstances are that—

(a) any person was, at the time of the relevant act or immediately before it began, using violence against the complainant or causing the complainant to fear that immediate violence would be used against him;

(b) any person was, at the time of the relevant act or immediately before it began, causing the complainant to fear that violence was being used, or that immediate violence would be used, against another person;

(c) the complainant was, and the defendant was not, unlawfully detained at the time of the relevant act;

(d) the complainant was asleep or otherwise unconscious at the time of the relevant act;

(e) because of the complainant's physical disability, the complainant would not have been able at the time of the relevant act to communicate to the defendant whether the complainant consented;

(f) any person had administered to or caused to be taken by the complainant, without the complainant's consent, a substance which, having regard to when it was administered or taken, was capable of causing or enabling the complainant to be stupefied or overpowered at the time of the relevant act.

(3) In subsection (2)(a) and (b), the reference to the time immediately before the relevant act began is, in the case of an act which is one of a continuous series of sexual activities, a reference to the time immediately before the first sexual activity began.

76 CONCLUSIVE PRESUMPTIONS ABOUT CONSENT

(1) If in proceedings for an offence to which this section applies it is proved that the defendant did the relevant act and that any of the circumstances specified in subsection (2) existed, it is to be conclusively presumed—
    (a) that the complainant did not consent to the relevant act, and
    (b) that the defendant did not believe that the complainant consented to the relevant act.

(2) The circumstances are that—
    (a) the defendant intentionally deceived the complainant as to the nature or purpose of the relevant act;
    (b) the defendant intentionally induced the complainant to consent to the relevant act by impersonating a person known personally to the complainant.

77 SECTIONS 75 AND 76: RELEVANT ACTS

In relation to an offence to which sections 75 and 76 apply, references in those sections to the relevant act and to the complainant are to be read as follows—

Offence	Relevant Act
An offence under section 1 (rape).	The defendant intentionally penetrating, with his penis, the vagina, anus or mouth of another person ("the complainant").
An offence under section 2 (assault by penetration).	The defendant intentionally penetrating, with a part of his body or anything else, the vagina or anus of another person ("the complainant"), where the penetration is sexual.
An offence under section 3 (sexual assault).	The defendant intentionally touching another person ("the complainant"), where the touching is sexual.
An offence under section 4 (causing a person to engage in sexual activity without consent).	The defendant intentionally causing another person ("the complainant") to engage in an activity, where the activity is sexual.

78 "SEXUAL"

For the purposes of this Part (except section 71), penetration, touching or any other activity is sexual if a reasonable person would consider that—

(a) whatever its circumstances or any person's purpose in relation to it, it is because of its nature sexual, or

(b) because of its nature it may be sexual and because of its circumstances or the purpose of any person in relation to it (or both) it is sexual.

79 PART 1: GENERAL INTERPRETATION

(1) The following apply for the purposes of this Part.

(2)   Penetration is a continuing act from entry to withdrawal.

(3)   References to a part of the body include references to a part surgically constructed (in particular, through gender reassignment surgery).

(4)   "Image" means a moving or still image and includes an image produced by any means and, where the context permits, a three-dimensional image.

(5)   References to an image of a person include references to an image of an imaginary person.

(6)   "Mental disorder" has the meaning given by section 1 of the Mental Health Act 1983 (c 20).

(7)   References to observation (however expressed) are to observation whether direct or by looking at an image.

(8)   Touching includes touching—
       (a) with any part of the body,
       (b) with anything else,
       (c) through anything,
       and in particular includes touching amounting to penetration.

(9)   "Vagina" includes vulva.

(10)   In relation to an animal, references to the vagina or anus include references to any similar part.

PART 2

NOTIFICATION AND ORDERS

Notification requirements

80 PERSONS BECOMING SUBJECT TO NOTIFICATION REQUIREMENTS

(1)   A person is subject to the notification requirements of this Part for the period set out in section 82 ("the notification period") if–
       (a) he is convicted of an offence listed in Schedule 3;
       (b) he is found not guilty of such an offence by reason of insanity;
       (c) he is found to be under a disability and to have done the act charged against him in respect of such an offence; or
       (d) in England and Wales or Northern Ireland, he is cautioned in respect of such an offence.

(2)   A person for the time being subject to the notification requirements of this Part is referred to in this Part as a "relevant offender".

81 PERSONS FORMERLY SUBJECT TO PART 1 OF THE SEX OFFENDERS ACT 1997

(1)   A person is, from the commencement of this Part until the end of the notification period, subject to the notification requirements of this Part if, before the commencement of this Part–

(a) he was convicted of an offence listed in Schedule 3;

(b) he was found not guilty of such an offence by reason of insanity;

(c) he was found to be under a disability and to have done the act charged against him in respect of such an offence; or

(d) in England and Wales or Northern Ireland, he was cautioned in respect of such an offence.

(2) Subsection (1) does not apply if the notification period ended before the commencement of this Part.

(3) Subsection (1)(a) does not apply to a conviction before 1st September 1997 unless, at the beginning of that day, the person–

(a) had not been dealt with in respect of the offence;

(b) was serving a sentence of imprisonment [. . .]1 or was subject to a community order, in respect of the offence;

(c) was subject to supervision, having been released from prison after serving the whole or part of a sentence of imprisonment in respect of the offence; or

(d) was detained in a hospital or was subject to a guardianship order, following the conviction.

(4) Paragraphs (b) and (c) of subsection (1) do not apply to a finding made before 1st September 1997 unless, at the beginning of that day, the person–

(a) had not been dealt with in respect of the finding; or

(b) was detained in a hospital, following the finding.

(5) Subsection (1)(d) does not apply to a caution given before 1st September 1997.

(6) A person who would have been within subsection (3)(b) or (d) or (4)(b) but for the fact that at the beginning of 1st September 1997 he was unlawfully at large or absent without leave, on temporary release or leave of absence, or on bail pending an appeal, is to be treated as being within that provision.

(7) Where, immediately before the commencement of this Part, an order under a provision within subsection (8) was in force in respect of a person, the person is subject to the notification requirements of this Part from that commencement until the order is discharged or otherwise ceases to have effect.

(8) The provisions are–

(a) section 5A of the Sex Offenders Act 1997 (c. 51) (restraining orders);

(b) section 2 of the Crime and Disorder Act 1998 (c. 37) (sex offender orders made in England and Wales);

(c) section 2A of the Crime and Disorder Act 1998 (interim orders made in England and Wales);

(d) section 20 of the Crime and Disorder Act 1998 (sex offender orders and interim orders made in Scotland);

(e) Article 6 of the Criminal Justice (Northern Ireland) Order 1998 (S.I. 1998/2839 (N.I. 20)) (sex offender orders made in Northern Ireland);

(f) Article 6A of the Criminal Justice (Northern Ireland) Order 1998 (interim orders made in Northern Ireland).

82 THE NOTIFICATION PERIOD

(1) The notification period for a person within section 80(1) or 81(1) is the period in the second column of the following Table opposite the description that applies to him.

TABLE

Description of relevant offender	Notification period
A person who, in respect of the offence, is or has been sentenced to imprisonment for life, to imprisonment for public protection under section 225 of the Criminal Justice Act 2003, to an indeterminate custodial sentence under Article 13(4)(a) of the Criminal Justice (Northern Ireland) Order 2008 or to imprisonment for a term of 30 months or more	An indefinite period beginning with the relevant date
A person who, in respect of the offence, has been made the subject of an order under section 210F(1) of the Criminal Procedure (Scotland) Act 1995 (order for lifelong restriction)	An indefinite period beginning with that date
A person who, in respect of the offence or finding, is or has been admitted to a hospital subject to a restriction order	An indefinite period beginning with that date
A person who, in respect of the offence, is or has been sentenced to imprisonment for a term of more than 6 months but less than 30 months	10 years beginning with that date
A person who, in respect of the offence, is or has been sentenced to imprisonment for a term of 6 months or less	7 years beginning with that date
A person who, in respect of the offence or finding, is or has been admitted to a hospital without being subject to a restriction order	7 years beginning with that date
A person within section 80(1)(d)	2 years beginning with that date
A person in whose case an order for conditional discharge or, in Scotland, a community payback order imposing an offender supervision requirement, is made in respect of the offence	The period of conditional discharge or, in Scotland, the specified period for the offender supervision requirement
A person of any other description	5 years beginning with the relevant date

(2)   Where a person is under 18 on the relevant date, subsection (1) has effect as if for any reference to a period of 10 years, 7 years, 5 years or 2 years there were substituted a reference to one-half of that period.

(3)   Subsection (4) applies where a relevant offender within section 80(1)(a) or 81(1)(a) is or has been sentenced, in respect of two or more offences listed in Schedule 3–

(a) to consecutive terms of imprisonment; or

(b) to terms of imprisonment which are partly concurrent.

(4) Where this subsection applies, subsection (1) has effect as if the relevant offender were or had been sentenced, in respect of each of the offences, to a term of imprisonment which–

(a) in the case of consecutive terms, is equal to the aggregate of those terms;

(b) in the case of partly concurrent terms (X and Y, which overlap for a period Z), is equal to X plus Y minus Z.

(5) Where a relevant offender the subject of a finding within section 80(1)(c) or 81(1)(c) is subsequently tried for the offence, the notification period relating to the finding ends at the conclusion of the trial.

(6) In this Part, "relevant date" means–

(a) in the case of a person within section 80(1)(a) or 81(1)(a), the date of the conviction;

(b) in the case of a person within section 80(1)(b) or (c) or 81(1)(b) or (c), the date of the finding;

(c) in the case of a person within section 80(1)(d) or 81(1)(d), the date of the caution;

(d) in the case of a person within section 81(7), the date which, for the purposes of Part 1 of the Sex Offenders Act 1997 (c. 51), was the relevant date in relation to that person.

83 NOTIFICATION REQUIREMENTS: INITIAL NOTIFICATION

(1) A relevant offender must, within the period of 3 days beginning with the relevant date (or, if later, the commencement of this Part), notify to the police the information set out in subsection (5).

(2) Subsection (1) does not apply to a relevant offender in respect of a conviction, finding or caution within section 80(1) if–

(a) immediately before the conviction, finding or caution, he was subject to the notification requirements of this Part as a result of another conviction, finding or caution or an order of a court ("the earlier event"),

(b) at that time, he had made a notification under subsection (1) in respect of the earlier event, and

(c) throughout the period referred to in subsection (1), he remains subject to the notification requirements as a result of the earlier event.

(3) Subsection (1) does not apply to a relevant offender in respect of a conviction, finding or caution within section 81(1) or an order within section 81(7) if the offender complied with section 2(1) of the Sex Offenders Act 1997 in respect of the conviction, finding, caution or order.

(4) Where a notification order is made in respect of a conviction, finding or caution, subsection (1) does not apply to the relevant offender in respect of the conviction, finding or caution if–

(a) immediately before the order was made, he was subject to the notification requirements of this Part as a result of another conviction, finding or caution or an order of a court ("the earlier event"),

(b) at that time, he had made a notification under subsection (1) in respect of the earlier event, and

(c) throughout the period referred to in subsection (1), he remains subject to the notification requirements as a result of the earlier event.

(5) The information is–

(a) the relevant offender's date of birth;

(b) his national insurance number;

(c) his name on the relevant date and, where he used one or more other names on that date, each of those names;

(d) his home address on the relevant date;

(e) his name on the date on which notification is given and, where he uses one or more other names on that date, each of those names;

(f) his home address on the date on which notification is given;

(g) the address of any other premises in the United Kingdom at which, at the time the notification is given, he regularly resides or stays;

(h) any prescribed information.

(5A) In subsection (5)(h) "prescribed" means prescribed by regulations made by the Secretary of State.

(6) When determining the period for the purpose of subsection (1), there is to be disregarded any time when the relevant offender is–

(a) remanded in or committed to custody by an order of a court or kept in service custody;

(b) serving a sentence of imprisonment or a term of service detention;

(c) detained in a hospital; or

(d) outside the United Kingdom.

(7) In this Part, "home address" means, in relation to any person–

(a) the address of his sole or main residence in the United Kingdom, or

(b) where he has no such residence, the address or location of a place in the United Kingdom where he can regularly be found and, if there is more than one such place, such one of those places as the person may select.

84 NOTIFICATION REQUIREMENTS: CHANGES

(1) A relevant offender must, within the period of 3 days beginning with–

(a) his using a name which has not been notified to the police under section 83(1), this subsection, or section 2 of the Sex Offenders Act 1997 (c. 51),

(b) any change of his home address,

(c) his having resided or stayed, for a qualifying period, at any premises in the United Kingdom the address of which has not been notified to the police under section 83(1), this subsection, or section 2 of the Sex Offenders Act 1997,

(ca) any prescribed change of circumstances, or

(d) his release from custody pursuant to an order of a court or from imprisonment, service detention or detention in a hospital, notify to the police that name, the new home address, the address of those premises, the prescribed details or (as the case may be) the fact that he has been released, and (in addition) the information set out in section 83(5).

(2) A notification under subsection (1) may be given before the name is used, the change of home address or the prescribed change of circumstances occurs or the qualifying period ends, but in that case the relevant offender must also specify the date when the event is expected to occur.

(3) If a notification is given in accordance with subsection (2) and the event to which it relates occurs more than 2 days before the date specified, the notification does not affect the duty imposed by subsection (1).

(4) If a notification is given in accordance with subsection (2) and the event to which it relates has not occurred by the end of the period of 3 days beginning with the date specified–

(a) the notification does not affect the duty imposed by subsection (1), and

(b) the relevant offender must, within the period of 6 days beginning with the date specified, notify to the police the fact that the event did not occur within the period of 3 days beginning with the date specified.

(5)   Section 83(6) applies to the determination of the period of 3 days mentioned in subsection (1) and the period of 6 days mentioned in subsection (4)(b), as it applies to the determination of the period mentioned in section 83(1).

(5A) In this section—
      (a) "prescribed change of circumstances" means any change—
           (i)   occurring in relation to any matter in respect of which information is required to be notified by virtue of section 83(5)(h), and
           (ii) of a description prescribed by regulations made by the Secretary of State;
      (b) "the prescribed details", in relation to a prescribed change of circumstances, means such details of the change as may be so prescribed.

(6)   In this section, "qualifying period" means–
      (a) a period of 7 days, or
      (b) two or more periods, in any period of 12 months, which taken together amount to 7 days.

85 NOTIFICATION REQUIREMENTS: PERIODIC NOTIFICATION

(1)   A relevant offender must, within the applicable period after each event within subsection (2), notify to the police the information set out in section 83(5), unless within that period he has given a notification under section 84(1).

(2)   The events are–
      (a) the commencement of this Part (but only in the case of a person who is a relevant offender from that commencement);
      (b) any notification given by the relevant offender under section 83(1) or 84(1); and
      (c) any notification given by him under subsection (1).

(3)   Where the applicable period would (apart from this subsection) end whilst subsection (4) applies to the relevant offender, that period is to be treated as continuing until the end of the period of 3 days beginning when subsection (4) first ceases to apply to him.

(4)   This subsection applies to the relevant offender if he is–
      (a) remanded in or committed to custody by an order of a court or kept in service custody,
      (b) serving a sentence of imprisonment or a term of service detention,
      (c) detained in a hospital, or
      (d) outside the United Kingdom.

(5)   In this section, "the applicable period" means—
      (a) in any case where subsection (6) applies to the relevant offender, such period as may be prescribed by regulations made by the Secretary of State, and
      (b) in any other case, the period of one year.

(6)   This subsection applies to the relevant offender if the last home address notified by him under section 83(1) or 84(1) or subsection (1) was the address or location of such a place as is mentioned in section 83(7)(b).

86 NOTIFICATION REQUIREMENTS: TRAVEL OUTSIDE THE UNITED KINGDOM

(1)   The Secretary of State may by regulations make provision requiring relevant offenders who leave the United Kingdom, or any description of such offenders–
      (a) to give in accordance with the regulations, before they leave, a notification under subsection (2);

(b) if they subsequently return to the United Kingdom, to give in accordance with the regulations a notification under subsection (3).

(2) A notification under this subsection must disclose–
(a) the date on which the offender will leave the United Kingdom;
(b) the country (or, if there is more than one, the first country) to which he will travel and his point of arrival (determined in accordance with the regulations) in that country;
(c) any other information prescribed by the regulations which the offender holds about his departure from or return to the United Kingdom or his movements while outside the United Kingdom.

(3) A notification under this subsection must disclose any information prescribed by the regulations about the offender's return to the United Kingdom.

87 METHOD OF NOTIFICATION AND RELATED MATTERS

(1) A person gives a notification under section 83(1), 84(1) or 85(1) by–
(a) attending at such police station in his local police area as the Secretary of State may by regulations prescribe or, if there is more than one, at any of them, and
(b) giving an oral notification to any police officer, or to any person authorised for the purpose by the officer in charge of the station.

(2) A person giving a notification under section 84(1)–
(a) in relation to a prospective change of home address, or
(b) in relation to premises referred to in subsection (1)(c) of that section, may give the notification at a police station that would fall within subsection (1) above if the change in home address had already occurred or (as the case may be) if the address of those premises were his home address.

(3) Any notification under this section must be acknowledged; and an acknowledgment under this subsection must be in writing, and in such form as the Secretary of State may direct.

(4) Where a notification is given under section 83(1), 84(1) or 85(1), the relevant offender must, if requested to do so by the police officer or person referred to in subsection (1)(b), allow the officer or person to–
(a) take his fingerprints,
(b) photograph any part of him, or
(c) do both these things.

(5) The power in subsection (4) is exercisable for the purpose of verifying the identity of the relevant offender.

88 SECTION 87: INTERPRETATION

(1) Subsections (2) to (4) apply for the purposes of section 87.

(2) "Photograph" includes any process by means of which an image may be produced.

(3) "Local police area" means, in relation to a person–
(a) the police area in which his home address is situated;
(b) in the absence of a home address, the police area in which the home address last notified is situated;
(c) in the absence of a home address and of any such notification, the police area in which the court which last dealt with the person in a way mentioned in subsection (4) is situated.

(4)   The ways are–
    (a)   dealing with a person in respect of an offence listed in Schedule 3 or a finding in relation to such an offence;
    (b)   dealing with a person in respect of an offence under section 128 or a finding in relation to such an offence;
    (c)   making, in respect of a person, a notification order, interim notification order, sexual offences prevention order or interim sexual offences prevention order;
    (d)   making, in respect of a person, an order under section 2, 2A or 20 of the Crime and Disorder Act 1998 (c. 37) (sex offender orders and interim orders made in England and Wales or Scotland) or Article 6 or 6A of the Criminal Justice (Northern Ireland) Order 1998 (S.I. 1998/2839 (N.I. 20)) (sex offender orders and interim orders made in Northern Ireland); and in paragraphs (a) and (b), "finding" in relation to an offence means a finding of not guilty of the offence by reason of insanity or a finding that the person was under a disability and did the act or omission charged against him in respect of the offence.

(5)   Subsection (3) applies as if Northern Ireland were a police area.

. . .

104 SEXUAL OFFENCES PREVENTION ORDERS: APPLICATIONS AND GROUNDS

(1)   A court may make an order under this section in respect of a person ("the defendant") where any of subsections (2) to (4) applies to the defendant and–
    (a)   where subsection (4) applies, it is satisfied that the defendant's behaviour since the appropriate date makes it necessary to make such an order, for the purpose of protecting the public or any particular members of the public from serious sexual harm from the defendant;
    (b)   in any other case, it is satisfied that it is necessary to make such an order, for the purpose of protecting the public or any particular members of the public from serious sexual harm from the defendant.

(2)   This subsection applies to the defendant where the court deals with him in respect of an offence listed in Schedule 3 or 5.

(3)   This subsection applies to the defendant where the court deals with him in respect of a finding–
    (a)   that he is not guilty of an offence listed in Schedule 3 or 5 by reason of insanity, or
    (b)   that he is under a disability and has done the act charged against him in respect of such an offence.

(4)   This subsection applies to the defendant where–
    (a)   an application under subsection (5) has been made to the court in respect of him, and
    (b)   on the application, it is proved that he is a qualifying offender.

(5)   A chief officer of police may by complaint to a magistrates' court apply for an order under this section in respect of a person who resides in his police area or who the chief officer believes is in, or is intending to come to, his police area if it appears to the chief officer that–
    (a)   the person is a qualifying offender, and
    (b)   the person has since the appropriate date acted in such a way as to give reasonable cause to believe that it is necessary for such an order to be made.

(6)   An application under subsection (5) may be made to any magistrates' court whose commission area includes–

(a) any part of the applicant's police area, or
(b) any place where it is alleged that the person acted in a way mentioned in subsection (5)(b).

. . .

123 RISK OF SEXUAL HARM ORDERS: APPLICATIONS, GROUNDS AND EFFECT

(1) A chief officer of police may by complaint to a magistrates' court apply for an order under this section (a "risk of sexual harm order") in respect of a person aged 18 or over ("the defendant") who resides in his police area or who the chief officer believes is in, or is intending to come to, his police area if it appears to the chief officer that–
  (a) the defendant has on at least two occasions, whether before or after the commencement of this Part, done an act within subsection (3), and
  (b) as a result of those acts, there is reasonable cause to believe that it is necessary for such an order to be made.

(2) An application under subsection (1) may be made to any magistrates' court whose commission area includes–
  (a) any part of the applicant's police area, or
  (b) any place where it is alleged that the defendant acted in a way mentioned in subsection (1)(a).

(3) The acts are–
  (a) engaging in sexual activity involving a child or in the presence of a child;
  (b) causing or inciting a child to watch a person engaging in sexual activity or to look at a moving or still image that is sexual;
  (c) giving a child anything that relates to sexual activity or contains a reference to such activity;
  (d) communicating with a child, where any part of the communication is sexual.

(4) On the application, the court may make a risk of sexual harm order if it is satisfied that–
  (a) the defendant has on at least two occasions, whether before or after the commencement of this section, done an act within subsection (3); and
  (b) it is necessary to make such an order, for the purpose of protecting children generally or any child from harm from the defendant.

(5) Such an order–
  (a) prohibits the defendant from doing anything described in the order;
  (b) has effect for a fixed period (not less than 2 years) specified in the order or until further order.

(6) The only prohibitions that may be imposed are those necessary for the purpose of protecting children generally or any child from harm from the defendant.

(7) Where a court makes a risk of sexual harm order in relation to a person already subject to such an order (whether made by that court or another), the earlier order ceases to have effect.

124 SECTION 123: INTERPRETATION

(1) Subsections (2) to (7) apply for the purposes of section 123.

(2) "Protecting children generally or any child from harm from the defendant" means protecting children generally or any child from physical or psychological harm, caused by the defendant doing acts within section 123(3).

(3) "Child" means a person under 16.

(4) "Image" means an image produced by any means, whether of a real or imaginary subject.

(5) "Sexual activity" means an activity that a reasonable person would, in all the circumstances but regardless of any person's purpose, consider to be sexual.

(6) A communication is sexual if–
   (a) any part of it relates to sexual activity, or
   (b) a reasonable person would, in all the circumstances but regardless of any person's purpose, consider that any part of the communication is sexual.

(7) An image is sexual if–
   (a) any part of it relates to sexual activity, or
   (b) a reasonable person would, in all the circumstances but regardless of any person's purpose, consider that any part of the image is sexual.

As amended Children and Young Persons Act 2008, s 8(2), Criminal Justice and Immigration Act 2008; Policing and Crime Act 2009.

CHILDREN ACT 2004

58 REASONABLE PUNISHMENT

(1) In relation to any offence specified in subsection (2), battery of a child cannot be justified on the ground that it constituted reasonable punishment.

(2) The offences referred to in subsection (1) are—
   (a) an offence under section 18 or 20 of the Offences against the Person Act 1861 (c. 100) (wounding and causing grievous bodily harm);
   (b) an offence under section 47 of that Act (assault occasioning actual bodily harm);
   (c) an offence under section 1 of the Children and Young Persons Act 1933 (c. 12) (cruelty to persons under 16).

(3) Battery of a child causing actual bodily harm to the child cannot be justified in any civil proceedings on the ground that it constituted reasonable punishment.

(4) For the purposes of subsection (3) "actual bodily harm" has the same meaning as it has for the purposes of section 47 of the Offences against the Person Act 1861.

DOMESTIC VIOLENCE, CRIME AND VICTIMS ACT 2004

5 THE OFFENCE

(1) A person ("D") is guilty of an offence if—
   (a) a child or vulnerable adult ("V") dies or suffers serious physical harm as a result of the unlawful act of a person who—
      (i) was a member of the same household as V, and
      (ii) had frequent contact with him,
   (b) D was such a person at the time of that act,

(c) at that time there was a significant risk of serious physical harm being caused to V by the unlawful act of such a person, and

(d) either D was the person whose act caused the death or serious physical harm or—

    (i)   D was, or ought to have been, aware of the risk mentioned in paragraph (c),

    (ii) D failed to take such steps as he could reasonably have been expected to take to protect V from the risk, and

    (iii) the act occurred in circumstances of the kind that D foresaw or ought to have foreseen.

(2) The prosecution does not have to prove whether it is the first alternative in subsection (1) (d) or the second (sub-paragraphs (i) to (iii)) that applies.

(3) If D was not the mother or father of V—

(a) D may not be charged with an offence under this section if he was under the age of 16 at the time of the act that caused the death or serious physical harm;

(b) for the purposes of subsection (1)(d)(ii) D could not have been expected to take any such step as is referred to there before attaining that age.

(4) For the purposes of this section—

(a) a person is to be regarded as a "member" of a particular household, even if he does not live in that household, if he visits it so often and for such periods of time that it is reasonable to regard him as a member of it;

(b) where V lived in different households at different times, "the same household as V" refers to the household in which V was living at the time of the act that caused the death or serious physical harm.

(5) For the purposes of this section an "unlawful" act is one that—

(a) constitutes an offence, or

(b) would constitute an offence but for being the act of—

    (i) a person under the age of ten, or

    (ii) a person entitled to rely on a defence of insanity.

Paragraph (b) does not apply to an act of D.

(6) In this section—

"act" includes a course of conduct and also includes omission;

"child" means a person under the age of 16;

"serious" harm means harm that amounts to grievous bodily harm for the purposes of the Offences against the Person Act 1861 (c. 100);

"vulnerable adult" means a person aged 16 or over whose ability to protect himself from violence, abuse or neglect is significantly impaired through physical or mental disability or illness, through old age or otherwise.

(7) A person guilty of an offence under this section of causing or allowing a peron's death is liable on conviction on indictment to imprisonment for a term not exceeding 14 years or to a fine, or to both.

(8) A person guilty of an offence under this section of causing or allowing a person to suffer serious physical harm is liable on conviction on indictment to imprisonment for a term not exceeding 10 years or to a fine, or to both.

As amended by Domestic Violence, Crime and Victims (Amendment) Act 2012.

GENDER RECOGNITION ACT 2004

9 GENERAL

(1) Where a full gender recognition certificate is issued to a person, the person's gender becomes for all purposes the acquired gender (so that, if the acquired gender is the male gender, the person's sex becomes that of a man and, if it is the female gender, the person's sex becomes that of a woman).

(2) Subsection (1) does not affect things done, or events occurring, before the certificate is issued; but it does operate for the interpretation of enactments passed, and instruments and other documents made, before the certificate is issued (as well as those passed or made afterwards).

(3) Subsection (1) is subject to provision made by this Act or any other enactment or any subordinate legislation.

20 GENDER-SPECIFIC OFFENCES

(1) Where (apart from this subsection) a relevant gender-specific offence could be committed or attempted only if the gender of a person to whom a full gender recognition certificate has been issued were not the acquired gender, the fact that the person's gender has become the acquired gender does not prevent the offence being committed or attempted.

(2) An offence is a "relevant gender-specific offence" if—
(a) either or both of the conditions in subsection (3) are satisfied, and
(b) the commission of the offence involves the accused engaging in sexual activity.

(3) The conditions are—
(a) that the offence may be committed only by a person of a particular gender, and
(b) that the offence may be committed only on, or in relation to, a person of a particular gender,
and the references to a particular gender include a gender identified by reference to the gender of the other person involved.

HUNTING ACT 2004

1 HUNTING WILD MAMMALS WITH DOGS

A person commits an offence if he hunts a wild mammal with a dog, unless his hunting is exempt.

2 EXEMPT HUNTING

(1) Hunting is exempt if it is within a class specified in Schedule 1.

(2) The Secretary of State may by order amend Schedule 1 so as to vary a class of exempt hunting.

3 HUNTING: ASSISTANCE

(1) A person commits an offence if he knowingly permits land which belongs to him to be entered or used in the course of the commission of an offence under section 1.

(2)   A person commits an offence if he knowingly permits a dog which belongs to him to be used in the course of the commission of an offence under section 1.

4 HUNTING: DEFENCE

It is a defence for a person charged with an offence under section 1 in respect of hunting to show that he reasonably believed that the hunting was exempt.

5 HARE COURSING

(1)   A person commits an offence if he—
 (a) participates in a hare coursing event,
 (b) attends a hare coursing event,
 (c) knowingly facilitates a hare coursing event, or
 (d) permits land which belongs to him to be used for the purposes of a hare coursing event.

(2)   Each of the following persons commits an offence if a dog participates in a hare coursing event—
 (a) any person who enters the dog for the event,
 (b) any person who permits the dog to be entered, and
 (c) any person who controls or handles the dog in the course of or for the purposes of the event.

(3)   A "hare coursing event" is a competition in which dogs are, by the use of live hares, assessed as to skill in hunting hares.

6 PENALTY

A person guilty of an offence under this Act shall be liable on summary conviction to a fine not exceeding level 5 on the standard scale.

11 INTERPRETATION

(1)   In this Act "wild mammal" includes, in particular—
 (a) a wild mammal which has been bred or tamed for any purpose,
 (b) a wild mammal which is in captivity or confinement,
 (c) a wild mammal which has escaped or been released from captivity or confinement, and
 (d) any mammal which is living wild.

(2)   For the purposes of this Act a reference to a person hunting a wild mammal with a dog includes, in particular, any case where—
 (a) a person engages or participates in the pursuit of a wild mammal, and
 (b) one or more dogs are employed in that pursuit (whether or not by him and whether or not under his control or direction).

(3)   For the purposes of this Act land belongs to a person if he—
 (a) owns an interest in it,
 (b) manages or controls it, or
 (c) occupies it.

(4)   For the purposes of this Act a dog belongs to a person if he—
 (a) owns it,
 (b) is in charge of it, or
 (c) has control of it.

SCHEDULE 1

Section 2 EXEMPT HUNTING

Stalking and flushing out

1   (1) Stalking a wild mammal, or flushing it out of cover, is exempt hunting if the conditions in this paragraph are satisfied.

   (2) The first condition is that the stalking or flushing out is undertaken for the purpose of—
     (a) preventing or reducing serious damage which the wild mammal would otherwise cause—
       (i)   to livestock,
       (ii)   to game birds or wild birds (within the meaning of section 27 of the Wildlife and Countryside Act 1981 (c. 69)),
       (iii) to food for livestock,
       (iv)   to crops (including vegetables and fruit),
       (v)   to growing timber,
       (vi)   to fisheries,
       (vii) to other property, or
       (viii) to the biological diversity of an area (within the meaning of the United Nations Environmental Programme Convention on Biological Diversity of 1992),
     (b) obtaining meat to be used for human or animal consumption, or
     (c) participation in a field trial.

   (3) In subparagraph (2)(c) "field trial" means a competition (other than a hare coursing event within the meaning of section 5) in which dogs—
     (a) flush animals out of cover or retrieve animals that have been shot (or both), and
     (b) are assessed as to their likely usefulness in connection with shooting.

   (4) The second condition is that the stalking or flushing out takes place on land—
     (a) which belongs to the person doing the stalking or flushing out, or
     (b) which he has been given permission to use for the purpose by the occupier or, in the case of unoccupied land, by a person to whom it belongs.

   (5) The third condition is that the stalking or flushing out does not involve the use of more than two dogs.

   (6) The fourth condition is that the stalking or flushing out does not involve the use of a dog below ground otherwise than in accordance with paragraph 2 below.

   (7) The fifth condition is that—
     (a) reasonable steps are taken for the purpose of ensuring that as soon as possible after being found or flushed out the wild mammal is shot dead by a competent person, and
     (b) in particular, each dog used in the stalking or flushing out is kept under sufficiently close control to ensure that it does not prevent or obstruct achievement of the objective in paragraph (a).

Use of dogs below ground to protect birds for shooting

2   (1) The use of a dog below ground in the course of stalking or flushing out is in accordance with this paragraph if the conditions in this paragraph are satisfied.

   (2) The first condition is that the stalking or flushing out is undertaken for the purpose of preventing or reducing serious damage to game birds or wild birds (within the meaning of section 27 of the Wildlife and Countryside Act 1981 (c. 69)) which a person is keeping or preserving for the purpose of their being shot.

(3) The second condition is that the person doing the stalking or flushing out—
    (a) has with him written evidence—
        (i) that the land on which the stalking or flushing out takes place belongs to him, or
        (ii) that he has been given permission to use that land for the purpose by the occupier or, in the case of unoccupied land, by a person to whom it belongs, and
    (b) makes the evidence immediately available for inspection by a constable who asks to see it.

(4) The third condition is that the stalking or flushing out does not involve the use of more than one dog below ground at any one time.

(5) In so far as stalking or flushing out is undertaken with the use of a dog below ground in accordance with this paragraph, paragraph 1 shall have effect as if for the condition in paragraph 1(7) there were substituted the condition that—
    (a) reasonable steps are taken for the purpose of ensuring that as soon as possible after being found the wild mammal is flushed out from below ground,
    (b) reasonable steps are taken for the purpose of ensuring that as soon as possible after being flushed out from below ground the wild mammal is shot dead by a competent person,
    (c) in particular, the dog is brought under sufficiently close control to ensure that it does not prevent or obstruct achievement of the objective in paragraph (b),
    (d) reasonable steps are taken for the purpose of preventing injury to the dog, and
    (e) the manner in which the dog is used complies with any code of practice which is issued or approved for the purpose of this paragraph by the Secretary of State.

Rats
3   The hunting of rats is exempt if it takes place on land—
    (a) which belongs to the hunter, or
    (b) which he has been given permission to use for the purpose by the occupier or, in the case of unoccupied land, by a person to whom it belongs.

Rabbits
4   The hunting of rabbits is exempt if it takes place on land—
    (a) which belongs to the hunter, or
    (b) which he has been given permission to use for the purpose by the occupier or, in the case of unoccupied land, by a person to whom it belongs.

Retrieval of hares
5   The hunting of a hare which has been shot is exempt if it takes place on land—
    (a) which belongs to the hunter, or
    (b) which he has been given permission to use for the purpose of hunting hares by the occupier or, in the case of unoccupied land, by a person to whom it belongs.

Falconry
6   Flushing a wild mammal from cover is exempt hunting if undertaken—
    (a) for the purpose of enabling a bird of prey to hunt the wild mammal, and
    (b) on land which belongs to the hunter or which he has been given permission to use for the purpose by the occupier or, in the case of unoccupied land, by a person to whom it belongs.

Recapture of wild mammal
7   (1) The hunting of a wild mammal which has escaped or been released from captivity or confinement is exempt if the conditions in this paragraph are satisfied.

(2) The first condition is that the hunting takes place—
   (a) on land which belongs to the hunter,
   (b) on land which he has been given permission to use for the purpose by the occupier or, in the case of unoccupied land, by a person to whom it belongs, or
   (c) with the authority of a constable.

(3) The second condition is that—
   (a) reasonable steps are taken for the purpose of ensuring that as soon as possible after being found the wild mammal is recaptured or shot dead by a competent person, and
   (b) in particular, each dog used in the hunt is kept under sufficiently close control to ensure that it does not prevent or obstruct achievement of the objective in paragraph (a).

(4) The third condition is that the wild mammal—
   (a) was not released for the purpose of being hunted, and
   (b) was not, for that purpose, permitted to escape.

Rescue of wild mammal

8 (1) The hunting of a wild mammal is exempt if the conditions in this paragraph are satisfied.

(2) The first condition is that the hunter reasonably believes that the wild mammal is or may be injured.

(3) The second condition is that the hunting is undertaken for the purpose of relieving the wild mammal's suffering.

(4) The third condition is that the hunting does not involve the use of more than two dogs.

(5) The fourth condition is that the hunting does not involve the use of a dog below ground.

(6) The fifth condition is that the hunting takes place—
   (a) on land which belongs to the hunter,
   (b) on land which he has been given permission to use for the purpose by the occupier or, in the case of unoccupied land, by a person to whom it belongs, or
   (c) with the authority of a constable.

(7) The sixth condition is that—
   (a) reasonable steps are taken for the purpose of ensuring that as soon as possible after the wild mammal is found appropriate action (if any) is taken to relieve its suffering, and
   (b) in particular, each dog used in the hunt is kept under sufficiently close control to ensure that it does not prevent or obstruct achievement of the objective in paragraph (a).

(8) The seventh condition is that the wild mammal was not harmed for the purpose of enabling it to be hunted in reliance upon this paragraph.

Research and observation

9 (1) The hunting of a wild mammal is exempt if the conditions in this paragraph are satisfied.

(2) The first condition is that the hunting is undertaken for the purpose of or in connection with the observation or study of the wild mammal.

(3) The second condition is that the hunting does not involve the use of more than two dogs.

(4) The third condition is that the hunting does not involve the use of a dog below ground.

(5) The fourth condition is that the hunting takes place on land—
  (a) which belongs to the hunter, or
  (b) which he has been given permission to use for the purpose by the occupier or, in the case of unoccupied land, by a person to whom it belongs.

(6) The fifth condition is that each dog used in the hunt is kept under sufficiently close control to ensure that it does not injure the wild mammal.

GAMBLING ACT 2005

42 CHEATING

(1) A person commits an offence if he—
  (a) cheats at gambling, or
  (b) does anything for the purpose of enabling or assisting another person to cheat at gambling.

(2) For the purposes of subsection (1) it is immaterial whether a person who cheats—
  (a) improves his chances of winning anything, or
  (b) wins anything.

(3) Without prejudice to the generality of subsection (1) cheating at gambling may, in particular, consist of actual or attempted deception or interference in connection with—
  (a) the process by which gambling is conducted, or
  (b) a real or virtual game, race or other event or process to which gambling relates.

(4) A person guilty of an offence under this section shall be liable—
  (a) on conviction on indictment, to imprisonment for a term not exceeding two years, to a fine or to both, or
  (b) on summary conviction, to imprisonment for a term not exceeding 51 weeks, to a fine not exceeding the statutory maximum or to both.

MENTAL CAPACITY ACT 2005

2 PEOPLE WHO LACK CAPACITY

(1) For the purposes of this Act, a person lacks capacity in relation to a matter if at the material time he is unable to make a decision for himself in relation to the matter because of an impairment of, or a disturbance in the functioning of, the mind or brain.

(2) It does not matter whether the impairment or disturbance is permanent or temporary.

(3) A lack of capacity cannot be established merely by reference to—
  (a) a person's age or appearance, or
  (b) a condition of his, or an aspect of his behaviour, which might lead others to make unjustified assumptions about his capacity.

(4) In proceedings under this Act or any other enactment, any question whether a person lacks capacity within the meaning of this Act must be decided on the balance of probabilities.

(5) No power which a person ("D") may exercise under this Act—
(a) in relation to a person who lacks capacity, or
(b) where D reasonably thinks that a person lacks capacity,
is exercisable in relation to a person under 16.

3 INABILITY TO MAKE DECISIONS

(1) For the purposes of section 2, a person is unable to make a decision for himself if he is unable—
(a) to understand the information relevant to the decision,
(b) to retain that information,
(c) to use or weigh that information as part of the process of making the decision, or
(d) to communicate his decision (whether by talking, using sign language or any other means).

(2) A person is not to be regarded as unable to understand the information relevant to a decision if he is able to understand an explanation of it given to him in a way that is appropriate to his circumstances (using simple language, visual aids or any other means).

(3) The fact that a person is able to retain the information relevant to a decision for a short period only does not prevent him from being regarded as able to make the decision.

(4) The information relevant to a decision includes information about the reasonably foreseeable consequences of—
(a) deciding one way or another, or
(b) failing to make the decision.

4 BEST INTERESTS

(1) In determining for the purposes of this Act what is in a person's best interests, the person making the determination must not make it merely on the basis of—
(a) the person's age or appearance, or
(b) a condition of his, or an aspect of his behaviour, which might lead others to make unjustified assumptions about what might be in his best interests.

(2) The person making the determination must consider all the relevant circumstances and, in particular, take the following steps.

(3) He must consider—
(a) whether it is likely that the person will at some time have capacity in relation to the matter in question, and
(b) if it appears likely that he will, when that is likely to be.

(4) He must, so far as reasonably practicable, permit and encourage the person to participate, or to improve his ability to participate, as fully as possible in any act done for him and any decision affecting him.

(5) Where the determination relates to life-sustaining treatment he must not, in considering whether the treatment is in the best interests of the person concerned, be motivated by a desire to bring about his death.

(6) He must consider, so far as is reasonably ascertainable—
(a) the person's past and present wishes and feelings (and, in particular, any relevant written statement made by him when he had capacity),
(b) the beliefs and values that would be likely to influence his decision if he had capacity, and
(c) the other factors that he would be likely to consider if he were able to do so.

(7) He must take into account, if it is practicable and appropriate to consult them, the views of—
    (a) anyone named by the person as someone to be consulted on the matter in question or on matters of that kind,
    (b) anyone engaged in caring for the person or interested in his welfare,
    (c) any donee of a lasting power of attorney granted by the person, and
    (d) any deputy appointed for the person by the court,
as to what would be in the person's best interests and, in particular, as to the matters mentioned in subsection (6).

(8) The duties imposed by subsections (1) to (7) also apply in relation to the exercise of any powers which—
    (a) are exercisable under a lasting power of attorney, or
    (b) are exercisable by a person under this Act where he reasonably believes that another person lacks capacity.

(9) In the case of an act done, or a decision made, by a person other than the court, there is sufficient compliance with this section if (having complied with the requirements of subsections (1) to (7)) he reasonably believes that what he does or decides is in the best interests of the person concerned.

(10) "Life-sustaining treatment" means treatment which in the view of a person providing health care for the person concerned is necessary to sustain life.

(11) "Relevant circumstances" are those—
    (a) of which the person making the determination is aware, and
    (b) which it would be reasonable to regard as relevant.
. . .

5 ACTS IN CONNECTION WITH CARE OR TREATMENT

(1) If a person ("D") does an act in connection with the care or treatment of another person ("P"), the act is one to which this section applies if—
    (a) before doing the act, D takes reasonable steps to establish whether P lacks capacity in relation to the matter in question, and
    (b) when doing the act, D reasonably believes—
        (i)   that P lacks capacity in relation to the matter, and
        (ii) that it will be in P's best interests for the act to be done.

(2) D does not incur any liability in relation to the act that he would not have incurred if P—
    (a) had had capacity to consent in relation to the matter, and
    (b) had consented to D's doing the act.

(3) Nothing in this section excludes a person's civil liability for loss or damage, or his criminal liability, resulting from his negligence in doing the act.

(4) Nothing in this section affects the operation of sections 24 to 26 (advance decisions to refuse treatment).

6 SECTION 5 ACTS: LIMITATIONS

(1) If D does an act that is intended to restrain P, it is not an act to which section 5 applies unless two further conditions are satisfied.

(2) The first condition is that D reasonably believes that it is necessary to do the act in order to prevent harm to P.

(3) The second is that the act is a proportionate response to—
     (a) the likelihood of P's suffering harm, and
     (b) the seriousness of that harm.

(4) For the purposes of this section D restrains P if he—
     (a) uses, or threatens to use, force to secure the doing of an act which P resists, or
     (b) restricts P's liberty of movement, whether or not P resists

(6) Section 5 does not authorise a person to do an act which conflicts with a decision made, within the scope of his authority and in accordance with this Part, by—
     (a) a donee of a lasting power of attorney granted by P, or
     (b) a deputy appointed for P by the court.

(7) But nothing in subsection (6) stops a person—
     (a) providing life-sustaining treatment, or
     (b) doing any act which he reasonably believes to be necessary to prevent a serious deterioration in P's condition,
     while a decision as respects any relevant issue is sought from the court.

24 ADVANCE DECISIONS TO REFUSE TREATMENT: GENERAL

(1) "Advance decision" means a decision made by a person ("P"), after he has reached 18 and when he has capacity to do so, that if—
     (a) at a later time and in such circumstances as he may specify, a specified treatment is proposed to be carried out or continued by a person providing health care for him, and
     (b) at that time he lacks capacity to consent to the carrying out or continuation of the treatment, the specified treatment is not to be carried out or continued.

(2) For the purposes of subsection (1)(a), a decision may be regarded as specifying a treatment or circumstances even though expressed in layman's terms.

(3) P may withdraw or alter an advance decision at any time when he has capacity to do so.

(4) A withdrawal (including a partial withdrawal) need not be in writing.

(5) An alteration of an advance decision need not be in writing (unless section 25(5) applies in relation to the decision resulting from the alteration).

25 VALIDITY AND APPLICABILITY OF ADVANCE DECISIONS

(1) An advance decision does not affect the liability which a person may incur for carrying out or continuing a treatment in relation to P unless the decision is at the material time—
     (a) valid, and
     (b) applicable to the treatment.

(2) An advance decision is not valid if P—
     (a) has withdrawn the decision at a time when he had capacity to do so,
     (b) has, under a lasting power of attorney created after the advance decision was made, conferred authority on the donee (or, if more than one, any of them) to give or refuse consent to the treatment to which the advance decision relates, or
     (c) has done anything else clearly inconsistent with the advance decision remaining his fixed decision.

(3) An advance decision is not applicable to the treatment in question if at the material time P has capacity to give or refuse consent to it.

(4)   An advance decision is not applicable to the treatment in question if—
    (a) that treatment is not the treatment specified in the advance decision,
    (b) any circumstances specified in the advance decision are absent, or
    (c) there are reasonable grounds for believing that circumstances exist which P did not anticipate at the time of the advance decision and which would have affected his decision had he anticipated them.

(5)   An advance decision is not applicable to life-sustaining treatment unless—
    (a) the decision is verified by a statement by P to the effect that it is to apply to that treatment even if life is at risk, and
    (b) the decision and statement comply with subsection (6).

(6)   A decision or statement complies with this subsection only if—
    (a) it is in writing,
    (b) it is signed by P or by another person in P's presence and by P's direction,
    (c) the signature is made or acknowledged by P in the presence of a witness, and
    (d) the witness signs it, or acknowledges his signature, in P's presence.

(7)   The existence of any lasting power of attorney other than one of a description mentioned in subsection (2)(b) does not prevent the advance decision from being regarded as valid and applicable.

26 EFFECT OF ADVANCE DECISIONS

(1)   If P has made an advance decision which is—
    (a) valid, and
    (b) applicable to a treatment,
the decision has effect as if he had made it, and had had capacity to make it, at the time when the question arises whether the treatment should be carried out or continued.

(2)   A person does not incur liability for carrying out or continuing the treatment unless, at the time, he is satisfied that an advance decision exists which is valid and applicable to the treatment.

(3)   A person does not incur liability for the consequences of withholding or withdrawing a treatment from P if, at the time, he reasonably believes that an advance decision exists which is valid and applicable to the treatment.

(4)   The court may make a declaration as to whether an advance decision—
    (a) exists;
    (b) is valid;
    (c) is applicable to a treatment.

(5)   Nothing in an apparent advance decision stops a person—
    (a) providing life-sustaining treatment, or
    (b) doing any act he reasonably believes to be necessary to prevent a serious deterioration in P's condition,
while a decision as respects any relevant issue is sought from the court.

SERIOUS ORGANISED CRIME AND POLICE ACT 2005

128 OFFENCE OF TRESPASSING ON DESIGNATED SITE

(1)   A person commits an offence if he enters, or is on, any protected site in England and Wales or Northern Ireland as a trespasser.

1A   In this section "protected site" means—
    (a)   a nuclear site; or
    (b)   a designated site.

1B   In this section "nuclear site" means—
    (a)   so much of any premises in respect of which a nuclear site licence (within the meaning of the Nuclear Installations Act 1965) is for the time being in force as lies within the outer perimeter of the protection provided for those premises; and
    (b)   so much of any other premises of which premises falling within paragraph (a) form a part as lies within that outer perimeter.

1C   For this purpose—
    (a)   the outer perimeter of the protection provided for any premises is the line of the outermost fences, walls or other obstacles provided or relied on for protecting those premises from intruders; and
    (b)   that line shall be determined on the assumption that every gate, door or other barrier across a way through a fence, wall or other obstacle is closed.

(2)   A "designated site" means a site—
    (a)   specified or described (in any way) in an order made by the Secretary of State, and
    (b)   designated for the purposes of this section by the order.

(3)   The Secretary of State may only designate a site for the purposes of this section if—
    (a)   it is comprised in Crown land; or
    (b)   it is comprised in land belonging to Her Majesty in Her private capacity or to the immediate heir to the Throne in his private capacity; or
    (c)   it appears to the Secretary of State that it is appropriate to designate the site in the interests of national security.

(4)   It is a defence for a person charged with an offence under this section to prove that he did not know, and had no reasonable cause to suspect, that the site in relation to which the offence is alleged to have been committed was a protected site.

(5)   A person guilty of an offence under this section is liable on summary conviction—
    (a)   to imprisonment for a term not exceeding 51 weeks, or
    (b)   to a fine not exceeding level 5 on the standard scale, or to both.

. . .

(7)   For the purposes of this section a person who is on any protected site as a trespasser does not cease to be a trespasser by virtue of being allowed time to leave the site.

(8)   In this section—
    (a)   "site" means the whole or part of any building or buildings, or any land, or both;
    (b)   "Crown land" means land in which there is a Crown interest or a Duchy interest.

(9)   For this purpose—

"Crown interest" means an interest belonging to Her Majesty in right of the Crown, and

"Duchy interest" means an interest belonging to Her Majesty in right of the Duchy of Lancaster or belonging to the Duchy of Cornwall.

132 DEMONSTRATING WITHOUT AUTHORISATION IN DESIGNATED AREA

(1)   Any person who—
    (a)   organises a demonstration in a public place in the designated area, or
    (b)   takes part in a demonstration in a public place in the designated area, or

(c) carries on a demonstration by himself in a public place in the designated area, is guilty of an offence if, when the demonstration starts, authorisation for the demonstration has not been given under section 134(2).

(2) It is a defence for a person accused of an offence under subsection (1) to show that he reasonably believed that authorisation had been given.

(3) Subsection (1) does not apply if the demonstration is—
 (a) a public procession of which notice is required to be given under subsection (1) of section 11 of the Public Order Act 1986 (c 64), or of which (by virtue of subsection (2) of that section) notice is not required to be given, or
 (b) a public procession for the purposes of section 12 or 13 of that Act.

(4) Subsection (1) also does not apply in relation to any conduct which is lawful under section 220 of the Trade Union and Labour Relations (Consolidation) Act 1992 (c 52).

(5) If subsection (1) does not apply by virtue of subsection (3) or (4), nothing in sections 133 to 136 applies either.

(6) Section 14 of the Public Order Act 1986 (imposition of conditions on public assemblies) does not apply in relation to a public assembly which is also a demonstration in a public place in the designated area.

(7) In this section and in sections 133 to 136—
 (a) "the designated area" means the area specified in an order under section 138,
 (b) "public place" means any highway or any place to which at the material time the public or any section of the public has access, on payment or otherwise, as of right or by virtue of express or implied permission,
 (c) references to any person organising a demonstration include a person participating in its organisation,
 (d) references to any person organising a demonstration do not include a person carrying on a demonstration by himself,
 (e) references to any person or persons taking part in a demonstration (except in subsection (1) of this section) include a person carrying on a demonstration by himself.

145 INTERFERENCE WITH CONTRACTUAL RELATIONSHIPS SO AS TO HARM AN ANIMAL RESEARCH ORGANISATION

(1) A person (A) commits an offence if, with the intention of harming an animal research organisation, he—
 (a) does a relevant act, or
 (b) threatens that he or somebody else will do a relevant act,
in circumstances in which that act or threat is intended or likely to cause a second person (B) to take any of the steps in subsection (2).

(2) The steps are—
 (a) not to perform any contractual obligation owed by B to a third person (C) (whether or not such non-performance amounts to a breach of contract);
 (b) to terminate any contract B has with C;
 (c) not to enter into a contract with C

(3) For the purposes of this section, a "relevant act" is—
 (a) an act amounting to a criminal offence, or
 (b) a tortious act causing B to suffer loss or damage of any description;
  but paragraph (b) does not include an act which is actionable on the ground only that it induces another person to break a contract with B.

(4)   For the purposes of this section, "contract" includes any other arrangement (and "contractual" is to be read accordingly).

(5)   For the purposes of this section, to "harm" an animal research organisation means—
(a) to cause the organisation to suffer loss or damage of any description, or
(b) to prevent or hinder the carrying out by the organisation of any of its activities.

(6)   This section does not apply to any act done wholly or mainly in contemplation or furtherance of a trade dispute.

(7)   In subsection (6) "trade dispute" has the same meaning as in Part 4 of the Trade Union and Labour Relations (Consolidation) Act 1992 (c 52), except that section 218 of that Act shall be read as if—
(a) it made provision corresponding to section 244(4) of that Act, and
(b) in subsection (5), the definition of "worker" included any person falling within paragraph (b) of the definition of "worker" in section 244(5).

146 INTIMIDATION OF PERSONS CONNECTED WITH AN ANIMAL RESEARCH ORGANISATION

(1)   A person (A) commits an offence if, with the intention of causing a second person (B) to abstain from doing something which B is entitled to do (or to do something which B is entitled to abstain from doing)—
(a) A threatens B that A or somebody else will do a relevant act, and
(b) A does so wholly or mainly because B is a person falling within subsection (2).

(2)   A person falls within this subsection if he is—
(a) an employee or officer of an animal research organisation;
(b) a student at an educational establishment that is an animal research organisation;
(c) a lessor or licensor of any premises occupied by an animal research organisation;
(d) a person with a financial interest in, or who provides financial assistance to, an animal research organisation;
(e) a customer or supplier of an animal research organisation;
(f) a person who is contemplating becoming someone within paragraph (c), (d) or (e);
(g) a person who is, or is contemplating becoming, a customer or supplier of someone within paragraph (c), (d), (e) or (f);
(h) an employee or officer of someone within paragraph (c), (d), (e), (f) or (g);
(i) a person with a financial interest in, or who provides financial assistance to, someone within paragraph (c), (d), (e), (f) or (g);
(j) a spouse, civil partner, friend or relative of, or a person who is known personally to, someone within any of paragraphs (a) to (i);
(k) a person who is, or is contemplating becoming, a customer or supplier of someone within paragraph (a), (b), (h), (i) or (j); or
(l) an employer of someone within paragraph (j).

(3)   For the purposes of this section, an "officer" of an animal research organisation or a person includes—
(a) where the organisation or person is a body corporate, a director, manager or secretary;
(b) where the organisation or person is a charity, a charity trustee (within the meaning of the Charities act 1993 (c 10);
(c) where the organisation or person is a partnership, a partner.

(4)   For the purposes of this section—
(a) a person is a customer or supplier of another person if he purchases goods, services or facilities from, or (as the case may be) supplies goods, services or facilities to, that other; and

(b) "supplier" includes a person who supplies services in pursuance of any enactment that requires or authorises such services to be provided.

(5) For the purposes of this section, a "relevant act" is—
(a) an act amounting to a criminal offence, or
(b) a tortious act causing B or another person to suffer loss or damage of any description.

(6) The Secretary of State may by order amend this section so as to include within subsection (2) any description of persons framed by reference to their connection with—
(a) an animal research organisation, or
(b) any description of persons for the time being mentioned in that subsection.

(7) This section does not apply to any act done wholly or mainly in contemplation or furtherance of a trade dispute.

(8) In subsection (7) "trade dispute" has the meaning given by section 145(7).

147 PENALTY FOR OFFENCES UNDER SECTIONS 145 AND 146

(1) A person guilty of an offence under section 145 or 146 is liable—
(a) on summary conviction, to imprisonment for a term not exceeding 12 months or to a fine not exceeding the statutory maximum, or to both;
(b) on conviction on indictment, to imprisonment for a term not exceeding five years or to a fine, or to both.

(2) No proceedings for an offence under either of those sections may be instituted except by or with the consent of the Director of Public Prosecutions.

148 ANIMAL RESEARCH ORGANISATIONS

(1) For the purposes of sections 145 and 146 "animal research organisation" means any person or organisation falling within subsection (2) or (3).

(2) A person or organisation falls within this subsection if he or it is the owner, lessee or licensee of premises constituting or including—
(a) a place specified in a licence granted under section 4 or 5 of the 1986 Act,
(b) a scientific procedure establishment designated under section 6 of that Act, or
(c) a breeding or supplying establishment designated under section 7 of that Act.

(3) A person or organisation falls within this subsection if he or it employs, or engages under a contract for services, any of the following in his capacity as such—
(a) the holder of a personal licence granted under section 4 of the 1986 Act,
(b) the holder of a project licence granted under section 5 of that Act,
(c) a person specified under section 6(5) of that Act, or
(d) a person specified under section 7(5) of that Act.

(4) The Secretary of State may by order amend this section so as to include a reference to any description of persons whom he considers to be involved in, or to have a direct connection with persons who are involved in, the application of regulated procedures.

(5) In this section—

"the 1986 Act" means the Animal (Scientific Procedures) Act 1986 (c14);

"organisation" includes any institution, trust, undertaking or association of persons;

"premises" includes any place within the meaning of the 1986 Act;

"regulated procedures" has the meaning given by section 2 of the 1986 Act.

VIOLENT CRIME REDUCTION ACT 2006

28 USING SOMEONE TO MIND A WEAPON

(1) A person is guilty of an offence if—
   (a) he uses another to look after, hide or transport a dangerous weapon for him; and
   (b) he does so under arrangements or in circumstances that facilitate, or are intended to facilitate, the weapon's being available to him for an unlawful purpose.

(2) For the purposes of this section the cases in which a dangerous weapon is to be regarded as available to a person for an unlawful purpose include any case where—
   (a) the weapon is available for him to take possession of it at a time and place; and
   (b) his possession of the weapon at that time and place would constitute, or be likely to involve or to lead to, the commission by him of an offence.

(3) In this section "dangerous weapon" means—
   (a) a firearm other than an air weapon or a component part of, or accessory to, an air weapon; or
   (b) a weapon to which section 141 or 141A of the Criminal Justice Act 1988 (c 33) applies (specified offensive weapons, knives and bladed weapons).

. . .

36 MANUFACTURE, IMPORT AND SALE OF REALISTIC IMITATION FIREARMS

(1) A person is guilty of an offence if—
   (a) he manufactures a realistic imitation firearm;
   (b) he modifies an imitation firearm so that it becomes a realistic imitation firearm;
   (c) he sells a realistic imitation firearm; or
   (d) he brings a realistic imitation firearm into Great Britain or causes one to be brought into Great Britain.

(2) Subsection (1) has effect subject to the defences in section 37.

. . .

37 SPECIFIC DEFENCES APPLYING TO THE OFFENCE UNDER S. 36

(1) It shall be a defence for a person charged with an offence under section 36 in respect of any conduct to show that the conduct was for the purpose only of making the imitation firearm in question available for one or more of the purposes specified in subsection (2).

(2) Those purposes are—
   (a) the purposes of a museum or gallery;
   (b) the purposes of theatrical performances and of rehearsals for such performances;
   (c) the production of films (within the meaning of Part 1 of the Copyright, Designs and Patents Act 1988 (c 48)_see section 5B of that Act);
   (d) the production of television programmes (within the meaning of the Communications Act 2003 (c21) see section 405(1) of that Act);
   (e) the organisation and holding of historical re-enactments organised and held by persons specified or described for the purposes of this section by regulations made by the Secretary of State;

(f)   the purposes of functions that a person has in his capacity as a person in the service of Her Majesty.

(3)   It shall also be a defence for a person charged with an offence under section 36 in respect of conduct falling within subsection (1)(d) of that section to show that the conduct—
(a)   was in the course of carrying on any trade or business; and
(b)   was for the purpose of making the imitation firearm in question available to be modified in a way which would result in its ceasing to be a realistic imitation firearm.

(4)   For the purposes of this section a person shall be taken to have shown a matter specified in subsection (1) or (3) if—
(a)   sufficient evidence of that matter is adduced to raise an issue with respect to it; and
(b)   the contrary is not proved beyond a reasonable doubt.

. . .

(7)   In this section—

"historical re-enactment" means any presentation or other event held for the purpose of re-enacting an event from the past or of illustrating conduct from a particular time or period in the past;

"museum or gallery" includes any institution which—

(a)   has as its purpose, or one of its purposes, the preservation, display and interpretation of material of historical, artistic or scientific interest; and
(b)   gives the public access to it.

38   MEANING OF "REALISTIC IMITATION FIREARM"

(1)   In sections 36 and 37 "realistic imitation firearm" means an imitation firearm which—
(a)   has an appearance that is so realistic as to make it indistinguishable, for all practical purposes, from a real firearm; and
(b)   is neither a de-activated firearm nor itself an antique.

(2)   For the purposes of this section, an imitation firearm is not (except by virtue of subsection (3)(b)) to be regarded as distinguishable from a real firearm for any practical purpose if it could be so distinguished only—
(a)   by an expert;
(b)   on a close examination; or
(c)   as a result of an attempt to load or to fire it.

(3)   In determining for the purposes of this section whether an imitation firearm is distinguishable from a real firearm—
(a)   the matters that must be taken into account include any differences between the size, shape and principal colour of the imitation firearm and the size, shape and colour in which the real firearm is manufactured; and
(b)   the imitation is to be regarded as distinguishable if its size, shape or principal colour is unrealistic for a real firearm.

. . .

(7)   In this section—

"colour" is to be construed in accordance with subsection (9);

"de-activated firearm" means an imitation firearm that consists in something which—
(a)   was a firearm; but
(b)   has been so rendered incapable of discharging a shot, bullet or other missile as no longer to be a firearm;

"real firearm" means—
- (a) a firearm of an actual make or model of modern firearm (whether existing or discontinued); or
- (b) something falling within a description which could be used for identifying, by reference to their appearance, the firearms falling within a category of actual modern firearms which, even though they include firearms of different makes or models (whether existing or discontinued) or both, all have the same or a similar appearance.

(8) In subsection (7) "modern firearm" means any firearm other than one the appearance of which would tend to identify it as having a design and mechanism of a sort first dating from before the year 1870.

(9) References in this section, in relation to an imitation firearm or a real firearm, to its colour include references to its being made of transparent material.

FRAUD ACT 2006

1 FRAUD

(1) A person is guilty of fraud if he is in breach of any of the sections listed in subsection (2) (which provide for different ways of committing the offence).

(2) The sections are—
- (a) section 2 (fraud by false representation),
- (b) section 3 (fraud by failing to disclose information), and
- (c) section 4 (fraud by abuse of position).

(3) A person who is guilty of fraud is liable—
- (a) on summary conviction, to imprisonment for a term not exceeding 12 months or to a fine not exceeding the statutory maximum (or to both);
- (b) on conviction on indictment, to imprisonment for a term not exceeding 10 years or to a fine (or to both).

(4) Subsection (3)(a) applies in relation to Northern Ireland as if the reference to 12 months were a reference to 6 months.

2 FRAUD BY FALSE REPRESENTATION

(1) A person is in breach of this section if he—
- (a) dishonestly makes a false representation, and
- (b) intends, by making the representation—
  - (i) to make a gain for himself or another, or
  - (ii) to cause loss to another or to expose another to a risk of loss.

(2) A representation is false if—
- (a) it is untrue or misleading, and
- (b) the person making it knows that it is, or might be, untrue or misleading.

(3) "Representation" means any representation as to fact or law, including a representation as to the state of mind of—
- (a) the person making the representation, or
- (b) any other person.

(4) A representation may be express or implied.

(5)   For the purposes of this section a representation may be regarded as made if it (or anything implying it) is submitted in any form to any system or device designed to receive, convey or respond to communications (with or without human intervention).

3 FRAUD BY FAILING TO DISCLOSE INFORMATION

A person is in breach of this section if he—

(a)   dishonestly fails to disclose to another person information which he is under a legal duty to disclose, and

(b)   intends, by failing to disclose the information—
       (i)   to make a gain for himself or another, or
       (ii) to cause loss to another or to expose another to a risk of loss.

4 FRAUD BY ABUSE OF POSITION

(1)   A person is in breach of this section if he—
       (a) occupies a position in which he is expected to safeguard, or not to act against, the financial interests of another person,
       (b) dishonestly abuses that position, and
       (c) intends, by means of the abuse of that position—
            (i)   to make a gain for himself or another, or
            (ii) to cause loss to another or to expose another to a risk of loss.

(2)   A person may be regarded as having abused his position even though his conduct consisted of an omission rather than an act.

5 "GAIN" AND "LOSS"

(1)   The references to gain and loss in sections 2 to 4 are to be read in accordance with this section.

(2)   "Gain" and "loss"—
       (a) extend only to gain or loss in money or other property;
       (b) include any such gain or loss whether temporary or permanent;
            and "property" means any property whether real or personal (including things in action and other intangible property).

(3)   "Gain" includes a gain by keeping what one has, as well as a gain by getting what one does not have.

(4)   "Loss" includes a loss by not getting what one might get, as well as a loss by parting with what one has.

6 POSSESSION ETC OF ARTICLES FOR USE IN FRAUDS

(1)   A person is guilty of an offence if he has in his possession or under his control any article for use in the course of or in connection with any fraud.

(2)   A person guilty of an offence under this section is liable—
       (a) on summary conviction, to imprisonment for a term not exceeding 12 months or to a fine not exceeding the statutory maximum (or to both);
       (b) on conviction on indictment, to imprisonment for a term not exceeding 5 years or to a fine (or to both).

. . .

7 MAKING OR SUPPLYING ARTICLES FOR USE IN FRAUDS

(1)   A person is guilty of an offence if he makes, adapts, supplies or offers to supply any article—
    (a)   knowing that it is designed or adapted for use in the course of or in connection with fraud, or
    (b)   intending it to be used to commit, or assist in the commission of, fraud.

(2)   A person guilty of an offence under this section is liable—
    (a)   on summary conviction, to imprisonment for a term not exceeding 12 months or to a fine not exceeding the statutory maximum (or to both);
    (b)   on conviction on indictment, to imprisonment for a term not exceeding 10 years or to a fine (or to both).

. . .

8 "ARTICLE"

(1)   For the purposes of—
    (a)   sections 6 and 7, and
    (b)   the provisions listed in subsection (2), so far as they relate to articles for use in the course of or in connection with fraud,
    "article" includes any program or data held in electronic form.

(2)   The provisions are—
    (a)   section 1(7)(b) of the Police and Criminal Evidence Act 1984 (c 60),
    (b)   section 2(8)(b) of the Armed Forces Act 2001 (c 19). . . .

9 PARTICIPATING IN FRAUDULENT BUSINESS CARRIED ON BY SOLE TRADER ETC

(1)   A person is guilty of an offence if he is knowingly a party to the carrying on of a business to which this section applies.

(2)   This section applies to a business which is carried on—
    (a)   by a person who is outside the reach of section 993 of the Companies Act 2006 (offence of fraudulent trading), and
    (b)   with intent to defraud creditors of any person or for any other fraudulent purpose.

(3)   The following are within the reach of that section—
    (a)   a company (within the meaning of the Companies Act 1985 or the Companies (Northern Ireland) Order 1986);
    (b)   a person to whom that section applies (with or without adaptations or modifications) as if the person were a company;
    (c)   a person exempted from the application of that section.

(2)   "Fraudulent purpose" has the same meaning as in that section.

(6)   A person guilty of an offence under this section is liable—
    (a)   on summary conviction, to imprisonment for a term not exceeding 12 months or to a fine not exceeding the statutory maximum (or to both);
    (b)   on conviction on indictment, to imprisonment for a term not exceeding 10 years or to a fine (or to both).

. . .

11 OBTAINING SERVICES DISHONESTLY

(1)   A person is guilty of an offence under this section if he obtains services for himself or another—
    (a) by a dishonest act, and
    (b) in breach of subsection (2).

(2)   A person obtains services in breach of this subsection if—
    (a) they are made available on the basis that payment has been, is being or will be made for or in respect of them,
    (b) he obtains them without any payment having been made for or in respect of them or without payment having been made in full, and
    (c) when he obtains them, he knows—
        (i)   that they are being made available on the basis described in paragraph (a), or
        (ii) that they might be,
    but intends that payment will not be made, or will not be made in full.

(3)   A person guilty of an offence under this section is liable—
    (a) on summary conviction, to imprisonment for a term not exceeding 12 months or to a fine not exceeding the statutory maximum (or to both);
    (b) on conviction on indictment, to imprisonment for a term not exceeding 5 years or to a fine (or to both).

. . .

12 LIABILITY OF COMPANY OFFICERS FOR OFFENCES BY COMPANY

(1)   Subsection (2) applies if an offence under this Act is committed by a body corporate.

(2)   If the offence is proved to have been committed with the consent or connivance of—
    (a) a director, manager, secretary or other similar officer of the body corporate, or
    (b) a person who was purporting to act in any such capacity,
        he (as well as the body corporate) is guilty of the offence and liable to be proceeded against and punished accordingly.

(3)   If the affairs of a body corporate are managed by its members, subsection (2) applies in relation to the acts and defaults of a member in connection with his functions of management as if he were a director of the body corporate.

TERRORISM ACT 2006

1 ENCOURAGEMENT OF TERRORISM

(1)   This section applies to a statement that is likely to be understood by some or all of the members of the public to whom it is published as a direct or indirect encouragement or other inducement to them to the commission, preparation or instigation of acts of terrorism or Convention offences.

(2)   A person commits an offence if—
    (a) he publishes a statement to which this section applies or causes another to publish such a statement; and
    (b) at the time he publishes it or causes it to be published, he—
        (i)   intends members of the public to be directly or indirectly encouraged or otherwise induced by the statement to commit, prepare or instigate acts of terrorism or Convention offences; or

(ii) is reckless as to whether members of the public will be directly or indirectly encouraged or otherwise induced by the statement to commit, prepare or instigate such acts or offences.

(3) For the purposes of this section, the statements that are likely to be understood by members of the public as indirectly encouraging the commission or preparation of acts of terrorism or Convention offences include every statement which—
(a) glorifies the commission or preparation (whether in the past, in the future or generally) of such acts or offences; and
(b) is a statement from which those members of the public could reasonably be expected to infer that what is being glorified is being glorified as conduct that should be emulated by them in existing circumstances.

(4) For the purposes of this section the questions how a statement is likely to be understood and what members of the public could reasonably be expected to infer from it must be determined having regard both—
(a) to the contents of the statement as a whole; and
(b) to the circumstances and manner of its publication.

(5) It is irrelevant for the purposes of subsections (1) to (3)—
(a) whether anything mentioned in those subsections relates to the commission, preparation or instigation of one or more particular acts of terrorism or Convention offences, of acts of terrorism or Convention offences of a particular description or of acts of terrorism or Convention offences generally; and
(b) whether any person is in fact encouraged or induced by the statement to commit, prepare or instigate any such act or offence.

(6) In proceedings for an offence under this section against a person in whose case it is not proved that he intended the statement directly or indirectly to encourage or otherwise induce the commission, preparation or instigation of acts of terrorism or Convention offences, it is a defence for him to show—
(a) that the statement neither expressed his views nor had his endorsement (whether by virtue of section 3 or otherwise); and
(b) that it was clear, in all the circumstances of the statement's publication, that it did not express his views and (apart from the possibility of his having been given and failed to comply with a notice under subsection (3) of that section) did not have his endorsement.

(7) A person guilty of an offence under this section shall be liable—
(a) on conviction on indictment, to imprisonment for a term not exceeding 7 years or to a fine, or to both;
(b) on summary conviction in England and Wales, to imprisonment for a term not exceeding 12 months or to a fine not exceeding the statutory maximum, or to both; . . .

2 DISSEMINATION OF TERRORIST PUBLICATIONS

(1) A person commits an offence if he engages in conduct falling within subsection (2) and, at the time he does so—
(a) he intends an effect of his conduct to be a direct or indirect encouragement or other inducement to the commission, preparation or instigation of acts of terrorism;
(b) he intends an effect of his conduct to be the provision of assistance in the commission or preparation of such acts; or
(c) he is reckless as to whether his conduct has an effect mentioned in paragraph (a) or (b).

(2)   For the purposes of this section a person engages in conduct falling within this subsection if he—

(a) distributes or circulates a terrorist publication;

(b) gives, sells or lends such a publication;

(c) offers such a publication for sale or loan;

(d) provides a service to others that enables them to obtain, read, listen to or look at such a publication, or to acquire it by means of a gift, sale or loan;

(e) transmits the contents of such a publication electronically; or

(f) has such a publication in his possession with a view to its becoming the subject of conduct falling within any of paragraphs (a) to (e).

(3)   For the purposes of this section a publication is a terrorist publication, in relation to conduct falling within subsection (2), if matter contained in it is likely—

(a) to be understood, by some or all of the persons to whom it is or may become available as a consequence of that conduct, as a direct or indirect encouragement or other inducement to them to the commission, preparation or instigation of acts of terrorism; or

(b) to be useful in the commission or preparation of such acts and to be understood, by some or all of those persons, as contained in the publication, or made available to them, wholly or mainly for the purpose of being so useful to them.

(4)   For the purposes of this section matter that is likely to be understood by a person as indirectly encouraging the commission or preparation of acts of terrorism includes any matter which—

(a) glorifies the commission or preparation (whether in the past, in the future or generally) of such acts; and

(b) is matter from which that person could reasonably be expected to infer that what is being glorified is being glorified as conduct that should be emulated by him in existing circumstances.

(5)   For the purposes of this section the question whether a publication is a terrorist publication in relation to particular conduct must be determined—

(a) as at the time of that conduct; and

(b) having regard both to the contents of the publication as a whole and to the circumstances in which that conduct occurs.

(6)   In subsection (1) references to the effect of a person's conduct in relation to a terrorist publication include references to an effect of the publication on one or more persons to whom it is or may become available as a consequence of that conduct.

(7)   It is irrelevant for the purposes of this section whether anything mentioned in subsections (1) to (4) is in relation to the commission, preparation or instigation of one or more particular acts of terrorism, of acts of terrorism of a particular description or of acts of terrorism generally.

(8)   For the purposes of this section it is also irrelevant, in relation to matter contained in any article whether any person—

(a) is in fact encouraged or induced by that matter to commit, prepare or instigate acts of terrorism; or

(b) in fact makes use of it in the commission or preparation of such acts.

(9)   In proceedings for an offence under this section against a person in respect of conduct to which subsection (10) applies, it is a defence for him to show—

(a) that the matter by reference to which the publication in question was a terrorist publication neither expressed his views nor had his endorsement (whether by virtue of section 3 or otherwise); and

(b) that it was clear, in all the circumstances of the conduct, that that matter did not express his views and (apart from the possibility of his having been given and failed to comply with a notice under subsection (3) of that section) did not have his endorsement.

(10) This subsection applies to the conduct of a person to the extent that—
   (a) the publication to which his conduct related contained matter by reference to which it was a terrorist publication by virtue of subsection (3)(a); and
   (b) that person is not proved to have engaged in that conduct with the intention specified in subsection (1)(a).

(11) A person guilty of an offence under this section shall be liable—
   (a) on conviction on indictment, to imprisonment for a term not exceeding 7 years or to a fine, or to both;
   (b) on summary conviction in England and Wales, to imprisonment for a term not exceeding 12 months or to a fine not exceeding the statutory maximum, or to both;
   (c) on summary conviction in Scotland or Northern Ireland, to imprisonment for a term not exceeding 6 months or to a fine not exceeding the statutory maximum, or to both.

. . .

(13) In this section—

"lend" includes let on hire, and "loan" is to be construed accordingly;

"publication" means an article or record of any description that contains any of the following, or any combination of them—
   (a) matter to be read;
   (b) matter to be listened to;
   (c) matter to be looked at or watched.

3 APPLICATION OF SS. 1 AND 2 TO INTERNET ACTIVITY ETC

(1) This section applies for the purposes of sections 1 and 2 in relation to cases where—
   (a) a statement is published or caused to be published in the course of, or in connection with, the provision or use of a service provided electronically; or
   (b) conduct falling within section 2(2) was in the course of, or in connection with, the provision or use of such a service.

(2) The cases in which the statement, or the article or record to which the conduct relates, is to be regarded as having the endorsement of a person ("the relevant person") at any time include a case in which—
   (a) a constable has given him a notice under subsection (3);
   (b) that time falls more than 2 working days after the day on which the notice was given; and
   (c) the relevant person has failed, without reasonable excuse, to comply with the notice.

(3) A notice under this subsection is a notice which—
   (a) declares that, in the opinion of the constable giving it, the statement or the article or record is unlawfully terrorism-related;
   (b) requires the relevant person to secure that the statement or the article or record, so far as it is so related, is not available to the public or is modified so as no longer to be so related;
   (c) warns the relevant person that a failure to comply with the notice within 2 working days will result in the statement, or the article or record, being regarded as having his endorsement; and

(d) explains how, under subsection (4), he may become liable by virtue of the notice if the statement, or the article or record, becomes available to the public after he has complied with the notice.

(4) Where—
(a) a notice under subsection (3) has been given to the relevant person in respect of a statement, or an article or record, and he has complied with it, but
(b) he subsequently publishes or causes to be published a statement which is, or is for all practical purposes, the same or to the same effect as the statement to which the notice related, or to matter contained in the article or record to which it related, (a "repeat statement");
the requirements of subsection (2)(a) to (c) shall be regarded as satisfied in the case of the repeat statement in relation to the times of its subsequent publication by the relevant person.

(5) In proceedings against a person for an offence under section 1 or 2 the requirements of subsection (2)(a) to (c) are not, in his case, to be regarded as satisfied in relation to any time by virtue of subsection (4) if he shows that he—
(a) has, before that time, taken every step he reasonably could to prevent a repeat statement from becoming available to the public and to ascertain whether it does; and
(b) was, at that time, a person to whom subsection (6) applied.

(6) This subsection applies to a person at any time when he—
(a) is not aware of the publication of the repeat statement; or
(b) having become aware of its publication, has taken every step that he reasonably could to secure that it either ceased to be available to the public or was modified as mentioned in subsection (3)(b).

(7) For the purposes of this section a statement or an article or record is unlawfully terrorism-related if it constitutes, or if matter contained in the article or record constitutes—
(a) something that is likely to be understood, by any one or more of the persons to whom it has or may become available, as a direct or indirect encouragement or other inducement to the commission, preparation or instigation of acts of terrorism or Convention offences; or
(b) information which—
(i) is likely to be useful to any one or more of those persons in the commission or preparation of such acts; and
(ii) is in a form or context in which it is likely to be understood by any one or more of those persons as being wholly or mainly for the purpose of being so useful.

(8) The reference in subsection (7) to something that is likely to be understood as an indirect encouragement to the commission or preparation of acts of terrorism or Convention offences includes anything which is likely to be understood as—
(a) the glorification of the commission or preparation (whether in the past, in the future or generally) of such acts or such offences; and
(b) a suggestion that what is being glorified is being glorified as conduct that should be emulated in existing circumstances.

(9) In this section "working day" means any day other than—
(a) a Saturday or a Sunday;
(b) Christmas Day or Good Friday; or
(c) a day which is a bank holiday under the Banking and Financial Dealings Act 1971 (c 80) in any part of the United Kingdom.

. . .

5 PREPARATION OF TERRORIST ACTS

(1)   A person commits an offence if, with the intention of—
    (a) committing acts of terrorism, or
    (b) assisting another to commit such acts,
    he engages in any conduct in preparation for giving effect to his intention.

(2)   It is irrelevant for the purposes of subsection (1) whether the intention and preparations relate to one or more particular acts of terrorism, acts of terrorism of a particular description or acts of terrorism generally.

(3)   A person guilty of an offence under this section shall be liable, on conviction on indictment, to imprisonment for life.

6 TRAINING FOR TERRORISM

(1)   A person commits an offence if—
    (a) he provides instruction or training in any of the skills mentioned in subsection (3); and
    (b) at the time he provides the instruction or training, he knows that a person receiving it intends to use the skills in which he is being instructed or trained—
        (i)   for or in connection with the commission or preparation of acts of terrorism or Convention offences; or
        (ii) for assisting the commission or preparation by others of such acts or offences.

(2)   A person commits an offence if—
    (a) he receives instruction or training in any of the skills mentioned in subsection (3); and
    (b) at the time of the instruction or training, he intends to use the skills in which he is being instructed or trained—
        (i)   for or in connection with the commission or preparation of acts of terrorism or Convention offences; or
        (ii) for assisting the commission or preparation by others of such acts or offences.

(3)   The skills are—
    (a) the making, handling or use of a noxious substance, or of substances of a description of such substances;
    (b) the use of any method or technique for doing anything else that is capable of being done for the purposes of terrorism, in connection with the commission or preparation of an act of terrorism or Convention offence or in connection with assisting the commission or preparation by another of such an act or offence; and
    (c) the design or adaptation for the purposes of terrorism, or in connection with the commission or preparation of an act of terrorism or Convention offence, of any method or technique for doing anything.

(4)   It is irrelevant for the purposes of subsections (1) and (2)—
    (a) whether any instruction or training that is provided is provided to one or more particular persons or generally;
    (b) whether the acts or offences in relation to which a person intends to use skills in which he is instructed or trained consist of one or more particular acts of terrorism or Convention offences, acts of terrorism or Convention offences of a particular description or acts of terrorism or Convention offences generally; and
    (c) whether assistance that a person intends to provide to others is intended to be provided to one or more particular persons or to one or more persons whose identities are not yet known.

(5)   A person guilty of an offence under this section shall be liable—
  (a) on conviction on indictment, to imprisonment for a term not exceeding 10 years or to a fine, or to both;
  (b) on summary conviction in England and Wales, to imprisonment for a term not exceeding 12 months or to a fine not exceeding the statutory maximum, or to both;
  (c) on summary conviction in Scotland or Northern Ireland, to imprisonment for a term not exceeding 6 months or to a fine not exceeding the statutory maximum, or to both.
  . . .

(7)   In this section—

  "noxious substance" means—
  (a) a dangerous substance within the meaning of Part 7 of the Anti-terrorism, Crime and Security Act 2001 (c 24); or
  (b) any other substance which is hazardous or noxious or which may be or become hazardous or noxious only in certain circumstances;
  "substance" includes any natural or artificial substance (whatever its origin or method of production and whether in solid or liquid form or in the form of a gas or vapour) and any mixture of substances.

8 ATTENDANCE AT A PLACE USED FOR TERRORIST TRAINING

(1)   A person commits an offence if—
  (a) he attends at any place, whether in the United Kingdom or elsewhere;
  (b) while he is at that place, instruction or training of the type mentioned in section 6(1) of this Act or section 54(1) of the Terrorism Act 2000 (c 11) (weapons training) is provided there;
  (c) that instruction or training is provided there wholly or partly for purposes connected with the commission or preparation of acts of terrorism or Convention offences; and
  (d) the requirements of subsection (2) are satisfied in relation to that person.

(2)   The requirements of this subsection are satisfied in relation to a person if—
  (a) he knows or believes that instruction or training is being provided there wholly or partly for purposes connected with the commission or preparation of acts of terrorism or Convention offences; or
  (b) a person attending at that place throughout the period of that person's attendance could not reasonably have failed to understand that instruction or training was being provided there wholly or partly for such purposes.

(3)   It is immaterial for the purposes of this section—
  (a) whether the person concerned receives the instruction or training himself; and
  (b) whether the instruction or training is provided for purposes connected with one or more particular acts of terrorism or Convention offences, acts of terrorism or Convention offences of a particular description or acts of terrorism or Convention offences generally.

(4)   A person guilty of an offence under this section shall be liable—
  (a) on conviction on indictment, to imprisonment for a term not exceeding 10 years or to a fine, or to both;
  (b) on summary conviction in England and Wales, to imprisonment for a term not exceeding 12 months or to a fine not exceeding the statutory maximum, or to both;
  (c) on summary conviction in Scotland or Northern Ireland, to imprisonment for a term not exceeding 6 months or to a fine not exceeding the statutory maximum, or to both.

. . .

(6) References in this section to instruction or training being provided include references to its being made available.

9 MAKING AND POSSESSION OF DEVICES OR MATERIALS

(1) A person commits an offence if—
(a) he makes or has in his possession a radioactive device, or
(b) he has in his possession radioactive material,
with the intention of using the device or material in the course of or in connection with the commission or preparation of an act of terrorism or for the purposes of terrorism, or of making it available to be so used.

(2) It is irrelevant for the purposes of subsection (1) whether the act of terrorism to which an intention relates is a particular act of terrorism, an act of terrorism of a particular description or an act of terrorism generally.

(3) A person guilty of an offence under this section shall be liable, on conviction on indictment, to imprisonment for life.

(4) In this section—

"radioactive device" means—
(a) a nuclear weapon or other nuclear explosive device;
(b) a radioactive material dispersal device;
(c) a radiation-emitting device;

"radioactive material" means nuclear material or any other radioactive substance which—
(a) contains nuclides that undergo spontaneous disintegration in a process accompanied by the emission of one or more types of ionising radiation, such as alpha radiation, beta radiation, neutron particles or gamma rays; and
(b) is capable, owing to its radiological or fissile properties, of—
(i)   causing serious bodily injury to a person;
(ii) causing serious damage to property;
(iii) endangering a person's life; or
(iv) creating a serious risk to the health or safety of the public.

(5) In subsection (4)—
"device" includes any of the following, whether or not fixed to land, namely, machinery, equipment, appliances, tanks, containers, pipes and conduits;

"nuclear material" has the same meaning as in the Nuclear Material (Offences) Act 1983 (c 18) (see section 6 of that Act).

10 MISUSE OF DEVICES OR MATERIAL AND MISUSE AND DAMAGE OF FACILITIES

(1) A person commits an offence if he uses—
(a) a radioactive device, or
(b) radioactive material,
in the course of or in connection with the commission of an act of terrorism or for the purposes of terrorism.

(2)   A person commits an offence if, in the course of or in connection with the commission of an act of terrorism or for the purposes of terrorism, he uses or damages a nuclear facility in a manner which—

(a)   causes a release of radioactive material; or

(b)   creates or increases a risk that such material will be released.

(3)   A person guilty of an offence under this section shall be liable, on conviction on indictment, to imprisonment for life.

(4)   In this section—

"nuclear facility" means—

(a)   a nuclear reactor, including a reactor installed in or on any transportation device for use as an energy source in order to propel it or for any other purpose; or

(b)   a plant or conveyance being used for the production, storage, processing or transport of radioactive material;

"radioactive device" and "radioactive material" have the same meanings as in section 9.

(5)   In subsection (4)—

"nuclear reactor" has the same meaning as in the Nuclear Installations Act 1965 (c 57) (see section 26 of that Act);

"transportation device" means any vehicle or any space object (within the meaning of the Outer Space Act 1986 (c 38)).

11   TERRORIST THREATS RELATING TO DEVICES, MATERIALS OR FACILITIES

(1)   A person commits an offence if, in the course of or in connection with the commission of an act of terrorism or for the purposes of terrorism—

(a)   he makes a demand—

(i)   for the supply to himself or to another of a radioactive device or of radioactive material;

(ii)   for a nuclear facility to be made available to himself or to another; or

(iii)   for access to such a facility to be given to himself or to another;

(b)   he supports the demand with a threat that he or another will take action if the demand is not met; and

(c)   the circumstances and manner of the threat are such that it is reasonable for the person to whom it is made to assume that there is real risk that the threat will be carried out if the demand is not met.

(2)   A person also commits an offence if—

(a)   he makes a threat falling within subsection (3) in the course of or in connection with the commission of an act of terrorism or for the purposes of terrorism; and

(b)   the circumstances and manner of the threat are such that it is reasonable for the person to whom it is made to assume that there is real risk that the threat will be carried out, or would be carried out if demands made in association with the threat are not met.

(3)   A threat falls within this subsection if it is—

(a)   a threat to use radioactive material;

(b)   a threat to use a radioactive device; or

(c)   a threat to use or damage a nuclear facility in a manner that releases radioactive material or creates or increases a risk that such material will be released.

(4) A person guilty of an offence under this section shall be liable, on conviction on indictment, to imprisonment for life.

(5) In this section—

"nuclear facility" has the same meaning as in section 10;

"radioactive device" and "radioactive material" have the same meanings as in section 9.

. . .

20 INTERPRETATION OF PART 1

(1) Expressions used in this Part and in the Terrorism Act 2000 (c 11) have the same meanings in this Part as in that Act.

(2) In this Part—

"act of terrorism" includes anything constituting an action taken for the purposes of terrorism, within the meaning of the Terrorism Act 2000 (see section 1(5) of that Act);

"article" includes anything for storing data;

"Convention offence" means an offence listed in Schedule 1 or an equivalent offence under the law of a country or territory outside the United Kingdom;

"glorification" includes any form of praise or celebration, and cognate expressions are to be construed accordingly;

"public" is to be construed in accordance with subsection (3);

"publish" and cognate expressions are to be construed in accordance with subsection (4);

"record" means a record so far as not comprised in an article, including a temporary record created electronically and existing solely in the course of, and for the purposes of, the transmission of the whole or a part of its contents;

"statement" is to be construed in accordance with subsection (6).

(3) In this Part references to the public—
(a) are references to the public of any part of the United Kingdom or of a country or territory outside the United Kingdom, or any section of the public; and
(b) except in section 9(4), also include references to a meeting or other group of persons which is open to the public (whether unconditionally or on the making of a payment or the satisfaction of other conditions).

(4) In this Part references to a person's publishing a statement are references to—
(a) his publishing it in any manner to the public;
(b) his providing electronically any service by means of which the public have access to the statement; or
(c) his using a service provided to him electronically by another so as to enable or to facilitate access by the public to the statement;
but this subsection does not apply to the references to a publication in section 2.

(5) In this Part references to providing a service include references to making a facility available; and references to a service provided to a person are to be construed accordingly.

(6) In this Part references to a statement are references to a communication of any description, including a communication without words consisting of sounds or images or both.

(7)   In this Part references to conduct that should be emulated in existing circumstances include references to conduct that is illustrative of a type of conduct that should be so emulated.

(8)   In this Part references to what is contained in an article or record include references—
    (a)   to anything that is embodied or stored in or on it; and
    (b)   to anything that may be reproduced from it using apparatus designed or adapted for the purpose.

. . .

As amended by Terrorism Act 2006, s 34.

WIRELESS TELEGRAPHY ACT 2006

47 MISLEADING MESSAGES

(1)   A person commits an offence if, by means of wireless telegraphy, he sends or attempts to send a message to which this section applies.

(2)   This section applies to a message which, to the person's knowledge—
    (a)   is false or misleading; and
    (b)   is likely to prejudice the efficiency of a safety of life service or to endanger the safety of a person or of a ship, aircraft or vehicle.

(3)   This section applies in particular to a message which, to the person's knowledge, falsely suggests that a ship or aircraft—
    (a)   is in distress or in need of assistance; or
    (b)   is not in distress or not in need of assistance.

(4)   A person who commits an offence under this section is liable—
    (a)   on summary conviction, to imprisonment for a term not exceeding 12 months or to a fine not exceeding the statutory maximum or to both;
    (b)   on conviction on indictment, to imprisonment for a term not exceeding two years or to a fine or to both.

. . .

48 INTERCEPTION AND DISCLOSURE OF MESSAGES

(1)   A person commits an offence if, otherwise than under the authority of a designated person—
    (a)   he uses wireless telegraphy apparatus with intent to obtain information as to the contents, sender or addressee of a message (whether sent by means of wireless telegraphy or not) of which neither he nor a person on whose behalf he is acting is an intended recipient, or
    (b)   he discloses information as to the contents, sender or addressee of such a message.

(2)   A person commits an offence under this section consisting in the disclosure of information only if the information disclosed by him is information that would not have come to his knowledge but for the use of wireless telegraphy apparatus by him or by another person.

(3)   A person does not commit an offence under this section consisting in the disclosure of information if he discloses the information in the course of legal proceedings or for the purpose of a report of legal proceedings.

(4)   A person who commits an offence under this section is liable on summary conviction to a fine not exceeding level 5 on the standard scale.

(5)   "Designated person" means—
   (a) the Secretary of State;
   (b) the Commissioners for Her Majesty's Revenue and Customs; or
   (c) any other person designated for the purposes of this section by regulations made by the Secretary of State.

CORPORATE MANSLAUGHTER AND CORPORATE HOMICIDE ACT 2007

1 THE OFFENCE

(1)   An organisation to which this section applies is guilty of an offence if the way in which its activities are managed or organised—
   (a) causes a person's death, and
   (b) amounts to a gross breach of a relevant duty of care owed by the organisation to the deceased.

(2)   The organisations to which this section applies are—
   (a) a corporation;
   (b) a department or other body listed in Schedule 1;
   (c) a police force;
   (d) a partnership, or a trade union or employers' association, that is an employer.

(3)   An organisation is guilty of an offence under this section only if the way in which its activities are managed or organised by its senior management is a substantial element in the breach referred to in subsection (1).

(4)   For the purposes of this Act—
   (a) "relevant duty of care" has the meaning given by section 2, read with sections 3 to 7;
   (b) a breach of a duty of care by an organisation is a "gross" breach if the conduct alleged to amount to a breach of that duty falls far below what can reasonably be expected of the organisation in the circumstances;
   (c) "senior management", in relation to an organisation, means the persons who play significant roles in—
      (i)   the making of decisions about how the whole or a substantial part of its activities are to be managed or organised, or
      (ii) the actual managing or organising of the whole or a substantial part of those activities.

(5)   The offence under this section is called—
   (a) corporate manslaughter, in so far as it is an offence under the law of England and Wales or Northern Ireland;
   (b) corporate homicide, in so far as it is an offence under the law of Scotland.

(6)   An organisation that is guilty of corporate manslaughter or corporate homicide is liable on conviction on indictment to a fine.

(7)   The offence of corporate homicide is indictable only in the High Court of Justiciary.

2 MEANING OF "RELEVANT DUTY OF CARE"

(1)   A "relevant duty of care", in relation to an organisation, means any of the following duties owed by it under the law of negligence—
   (a)   a duty owed to its employees or to other persons working for the organisation or performing services for it;
   (b)   a duty owed as occupier of premises;
   (c)   a duty owed in connection with—
      (i)   the supply by the organisation of goods or services (whether for consideration or not),
      (ii)   the carrying on by the organisation of any construction or maintenance operations,
      (iii)   the carrying on by the organisation of any other activity on a commercial basis, or
      (iv)   the use or keeping by the organisation of any plant, vehicle or other thing;
   (d)   a duty owed to a person who, by reason of being a person within subsection (2), is someone for whose safety the organisation is responsible.

(2)   A person is within this subsection if—
   (a)   he is detained at a custodial institution or in a custody area at a court or police station;
   (b)   he is detained at a removal centre or short-term holding facility;
   (c)   he is being transported in a vehicle, or being held in any premises, in pursuance of prison escort arrangements or immigration escort arrangements;
   (d)   he is living in secure accommodation in which he has been placed;
   (e)   he is a detained patient.

(3)   Subsection (1) is subject to sections 3 to 7.

(4)   A reference in subsection (1) to a duty owed under the law of negligence includes a reference to a duty that would be owed under the law of negligence but for any statutory provision under which liability is imposed in place of liability under that law.

(5)   For the purposes of this Act, whether a particular organisation owes a duty of care to a particular individual is a question of law. The judge must make any findings of fact necessary to decide that question.

(6)   For the purposes of this Act there is to be disregarded—
   (a)   any rule of the common law that has the effect of preventing a duty of care from being owed by one person to another by reason of the fact that they are jointly engaged in unlawful conduct;
   (b)   any such rule that has the effect of preventing a duty of care from being owed to a person by reason of his acceptance of a risk of harm.

(7)   In this section—

"construction or maintenance operations" means operations of any of the following descriptions—
   (a)   construction, installation, alteration, extension, improvement, repair, maintenance, decoration, cleaning, demolition or dismantling of—
      (i)   any building or structure,
      (ii)   anything else that forms, or is to form, part of the land, or
      (iii)   any plant, vehicle or other thing;
   (b)   operations that form an integral part of, or are preparatory to, or are for rendering complete, any operations within paragraph (a);

"custodial institution" means a prison, a young offender institution, a secure training centre, a young offenders institution, a young offenders centre, a juvenile justice centre or a remand centre;

"detained patient" means—

(a) a person who is detained in any premises under—
    (i) Part 2 or 3 of the Mental Health Act 1983 (c. 20) ("the 1983 Act"), . . .

"immigration escort arrangements" means arrangements made under section 156 of the Immigration and Asylum Act 1999 (c. 33);

"the law of negligence" includes—
in relation to England and Wales, the Occupiers' Liability Act 1957 (c. 31), the Defective Premises Act 1972 (c. 35) and the Occupiers' Liability Act 1984 (c. 3); . . .

"removal centre" and "short-term holding facility" have the meaning given by section 147 of the Immigration and Asylum Act 1999;

"secure accommodation" means accommodation, not consisting of or forming part of a custodial institution, provided for the purpose of restricting the liberty of persons under the age of 18.

3 PUBLIC POLICY DECISIONS, EXCLUSIVELY PUBLIC FUNCTIONS AND STATUTORY INSPECTIONS

(1)   Any duty of care owed by a public authority in respect of a decision as to matters of public policy (including in particular the allocation of public resources or the weighing of competing public interests) is not a "relevant duty of care".

(2)   Any duty of care owed in respect of things done in the exercise of an exclusively public function is not a "relevant duty of care" unless it falls within section 2(1)(a), (b) or (d).

(3)   Any duty of care owed by a public authority in respect of inspections carried out in the exercise of a statutory function is not a "relevant duty of care" unless it falls within section 2(1)(a) or (b).

(4)   In this section—

"exclusively public function" means a function that falls within the prerogative of the Crown or is, by its nature, exercisable only with authority conferred—
(a) by the exercise of that prerogative, or
(b) by or under a statutory provision;
"statutory function" means a function conferred by or under a statutory provision.

4 MILITARY ACTIVITIES

(1)   Any duty of care owed by the Ministry of Defence in respect of—
(a) operations within subsection (2),
(b) activities carried on in preparation for, or directly in support of, such operations, or
(c) training of a hazardous nature, or training carried out in a hazardous way, which it is considered needs to be carried out, or carried out in that way, in order to improve or maintain the effectiveness of the armed forces with respect to such operations,
is not a "relevant duty of care".

(2)   The operations within this subsection are operations, including peacekeeping operations and operations for dealing with terrorism, civil unrest or serious public disorder, in the course of which members of the armed forces come under attack or face the threat of attack or violent resistance.

(3)   Any duty of care owed by the Ministry of Defence in respect of activities carried on by members of the special forces is not a "relevant duty of care".

(4)   In this section "the special forces" means those units of the armed forces the maintenance of whose capabilities is the responsibility of the Director of Special Forces or which are for the time being subject to the operational command of that Director.

5 POLICING AND LAW ENFORCEMENT

(1)   Any duty of care owed by a public authority in respect of—
   (a) operations within subsection (2),
   (b) activities carried on in preparation for, or directly in support of, such operations, or
   (c) training of a hazardous nature, or training carried out in a hazardous way, which it is considered needs to be carried out, or carried out in that way, in order to improve or maintain the effectiveness of officers or employees of the public authority with respect to such operations,
is not a "relevant duty of care".

(2)   Operations are within this subsection if—
   (a) they are operations for dealing with terrorism, civil unrest or serious disorder,
   (b) they involve the carrying on of policing or law-enforcement activities, and
   (c) officers or employees of the public authority in question come under attack, or face the threat of attack or violent resistance, in the course of the operations.

(3)   Any duty of care owed by a public authority in respect of other policing or law-enforcement activities is not a "relevant duty of care" unless it falls within section 2(1)(a), (b) or (d).

(4)   In this section "policing or law-enforcement activities" includes—
   (a) activities carried on in the exercise of functions that are—
       (i)   functions of police forces, or
       (ii) functions of the same or a similar nature exercisable by public authorities other than police forces;
   (b) activities carried on in the exercise of functions of constables employed by a public authority;
   (c) activities carried on in the exercise of functions exercisable under Chapter 4 of Part 2 of the Serious Organised Crime and Police Act 2005 (c. 15) (protection of witnesses and other persons);
   (d) activities carried on to enforce any provision contained in or made under the Immigration Acts.

6 EMERGENCIES

(1)   Any duty of care owed by an organisation within subsection (2) in respect of the way in which it responds to emergency circumstances is not a "relevant duty of care" unless it falls within section 2(1)(a) or (b).

(2)   The organisations within this subsection are—
      (a) a fire and rescue authority in England and Wales; . . .
      (d) any other organisation providing a service of responding to emergency circumstances
           either—
           (i)   in pursuance of arrangements made with an organisation within paragraph (a),
                 (b) or (c), or
           (ii) (if not in pursuance of such arrangements) otherwise than on a commercial
                 basis;
      (e) a relevant NHS body;
      (f) an organisation providing ambulance services in pursuance of arrangements—
           (i)   made by, or at the request of, a relevant NHS body, or
           (ii) made with the Secretary of State or with the Welsh Ministers;
      (g) an organisation providing services for the transport of organs, blood, equipment or
           personnel in pursuance of arrangements of the kind mentioned in paragraph (f);
      (h) an organisation providing a rescue service;
      (i) the armed forces.

(3)   For the purposes of subsection (1), the way in which an organisation responds to
      emergency circumstances does not include the way in which—
      (a) medical treatment is carried out, or
      (b) decisions within subsection (4) are made.

(4)   The decisions within this subsection are decisions as to the carrying out of medical
      treatment, other than decisions as to the order in which persons are to be given such
      treatment.

(5)   Any duty of care owed in respect of the carrying out, or attempted carrying out, of a
      rescue operation at sea in emergency circumstances is not a "relevant duty of care" unless
      it falls within section 2(1)(a) or (b).

(6)   Any duty of care owed in respect of action taken—
      (a) in order to comply with a direction under Schedule 3A to the Merchant Shipping
           Act 1995 (c. 21) (safety directions), or
      (b) by virtue of paragraph 4 of that Schedule (action in lieu of direction),
           is not a "relevant duty of care" unless it falls within section 2(1)(a) or (b).

(7)   In this section—

      "emergency circumstances" means circumstances that are present or imminent and—
      (a) are causing, or are likely to cause, serious harm or a worsening of such harm, or
      (b) are likely to cause the death of a person;

      "medical treatment" includes any treatment or procedure of a medical or similar
      nature;

      "relevant NHS body" means—
      (a) a Strategic Health Authority, Primary Care Trust, NHS trust, Special Health
           Authority or NHS foundation trust in England; . . .

      "serious harm" means—
      (a) serious injury to or the serious illness (including mental illness) of a person;
      (b) serious harm to the environment (including the life and health of plants and
           animals);
      (c) serious harm to any building or other property.

(8)   A reference in this section to emergency circumstances includes a reference to
      circumstances that are believed to be emergency circumstances.

7 CHILD-PROTECTION AND PROBATION FUNCTIONS

(1)   A duty of care to which this section applies is not a "relevant duty of care" unless it falls within section 2(1)(a), (b) or (d).

(2)   This section applies to any duty of care that a local authority or other public authority owes in respect of the exercise by it of functions conferred by or under—
(a) Parts 4 and 5 of the Children Act 1989 (c. 41) . . .

(3)   This section also applies to any duty of care that a local probation board or other public authority owes in respect of the exercise by it of functions conferred by or under—
(a) Chapter 1 of Part 1 of the Criminal Justice and Court Services Act 2000 (c. 43) . . .

8 FACTORS FOR JURY

(1)   This section applies where—
(a) it is established that an organisation owed a relevant duty of care to a person, and
(b) it falls to the jury to decide whether there was a gross breach of that duty.

(2)   The jury must consider whether the evidence shows that the organisation failed to comply with any health and safety legislation that relates to the alleged breach, and if so—
(a) how serious that failure was;
(b) how much of a risk of death it posed.

(3)   The jury may also—
(a) consider the extent to which the evidence shows that there were attitudes, policies, systems or accepted practices within the organisation that were likely to have encouraged any such failure as is mentioned in subsection (2), or to have produced tolerance of it;
(b) have regard to any health and safety guidance that relates to the alleged breach.

(4)   This section does not prevent the jury from having regard to any other matters they consider relevant.

(5)   In this section "health and safety guidance" means any code, guidance, manual or similar publication that is concerned with health and safety matters and is made or issued (under a statutory provision or otherwise) by an authority responsible for the enforcement of any health and safety legislation.

. . .

18 NO INDIVIDUAL LIABILITY

(1)   An individual cannot be guilty of aiding, abetting, counselling or procuring the commission of an offence of corporate manslaughter.

(2)   An individual cannot be guilty of aiding, abetting, counselling or procuring, or being art and part in, the commission of an offence of corporate homicide.

. . .

20 ABOLITION OF LIABILITY OF CORPORATIONS FOR MANSLAUGHTER AT COMMON LAW

The common law offence of manslaughter by gross negligence is abolished in its application to corporations, and in any application it has to other organisations to which section 1 applies.

SERIOUS CRIME ACT 2007

44 INTENTIONALLY ENCOURAGING OR ASSISTING AN OFFENCE

(1) A person commits an offence if—
  (a) he does an act capable of encouraging or assisting the commission of an offence; and
  (b) he intends to encourage or assist its commission.

(2) But he is not to be taken to have intended to encourage or assist the commission of an offence merely because such encouragement or assistance was a foreseeable consequence of his act.

45 ENCOURAGING OR ASSISTING AN OFFENCE BELIEVING IT WILL BE COMMITTED

A person commits an offence if—
(a) he does an act capable of encouraging or assisting the commission of an offence; and

(b) he believes—
  (i) that the offence will be committed; and
  (ii) that his act will encourage or assist its commission.

46 ENCOURAGING OR ASSISTING OFFENCES BELIEVING ONE OR MORE WILL BE COMMITTED

(1) A person commits an offence if—
  (a) he does an act capable of encouraging or assisting the commission of one or more of a number of offences; and
  (b) he believes—
    (i) that one or more of those offences will be committed (but has no belief as to which); and
    (ii) that his act will encourage or assist the commission of one or more of them.

(2) It is immaterial for the purposes of subsection (1)(b)(ii) whether the person has any belief as to which offence will be encouraged or assisted.

(3) If a person is charged with an offence under subsection (1)—
  (a) the indictment must specify the offences alleged to be the "number of offences" mentioned in paragraph (a) of that subsection; but
  (b) nothing in paragraph (a) requires all the offences potentially comprised in that number to be specified.

(4) In relation to an offence under this section, reference in this Part to the offences specified in the indictment is to the offences specified by virtue of subsection (3)(a).

47 PROVING AN OFFENCE UNDER THIS PART

(1) Sections 44, 45 and 46 are to be read in accordance with this section.

(2) If it is alleged under section 44(1)(b) that a person (D) intended to encourage or assist the commission of an offence, it is sufficient to prove that he intended to encourage or assist the doing of an act which would amount to the commission of that offence.

(3) If it is alleged under section 45(b) that a person (D) believed that an offence would be committed and that his act would encourage or assist its commission, it is sufficient to prove that he believed—
 (a) that an act would be done which would amount to the commission of that offence; and
 (b) that his act would encourage or assist the doing of that act.

(4) If it is alleged under section 46(1)(b) that a person (D) believed that one or more of a number of offences would be committed and that his act would encourage or assist the commission of one or more of them, it is sufficient to prove that he believed—
 (a) that one or more of a number of acts would be done which would amount to the commission of one or more of those offences; and
 (b) that his act would encourage or assist the doing of one or more of those acts.

(5) In proving for the purposes of this section whether an act is one which, if done, would amount to the commission of an offence—
 (a) if the offence is one requiring proof of fault, it must be proved that—
  (i) D believed that, were the act to be done, it would be done with that fault;
  (ii) D was reckless as to whether or not it would be done with that fault; or
  (iii) D's state of mind was such that, were he to do it, it would be done with that fault; and
 (b) if the offence is one requiring proof of particular circumstances or consequences (or both), it must be proved that—
  (i) D believed that, were the act to be done, it would be done in those circumstances or with those consequences; or
  (ii) D was reckless as to whether or not it would be done in those circumstances or with those consequences.

(6) For the purposes of subsection (5)(a)(iii), D is to be assumed to be able to do the act in question.

(7) In the case of an offence under section 44—
 (a) subsection (5)(b)(i) is to be read as if the reference to "D believed" were a reference to "D intended or believed"; but
 (b) D is not to be taken to have intended that an act would be done in particular circumstances or with particular consequences merely because its being done in those circumstances or with those consequences was a foreseeable consequence of his act of encouragement or assistance.

(8) Reference in this section to the doing of an act includes reference to—
 (a) a failure to act;
 (b) the continuation of an act that has already begun;
 (c) an attempt to do an act (except an act amounting to the commission of the offence of attempting to commit another offence).

(9) In the remaining provisions of this Part (unless otherwise provided) a reference to the anticipated offence is—
 (a) in relation to an offence under section 44, a reference to the offence mentioned in subsection (2); and
 (b) in relation to an offence under section 45, a reference to the offence mentioned in subsection (3).

48 PROVING AN OFFENCE UNDER SECTION 46

(1) This section makes further provision about the application of section 47 to an offence under section 46.

(2)   It is sufficient to prove the matters mentioned in section 47(5) by reference to one offence only.

(3)   The offence or offences by reference to which those matters are proved must be one of the offences specified in the indictment.

(4)   Subsection (3) does not affect any enactment or rule of law under which a person charged with one offence may be convicted of another and is subject to section 57.

49 SUPPLEMENTAL PROVISIONS

(1)   A person may commit an offence under this Part whether or not any offence capable of being encouraged or assisted by his act is committed.

(2)   If a person's act is capable of encouraging or assisting the commission of a number of offences—
(a)   section 44 applies separately in relation to each offence that he intends to encourage or assist to be committed; and
(b)   section 45 applies separately in relation to each offence that he believes will be encouraged or assisted to be committed.

(3)   A person may, in relation to the same act, commit an offence under more than one provision of this Part.

(4)   In reckoning whether—
(a)   for the purposes of section 45, an act is capable of encouraging or assisting the commission of an offence; or
(b)   for the purposes of section 46, an act is capable of encouraging or assisting the commission of one or more of a number of offences;
offences under this Part and listed offences are to be disregarded.

(5)   "Listed offence" means—
(a)   in England and Wales, an offence listed in Part 1, 2 or 3 of Schedule 3;

. . .

(7)   For the purposes of sections 45(b)(i) and 46(1)(b)(i) it is sufficient for the person concerned to believe that the offence (or one or more of the offences) will be committed if certain conditions are met.

50 DEFENCE OF ACTING REASONABLY

(1)   A person is not guilty of an offence under this Part if he proves—
(a)   that he knew certain circumstances existed; and
(b)   that it was reasonable for him to act as he did in those circumstances.

(2)   A person is not guilty of an offence under this Part if he proves—
(a)   that he believed certain circumstances to exist;
(b)   that his belief was reasonable; and
(c)   that it was reasonable for him to act as he did in the circumstances as he believed them to be.

(3)   Factors to be considered in determining whether it was reasonable for a person to act as he did include—
(a)   the seriousness of the anticipated offence (or, in the case of an offence under section 46, the offences specified in the indictment);

(b) any purpose for which he claims to have been acting;

(c) any authority by which he claims to have been acting.

51 PROTECTIVE OFFENCES: VICTIMS NOT LIABLE

(1) In the case of protective offences, a person does not commit an offence under this Part by reference to such an offence if—

(a) he falls within the protected category; and

(b) he is the person in respect of whom the protective offence was committed or would have been if it had been committed.

(2) "Protective offence" means an offence that exists (wholly or in part) for the protection of a particular category of persons ("the protected category").

51A EXCEPTIONS TO SECTION 44 FOR ENCOURAGING OR ASSISTING SUICIDE

Section 44 does not apply to an offence under section 2(1) of the Suicide Act 1961 . . .

58 PENALTIES

(1) Subsections (2) and (3) apply if—

(a) a person is convicted of an offence under section 44 or 45; or

(b) a person is convicted of an offence under section 46 by reference to only one offence ("the reference offence").

(2) If the anticipated or reference offence is murder, he is liable to imprisonment for life.

(3) In any other case he is liable to any penalty for which he would be liable on conviction of the anticipated or reference offence.

(4) Subsections (5) to (7) apply if a person is convicted of an offence under section 46 by reference to more than one offence ("the reference offences").

(5) If one of the reference offences is murder, he is liable to imprisonment for life.

(6) If none of the reference offences is murder but one or more of them is punishable with imprisonment, he is liable—

(a) to imprisonment for a term not exceeding the maximum term provided for any one of those offences (taking the longer or the longest term as the limit for the purposes of this paragraph where the terms provided differ); or

(b) to a fine.

(7) In any other case he is liable to a fine.

(8) Subsections (3), (6) and (7) are subject to any contrary provision made by or under—

(a) an Act . . .

(9) In the case of an offence triable either way, the reference in subsection (6) to the maximum term provided for that offence is a reference to the maximum term so provided on conviction on indictment.

59 ABOLITION OF COMMON LAW REPLACED BY THIS PART

The common law offence of inciting the commission of another offence is abolished.

65 BEING CAPABLE OF ENCOURAGING OR ASSISTING

(1) A reference in this Part to a person's doing an act that is capable of encouraging the commission of an offence includes a reference to his doing so by threatening another person or otherwise putting pressure on another person to commit the offence.

(2) A reference in this Part to a person's doing an act that is capable of encouraging or assisting the commission of an offence includes a reference to his doing so by—
(a) taking steps to reduce the possibility of criminal proceedings being brought in respect of that offence;
(b) failing to take reasonable steps to discharge a duty.

(3) But a person is not to be regarded as doing an act that is capable of encouraging or assisting the commission of an offence merely because he fails to respond to a constable's request for assistance in preventing a breach of the peace.

66 INDIRECTLY ENCOURAGING OR ASSISTING

If a person (D1) arranges for a person (D2) to do an act that is capable of encouraging or assisting the commission of an offence, and D2 does the act, D1 is also to be treated for the purposes of this Part as having done it.

As amended Coroners and Justice Act 2009, sch 21.

UK BORDERS ACT 2007

22 ASSAULTING AN IMMIGRATION OFFICER: OFFENCE

(1) A person who assaults an immigration officer commits an offence.

(2) A person guilty of an offence under this section shall be liable on summary conviction to—
(a) imprisonment for a period not exceeding 51 weeks,
(b) a fine not exceeding level 5 on the standard scale, or
(c) both.

CRIMINAL JUSTICE AND IMMIGRATION ACT 2008

63 POSSESSION OF EXTREME PORNOGRAPHIC IMAGES

(1) It is an offence for a person to be in possession of an extreme pornographic image.

(2) An "extreme pornographic image" is an image which is both—
(a) pornographic, and
(b) an extreme image.

(3) An image is "pornographic" if it is of such a nature that it must reasonably be assumed to have been produced solely or principally for the purpose of sexual arousal.

(4) Where (as found in the person's possession) an image forms part of a series of images, the question whether the image is of such a nature as is mentioned in subsection (3) is to be determined by reference to—

    (a) the image itself, and

    (b) (if the series of images is such as to be capable of providing a context for the image) the context in which it occurs in the series of images.

(5)   So, for example, where—

    (a) an image forms an integral part of a narrative constituted by a series of images, and

    (b) having regard to those images as a whole, they are not of such a nature that they must reasonably be assumed to have been produced solely or principally for the purpose of sexual arousal,

    the image may, by virtue of being part of that narrative, be found not to be pornographic, even though it might have been found to be pornographic if taken by itself.

(6)   An "extreme image" is an image which—

    (a) falls within subsection (7), and

    (b) is grossly offensive, disgusting or otherwise of an obscene character.

(7)   An image falls within this subsection if it portrays, in an explicit and realistic way, any of the following—

    (a) an act which threatens a person's life,

    (b) an act which results, or is likely to result, in serious injury to a person's anus, breasts or genitals,

    (c) an act which involves sexual interference with a human corpse, or

    (d) a person performing an act of intercourse or oral sex with an animal (whether dead or alive),

    and a reasonable person looking at the image would think that any such person or animal was real.

(8)   In this section "image" means—

    (a) a moving or still image (produced by any means); or

    (b) data (stored by any means) which is capable of conversion into an image within paragraph (a).

(9)   In this section references to a part of the body include references to a part surgically constructed (in particular through gender reassignment surgery).

(10) Proceedings for an offence under this section may not be instituted—

    (a) in England and Wales, except by or with the consent of the Director of Public Prosecutions . . .

64 EXCLUSION OF CLASSIFIED FILMS ETC.

(1)   Section 63 does not apply to excluded images.

(2)   An "excluded image" is an image which forms part of a series of images contained in a recording of the whole or part of a classified work.

(3)   But such an image is not an "excluded image" if—

    (a) it is contained in a recording of an extract from a classified work, and

    (b) it is of such a nature that it must reasonably be assumed to have been extracted (whether with or without other images) solely or principally for the purpose of sexual arousal.

(4)   Where an extracted image is one of a series of images contained in the recording, the question whether the image is of such a nature as is mentioned in subsection (3)(b) is to be determined by reference to—

(a) the image itself, and
(b) (if the series of images is such as to be capable of providing a context for the image) the context in which it occurs in the series of images; and section 63(5) applies in connection with determining that question as it applies in connection with determining whether an image is pornographic.

(5)   In determining for the purposes of this section whether a recording is a recording of the whole or part of a classified work, any alteration attributable to—
(a) a defect caused for technical reasons or by inadvertence on the part of any person, or
(b) the inclusion in the recording of any extraneous material (such as advertisements), is to be disregarded.

(6)   Nothing in this section is to be taken as affecting any duty of a designated authority to have regard to section 63 (along with other enactments creating criminal offences) in determining whether a video work is suitable for a classification certificate to be issued in respect of it.

(7)   In this section—

"classified work" means (subject to subsection (8)) a video work in respect of which a classification certificate has been issued by a designated authority (whether before or after the commencement of this section);

"classification certificate" and "video work" have the same meanings as in the Video Recordings Act 1984 (c. 39);

"designated authority" means an authority which has been designated by the Secretary of State under section 4 of that Act;

"extract" includes an extract consisting of a single image;

"image" and "pornographic" have the same meanings as in section 63;

"recording" means any disc, tape or other device capable of storing data electronically and from which images may be produced (by any means).

65 DEFENCES: GENERAL

(1)   Where a person is charged with an offence under section 63, it is a defence for the person to prove any of the matters mentioned in subsection (2).

(2)   The matters are—
(a) that the person had a legitimate reason for being in possession of the image concerned;
(b) that the person had not seen the image concerned and did not know, nor had any cause to suspect, it to be an extreme pornographic image;
(c) that the person—
(i)   was sent the image concerned without any prior request having been made by or on behalf of the person, and
(ii) did not keep it for an unreasonable time.

(3)   In this section "extreme pornographic image" and "image" have the same meanings as in section 63.

66 DEFENCE: PARTICIPATION IN CONSENSUAL ACTS

(1)   This section applies where—
   (a) a person ("D") is charged with an offence under section 63, and
   (b) the offence relates to an image that portrays an act or acts within paragraphs (a) to (c) (but none within paragraph (d)) of subsection (7) of that section.

(2)   It is a defence for D to prove—
   (a) that D directly participated in the act or any of the acts portrayed, and
   (b) that the act or acts did not involve the infliction of any non-consensual harm on any person, and
   (c) if the image portrays an act within section 63(7)(c), that what is portrayed as a human corpse was not in fact a corpse.

(3)   For the purposes of this section harm inflicted on a person is "non-consensual" harm if—
   (a) the harm is of such a nature that the person cannot, in law, consent to it being inflicted on himself or herself; or
   (b) where the person can, in law, consent to it being so inflicted, the person does not in fact consent to it being so inflicted.

67 PENALTIES ETC. FOR POSSESSION OF EXTREME PORNOGRAPHIC IMAGES

(1)   This section has effect where a person is guilty of an offence under section 63.

(2)   Except where subsection (3) applies to the offence, the offender is liable—
   (a) on summary conviction, to imprisonment for a term not exceeding the relevant period or a fine not exceeding the statutory maximum or both;
   (b) on conviction on indictment, to imprisonment for a term not exceeding 3 years or a fine or both.

(3)   If the offence relates to an image that does not portray any act within section 63(7)(a) or (b), the offender is liable—
   (a) on summary conviction, to imprisonment for a term not exceeding the relevant period or a fine not exceeding the statutory maximum or both;
   (b) on conviction on indictment, to imprisonment for a term not exceeding 2 years or a fine or both.

(4)   In subsection (2)(a) or (3)(a) "the relevant period" means—
   (a) in relation to England and Wales, 12 months; . . .

76 REASONABLE FORCE FOR PURPOSES OF SELF-DEFENCE ETC.

(1)   This section applies where in proceedings for an offence—
   (a) an issue arises as to whether a person charged with the offence ("D") is entitled to rely on a defence within subsection (2), and
   (b) the question arises whether the degree of force used by D against a person ("V") was reasonable in the circumstances.

(2)   The defences are—
   (a) the common law defence of self-defence; and
   (b) the defences provided by section 3(1) of the Criminal Law Act 1967 (c. 58) or section 3(1) of the Criminal Law Act (Northern Ireland) 1967 (c. 18 (N.I.)) (use of force in prevention of crime or making arrest).

(3)   The question whether the degree of force used by D was reasonable in the circumstances is to be decided by reference to the circumstances as D believed them to be, and subsections (4) to (8) also apply in connection with deciding that question.

(4)   If D claims to have held a particular belief as regards the existence of any circumstances—
    (a) the reasonableness or otherwise of that belief is relevant to the question whether D genuinely held it; but
    (b) if it is determined that D did genuinely hold it, D is entitled to rely on it for the purposes of subsection (3), whether or not—
        (i)   it was mistaken, or
        (ii) (if it was mistaken) the mistake was a reasonable one to have made.

(5)   But subsection (4)(b) does not enable D to rely on any mistaken belief attributable to intoxication that was voluntarily induced.

(6)   The degree of force used by D is not to be regarded as having been reasonable in the circumstances as D believed them to be if it was disproportionate in those circumstances.

(7)   In deciding the question mentioned in subsection (3) the following considerations are to be taken into account (so far as relevant in the circumstances of the case)—
    (a) that a person acting for a legitimate purpose may not be able to weigh to a nicety the exact measure of any necessary action; and
    (b) that evidence of a person's having only done what the person honestly and instinctively thought was necessary for a legitimate purpose constitutes strong evidence that only reasonable action was taken by that person for that purpose.

(8)   Subsection (7) is not to be read as preventing other matters from being taken into account where they are relevant to deciding the question mentioned in subsection (3).

(9)   This section is intended to clarify the operation of the existing defences mentioned in subsection (2).

(10)   In this section—
    (a) "legitimate purpose" means—
        (i)   the purpose of self-defence under the common law, or
        (ii) the prevention of crime or effecting or assisting in the lawful arrest of persons mentioned in the provisions referred to in subsection (2)(b);
    (b) references to self-defence include acting in defence of another person; and
    (c) references to the degree of force used are to the type and amount of force used.

As amended by Video Recordings Act 2010.

CORONERS AND JUSTICE ACT 2009

54 PARTIAL DEFENCE TO MURDER: LOSS OF CONTROL

(1)   Where a person ("D") kills or is a party to the killing of another ("V"), D is not to be convicted of murder if—
    (a) D's acts and omissions in doing or being a party to the killing resulted from D's loss of self-control,
    (b) the loss of self-control had a qualifying trigger, and
    (c) a person of D's sex and age, with a normal degree of tolerance and self-restraint and in the circumstances of D, might have reacted in the same or in a similar way to D.

(2)   For the purposes of subsection (1)(a), it does not matter whether or not the loss of control was sudden.

(3)   In subsection (1)(c) the reference to "the circumstances of D" is a reference to all of D's circumstances other than those whose only relevance to D's conduct is that they bear on D's general capacity for tolerance or self-restraint.

(4)   Subsection (1) does not apply if, in doing or being a party to the killing, D acted in a considered desire for revenge.

(5)   On a charge of murder, if sufficient evidence is adduced to raise an issue with respect to the defence under subsection (1), the jury must assume that the defence is satisfied unless the prosecution proves beyond reasonable doubt that it is not.

(6)   For the purposes of subsection (5), sufficient evidence is adduced to raise an issue with respect to the defence if evidence is adduced on which, in the opinion of the trial judge, a jury, properly directed, could reasonably conclude that the defence might apply.

(7)   A person who, but for this section, would be liable to be convicted of murder is liable instead to be convicted of manslaughter.

(8)   The fact that one party to a killing is by virtue of this section not liable to be convicted of murder does not affect the question whether the killing amounted to murder in the case of any other party to it.

55 MEANING OF "QUALIFYING TRIGGER"

(1)   This section applies for the purposes of section 54.

(2)   A loss of self-control had a qualifying trigger if subsection (3), (4) or (5) applies.

(3)   This subsection applies if D's loss of self-control was attributable to D's fear of serious violence from V against D or another identified person.

(4)   This subsection applies if D's loss of self-control was attributable to a thing or things done or said (or both) which—
       (a) constituted circumstances of an extremely grave character, and
       (b) caused D to have a justifiable sense of being seriously wronged.

(5)   This subsection applies if D's loss of self-control was attributable to a combination of the matters mentioned in subsections (3) and (4).

(6)   In determining whether a loss of self-control had a qualifying trigger—
       (a) D's fear of serious violence is to be disregarded to the extent that it was caused by a thing which D incited to be done or said for the purpose of providing an excuse to use violence;
       (b) a sense of being seriously wronged by a thing done or said is not justifiable if D incited the thing to be done or said for the purpose of providing an excuse to use violence;
       (c) the fact that a thing done or said constituted sexual infidelity is to be disregarded.

(7)   In this section references to "D" and "V" are to be construed in accordance with section 54.

56 ABOLITION OF COMMON LAW DEFENCE OF PROVOCATION

(1)   The common law defence of provocation is abolished and replaced by sections 54 and 55.

. . .

62 POSSESSION OF PROHIBITED IMAGES OF CHILDREN

(1)   It is an offence for a person to be in possession of a prohibited image of a child.

(2)   A prohibited image is an image which—
(a) is pornographic,
(b) falls within subsection (6), and
(c) is grossly offensive, disgusting or otherwise of an obscene character.

(3)   An image is "pornographic" if it is of such a nature that it must reasonably be assumed to have been produced solely or principally for the purpose of sexual arousal.

(4)   Where (as found in the person's possession) an image forms part of a series of images, the question whether the image is of such a nature as is mentioned in subsection (3) is to be determined by reference to—
(a) the image itself, and
(b) (if the series of images is such as to be capable of providing a context for the image) the context in which it occurs in the series of images.

(5)   So, for example, where—
(a) an image forms an integral part of a narrative constituted by a series of images, and
(b) having regard to those images as a whole, they are not of such a nature that they must reasonably be assumed to have been produced solely or principally for the purpose of sexual arousal,
the image may, by virtue of being part of that narrative, be found not to be pornographic, even though it might have been found to be pornographic if taken by itself.

(6)   An image falls within this subsection if it—
(a) is an image which focuses solely or principally on a child's genitals or anal region, or
(b) portrays any of the acts mentioned in subsection (7).

(7)   Those acts are—
(a) the performance by a person of an act of intercourse or oral sex with or in the presence of a child;
(b) an act of masturbation by, of, involving or in the presence of a child;
(c) an act which involves penetration of the vagina or anus of a child with a part of a person's body or with anything else;
(d) an act of penetration, in the presence of a child, of the vagina or anus of a person with a part of a person's body or with anything else;
(e) the performance by a child of an act of intercourse or oral sex with an animal (whether dead or alive or imaginary);
(f) the performance by a person of an act of intercourse or oral sex with an animal (whether dead or alive or imaginary) in the presence of a child.

(8)   For the purposes of subsection (7), penetration is a continuing act from entry to withdrawal.

(9)   Proceedings for an offence under subsection (1) may not be instituted—
(a) in England and Wales, except by or with the consent of the Director of Public Prosecutions;

. . .

63 EXCLUSION OF CLASSIFIED FILM ETC

(1)   Section 62(1) does not apply to excluded images.

(2)   An "excluded image" is an image which forms part of a series of images contained in a recording of the whole or part of a classified work.

(3) But such an image is not an "excluded image" if—
(a) it is contained in a recording of an extract from a classified work, and
(b) it is of such a nature that it must reasonably be assumed to have been extracted (whether with or without other images) solely or principally for the purpose of sexual arousal.

(4) Where an extracted image is one of a series of images contained in the recording, the question whether the image is of such a nature as is mentioned in subsection (3)(b) is to be determined by reference to—
(a) the image itself, and
(b) (if the series of images is such as to be capable of providing a context for the image) the context in which it occurs in the series of images;
and section 62(5) applies in connection with determining that question as it applies in connection with determining whether an image is pornographic.

(5) In determining for the purposes of this section whether a recording is a recording of the whole or part of a classified work, any alteration attributable to—
(a) a defect caused for technical reasons or by inadvertence on the part of any person, or
(b) the inclusion in the recording of any extraneous material (such as advertisements), is to be disregarded.

(6) Nothing in this section is to be taken as affecting any duty of a designated authority to have regard to section 62 (along with other enactments creating criminal offences) in determining whether a video work is suitable for a classification certificate to be issued in respect of it.

(7) In this section—
• "classified work" means (subject to subsection (8)) a video work in respect of which a classification certificate has been issued by a designated authority (whether before or after the commencement of this section);
• "classification certificate" and "video work" have the same meaning as in the Video Recordings Act 1984 (c. 39);
• "designated authority" means an authority which has been designated by the Secretary of State under section 4 of that Act;
• "extract" includes an extract consisting of a single image;
• "pornographic" has the same meaning as in section 62;
• "recording" means any disc, tape or other device capable of storing data electronically and from which images may be produced (by any means).

64 DEFENCES

(1) Where a person is charged with an offence under section 62(1), it is a defence for the person to prove any of the following matters—
(a) that the person had a legitimate reason for being in possession of the image concerned;
(b) that the person had not seen the image concerned and did not know, nor had any cause to suspect, it to be a prohibited image of a child;
(c) that the person—
(i) was sent the image concerned without any prior request having been made by or on behalf of the person, and
(ii) did not keep it for an unreasonable time.

(2) In this section "prohibited image" has the same meaning as in section 62.

65 MEANING OF "IMAGE" AND "CHILD"

(1)   The following apply for the purposes of sections 62 to 64.

(2)   "Image" includes—
    (a) a moving or still image (produced by any means), or
    (b) data (stored by any means) which is capable of conversion into an image within paragraph (a).

(3)   "Image" does not include an indecent photograph, or indecent pseudo-photograph, of a child.

(4)   In subsection (3) "indecent photograph" and "indecent pseudo-photograph" are to be construed—
    (a) in relation to England and Wales, in accordance with the Protection of Children Act 1978 . . .

(5)   "Child", subject to subsection (6), means a person under the age of 18.

(6)   Where an image shows a person the image is to be treated as an image of a child if—
    (a) the impression conveyed by the image is that the person shown is a child, or
    (b) the predominant impression conveyed is that the person shown is a child despite the fact that some of the physical characteristics shown are not those of a child.

(7)   References to an image of a person include references to an image of an imaginary person.

(8)   References to an image of a child include references to an image of an imaginary child.

. . .

73 ABOLITION OF COMMON LAW LIBEL OFFENCES ETC

The following offences under the common law of England and Wales and the common law of Northern Ireland are abolished—

(a)   the offences of sedition and seditious libel;

(b)   the offence of defamatory libel;

(c)   the offence of obscene libel.

As amended Video Recordings Act 2010.

POLICING AND CRIME ACT 2009

30 OFFENCE OF PERSISTENTLY POSSESSING ALCOHOL IN A PUBLIC PLACE

(1)   A person under the age of 18 is guilty of an offence if, without reasonable excuse, the person is in possession of alcohol in any relevant place on 3 or more occasions within a period of 12 consecutive months.

(2)   "Relevant place", in relation to a person, means—
    (a) any public place, other than excluded premises, or
    (b) any place, other than a public place, to which the person has unlawfully gained access.

(3)   A person guilty of an offence under this section is liable on summary conviction to a fine not exceeding level 2 on the standard scale.

(4)   For the purposes of subsection (2) a place is a public place if at the material time the public or any section of the public has access to it, on payment or otherwise, as of right or by virtue of express or implied permission.

(5)   In subsection (2) "excluded premises"—
    (a)   in relation to England and Wales, means—
        (i)   premises which may by virtue of Part 3 or 5 of the Licensing Act 2003 (c. 17) (premises licence or permitted temporary activity) be used for the supply of alcohol,
        (ii)   premises which may by virtue of Part 4 of that Act (club premises certificate) be used for the supply of alcohol to members or guests.

BRIBERY ACT 2010

General bribery offences

1 OFFENCES OF BRIBING ANOTHER PERSON

(1)   A person ("P") is guilty of an offence if either of the following cases applies.

(2)   Case 1 is where—
    (a)   P offers, promises or gives a financial or other advantage to another person, and
    (b)   P intends the advantage—
        (i)   to induce a person to perform improperly a relevant function or activity, or
        (ii)   to reward a person for the improper performance of such a function or activity.

(3)   Case 2 is where—
    (a)   P offers, promises or gives a financial or other advantage to another person, and
    (b)   P knows or believes that the acceptance of the advantage would itself constitute the improper performance of a relevant function or activity.

(4)   In case 1 it does not matter whether the person to whom the advantage is offered, promised or given is the same person as the person who is to perform, or has performed, the function or activity concerned.

(5)   In cases 1 and 2 it does not matter whether the advantage is offered, promised or given by P directly or through a third party.

2 OFFENCES RELATING TO BEING BRIBED

(1)   A person ("R") is guilty of an offence if any of the following cases applies.

(2)   Case 3 is where R requests, agrees to receive or accepts a financial or other advantage intending that, in consequence, a relevant function or activity should be performed improperly (whether by R or another person).

(3)   Case 4 is where—
    (a)   R requests, agrees to receive or accepts a financial or other advantage, and
    (b)   the request, agreement or acceptance itself constitutes the improper performance by R of a relevant function or activity.

(4)   Case 5 is where R requests, agrees to receive or accepts a financial or other advantage as a reward for the improper performance (whether by R or another person) of a relevant function or activity.

(5)   Case 6 is where, in anticipation of or in consequence of R requesting, agreeing to receive or accepting a financial or other advantage, a relevant function or activity is performed improperly—
       (a) by R, or
       (b) by another person at R's request or with R's assent or acquiescence.

(6)   In cases 3 to 6 it does not matter—
       (a) whether R requests, agrees to receive or accepts (or is to request, agree to receive or accept) the advantage directly or through a third party,
       (b) whether the advantage is (or is to be) for the benefit of R or another person.

(7)   In cases 4 to 6 it does not matter whether R knows or believes that the performance of the function or activity is improper.

(8)   In case 6, where a person other than R is performing the function or activity, it also does not matter whether that person knows or believes that the performance of the function or activity is improper.

3 FUNCTION OR ACTIVITY TO WHICH BRIBE RELATES

(1)   For the purposes of this Act a function or activity is a relevant function or activity if—
       (a) it falls within subsection (2), and
       (b) meets one or more of conditions A to C.

(2)   The following functions and activities fall within this subsection—
       (a) any function of a public nature,
       (b) any activity connected with a business,
       (c) any activity performed in the course of a person's employment,
       (d) any activity performed by or on behalf of a body of persons (whether corporate or unincorporate).

(3)   Condition A is that a person performing the function or activity is expected to perform it in good faith.

(4)   Condition B is that a person performing the function or activity is expected to perform it impartially.

(5)   Condition C is that a person performing the function or activity is in a position of trust by virtue of performing it.

(6)   A function or activity is a relevant function or activity even if it—
       (a) has no connection with the United Kingdom, and
       (b) is performed in a country or territory outside the United Kingdom.

(7)   In this section "business" includes trade or profession.

4 IMPROPER PERFORMANCE TO WHICH BRIBE RELATES

(1)   For the purposes of this Act a relevant function or activity—
       (a) is performed improperly if it is performed in breach of a relevant expectation, and
       (b) is to be treated as being performed improperly if there is a failure to perform the function or activity and that failure is itself a breach of a relevant expectation.

(2) In subsection (1) "relevant expectation"—
   (a) in relation to a function or activity which meets condition A or B, means the expectation mentioned in the condition concerned, and
   (b) in relation to a function or activity which meets condition C, means any expectation as to the manner in which, or the reasons for which, the function or activity will be performed that arises from the position of trust mentioned in that condition.

(3) Anything that a person does (or omits to do) arising from or in connection with that person's past performance of a relevant function or activity is to be treated for the purposes of this Act as being done (or omitted) by that person in the performance of that function or activity.

5 EXPECTATION TEST

(1) For the purposes of sections 3 and 4, the test of what is expected is a test of what a reasonable person in the United Kingdom would expect in relation to the performance of the type of function or activity concerned.

(2) In deciding what such a person would expect in relation to the performance of a function or activity where the performance is not subject to the law of any part of the United Kingdom, any local custom or practice is to be disregarded unless it is permitted or required by the written law applicable to the country or territory concerned.

(3) In subsection (2) "written law" means law contained in—
   (a) any written constitution, or provision made by or under legislation, applicable to the country or territory concerned, or
   (b) any judicial decision which is so applicable and is evidenced in published written sources.

Bribery of foreign public officials

6 BRIBERY OF FOREIGN PUBLIC OFFICIALS

(1) A person ("P") who bribes a foreign public official ("F") is guilty of an offence if P's intention is to influence F in F's capacity as a foreign public official.

(2) P must also intend to obtain or retain—
   (a) business, or
   (b) an advantage in the conduct of business.

(3) P bribes F if, and only if—
   (a) directly or through a third party, P offers, promises or gives any financial or other advantage—
       (i) to F, or
       (ii) to another person at F's request or with F's assent or acquiescence, and
   (b) F is neither permitted nor required by the written law applicable to F to be influenced in F's capacity as a foreign public official by the offer, promise or gift.

(4) References in this section to influencing F in F's capacity as a foreign public official mean influencing F in the performance of F's functions as such an official, which includes—
   (a) any omission to exercise those functions, and
   (b) any use of F's position as such an official, even if not within F's authority.

(5) "Foreign public official" means an individual who—

(a) holds a legislative, administrative or judicial position of any kind, whether appointed or elected, of a country or territory outside the United Kingdom (or any subdivision of such a country or territory),

(b) exercises a public function—

    (i) for or on behalf of a country or territory outside the United Kingdom (or any subdivision of such a country or territory), or

    (ii) for any public agency or public enterprise of that country or territory (or subdivision), or

(c) is an official or agent of a public international organisation.

(6) "Public international organisation" means an organisation whose members are any of the following—

(a) countries or territories,

(b) governments of countries or territories,

(c) other public international organisations,

(d) a mixture of any of the above.

(7) For the purposes of subsection (3)(b), the written law applicable to F is—

(a) where the performance of the functions of F which P intends to influence would be subject to the law of any part of the United Kingdom, the law of that part of the United Kingdom,

(b) where paragraph (a) does not apply and F is an official or agent of a public international organisation, the applicable written rules of that organisation,

(c) where paragraphs (a) and (b) do not apply, the law of the country or territory in relation to which F is a foreign public official so far as that law is contained in—

    (i) any written constitution, or provision made by or under legislation, applicable to the country or territory concerned, or

    (ii) any judicial decision which is so applicable and is evidenced in published written sources.

(8) For the purposes of this section, a trade or profession is a business.

Failure of commercial organisations to prevent bribery

7 FAILURE OF COMMERCIAL ORGANISATIONS TO PREVENT BRIBERY

(1) A relevant commercial organisation ("C") is guilty of an offence under this section if a person ("A") associated with C bribes another person intending—

(a) to obtain or retain business for C, or

(b) to obtain or retain an advantage in the conduct of business for C.

(2) But it is a defence for C to prove that C had in place adequate procedures designed to prevent persons associated with C from undertaking such conduct.

(3) For the purposes of this section, A bribes another person if, and only if, A—

(a) is, or would be, guilty of an offence under section 1 or 6 (whether or not A has been prosecuted for such an offence), or

(b) would be guilty of such an offence if section 12(2)(c) and (4) were omitted.

(4) See section 8 for the meaning of a person associated with C and see section 9 for a duty on the Secretary of State to publish guidance.

(5) In this section—

"partnership" means—
(a) a partnership within the Partnership Act 1890, or
(b) a limited partnership registered under the Limited Partnerships Act 1907,
or a firm or entity of a similar character formed under the law of a country or territory outside the United Kingdom,

"relevant commercial organisation" means—
(a) a body which is incorporated under the law of any part of the United Kingdom and which carries on a business (whether there or elsewhere),
(b) any other body corporate (wherever incorporated) which carries on a business, or part of a business, in any part of the United Kingdom,
(c) a partnership which is formed under the law of any part of the United Kingdom and which carries on a business (whether there or elsewhere), or
(d) any other partnership (wherever formed) which carries on a business, or part of a business, in any part of the United Kingdom, and, for the purposes of this section, a trade or profession is a business.

8 MEANING OF ASSOCIATED PERSON

(1) For the purposes of section 7, a person ("A") is associated with C if (disregarding any bribe under consideration) A is a person who performs services for or on behalf of C.

(2) The capacity in which A performs services for or on behalf of C does not matter.

(3) Accordingly A may (for example) be C's employee, agent or subsidiary.

(4) Whether or not A is a person who performs services for or on behalf of C is to be determined by reference to all the relevant circumstances and not merely by reference to the nature of the relationship between A and C.

(5) But if A is an employee of C, it is to be presumed unless the contrary is shown that A is a person who performs services for or on behalf of C.

. . .

Prosecution and penalties

10 CONSENT TO PROSECUTION

(1) No proceedings for an offence under this Act may be instituted in England and Wales except by or with the consent of—
(a) the Director of Public Prosecutions,
(b) the Director of the Serious Fraud Office, or
(c) the Director of Revenue and Customs Prosecutions.

. . .

Other provisions about offences

12 OFFENCES UNDER THIS ACT: TERRITORIAL APPLICATION

(1) An offence is committed under section 1, 2 or 6 in England and Wales, Scotland or Northern Ireland if any act or omission which forms part of the offence takes place in that part of the United Kingdom.

(2) Subsection (3) applies if—

(a) no act or omission which forms part of an offence under section 1, 2 or 6 takes place in the United Kingdom,

(b) a person's acts or omissions done or made outside the United Kingdom would form part of such an offence if done or made in the United Kingdom, and

(c) that person has a close connection with the United Kingdom.

(3) In such a case—

(a) the acts or omissions form part of the offence referred to in subsection (2)(a), and

(b) proceedings for the offence may be taken at any place in the United Kingdom.

(4) For the purposes of subsection (2)(c) a person has a close connection with the United Kingdom if, and only if, the person was one of the following at the time the acts or omissions concerned were done or made—

(a) a British citizen,

(b) a British overseas territories citizen,

(c) a British National (Overseas),

(d) a British Overseas citizen,

(e) a person who under the British Nationality Act 1981 was a British subject,

(f) a British protected person within the meaning of that Act,

(g) an individual ordinarily resident in the United Kingdom,

(h) a body incorporated under the law of any part of the United Kingdom,

(i) a Scottish partnership.

(5) An offence is committed under section 7 irrespective of whether the acts or omissions which form part of the offence take place in the United Kingdom or elsewhere.

(6) Where no act or omission which forms part of an offence under section 7 takes place in the United Kingdom, proceedings for the offence may be taken at any place in the United Kingdom.

. . .

13 DEFENCE FOR CERTAIN BRIBERY OFFENCES ETC.

(1) It is a defence for a person charged with a relevant bribery offence to prove that the person's conduct was necessary for—

(a) the proper exercise of any function of an intelligence service, or

(b) the proper exercise of any function of the armed forces when engaged on active service.

(2) The head of each intelligence service must ensure that the service has in place arrangements designed to ensure that any conduct of a member of the service which would otherwise be a relevant bribery offence is necessary for a purpose falling within subsection (1)(a).

(3) The Defence Council must ensure that the armed forces have in place arrangements designed to ensure that any conduct of—

(a) a member of the armed forces who is engaged on active service, or

(b) a civilian subject to service discipline when working in support of any person falling within paragraph (a),

which would otherwise be a relevant bribery offence is necessary for a purpose falling within subsection (1)(b).

(4) The arrangements which are in place by virtue of subsection (2) or (3) must be arrangements which the Secretary of State considers to be satisfactory.

(5) For the purposes of this section, the circumstances in which a person's conduct is necessary for a purpose falling within subsection (1)(a) or (b) are to be treated as including any circumstances in which the person's conduct—

(a) would otherwise be an offence under section 2, and

(b) involves conduct by another person which, but for subsection (1)(a) or (b), would be an offence under section 1.

(6) In this section—

"active service" means service in—

(a) an action or operation against an enemy,

(b) an operation outside the British Islands for the protection of life or property, or

(c) the military occupation of a foreign country or territory,

"armed forces" means Her Majesty's forces (within the meaning of the Armed Forces Act 2006),

"civilian subject to service discipline" and "enemy" have the same meaning as in the Act of 2006,

"GCHQ" has the meaning given by section 3(3) of the Intelligence Services Act 1994,

"head" means—

(a) in relation to the Security Service, the Director General of the Security Service,

(b) in relation to the Secret Intelligence Service, the Chief of the Secret Intelligence Service, and

(c) in relation to GCHQ, the Director of GCHQ,

"intelligence service" means the Security Service, the Secret Intelligence Service or GCHQ,

"relevant bribery offence" means—

(a) an offence under section 1 which would not also be an offence under section 6,

(b) an offence under section 2,

(c) an offence committed by aiding, abetting, counselling or procuring the commission of an offence falling within paragraph (a) or (b),

(d) an offence of attempting or conspiring to commit, or of inciting the commission of, an offence falling within paragraph (a) or (b), or

(e) an offence under Part 2 of the Serious Crime Act 2007 (encouraging or assisting crime) in relation to an offence falling within paragraph (a) or (b).

14 OFFENCES UNDER SECTIONS 1, 2 AND 6 BY BODIES CORPORATE ETC.

(1) This section applies if an offence under section 1, 2 or 6 is committed by a body corporate or a Scottish partnership.

(2) If the offence is proved to have been committed with the consent or connivance of—

(a) a senior officer of the body corporate or Scottish partnership, or

(b) a person purporting to act in such a capacity,

the senior officer or person (as well as the body corporate or partnership) is guilty of the offence and liable to be proceeded against and punished accordingly.

(3) But subsection (2) does not apply, in the case of an offence which is committed under section 1, 2 or 6 by virtue of section 12(2) to (4), to a senior officer or person purporting to act in such a capacity unless the senior officer or person has a close connection with the United Kingdom (within the meaning given by section 12(4)).

(4)   In this section—

"director", in relation to a body corporate whose affairs are managed by its members, means a member of the body corporate,

"senior officer" means—
(a) in relation to a body corporate, a director, manager, secretary or other similar officer of the body corporate, and
(b) in relation to a Scottish partnership, a partner in the partnership.

CRIME AND SECURITY ACT 2010

24 POWER TO ISSUE A DOMESTIC VIOLENCE PROTECTION NOTICE

(1)   A member of a police force not below the rank of superintendent ("the authorising officer") may issue a domestic violence protection notice ("a DVPN") under this section.

(2)   A DVPN may be issued to a person ("P") aged 18 years or over if the authorising officer has reasonable grounds for believing that—
(a) P has been violent towards, or has threatened violence towards, an associated person, and
(b) the issue of the DVPN is necessary to protect that person from violence or a threat of violence by P.

(3)   Before issuing a DVPN, the authorising officer must, in particular, consider—
(a) the welfare of any person under the age of 18 whose interests the officer considers relevant to the issuing of the DVPN (whether or not that person is an associated person),
(b) the opinion of the person for whose protection the DVPN would be issued as to the issuing of the DVPN,
(c) any representations made by P as to the issuing of the DVPN, and
(d) in the case of provision included by virtue of subsection (8), the opinion of any other associated person who lives in the premises to which the provision would relate.

(4)   The authorising officer must take reasonable steps to discover the opinions mentioned in subsection (3).

(5)   But the authorising officer may issue a DVPN in circumstances where the person for whose protection it is issued does not consent to the issuing of the DVPN.

(6)   A DVPN must contain provision to prohibit P from molesting the person for whose protection it is issued.

(7)   Provision required to be included by virtue of subsection (6) may be expressed so as to refer to molestation in general, to particular acts of molestation, or to both.

(8)   If P lives in premises which are also lived in by a person for whose protection the DVPN is issued, the DVPN may also contain provision—
(a) to prohibit P from evicting or excluding from the premises the person for whose protection the DVPN is issued,
(b) to prohibit P from entering the premises,
(c) to require P to leave the premises, or

(d) to prohibit P from coming within such distance of the premises as may be specified in the DVPN.

(9) An "associated person" means a person who is associated with P within the meaning of section 62 of the Family Law Act 1996.

(10) Subsection (11) applies where a DVPN includes provision in relation to premises by virtue of subsection (8)(b) or (8)(c) and the authorising officer believes that—
(a) P is a person subject to service law in accordance with sections 367 to 369 of the Armed Forces Act 2006, and
(b) the premises fall within paragraph (a) of the definition of "service living accommodation" in section 96(1) of that Act.

(11) The authorising officer must make reasonable efforts to inform P's commanding officer (within the meaning of section 360 of the Armed Forces Act 2006) of the issuing of the notice.

25 CONTENTS AND SERVICE OF A DOMESTIC VIOLENCE PROTECTION NOTICE

(1) A DVPN must state—
(a) the grounds on which it has been issued,
(b) that a constable may arrest P without warrant if the constable has reasonable grounds for believing that P is in breach of the DVPN,
(c) that an application for a domestic violence protection order under section 27 will be heard within 48 hours of the time of service of the DVPN and a notice of the hearing will be given to P,
(d) that the DVPN continues in effect until that application has been determined, and
(e) the provision that a magistrates' court may include in a domestic violence protection order.

(2) A DVPN must be in writing and must be served on P personally by a constable.

(3) On serving P with a DVPN, the constable must ask P for an address for the purposes of being given the notice of the hearing of the application for the domestic violence protection order.

26 BREACH OF A DOMESTIC VIOLENCE PROTECTION NOTICE

(1) A person arrested by virtue of section 25(1)(b) for a breach of a DVPN must be held in custody and brought before the magistrates' court which will hear the application for the DVPO under section 27—
(a) before the end of the period of 24 hours beginning with the time of the arrest, or
(b) if earlier, at the hearing of that application.

(2) If the person is brought before the court by virtue of subsection (1)(a), the court may remand the person.

(3) If the court adjourns the hearing of the application by virtue of section 27(8), the court may remand the person.

(4) In calculating when the period of 24 hours mentioned in subsection (1)(a) ends, Christmas Day, Good Friday, any Sunday and any day which is a bank holiday in England and Wales under the Banking and Financial Dealings Act 1971 are to be disregarded.

27 APPLICATION FOR A DOMESTIC VIOLENCE PROTECTION ORDER

(1)   If a DVPN has been issued, a constable must apply for a domestic violence protection order ("a DVPO").

(2)   The application must be made by complaint to a magistrates' court.

(3)   The application must be heard by the magistrates' court not later than 48 hours after the DVPN was served pursuant to section 25(2).

(4)   In calculating when the period of 48 hours mentioned in subsection (3) ends, Christmas Day, Good Friday, any Sunday and any day which is a bank holiday in England and Wales under the Banking and Financial Dealings Act 1971 are to be disregarded.

(5)   A notice of the hearing of the application must be given to P.

(6)   The notice is deemed given if it has been left at the address given by P under section 25(3).

(7)   But if the notice has not been given because no address was given by P under section 25(3), the court may hear the application for the DVPO if the court is satisfied that the constable applying for the DVPO has made reasonable efforts to give P the notice.

(8)   The magistrates' court may adjourn the hearing of the application.

(9)   If the court adjourns the hearing, the DVPN continues in effect until the application has been determined.

(10) On the hearing of an application for a DVPO, section 97 of the Magistrates' Courts Act 1980 (summons to witness and warrant for his arrest) does not apply in relation to a person for whose protection the DVPO would be made, except where the person has given oral or written evidence at the hearing.

28 CONDITIONS FOR AND CONTENTS OF A DOMESTIC VIOLENCE PROTECTION ORDER

(1)   The court may make a DVPO if two conditions are met.

(2)   The first condition is that the court is satisfied on the balance of probabilities that P has been violent towards, or has threatened violence towards, an associated person.

(3)   The second condition is that the court thinks that making the DVPO is necessary to protect that person from violence or a threat of violence by P.

(4)   Before making a DVPO, the court must, in particular, consider—
      (a) the welfare of any person under the age of 18 whose interests the court considers relevant to the making of the DVPO (whether or not that person is an associated person), and
      (b) any opinion of which the court is made aware—
           (i) of the person for whose protection the DVPO would be made, and
           (ii) in the case of provision included by virtue of subsection (8), of any other associated person who lives in the premises to which the provision would relate.

(5)   But the court may make a DVPO in circumstances where the person for whose protection it is made does not consent to the making of the DVPO.

(6)   A DVPO must contain provision to prohibit P from molesting the person for whose protection it is made.

(7)   Provision required to be included by virtue of subsection (6) may be expressed so as to refer to molestation in general, to particular acts of molestation, or to both.

(8)   If P lives in premises which are also lived in by a person for whose protection the DVPO is made, the DVPO may also contain provision—
   (a) to prohibit P from evicting or excluding from the premises the person for whose protection the DVPO is made,
   (b) to prohibit P from entering the premises,
   (c) to require P to leave the premises, or
   (d) to prohibit P from coming within such distance of the premises as may be specified in the DVPO.

(9)   A DVPO must state that a constable may arrest P without warrant if the constable has reasonable grounds for believing that P is in breach of the DVPO.

(10)   A DVPO may be in force for—
   (a) no fewer than 14 days beginning with the day on which it is made, and
   (b) no more than 28 days beginning with that day.

(11)   A DVPO must state the period for which it is to be in force.

29 BREACH OF A DOMESTIC VIOLENCE PROTECTION ORDER

(1)   A person arrested by virtue of section 28(9) for a breach of a DVPO must be held in custody and brought before a magistrates' court within the period of 24 hours beginning with the time of the arrest.

(2)   If the matter is not disposed of when the person is brought before the court, the court may remand the person.

(3)   In calculating when the period of 24 hours mentioned in subsection (1) ends, Christmas Day, Good Friday, any Sunday and any day which is a bank holiday in England and Wales under the Banking and Financial Dealings Act 1971 are to be disregarded.

SUNBEDS (REGULATION) ACT 2010

1 MAIN INTERPRETATIVE PROVISIONS

(1)   The following provisions apply for the interpretation of this Act.

(2)   "Sunbed" means an electrically-powered device designed to produce tanning of the human skin by the emission of ultra-violet radiation.

(3)   A "sunbed business" is a business that involves making one or more sunbeds available for use on premises that are occupied by, or are to any extent under the management or control of, the person who carries on the business; and those sunbeds are the sunbeds to which the business relates.

2 DUTY TO PREVENT SUNBED USE BY CHILDREN

(1)   A person who carries on a sunbed business ("P") must secure—
   (a) that no person aged under 18 uses on relevant premises a sunbed to which the business relates;
   (b) that no offer is made by P or on P's behalf to make a sunbed to which the business relates available for use on relevant premises by a person aged under 18;

(c)   that no person aged under 18 is at any time present, otherwise than in the course of providing services to P for the purposes of the business, in a restricted zone.

(2)   In this section "relevant premises" means premises which—
(a)   are occupied by P or are to any extent under P's management or control, and
(b)   are not domestic premises.

(3)   Subsections (4) and (5) have effect for determining what is for the purposes of subsection (1)(c) a "restricted zone".

(4)   If a sunbed to which the business relates is in a wholly or partly enclosed space on relevant premises that is reserved for users of that sunbed, every part of that space is a restricted zone.

(5)   If a sunbed to which the business relates is in a room on relevant premises, but not in a space falling within subsection (4), every part of that room is a restricted zone.

(6)   If P fails to comply with subsection (1), P commits an offence and is liable on summary conviction to a fine not exceeding £20,000.

(7)   It is a defence for a person ("D") charged with an offence under this section to show that D took all reasonable precautions and exercised all due diligence to avoid committing it.

(8)   This section is subject to section 3 (exemption for medical treatment).

PROTECTION OF FREEDOMS ACT 2012

54. OFFENCE OF IMMOBILISING ETC. VEHICLES

(1)   A person commits an offence who, without lawful authority—
(a)   immobilises a motor vehicle by the attachment to the vehicle, or a part of it, of an immobilising device, or
(b)   moves, or restricts the movement of, such a vehicle by any means, intending to prevent or inhibit the removal of the vehicle by a person otherwise entitled to remove it.

(2)   The express or implied consent (whether or not legally binding) of a person otherwise entitled to remove the vehicle to the immobilisation, movement or restriction concerned is not lawful authority for the purposes of subsection (1).

(3)   But, where the restriction of the movement of the vehicle is by means of a fixed barrier and the barrier was present (whether or not lowered into place or otherwise restricting movement) when the vehicle was parked, any express or implied consent (whether or not legally binding) of the driver of the vehicle to the restriction is, for the purposes of subsection (1), lawful authority for the restriction.

(4)   A person who is entitled to remove a vehicle cannot commit an offence under this section in relation to that vehicle.

(5)   A person guilty of an offence under this section is liable—
(a)   on conviction on indictment, to a fine,
(b)   on summary conviction, to a fine not exceeding the statutory maximum.

(6)   In this section "motor vehicle" means a mechanically propelled vehicle or a vehicle designed or adapted for towing by a mechanically propelled vehicle.

Thematic Index

Accomplices
Accessories and Abettors Act 1861   1

Harassment and Stalking
Communications Act 2003   146–147
Malicious Communications
    Act 1988   86
Protection from Harassment
    Act 1997   110–112
Wireless Telegraphy Act 2006   218–219

Inchoate Offences
Criminal Attempts Act 1981   65–68
Serious Crime Act 2007   225–229

Offences against the Person
Abortion Act 1967   20–21
Child Abduction Act 1984   71–73
Children Act 2004   187
Children and Young Persons
    Act 1933   11–12
Coroners and Justice Act 2009   233–237
Corporate Manslaughter and
    Corporate Homicide Act 2007   219–224
Crime and Security Act 2010   245–248
Domestic Violence, Crime and
    Victims Act 2004   187–188
Family Law Act 1996   107–108
Female Genital Mutilation Act 2003   147–148
Homicide Act 1957   14–15
Infant Life (Preservation) Act 1929   10–11
Infanticide Act 1938   12–13
Law Reform (Year and a Day Rule)
    Act 1996   108
Mental Capacity Act 2005   194–198
Murder (Abolition of Death Penalty)
    Act 1965   19
Offences Against the Person
    Act 1861   1–6
Police Act 1996   108–109
Prevention of Crime Act 1953   13
Protection of Children Act 1978   63–64
Road Traffic Act 1988   86–89
Suicide Act 1961   18–19
Taking of Hostages Act 1982   71
Tattooing of Minors Act 1969   51
UK Borders Act 2007   229
Violent Crime Reduction Act 2006   203–205

Offences against Public Order
Crime and Disorder Act 1998   115–118
Criminal Justice and Immigration
    Act 2008   229–233
Criminal Justice and Public Order
    Act 1994   107
Dangerous Dogs Act 1991   102–105
Firearms Act 1968   27–39
Firearms (Amendment) Act 1988   85–86
Firearms (Amendment) Act 1997   112–113
Football (Offences) Act 1991   105–106
Hunting Act 2004   189–194
Intoxicating Substances (Supply)
    Act 1985   73–74
Knives Act 1997   113–115
Licensing Act 2003   148–150
Misuse of Drugs Act 1971   54–59
Obscene Publications Act 1959   15–17
Policing and Crime Act 2009   237–238
Public Order Act 1936   12
Public Order Act 1986   75–82
Street Offences Act 1959   17–18
Sunbeds (Regulation) Act 2010   248–249

Offences against the State
Anti-Terrorism, Crime and Security
    Act 2001   143–145
Bribery Act 2010   238–245
Explosive Substances Act 1883   6–8
Finance Act 2000   134
Official Secrets Act 1911   8–9
Official Secrets Act 1989   89–97
Serious Organised Crime and Police
    Act 2005   198–202
Terrorism Act 2000   134–143
Terrorism Act 2006   208–218

Procedural and General
Criminal Appeals Act 1968   24–26
Criminal Justice Act 1925   10
Criminal Justice Act 1967   21
Criminal Justice Act 1987   82–85
Criminal Law Act 1967   21–24
Criminal Law Act 1977   59–62
Criminal Procedure (Insanity)
    Act 1964   19
Criminal Procedure (Insanity and
    Unfitness to Plead) Act 1991   102

Gender Recognition Act 2004   189
Human Rights Act 1998   118–126
Interpretation Act 1978   62–63
Magistrates' Courts Act 1980   65
Perjury Act 1911   9–10
Trial of Lunatics Act 1883   8
Youth Justice and Criminal
    Evidence Act 1999   126–133

Property Offences
Computer Misuse Act 1990   97–102
Criminal Damage Act 1971   51–53
Forgery and Counterfeiting
    Act 1981   68–71

Fraud Act 2006   205–208
Gambling Act 2005   194
Mobile Telephones (Re-programming)
    Act 2002   145–146
Protection of Freedoms Act 2012   249
Theft Act 1968   40–51
Theft Act 1978   64–65

Sexual Offences
Sexual Offences Act 1956   13–14
Sexual Offences Act 1967   24
Sexual Offences Act 1985   74–75
Sexual Offences Act 1993   106
Sexual Offences Act 2003   151–187